KATHMANDU

KATHMANDU

Thomas Bell

First published in the UK in 2016 by
Haus Publishing Ltd
70 Cadogan Place
London SW1 9AH
www.hauspublishing.com

ISBN: 978-1-910376-38-6
eISBN: 978-1-910376-39-3

All photographs except where otherwise stated by courtesy of the author.

Printed in the Czech Republic via Akcent Media Limited

Typeset by MacGuru Ltd
info@macguru.org.uk

For Subina

The past is never dead. It's not even past.

– William Faulkner

Contents

PART II – THE REVOLUTIONS

Photos and illustrations

All photographs by the author unless otherwise stated.

Preface

I found myself sitting in the upstairs room of an old house at around eight in the morning. I'd been walking past it for nearly ten years. I knew the outside well, for the stucco columns in the form of palm trees, and I knew that it belonged to a medical family who also owned the pharmacy across the road. A member of the family had once treated me in a hospital across town, and when he started talking (to take my mind off the endoscopy) I understood exactly where he was from.

It was the day after we'd flown back from England. My wife and I had woken early and gone out to buy fruit and bread. While we were away the monsoon had begun. The streets were muddy and plants had sprouted on the buildings, which were turning green in places. There were piles of wet sand at the building sites, punched frequently into the crowded rows of old houses, and there were piles of sodden trash in the gutters. People were picking their way among the puddles.

My wife was pregnant and she'd been told to get a tetanus shot. Since we were walking past the pharmacy, just around the corner from the fruit market, we bought a phial and a needle and took them up the steep wooden stairs of the doctor's house to the waiting room at the top. I sat down while my wife went through to get her injection, and up the stairs after us came two women with three children. A boy of about ten stood in front of me. He was a goofy-looking kid.

'Hello,' I said. 'What's your name?' but he didn't have any words, only noises. He was pointing at the small terrace, supported by the stucco palms. I followed him outside. 'Can you see your house from here?' I asked, but he just pointed at my head and made his sounds.

Inside the doctor's room I could hear my wife and the doctor speaking their own language – Newari, not Nepali – which neither I nor the women in the waiting room could understand. Then I saw, on the beam beside where my head had been, there was a wasps' nest, crawling with wasps.

'Oh yes,' I said. 'Insects! Are you afraid of them?'

The boy's mother and the other woman came and repeated what I'd said and laughed, and congratulated him on his discovery. My wife was finished and we left.

She said, 'In this country, even doctors are so narrow-minded.'

'What makes you say that?'

'I told the doctor, "I think that boy's deaf." "He's just slow," the doctor said. I told him I thought the boy was deaf and he said, "Deaf people are slow anyway."'

'You should have said something to his mother,' I said, then after a while, 'If he was diagnosed as deaf I suppose that would make a big difference to him.'

'It would change his life.'

A while later she said, 'My cousin Dinesh used to live next door to a family; half of them were deaf. Very well-educated, the whole lot.'

When we got home I said, 'They must be regular patients.'

'He'd never seen them before. I asked.'

'Let's go back.'

'They'll have gone.'

I dragged her back. She followed me puffing up the stairs. They were still there, pleased and surprised to see us again. 'He pestered me to find out what's wrong with the little brother,' my wife said. 'Can he hear?'

'He can hear,' said the boy's mother. And now that he had heard us the boy was out of the doctor's room, squirming from his mother's grip, refusing to let go of my legs. I had to lure him back inside. We left as soon as we could. It was an awkward situation; a decade hasn't been long enough to learn to avoid those.

When I was a student I wanted to go to Africa to become a foreign correspondent, but I realized there are very few African countries that British people are ever at all interested in, and those were already covered. I considered Cairo (it seemed like an important place without many foreign journalists) but I settled on Pakistan – until the September 11 attacks filled it with more qualified rivals. By then I was back home in Newcastle, working in a call centre, paying off my student overdraft by selling boiler insurance.

The call centre manager was a barrel-chested Geordie hardman, partly raised in Delaware, who'd been a US Marine. If he caught me reading at work he would creep up and slam the desk so the book leapt from my hands. When he heard about the life I was planning he said I must learn to protect myself. I went to his house on a Saturday. We smoked joints and drank beer, and he hurled me around his sitting room, demonstrating good ways to fuck people up. Around Christmas that year, in a friend's kitchen in Kew, someone said, 'What about Nepal?' The country had already crossed my mind, but for some reason I'd dismissed it. Now it seemed a good idea. There were Maoist rebels, getting in the news with growing frequency. Earlier that year the crown prince had massacred the royal family, proving what a big story Nepal could be if something crazy happened. Crazy things seemed to be the Nepali style. That was all I knew about the place when I decided to go there. I arrived in May 2002, on a one-way ticket with my first laptop in my bag, and I stayed for five years, until the *Daily Telegraph* sent me to Bangkok.

Thousands of years ago, in legend and reality, the Kathmandu Valley was a lake, coursing with serpents. The stories describing it may be a memory passed down over numberless generations, from the unknown people who left stone tools on the shore. The clays of the ancient lakebed were laid down, between sandy and gravelly horizons, and mingled with minerals from

the neighbouring hills. The red earth is used by some castes to paint the outside of their houses. 'Sky-coloured earth', found in the banks of a few streams, was used by women to wash their hair. Three different types of clay are used in successive coatings, mixed with cow dung and rice husks, to mould copper statues of the gods. Brick- and tile-makers find their clay in their own fields. After the harvest the soil is quarried, packed into moulds and dried before firing. In the next planting season the field can be sown again, and its level will be a metre lower.

Until recently the term 'Nepal' applied only to this lush basin of rice fields, 250 square miles, ringed by green hills, with the white peaks of the Himalaya strung across the northern horizon. 'A lovelier spot than this the heart of man could scarce desire,' wrote Sir Henry Lawrence, a British official posted there in the 1840s.[1] The moderate climate and rich soils yielded three crops a year and made Kathmandu the greatest cradle of urban civilization in the Himalaya.

The standard account begins on the full moon in the month of Chaitra, when a buddha came and sowed a lotus seed in the ancient lake. From the flower a beam of light appeared, which was the self-created god Swayambhu. Another enlightened one, called Manjushree, came from the north and, seeing the Swayambhu light, used his sword to carve the Kotwal gorge and drain the lake. He brought people to the Valley. As the age of Kali approached, a holy man covered the Swayambhu light with a stone to protect it, and built the city's greatest Buddhist shrine on top. Astrologers announced the victory of injustice over justice. At midnight on 14 January 3102 BC the age of Kali began and the world became one-quarter virtue and three-quarters sin. It will last for 4,32,000 years.

In an alternative Hindu account, the valley floor was covered by a sacred forest of blossoming trees and birdsong. The great god Shiva and his consort Parvati lived there in the form of two deer. They sported themselves in the pristine groves and the crystalline waters of the Bagmati River while all the other deer kissed and licked his body all over. In this avatar Shiva was Pashupati, the Lord of the Animals, and the burbling of the river was the sound of his laughter. The other gods came and begged Shiva to live among them again and he agreed, but before he left he declared that the Valley would be a holy land of many holy places. He would remain there in the form of a luminous phallus, or lingam, on the bank of his holy river.

Hearing this Parvati said that she also wished to stay, and Shiva told her the story of one of her previous lives. She had been called Sati and had sacrificed herself on a fire for her husband. Stricken with grief Shiva flew around the world with her corpse, littering body parts. A toe landed near Calcutta, her three eyes near Karachi and her tongue in the Punjab – there are dozens of these holy places. Her vulva fell to earth at Gujeshwori in Kathmandu. It still lies there, a hole in the ground fringed with stone petals, on the river bank just upstream from where Shiva made his lingam.[2] By the beginning of the age of Kali the lingam had sunk entirely into the ground, but thousands of years ago the place was rediscovered and the Pashupati temple, Nepal's holiest Hindu shrine, was built.

There are many versions of Kathmandu's early history and they sometimes seem to contradict themselves, which is readily accepted, in fact hardly even noticed. An event can take place when, according to another page, the valley should still have been full of water. The same shrine seems to be founded by different people at different times, in the same text. And a certain king or mystic can pop up in different centuries, as if time didn't run in a line in the old days, or as if contradictory stories can both be true, and the order of events and the gaps between them are just one way of seeing things. A chronicle that starts with Swayambhu and Manjushree ends with the death of a prime minister in 1839. Somewhere in between it changes from a record of belief into a record of events, and the difference is only as great as you please.

Three cities stand in the Valley. Each was once a city state, which competed with the others in the beauty of its buildings. In the east there is Bhaktapur, which still stands 10 miles from the modern capital. Patan is on the south bank of the Bagmati River and opposite, on the north bank, is Kathmandu itself.

As you fly in there's an area of unpleasant dipping and juddering, which brings sweat to the palms. The plane ploughs through the vectors rising off the hills and the low clouds settled over them. You see the steep slopes, extraordinarily green, with white wisps hanging on their shoulders. There are pretty cottages with zinc roofs reflecting brightly. Then you see the flat of the valley floor. There are villages, roads and brick kilns in the rice fields, their iron chimneys streaming black muck. New neighbourhoods are spreading, which look as if a sack of brick and concrete blocks has been shaken across the fields. For a moment the old agriculture mingles with the new metropolis.

Kathmandu and Patan have fused together in recent decades to make a single conurbation with two ancient cores, like an egg with two yolks. It's normal to speak of this whole sprawling settlement of about three million people as 'Kathmandu', with Patan as its southern part. In the living memory of a thirty-year-old the fields between the two towns and all around have been consumed in a jagged maze of unplanned, dusty concrete. Alongside the runway there used to be a dusty road, where the packed vehicles were stuck tight like armies that had merged, hacking their way through each other. You bump down at perhaps the worst airport of any Asian capital.

I rented two rooms above a statue shop in Patan. Downstairs Hirakaji Shakya and his son Sunil, like all of their relatives on the street, sold copper statues of the Buddha and other gods, copulating or sitting in meditation, gilded beneath dust on the shelves in the window. The statue sellers stood about on their steps all day, in desultory conversation or minding one another's shops.

I took a P.O. Box to receive letters, and the torrent of cheques I was soon hoping to receive. For £250 I bought a mattress, a pillow, two cane chairs, a cane bookshelf and a hat stand to hang my clothes on, a couple of books on Nepal, settled my initial hotel bill, paid three months' rent on Hirakaji's flat and bought the carpet, which he insisted I do before I stain it. With the change I went out for a pizza and that night I worried at the rate I was getting through money, before writing even a single piece. I was still trying to get a phone line installed, so I could dial up the internet. Getting it took three months, which seemed to be some kind of record.

I also needed a press card. The guards at the gate of the government complex were amused when I climbed out of a taxi and put a tie on. A pretty policewoman showed me that my collar was bent. I wandered around the vast compound, a kind of forbidden city of dozing bureaucrats, with grass growing between the slabs and beneath dusty government cars. There were stray dogs but I didn't pass anyone to ask directions. With difficulty I found the Ministry of Information and Communications, where there were no papers on the desks, and was brought directly into the presence of a minister. He gave me a glass of tea and flicked through a copy of *World Water*, the bimonthly journal full of advertisements for pumps which had accredited me as its Nepal Correspondent.

Eventually someone worked out I was in the wrong place and I was directed to the ministry's outpost, miles away. The minister wrote the address for me on the back of a receipt. The bottom two storeys of this other office had clearly been in long use. The halls were stacked to the roof with ledgers and bundles of files, knotted in squares of cloth, but the top two floors were incomplete and damp, with miserable-looking women hauling bricks about in baskets. The staff seemed surprised to have had the minister on the phone about my case. I entered a process of exchanging passport photographs, forms in triplicate, my letter of accreditation and nominal fees paid in postage stamps.

I didn't know any more about journalism than I knew about Kathmandu, but in the following years I learned the techniques of a foreign correspondent. My only training was what I had received as a student, in history, so I turned to history to understand Kathmandu. When a man told me the history of his favourite shrine, he casually placed the story in three different periods, ranged over millennia, without seeming to notice. It was the same when I asked an old woman why a ritual (bewilderingly elaborate in my eyes, though hardly out of the ordinary) was done the way it was. Her answer was duly translated: 'for the same reason you wash your arse after shitting.'

The stories were like the ritual, they relate the nature of things that are essential, which have not changed for so long that it's the same thing as forever. But I wanted to know how old what I saw really was, to understand how this intricate edifice had been erected, because I could see that it was changing faster than it ever had. Years later, when I began to write this book, I wanted to reveal the city's texture through the texts that compose its history (its 'written monuments'); to simulate the connections that run through all its parts, and to reproduce the cycles of repetition and reinvention that are the structure of its life. I sometimes thought of Kathmandu as like the model of a molecule, all the nodes connected by little rods, with everything there, all linked, at the same time.

To the south, malarial forests separated Kathmandu from India, passable only in the winter until the jungle was sprayed with insecticide by an American aid project in the 1950s. To the north, across the world's highest mountains, lie Tibet and China. The Valley stands at the edge of two worlds, at one of the fundamental frontiers, and its DNA splits both ways.

From the north comes the Tibeto-Burmese language of the city's native Newar people. It has tricks to terrify and appal an English speaker. The numbers are different according to the shape of the objects being counted. Instead of using a first person, a second person and a third person, Newars conjugate their verbs to speak of themselves, to speak of someone close to them or to speak of someone only tenuously connected. It's spoken in the old inner-cities and in the rich suburban villas where Newars live. Sanskrit, an Indo-European language distantly related to English, has also been used in the Valley since the earliest times. Modern Nepali is derived from Sanskrit and an English speaker finds occasional resonances in everyday words. The word for 'name' is 'nam', a snake is a 'sarpa' and teeth are 'dant'. Several of the numbers from one to ten sound similar to French.

Clearly Kathmandu hasn't spent its whole life cut off from the world. It gained its two religions, Hinduism and Buddhism, from the Ganges plains to the south. But its relative isolation meant it was spared the Muslim conquests that changed India forever after the twelfth century. The first Western orientalists who visited Nepal in the nineteenth century discovered in Kathmandu's Buddhism a relic of the Buddhism that had disappeared from India centuries earlier. They saw the exotic trials by water to settle property disputes, and recognized a unique survival of the Hindu culture which might have existed in India before Islamic influence. The city has been behind the times since the Middle Ages.

Nepal was never colonized by Europeans. Until 1951 foreigners were mostly excluded from the country, which was ruled as a kind of feudal theocracy. The first motorable road to Kathmandu was completed in 1956. Now the city is supplied by two slender mountain highways, both with a single lane in each direction. Television arrived in 1985, bringing the outside world closer again. Five years later the absolute monarchy yielded to parliamentary democracy, under pressure from massive street protests inspired by the fall of the Berlin Wall. Few people have ever lived through changes so dramatic as an old woman in Kathmandu has seen.

The result of this shrinking time lag is a city that feels at once abandoned by the modern world and buffeted by it. The failed introduction of democracy, the failure of foreign aid, the crisis of social values, the environmental catastrophe: these things have their equivalent in many old cities' experience of modernity and globalization, but probably no other city was woken so rudely from mediaeval sleep, to find itself exposed in the electric light of the later twentieth century.[3] Suddenly Kathmandu is possessed by new spirits, of individuality, consumerism, class struggle, and identity politics.

Nearly three weeks after I applied for my press card I received a call on my mobile phone from one of the officials at the Department. He was having a celebration at his home, he explained. Could I help?

I mumbled that I might be able to contribute something.

'Contribute? What?'

I ventured a bottle of whisky. He suggested two and I agreed. The next evening we met at a busy junction away from his office.

FRIED
VALLEY
CAFE'

I handed over the drinks and asked about the celebration. On the tape, which I recorded in my pocket, over the sound of the traffic and the rustle of my clothes, the official can be heard to claim that he is marking the recent birth of a son to the new crown prince. In the morning I went to his office and picked up my press card. My telephone line was installed the following day. It was my twenty-fourth birthday.

PART ONE

The Beginnings

1

> 'I doubt that an opium eater has ever dreamt, in his wildest dreams, of a more fantastic architecture than the one of this strange city.'
>
> – Gustav Le Bon, *Voyage to Nepal* (1886)

On my first day the haze stopped me from seeing beyond the rooftops. That night the dogs fighting in the street seemed so loud that in my half-sleep I dreamt they were in the passage outside, crashing against my hotel-room door. In the morning I was surprised to see the hills so close. It was months before the true mountains were revealed behind the filthy air.

At ground level Patan still feels old, despite the replacement of low brick-and-timber houses with high brick-and-concrete ones. At roof level, five or six floors up, it's like a mouth full of broken teeth. New storeys are slapped on top of old houses; new houses are crenellated with water tanks, aerials and unfinished concrete pillars, ready to add another level when the family grows. Near the top of every building – next to the kitchen – is the tiny puja room where the old woman of the house performs her daily worship. And on the roof, in the Buddhist households of the Shakya caste, a small dome called a chaitya is screwed down, where she worships again, smearing it with vermilion, tying threads around it and sprinkling rice. On each Buddhist rooftop flies the stripy flag, like a gay pride banner, of Theravada Buddhism.

Early in the morning people stand on the terrace outside the kitchen door to hack loudly at the black deposits in their lungs and spit. Later they bathe one another from basins, and in the warm winter sun the women oil their hair. On summer evenings people gather in pairs to look out from their building's highest point across the other roofs, clothes lines and flower pots, towards the Swayambhu temple on its hill in the west. Beyond are the surrounding ridges, and villages where no lights come on after dark.

In my early days, absorbed in the rooftops, I imagined a giant photographic collage, requiring at least three or four rolls of film. I would perch on the water tank, seven storeys above the street, zooming in and out on different elements to heighten the already jumbled effect, and compose a great wheel of all the roofs around me inside the ring of hills. I called the idea 'Kathmandu Mandala' and I only completed one section. I didn't realize that the city was already seen as a mandala by its residents.

At the tea-shop, where I asked for a glass of tea, the man behind the stove smiled and wagged his head from side to side. I couldn't understand the problem: everyone else had one. There was a shop where I bought pieces of cheese and bad sausage, noodles and sweet brown whisky for my unpleasant dinners at home. And there was a shop selling steamed dumplings. In there, sitting on the bench, I watched the shopkeeper standing at the greasy curtain in the doorway, anxiously observing the soldiers checking vehicles at the junction.

The old parts of the city are a pattern of squares and courtyards. The streets, where they exist, don't so much connect the squares as keep them apart, and many of the paved alleys were drains until recently, so a man born in 1944 can say 'there were no streets when we were growing up'. Dank gullies are only a couple of yards across at ground level and much narrower above, because modern houses are outrageously heaped on cantilevers to make the upper floors more spacious than the ones below. Turning into a covered passage five feet high you step into a sunlit square. Walking through the thoroughfares reminded me of Oxford, as my head was turned by the glimpse of pretty quadrangles through dark openings. A new friend said, 'No wonder the riot police don't stand a chance in Kathmandu's gullies. They have no idea. They come from the villages, hired because they

are the third cousin of some government MP.' In a city like that everyone knows everyone's business. There's hardly a window that is not face to face with another window.

Apart from the barking of street dogs, it's silent at night. After some steel plates fell from my sill with an awful sound I found them piled on the step in the morning. When there was a brawl, crashing between the pools of electric light beneath the houses, the whole street watched from its windows. In the morning they said it was two drunk brothers contesting their inheritance. Another new friend sent me a poem, written on the other side of the world. 'Living in Kathmandu is like this,' she wrote in the subject line.

Everyone pries under your sheets, everyone interferes with
your loving.
They say terrible things about a man and a woman,
who after much milling about,
all sorts of compunctions,
do something unique,
they both lie with each other in one bed.[1]

Hirakaji, my landlord, was pot-bellied and bald, shiny and round. He looked like some kind of chubby buddha. My rental agreement was a piece of paper, which I kept folded in my wallet. Each time I paid for the next quarter Hirakaji wrote the names of three more months on it: *Jestha, Asar, Shrawan; Bhadra, Asoj, Kartik*...Thirty pounds a month, electricity included, no hot running water in the building. By the time I moved on more than three years later every part of that tattered scrap was covered with the names of months written at every angle. In all that time, with dozens of people sleeping within a few yards of me, only once did I hear a woman moan in the night.

Hirakaji's son Sunil taught me to ride a motorcycle. Superbikes and sports cars were his passion because there were none of either in Nepal. While I was riding behind him he loved to swerve and dip around the market-goers and the other vehicles. He pitched his body from side to side to enhance the sensation. On the country roads where I took the controls he climbed all over my back, urging me to go faster. Then I ventured out by myself, and the city traffic made me furious. I swept around the side of a tempo on a broad, quick stretch and almost cut down a terrified couple, perched on tiptoes where the white line might have been, waiting to cross another lane.

I learned a new set of rules. Anything might happen in front of you, but you can also do anything you like: the guy behind you is expecting it. There is never any right of way, which means you can never be completely wrong. If a bus stops in the middle of the road, passengers will start disembarking from the door on the left, so don't cut past it on the inside. It goes on like this, a set of expectations that every road user shares, and until there are too many vehicles it works. Accidents are few. I wasn't slow to learn what to be wary of, nor to recognize the freedom the system gave me, and as I began to know it I found I liked the traffic. The chauffeur-driven ministerial Toyota, with a frilly box of hankies on the back shelf; the vast SUVs of parliamentarians (they passed a law so each could buy one tax-free); the gleaming white SUVs of the donor agencies (perhaps a foreign bureaucrat in the back seat, going to a workshop, or Mum taking the kids to the pool); the taxis, driven by impatient young men from the countryside; and the two-wheeled Chinese tractors, like mechanical oxen, dragging trailers of steel rebar to building sites. There were always traffic cops, blocking the traffic by flagging down a bus for a bribe.

The weather was dry. It was hot, and the fumes stank. The dust got in my eyes, but if I lowered my visor the scene lost its immediacy and I was afraid I would make a mistake. Everywhere the motorbikes were swarming around, enjoying their freedom. It is one of the city's elementary spectacles: a lovely girl, wrapped around her boy on the back of his badly driven bike.

I didn't have any articles to write, so I would sit at my table upstairs above the statue shop, reading Nepali short stories in translation or books of social science, anything that offered to describe the place. Such seeming chaos, yet so many rules. I read:

> Mali work as gardeners and florists and also play an important role in the ritual life of the temples by performing as the masked and costumed dancers ... Nau are barbers and nail cutters, but they leave the cutting of toe nails of anyone below the Jyapu in caste to the Nay caste of butchers ... Bha have the specific role of pipers during funeral processions. Pore are the keepers of the temples of Tantric deities in addition to being sweepers. Kulu, Pore, Chame and Halahulu are considered the lowest of the Newar caste hierarchy.[2]

Sometimes I would sit in the shop downstairs and talk to Sunil about the neighbourhood. On our side of the street, and along half of the other side, the people were Buddhists of the Shakya caste and they all made or sold copper statues. Every family – and they all seemed to be more or less distant cousins – had a shop with the same gods in the window. On the other side were Hindus of the Shrestha caste who did 'import-export'.

The Hindus observed different festivals, or the same festivals differently.

Sunil and his cousins thought that the Shrestha family opposite overworked the little girl who was their maid, bathing the family and oiling their hair on the rooftop, and tramping to the fountain at the end of the street to fill copper jars with water. The two groups didn't mix much, or much less than one might expect since they both spent so much time sitting in the street. As far as anyone knew, they'd always been neighbours.

At several places in Patan there were enclaves of priestly Vajracharyas, the highest of the Buddhist castes. Many of them were silversmiths. There was a community of Jyapu farmers around the corner, who still kept fields outside the city and winnowed rice in the square in the autumn. Half a mile away lived copper beaters, with the water-jars that women carried to the fountains displayed outside their homes. At the margins of the old town blacksmiths, cobblers, and butchers lived. Soft, bloody hides were piled on handcarts and there was shit and blood on the road every morning.

These were all Newar castes, speaking Newari and living in the old parts. But although my neighbourhood was almost entirely Newar most of the city was not. People from all over the country had moved in and entered the hierarchy above and below the aboriginals. The neighbours' overworked house-girl, by her narrow eyes and round face, clearly came from the hills beyond. The ragged porters, who waited to be hired on the temple steps, were from outside the city too; middle-aged men who looked older than they were, with families to feed in the village.

The Madhesis were conspicuously different. They were dark-skinned people from the southern plains, who sharpened the neighbourhood's knives, squatted in the courtyards with their harps to beat and fluff the neighbourhood's cotton mattresses, and sold fruit along the passageways and squares from baskets tied to their bicycles. People told me they were Indians. A few years later, when the people of the plains rose up in anger at their treatment by the government in the hills, rioters burnt the businesses of hill migrants who had settled there, and I found that some of the angriest men had worked in Kathmandu for a while and endured the complacent racism of the capital's housewives and policemen.

The high castes of the hill villages had ruled the city, and the rest of the country, for the last few hundred years. Politicians, bureaucrats, lawyers, and journalists were overwhelmingly Brahmins. Chhetris – one step below them in the hierarchy – provided the old elite of the monarchy, aristocracy and army officers. About a sixth of the national population were Dalits. The formal abolition of untouchability had not been enough to release them; recognized as the bottom of the heap by everyone else, they operated an intricate system of discrimination among themselves. There were about 100 castes, linguistic and ethnic groups in Nepal, most with further subdivisions among them, all living together in Kathmandu and regarding one another with a mixture of tolerance, anxiety, mild bemusement, indifference, and contempt. My Shakya landlords may have been unsure how our Shrestha neighbours celebrated their festivals, but to non-Newars all Newars were more or less the same. On Hirakaji's roof, drinking beer in the evening, a new friend – a Brahmin – described them.

'They're like frogs!' she trilled. 'They are frogs! They're the frogs of the Valley!'

If a community of frogs is trapped in a well it's said that they will drag back any individual that tries to escape, just like the insular and conservative Newars living in their old quarters while the city has been overtaken by new rulers, become modern and exploded around them. It's a description not even Newars dispute.

'They've been here since the Valley was a lake and they never leave,' she said. 'I was sitting on a plane once with so-and-so,' she mentioned a Newar name, 'on an aeroplane, a jet plane mind you, we were going to a conference in Bangkok, and he said, "Dinita, what's beyond Thankot?"'

Hirakaji was about sixty years old and he'd left the Valley only twice, once to visit the wish-granting temple of Manakamana, and once with a delegation of statue makers to Lumbini, where the Buddha was born. I guessed that after a couple of years living in his house I'd crossed the river from Patan into Kathmandu-proper more times than he had.

☀

When Hirakaji showed me a small black snake, like a writhing bootlace, which his family had caught in the kitchen, I asked if he was going to kill it.

'No,' he told me, 'we are Buddhists.'

But there were no such moral qualms against putting out glue-traps, on which screaming rats tore themselves apart at night. Like other Newar Buddhists Hirakaji would never have dreamt of eating a cow, and he also drew the line at chicken, which his caste holds to be a dirty animal. Yet there were no ritual objections to eating goat meat nor, especially, buffalo. When I was invited to join the family for the feast of Bhai Tika I was given one – then to my dismay another – firm, marbled slice of buffalo brain.

A few weeks after I arrived, the greatest festival in Patan passed down our street. There was an enormous cart, with four solid wooden wheels taller than a man, and an enormous wooden

beam riding out of the front. On top of it was a spire of wooden poles, bound with vines and ropes and cane, and decked with green juniper branches, as high as the highest house and leaning badly. The pot-holed road had been resurfaced, and perhaps the tar was still soft, because wherever it had been the studs on the great wheels had printed miles-long strands of divots in the surface. Every year the creaking structure is rebuilt and it takes weeks to drag around Patan, spending a few days at each of several stations, where the small red god inside is worshipped until the astrologers determine that it should move again.

The wires across the street had been disconnected so it could pass. The windows were full of women's heads and the street was full of the men, dancing with their drums and cymbals in the hot afternoon. The crowd was too tight to walk among, smelly and wet with sweat and booze. A platoon of soldiers in antique uniforms arrived and marched twice around the chariot. A musket shot gave the sign and a deep, long roar went up. Upstairs, Hirakaji handed me a plate of milky sweets, prawn crackers, spiced meat, a boiled egg and a slice of cake. Mrs Hirakaji poured me a glass of her homemade rice gin, eighty per cent ethanol. With a surge the huge cart made it round the corner and advanced. People threw water from their windows to cool the teams who were pulling it.

The leaning spire was blocked by the edges of the buildings. Young men swarmed onto the rooftops. Lines were thrown and ropes were attached. They pulled the thing upright and it advanced again. The teams in the street were right below us, and I could see the brake-men, with the wooden blocks they thrust beneath the wheels to stop it. One wheel had ridden onto the kerb and two men appeared with iron poles to smash the brick and concrete away. Kids swarmed over more houses extending more ropes to drag the spire upright, and it was sharply off again, breaking the tiles on the next-door house, which could have but didn't fall six storeys into the crowd.

'Many people have died,' Sunil said mildly.

After the crowds moved on to further rooftops the girls and the boys took the chance to stand close and watch it go. The

chariot swayed away down the street with a few brave men clinging to its pinnacle. It meant bad luck for the kingdom if the thing fell over, as it did quite frequently, and the kingdom's luck was bad. But the men clinging to the top received special protection, and in recent years they had always come through.

Patan's greatest festival is composed of Patan's elaborate social distinctions. The red god is a Buddhist god (known as Bungadya or Karunamaya), who is supposed to bring the rain. His guardians are members of the high Buddhist castes, Shakya and Vajracarya. His chariot is built by members of the Jyapu farming caste, who have a special interest in a timely monsoon, and it is only they who are allowed to climb the spire and direct the teams pulling it. Hindus worship the same god as a Hindu saint, called Matsyendranath, and the wheels are also recognized as a Hindu god, Bhairab. A member of the butcher caste slaughters a goat in offering to the wheels, because they will have blood by crushing someone if they're not satisfied.[3] Each year the chariot rests for a few weeks in a neighbourhood of sweepers, and it is said that Bungadya (who feels lonely on his long journey) slips away in the night to seek company with their women. The opposite has also been observed: in the middle of the night the sweeper women leave their homes and lie naked beneath the god's carriage.[4]

I had an image of the complexity, multiplying in every dimension like the reflections of a complicated object surrounded by mirrors, in which every iteration was different, related to the other images by an inconstant law. I used to tell myself, in connection with everything, 'Don't take anything for granted.' What I meant was, 'If you make an assumption, you're probably wrong.'

At the end of the day the soldiers slung their muskets on their shoulders, climbed into a green army truck and were driven away. I happened to be behind them on Sunil's motorbike. Glowing cigarette tips appeared in the gloom inside. It was raining slightly. The soldiers sat in silence, except for one near the tailgate who began to play his flute, and the noise drifted over the engines and the horns and the clamour. It was enchanting, and I followed the truck out of my way, all the way down to the river.

The monsoon began at night, making a great noise and turning the air cool. Fresh grass sprouted among the roof tiles and brick paving. Sometimes a downpour brought down the rotten roof of an old house. Roads filled with dark water, a foot deep, and the motorcyclists under coloured ponchos drove through it slowly with their feet in the air. When it had been raining continuously for a day or more people stood on the bridge to watch the river race through, composed mostly of water again for a few months every year. And after the downpour had cleared, the giant green hills appeared in startling detail at the end of every street, the minute pattern of the rice terraces, villages and jungle magnified by the clean bright air. I couldn't believe that I lived there.

2

After turning off my alarm at 8.30 I was woken again by an explosion. I stumbled onto the sunny rooftop in my underwear. There was white smoke rising at the end of the street, although I thought it was further away, and pigeons were wheeling around the sky. Other people began to appear on their roofs. I went downstairs, put some clothes on, brushed my teeth (which immediately struck me as absurd) and went outside. The police were already shooing people back and trucks of soldiers were arriving. Whichever route I tried I couldn't get to the scene of the blast, and in that way I realized where it was.

I went to the teashop, ordered a glass of tea and some biscuits. In the newspaper there was a story about the beginning of the bombing campaign the previous day. Nobody had been hurt. An early drunk disturbed me from reading about it so I went outside again. This seemed to be a story; I felt I should do something, but I didn't know what. A taxi driver, whom I'd met before, said that two people had just been killed. The policeman guarding the road said only one. After the police had gone I joined my neighbours as they gathered at the bombsite.

The army had been called following the sinister appearance overnight of a large, new teddy bear. It was leaning against a concrete post. There had been a teddy bear bomb before. The bear exploded when a soldier approached, blowing out the base of the post, leaving it standing on four strands of steel inside. Chunks of concrete were lying about. The puddle beside had clouds of blood hanging in the water. When the smoke had cleared the soldier was lying on the ground, still moving, but with no hands, and he soon died.

I emailed *The Scotsman*, who asked for 400 words 'along the lines of terror comes to Shangri-la'. I declined, saying I didn't really see it that way. I'd hardly got started as a journalist, and in my innocence I thought it was a dubious cliché. Astonishingly the editor asked me to write whatever I thought best. It wasn't published.

Nepal's Maoist revolution began in the mid-nineties, in the hilly districts of the mid-west, where incomes were five times lower than in Kathmandu.[1] By the first years of the new century the rebels had advanced impressively towards achieving the objective, which they announced at the outset, of encircling the city from the countryside:

> This plan of ours is based on the lessons of Marxism-Leninism-Maoism regarding revolutionary violence. On the occasion of the formulation of the plan for ... protracted people's war based on the strategy of encircling the city

> from the countryside according to the specificities of our country, the Party once again reiterates its eternal commitment to the theory of people's war developed by Mao as the universal and invincible Marxist theory of war.[2]

Karl Marx thought that communist revolution would be wrought by the proletariat against the contradictions of industrial capitalism, but (apart from the conquests of the Red Army in 1945) it has flourished in peasant societies. Mao Tse Tung developed the military techniques of a peasant revolution. He drew on the ancient sage Sun Tzu, who'd recommended 2,500 years earlier that a commander should manipulate the enemy, such as by lulling him into untenable positions, or attacking him when he is exhausted.[3] 'Uproar in the east. Strike in the west,' was Mao's tactical doctrine. Protracted people's war was his strategy, his fighters living among the peasants like fish in water, drawing on the peasants' strength and radicalizing them at the same time, so that the war and the political revolution advanced together, until the old order was weakened, put into retreat, swept away, and replaced with communism.

The hills of the revolution's mid-western cradle were less than two hundred miles away from Kathmandu, but far more remote than that from the capital's consciousness. The region had a recent tradition of radical leftism, but had been controlled for centuries by a few families of minor kings. Direct royal government ended and parliamentary democracy arrived in Nepal in 1990. Many of the petty rajas quickly joined the newly empowered Nepali Congress party, taking the vote banks of their peasants with them. The radicals preached that the new parliamentary politics was a false semblance, masking the same feudalism as before. In the early nineties the mid-west began to bubble with communist protests, public meetings and attacks on class enemies. The police, who were loyal to the Congress party, responded by arresting agitators on false charges, torturing them, raping women, beating people up and stealing their animals. Unknown to the government, an obscure committee of Maoists had already written their 'Plan for the Historic

Initiation of the People's War' when a new police action was launched under the code name Operation Romeo in 1995.

Hundreds of police entered the Maoists' mid-western stronghold and swept up hundreds of villagers, almost at random. Thousands of people fled from the rapes, torture and extrajudicial killings. It was a perfect beginning for the rebels. 'They picked up a rock to drop it on their own feet,' said a party worker, paraphrasing Mao.[4] The Maoists only had two guns, only one of which worked, when they launched their people's war in February 1996, overrunning three police stations and an agricultural bank. 'I am confident we will be able to bring the present activities under control within four or five days,' said the home minister.[5]

Two anthropologists later collected the following recollection, of the time when news of the insurrection reached peasants in the east of the country:

> In 1996 we heard that the Maoists were starting to break into the houses of wealthy people, tax collectors and money lenders, stealing their money and property and distributing it to the poor. What amazing news, we had never heard anything like that before! ... We heard that the Maoists were breaking the arms and legs of money lenders and tax collectors in the west of the country and were taking control of villages. How amazing![6]

Sometimes the Maoists would take a villager from his house, whom they accused of being a local thug, an exploiter or an informant, and kill him in front of the assembled people. The village representatives of rival parties fled to the towns. The Maoists took the records of moneylenders, marked with the thumbprints of illiterate villagers, and burned them. They banned the teaching of Sanskrit in schools, because it represented Brahminism and the caste system. They banned alcohol, and the wives and daughters of abusive drunks joined them in hundreds. They made gamblers eat their cards. Many of the Maoists' targets had no moral authority to protect them. Because government schools were so bad private schools had flourished across the country, but only rich villagers could afford them. The Maoists demanded that they make donations to the party and forced them to close. Foreign development projects were notorious for their corruption and for failing the poor, so the Maoists drove them out too.

The Maoists targeted all sorts of people for extortion; from villagers who were obliged to quarter their militia, to village teachers who must give up part of their salary, to rich business men and members of the government, who received threats, and paid. School children were led away for indoctrination programmes lasting days. The rebellion relied partly on coercion and fear, and it also gained support as a result of the state's more indiscriminate, less well calculated violence.

By 2001 the rebels were hitting police stations regularly and slaughtering scores of policemen. Then, on the first of June that year, something extraordinary happened. King Birendra and eight other members of the royal family were shot and killed at a dinner party inside the palace. Civil servants were ordered to shave their heads in mourning, and eat no salt for three days. Indeed, the whole city was cast into deep, hysterical grief. Barbers shaved people's heads for free. Twenty-four hours after the massacre half a million lined the streets, as the cortège crawled from the army hospital to the cremation place on the riverbank at Pashupati.

The crown prince initially survived his head wound, in a coma, and was briefly recognized as the new king. After he died his uncle Prince Gyanendra succeeded him, the third king in four days. But throughout all of this there was no official explanation. 'According to a report received by us,' Gyanendra announced by radio to a half-mad public, 'an automatic weapon went off suddenly, seriously injuring His Majesty ...'[7]

Others supplied their own reasons. The Maoists claimed that the massacre was orchestrated by the CIA and Indian intelligence, because the dead King Birendra was unwilling to unleash the army against them.[8] Most people were bound to conclude that the author of the killings must be the ultimate beneficiary, the new king. He was already an unpopular man. His hooded eyes gave a reptilian cast to his features. The streets were still full of riotous mourners when he sat hunched and scowling for his grim coronation. As he was driven back to the palace the crowds denounced Gyanendra as the murderer. Stones were thrown at the palace gate. Tear gas was fired. A curfew was imposed. Two people were shot. The hardest explanation to accept was the one that was true. The crown prince had murdered his family, because they wouldn't let him marry his girlfriend.

That November (terminating without warning a brief ceasefire and peace talks) the Maoists attacked an army camp, the government declared a state of emergency, and Gyanendra ordered the army into the war. Independent reporting was banned. I arrived a few months later. The newspapers were running daily articles beginning with the same formula, 'A press release issued by the defence ministry said ...' stating the army's count of yesterday's casualties. Hundreds of people were being killed but it was hard to tell who they were, or how these encounters were being fought. By August, 9,900 people had been arrested under the emergency but many of them had no connection to the Maoists, like the *Kathmandu Post* reporter taken in for writing that soldiers in a village had shot a handicapped child. Across the country, deaf mutes and village simpletons were shot as they ran in panic from army patrols. People were arrested and tortured, and disappeared. The Maoists kept hitting police stations, killing the police and stealing their rifles, blowing up government buildings, and sometimes hacking an enemy to death. Plain-clothed soldiers infiltrated Kathmandu colleges to monitor the students' politics. On anti-Maoist operations, the army rounded up 35 labourers building a remote airstrip and executed them.

At the beginning of 2002 the *Kathmandu Post* reported:

> The opposition leaders alleged that the security forces have been 'shooting innocent people suspecting them of being Maoists, torturing the arrested civilians and harassing them.'
>
> They also alleged that the indiscriminate arrests were done without any proper investigation and guided by personal vendetta.

> 'Sick people being taken to hospital have been shot and also those in social and religious gatherings.'[9]

The emergency lasted seven months more. To keep it going the prime minister dissolved parliament, because he knew he would lose the vote. The parliamentary system, which the rebels claimed was an illusion concealing the true, feudal character of politics, had been suspended by the elected government. The rulers in Kathmandu had picked up another rock, and dropped it on their own feet again.

The countryside was in a condition of terror and rebellion, but in the city a picture of the situation emerged only gradually and from fragments. Among the diplomats, human rights people and analysts I talked to it was a matter of keen speculation: the rebels' military strength and tactics; their popular support, or lack of it; the significance of the reports in the newspapers. With parliament dissolved, the Constitution demanded a fresh election by the autumn. Could it be held on time? Kathmandu's insularity and indifference to the rest of the country was notorious. It was frequently cited as one of the capital's salient characteristics. As the city was encircled the rest of the country became harder to ignore, but in the summer of 2002 people still hadn't learned to take the situation outside too much to heart.

I bought Sunil's motorbike and he bought a new one. Three weeks after the teddy bear bombing I rode it 140 miles west, through towering jungle-covered hills to Baglung, to try to meet some Maoists. In most of the neighbouring districts they'd declared 'people's governments', but Baglung was still supposed to be in the state's control. At the district headquarters, in the bare hotel where I stayed, the local reporters gathered to welcome me, but none of them wanted to leave the safety of the town. Instead they found a primary school teacher called Chandra who agreed to be my translator.

Chandra's home was outside the town anyway, so he shared my room that night and in the morning we went there together, to pick up a spare shirt and say goodbye to his wife. Then we set off on foot, along a deep valley of shining greenery. Everything was bright. The path was a highway of school children and porters, an army patrol, people carrying invalids in baskets on their backs; passing in and out between the district headquarters and the villages. There were Maoist slogans painted on the cliffs.

'Informants, be careful.'

'The people's war continues! Long live the C.P.N. (M)!'

In a few hours we reached a stretch of rutted track, apparently unconnected to another road at either end, where a public jeep was running. We travelled out faster, past gurgling irrigation channels through terraced fields. The tape in the car was playing folk music. The passengers wrapped scarves around their faces against the dust and swayed together to the holes in the road. I probably didn't realize, because I didn't know that the Maoists had recording studios, but they must have been Maoist songs on the tape. Between the tracks a piercing male voice shrieked, 'The government kills innocent people, the Maoists kill only the police and army.' According to the voice, the blame for Nepal's misery fell first and second on the government, third on the rebels and last on the people themselves.

In the jeep we met a young health worker called Binod, who was travelling home with his silent young wife. They became our companions. That night we slept in a smoky guest house, on straw mats under heavy blankets, then walked all of the next day. The way followed the valleys through jungle, and the paths were busy. It was hot and damp. Binod questioned the people passing us on their way in about the troop movements further out. At a bend on a muddy, steep stretch we came upon a startling sight which remains fresh in my memory, because I've never seen anything like it again. A striking woman with high cheek bones, her hair covered by a scarf, appeared on horseback. She stood still for a moment, looked at us, then kicked her pony and clattered through the trees.

Nepali hill villages are almost always picturesque, bearing no relation to how sad they are. There are rows and clusters of sturdy stone cottages with low slate roofs, flowers planted

at the front, winding paved pathways and mossy steps, artfully arranged in the huge green landscape. Chandra found a teacher who had been tortured by the army.

'They tied my eyes and hands and they beat me with sticks for forty to fifty rounds,' he translated. 'Nineteen hours was my unconscious period.

'I think the Maoists are also not good,' the teacher said. 'Mr Madhav Malla. They killed him. In my opinion he is innocent. In Maoist opinion he is connected with army.'

Madhav Malla had been a landowner, who was beaten to death with hammers a month earlier. The teacher pointed out the shuttered shops in the village bazaar, whose owners had been driven out by the rebels. They had sold things to soldiers after an army camp was built on a hill above the village. Our teacher had become the headmaster after his two predecessors fled, and now he was leaving too, because neither the army nor the Maoists trusted teachers.

The teachers led us around the village introducing people whom they said I should interview. Afterwards they told us things about these people that the people hadn't said themselves. We were taken to a tailor in the bazaar who had been arrested by the army. Bolts of striped cotton and dark polyester, for making the villagers' shirts and trousers, were leaning against the front of his house. His shop was still open. The army had released him, but the teachers said he really was a Maoist. Congress party members had vouched for his innocence and got him out, because they knew if he was killed the Maoists' revenge would be on them.

I had lunch in the camp. From its eminence, surrounded by barbed wire, the captain and I looked out over the huge forested hills, above us and below us, half covered in cloud. The landscape would have been full of menace to him.

'Look at the geographical conditions,' he said. 'We have no resources ...'

He trailed off. I asked if he was afraid.

'Why not?' he said. He was smiling, young, a bit sheepish. 'They are not the enemy,' he continued. 'They are also Nepalis, our brothers. We have to make them join the correct path.' He turned to the village below. 'Have you seen our poor people? They have to work very hard ... these fields ... it's tough.'

After lunch, in the village, they talked about the army. There was a water pit up there, they said, in which the soldiers tortured people. 'Sometimes they catch an innocent person and they ask random questions, and sometimes, though they are innocent, they give wrong answers. After getting reliable proof, they kill. The radio broadcasts information of Maoists killed in encounters and we know – they have killed that one and that one.'

It was the outermost army camp. The areas where we might find rebels still lay ahead, up the valleys that led north-west. At dusk I wanted to push on to the next village, but then we heard about an army patrol and stayed put. It only gradually dawned on me that I was not simply travelling towards them; I had been surrounded by the Maoists' friends since the beginning of the journey. That night, sitting on the mud floor in a candlelit kitchen, we drank *raksi* and ate curried minnows, and Binod made a speech in his broken English.

He would accompany us to the edge of the high country. His village was out there.

The army had gone up one valley and in the morning we took the other, which led to his home. His had been a love marriage, an inter-caste marriage. As we approached their village his wife produced an immaculate red sari from her small bag and, wearing it, drifted about ahead of us. When we had been walking for a while we would come across her again, sitting on a rock beside the path in her perfect clothes. The trees were smaller and so were the rivers, which ran steeply over stones. Binod began disappearing and leaving us to wait while he went to greet his relatives and hers.

We found the Maoists at the top of the valley. Binod's father, who was a teacher, took me to a house where a commissar's wife was hiding with her baby. I waited there alone, while Chandra and Binod went to the school. Perhaps they were sending more messages.

The commissar's wife was a pretty woman, surrounded by other women also with babies. Apparently she was a fighter herself, on maternity leave. She said that soldiers had been to her home and killed her family's animals. They told her she would be doing everyone a favour if she killed her baby too. We didn't talk much. After a few hours her husband arrived. He was an earnest young man in a checked shirt and glasses, who had a naivety about him, or innocence, which sat quite easily with the menace of an organization that kills people. He was suspicious to begin with and he had an aggressive bodyguard, who was dressed in a tracksuit, with a towel wrapped around his head.

The interview was conventional and dull. The commissar joined the party after seeing the good work it did for the people. It was their policy to oppose American imperialism and develop a new society for the poor. His rebel life brought him no hardship because 'the main thing is thought'. He read my notes as I made them, sitting beside me on the bed. 'I have a clear thought of Marxism-Leninism-Maoism and Prachandapath and the party line is clear and correct,' he confirmed.

Afterwards I bought some noodles and the commissar produced a bag of roasted maize. 'Tiffin,' he said.

We shared the food. The bodyguard took two homemade grenades from his bag, which they called socket bombs. They were pieces of steel pipe, with fittings screwed to seal the ends, a few inches around and a few inches deep. He showed me how, if he removed a piece of tape and held the bomb upside down, a pin like a matchstick dropped out a little. He demonstrated how he would pull it with his teeth and throw, if he and the commissar needed to escape. The tape didn't stick back on again so I gave him a sticking plaster. Then I gave him the rest of my medical kit – minus the condoms ('not necessary') and ('does it cure acne?') the sun-block.

☀

That was the furthest point we reached. Binod and his wife stayed, and Chandra and I turned back down. Another three days' walk, mostly downhill now. A long motorcycle ride. When I got back to Kathmandu what was obvious to me had not yet sunk into the insular city. Holding elections would not be possible in the countryside that autumn. It was sometime around then that I went to see an exhibition of performance art. In both Kathmandu and Patan there is an old palace at the

centre of the ancient core. It has fine brickwork and intricately carved windows. The pagoda roofs of royal temples rise over the palace courtyards. In the surrounding plaza there are high stepped plinths like ziggurats, each with a pagoda set on top of it. Around the many edges of their tiered roofs there is a skirt of scarlet and golden cloth, which runs in little waves with the breeze. Under the eaves there are small bells, with a copper leaf to catch the wind hanging from each clapper.

At the top of a temple's steps a young woman dressed in white, the widow's colour, was sitting in a posture of meditation, like the Buddha. There were some grubby kids staring at her but she ignored them. Hanging above her head was a bag of blood, like a hospital drip, slowly emptying like a sand timer, running through her hair, staining her clothes, first her shoulders, then down her breast. Years later, when I happened to mention the memory, I discovered it was the first time I saw my wife.

3

In any place, presumably, one has to peel back the layers to see how the surface was constructed, but in Kathmandu it was more difficult because so many aspects of the place are not what they purport to be. It's like the puzzle an archaeologist would face who, after discovering an ancient burial, digs beneath it to uncover a beer bottle and a typewriter. Old things overlay what's new, or they are brought to the surface without a true record of their original depth.

In the national museum there are goddesses whose extraordinary breasts are polished every day by visitors who can't resist sticking out a hand. Temples have stones so worn that they must have been trodden and rubbed for centuries. There are bits of ancient masonry all over the place: old statues are stuck into newer walls; waterspouts are reused as steps or bollards, or laid on the ground to stop people from parking; carved stones are dumped among other rubble and reburied. At Jhatapol in Patan, mostly unremarked, there was a smooth monolith standing 10 feet above the ground, as straight and slender as a tree. It carried electric wires but it looked like it could have been there a thousand years. It was in these stones that the city's history lay, indifferent to whether anyone possessed the key to unlock it.

The first account I found of Kathmandu in the past was *A Journey of Literary and Archaeological Research in Nepal and Northern India During the Winter of 1884–85* by Cecil Bendall M.A. of Cambridge University; a slender facsimile hardback of 100 pages, including a few murky photographs. It was a lucky find, and a good place to start, because Bendall's book was the first to examine the stones that are lying around.

In those days the British resident and his small staff were the only foreigners allowed inside the Valley. The government feared that by opening the door to Europeans any further they would invite outright colonization. Bendall must have applied for a special visa. He 'passed the Nepalese frontier, not without considerable annoyance from the officials, and arrived in Kathmandu on November 9th', where he put up at the residency bungalow.[1] He seems to have had a meticulous character, and was possibly pedantic or prickly. In his short text he described in detail the exact nature of the relations that existed between himself and every priest, official or local ruler whom he met, and he offered them disparagement or praise.[2]

Bendall wasn't quite the first to have followed this path. After he arrived he was forced to endure three days of confinement inside the residency, while the resident assured the authorities that he was harmless. Then he set out to read an inscription discovered by an Indian pandit four years earlier, near the water tank called Rani Pokhari on the eastern edge of the city.[3] Reaching there he found that 'the whole masonry of the place... seems quite recently to have been demolished, and heaps of brick rubbish are lying about in all directions, the whole spot as far as the tank now being included in the parade ground.'[4] Next he followed the pandit's footsteps to a stone fountain at Lagantol, and was pleased to confirm his predecessor's view that it recorded the establishment of the conduit by a wealthy benefactor, for the perpetual benefit of the neighbourhood, in AD 657.

Wherever Bendall went his Western dress was enough to attract a crowd of thirty or forty gawping idlers, 'which would soon be doubled if an object like a photographic camera were produced'.[5] In case he engaged in some covert reconnaissance he was accompanied at all times by several guards, but 'far from acting as spies ... they were of great use in overcoming the stupid prejudices against strangers manifested especially by the Buddhists of this country'.[6] He went to the Swayambhu temple, on its hill to the west of the city. The priests refused to show him their manuscripts, and Bendall concluded that they probably weren't put to any intelligent use, since even the chief priest 'to whom I addressed

some simple Sanskrit phrases, did not so much as attempt to answer me in the classical language'.[7] He did at least spot a few lines of archaic writing carved on a fallen column which, by the form of the letters, he attributed to the fourth or fifth century. Unfortunately it had been partly overwritten and illegible.

On the 16th of November Bendall went to Patan and he was impressed by the picturesque effect of the temples in the palace square. On a street leading east from there, past 'a small drill ground' (I guessed it must have been where the police station now stood), he found an inscription dated 688 that could be made out, although it was too smooth to make a rubbing. (Here he noted the advantages of photography in fieldwork, and its drawbacks. His glass negative broke so the photograph remained unpublished, and I couldn't search for the stone he found.) He came to the end of my street. Beside the public fountain he found an inscription whose date he converted to AD 640, recording a royal gift for the restoration of a temple.[8] Nearby was a fine statue of Surya, the sun god, made in 1082, which he also photographed. Then he turned south (along my street) and noted 'a conduit stone with a line or two of chipped and obliterated letters of the archaic type'.

The lane had been black-topped and the houses along it almost all rebuilt since then, but I found some steps made of old spouts, which might have been Bendall's conduits. The inscription of 640 was still there, embedded in the corner of a new brick wall beside the fountain. An old man watched me examine it and he helped me find the Surya statue, outside a temple a hundred yards away. It looked cruder than in Bendall's photograph. We took a cup of water from a shop to clean away the vermilion that caked the inscription.

When Bendall deciphered it, it said:

> When two hundred years were joined with three [i.e. Nepal Era 203 or AD 1082], on the 7th of the bright half of Baishakh, on Wednesday, Pushya [a sign of the zodiac] was auspicious in its rising. Vanadeva, son of king Yacodeva, religiously disposed, made this image well set up in honour of the sun, which had previously been planned by his mother with great rejoicing. Therefore to the maker may there ever accrue supreme increase of glory![9]

Another man came over and joined us in peering at and fingering the text. Even I could make out the figures of the date 203. Together we copied it and later I had it translated. Now the inscription reads:

> Vanadeva's statue which existed in this place, made on Wednesday 7th Baishakh 203 Nepal Sambat, got lost and in the same place Mr Ishwor Man Pradhan, from this neighbourhood, in the memory of his father Govinda Man Pradhan, with the hope that he would obtain salvation in paradise, made this statue ... given to the god Surya with the hope of the betterment of the people NS 1102 [AD 1981].

Local feelings seemed to have changed slowly in nine hundred years, but the statue has been transported to somewhere completely different, to America probably, or Europe, to the basements of a museum or the exquisite den of an anonymous connoisseur.[10]

After three weeks Bendall was sent away. One day the Maharaja promised him a thrilling glimpse of his manuscript collection, the next day he had to go, 'owing to an intimation from the Resident ... to leave the Government bungalow. The reason of this was an official visit by an officer of the Public Works Department.'

He depended mostly upon a single source to interpret his inscriptions. His references introduced me to a book entitled *History of Nepal,* which is also known as the Wright chronicle. Daniel Wright was the surgeon at the British residency between 1866–1876, a decade before Bendall's visit. During his posting Wright bought and had translated an 'antique chronicle', which was published, with his introduction and notes, by Cambridge University Press in 1877. 'Dr Wright's data are on the whole trustworthy,' Bendall believed. 'I think that the new matter I have now brought to light tends to give remarkable confirmation of these native records which are not to be lightly set aside.'[11]

Wright's book was something weirder and greater than Bendall's isolated findings. The chronicle stretched unbelievably far back into prehistory, but Wright had been able to link ancient sites with real places that still existed. It began with the Swayambhu light shining from a lotus, then Manjushree drained the lake with his sword. Various cities rose and fell. In those days a king could still reign for a thousand years, and the gods founded a long-vanished capital near Bhatbhateni, the location of Kathmandu's favourite supermarket. In Wright's day the place was less well known, but in a footnote the British surgeon identified it with a temple in some fields east of the residency: 'persons afflicted with paralysis are supposed to have incurred the displeasure of these deities,' he wrote.[12]

The history relates an incident at a fountain called Narayanhiti, which is the same name as the modern palace, where the crown prince had recently slaughtered his family. In ancient times there had been a drought and a king had offered himself in disguise as a sacrifice to end it. Not recognizing the victim, his own son took up the blade and killed him. The stone head of the fountain turned away in disgust, and when the prince tried to wash his hands the water swarmed with clouds of worms.

At first I browsed in a disconnected way and then I started over, combing the book for references to the way the city had developed. The first that I could recognize came when a Brahmin known as Sunayasri Mishra arrived from the south. He visited Lhasa, the capital of Tibet, to acquire greater powers, then he returned to establish a monastery, which still stands in Patan.[13] The story suggested a clue to the chronicle's ambiguous factual quality. I could see the dates were mixed up.[14] Nevertheless, Wright wrote in a footnote that he went to Mishra's monastery and found Mishra's descendants still living there: he bought another old manuscript from them for his collection. He described the location, at the northern edge of the city, by the road leading down to the river, so I went to Mishra's monastery, to discover what the people there (Mishra's descendants, as I hoped) believed about its history. The sign above the door read

'SUNAYA SHREE MISHRA YEMPI MAHABIHAR *Established First Century AD*'.

That evening there was a power cut. A group of teenagers was chatting in the dark quadrangle. In the second courtyard there was a house, with buddhas painted around the door. When I knocked a child called out from inside, then an old woman appeared with a torch.

'I don't know,' she said. 'I'll take you to the boy's mother.'

The mother was across the road in a darkened tailor's shop. A candle was burning; there was a sewing machine and kurtas on hangers on the wall. There wasn't much the woman could do in a power cut, besides sit in the gloom. Now she found herself being asked strange questions! For a few seconds she couldn't think of a single thing to say.

'We don't know about that,' the man in the next shop interrupted. 'There's only a monk who lives there.'

'I'm looking for Mishra's family,' I repeated. 'I read about them in a book.'

'We've also read about it in a book,' he said, 'but we've never seen any family.'

They said that there was someone else who might know more. They would try to find his telephone number. I should come back another day to collect it. When I did come back, a few days later, I found the same woman sitting in the shop with her sister. They were both stout, round-faced and plain, in their mid-thirties.

'We are supposed to be the ones who are Mishra,' said the sister. 'We don't know anything about it, but we were told that when Mishra built the monastery there was no one to take care of it so the old man married and we are the descendants.'

'But that was so long ago!' said the woman who was there the first time. 'It must have been twenty-five years!'

'Oh no,' said the sister. 'It was muuuuuch longer ago than that!'

It was quite obvious that the confusion over dates wasn't getting any attention here, but however difficult it was to understand, the Wright chronicle did belong to some kind of consensus.

☀

Many centuries pass in lists of kings, each succeeded by his son. Chronicles like Wright's are above all records of genealogy; it is a form known as vamshavali. Against some reigns no information is recorded except the monarch's name and his descent from his father. Some monasteries, such as Mishra's, were there already, but it's only after several more pages of kings that the Wright chronicle says the city of Patan was actually founded.

A leprous farmer went to gather grass on the south bank of the river, thrust his bamboo pole into the ground and went to look for water. When he drank from the spring he found nearby he was miraculously cured of his ugliness. The king renamed the farmer 'Lalita', meaning 'beautiful'. That night the king received instructions in a dream, and after he awoke he founded a city of twenty thousand people near Lalita's spring.

> He built and peopled it according to the following rules observed on such occasions. In the middle of the city he built a tank underground and in it he worshipped the snakes and many other deities. He then covered the tank and the water-courses for introducing and carrying away the water … He then built a *Dharma-sala*, for entertaining thirty-three crores of gods, and called it Lalitapur.[15]

Patan has many names, three of which are still in common use – Patan, Yala and Lalitpur – and others that are archaic, such as Lalitapattana. The stone monolith, as slender as a tree trunk and carrying electric wires, is the bamboo pole Lalita thrust into the ground, petrified, holy, and still rooted there. It is certainly a fact that the stone fountains are Patan's oldest and most important public amenity. And Lalita's farming caste still live there; the guardians, as anthropologists now believe, of the city's deepest layer of tradition.

Kathmandu proper was established later, near the sacred junction of the Bagmati and Vishnumati rivers, after another king had a dream in which the Hindu goddess of wealth, Laksmi, appeared.

> The new city was to be built in the shape of a sword ... and dealings to the amount of a lakh of rupees were to be transacted in it daily. The Raja, being thus directed, founded the city at an auspicious moment, and removed his court from Patan to Kathmandu. This took place in the 3824th year of the age of Kali [AD 722]. The city contained 18,000 houses ... He then peopled it with various castes.[16]

It's important to notice that the old part of Kathmandu is long and thin, a bit like a sword, and business *is* transacted there. Amongst all the other stuff, I could find three more passages which emphasized the city's physical development. The first described the reign of Jayastithiti Malla (AD 1381–95 – by this period the chronicle's dates were only a few decades out). Jayasthiti is praised as a wise king and a reformer:

> He made many laws regarding the rights of property in houses, lands, and *birthas,* which hereafter became saleable. In former reigns criminals were allowed to escape with blows and reprimands, but this Raja imposed fines according to the degree of their crimes.[17]

There were three types of houses in the city: those on lanes, those on streets and those in the city centre. The unit of measurement was a *kha* and its size varied depending on the class of house: for a first-class house it was about 15 per cent smaller than for a third-class one. Two new castes were created, one to measure houses and the other to measure land. In a footnote Wright describes how a system like this was operating in the nineteenth century:

> It may seem an extraordinary arrangement, and to a European a very absurd one, that a measure should vary in dimensions according to the quality of the thing to be measured.

> Such, however, is still the rule in Nepal. There is a special class of people who determine the value of houses and lands. These people are now called Chhibhandail, and they make a mystery of their trade.[18]

In Wright's chronicle Jayasthiti also goes down as the king who codified the caste system, and a list is provided of the sixty-four categories he supposedly defined.[19]

> Every caste followed its own customs. To the low castes dwellings, dress and ornaments were assigned according to certain rules ... Butchers, sweepers and leather-workers were not allowed to have houses roofed with tiles, and they were obliged to show proper respect to the people of castes higher than their own.[20]

The city's planning apparently took another step forward during the mid-sixteenth-century reign of Mahindra Malla, who built a temple and consecrated it with great rejoicing and the giving of land to many Brahmins. 'From this time people were allowed to build high houses in the city,' the vamshavali records.

The final reference I could find was in the reign of Pratap Malla, who became king in 1641. He collected 4,00,00,000 rupees and, in the ritual for laying foundations, buried it beneath his new palace courtyard. To protect himself from evil spirits, witches and epidemics, he put an image of the monkey-god Hanuman beside his palace gate.

These scraps about building the city seemed to be by the way, slipped into the story about gods and kings, which was the author's outward concern. But in this way the vamshavali established some of Kathmandu's most important characteristics: the vigour of trade, the all-pervasive religious significance of its buildings and organization, the tricky and obscure real estate market, caste divisions reflected in the planning, and a fondness for building upwards.

☀

Wright's text also held clues to its own origin, which I could hope to follow. One of its translators, almost 150 years ago, had been a man named Pandit Gunananda, 'residing at Patan, whose ancestors, for many generations, have been compilers of this History.'[21] It was also written, in the course of the chronicle, that during the sixteenth century the family's name was Buddhacharya, and that one of its members had founded the Mahabuddha temple.[22]

I could see the pinnacle of that temple's spire from Hirakaji's roof. I went there, hoping to discover something about the nature of the chronicle, or whether its traditions were upheld (was someone still updating it?), and I started asking people if there were still any Buddhacharyas around. A statue seller in the temple square directed me through a low passage, to a small yard that was sunless and damp. All the houses around it had been rebuilt in bleak concrete. When I rang a bell people put their heads out of the upper windows and looked down from all four sides.

'There are no Buddhacharyas here,' they said, 'but we are pandits.'

I tried the name of Wright's collaborator, the Pandit Gunananda, and they said they were his people. A thin man of about 40, with crooked black teeth and a black leather jacket, led me upstairs through his small shop. His sitting room was furnished with a padlocked wardrobe and a television in a glass cabinet. The walls were painted bright pink and decorated with a studio photograph of himself with his wife, and with a string of plastic flowers. He invited me to sit on a cushion on the floor. I asked him about Gunananda's book.

'Nobody remembers,' he said. 'This family has written so many books.'

It was disappointing, so I asked the same question again in a different way.

'Everyone is dead.'

I asked about his family's bookish history. His father had been the last of the writers, he said, and he wrote his books in Sanskrit, but in the Newari script, a combination that meant almost nobody could read them.

'Where are the books?' I asked, and the man and his wife produced a cardboard box of handwritten manuscripts, tied in scraps and patchwork pieces of cloth. There was the pestle his father used to grind pigments for his ink and two glass flasks he mixed and stored it in. The father made his own paper too, by sticking together translucent thin sheets to compile pages as stiff as board. They brought out a black and white photograph of the old man, in his topi and thick-framed spectacles, with a tika on the glass over his forehead. When he was alive he never allowed his son to touch the writing things. Then they brought more handfuls of loose manuscript, which they shuffled as they spread them on the floor and displayed them to me. It was not all in his father's handwriting, so he thought some of it might have been written by his grandfather.

The son was born when his father was already old. The family was poor and he received little education. There was no money in writing books then, either, so he learnt to decorate statues for a living, and although he had learnt one of the manuscripts by heart he had no idea what it meant. When the father died there had been a list of his scholarly ancestors, including the Pandit

Gunananda, in the obituary notice in the newspaper, but now that he looked for it he couldn't find the clipping.

In a storeroom downstairs, with a painting of a wrathful god on the wall next to a postcard of Saraswati, the couple kept a hessian sack stuffed with crumpled scraps of manuscript. There was a wooden chest stuffed with more. Insects had been inside and the sheets were falling apart.

The couple's daughter appeared in her school uniform, the heiress of a scholarly dynasty. She was studying commerce at a nearby college. I asked her if she ever thought of studying history and the girl cast her eyes down and blew out of the corner of her mouth, as if I'd suggested a long talk with a senile relative. Then she sat down and started diffidently leafing through the sheets strewn across her sitting room floor.

When I was leaving I suggested that I might come back with a scholar, if I could find one, who would decipher the texts. The mother seemed pleased. 'If we can sell them, we will,' she said. 'Because we don't know what to do with them!'

4

In Asia old objects are not generally considered beautiful for their age, which is a peculiarly Western taste. New things are preferred, so ancient wooden carvings are periodically touched up with colourful enamel paints. The fabric of the temples is layered, as they are renewed with fresh donations. When temples are rebuilt after an earthquake, which occur on average about once a century, old pieces of carved timber might be reused even as the structure is altered and worn-out parts replaced. In this way these holy buildings are neither old nor new. Rather, like other things in nature, such as a whirlpool, a forest, or a coral reef, they are constantly occurring in the same place. It is possible, up to a point, to look at the whole city as just such an eternal system.

When Sundar Man Shrestha was a teenager in the early 1960s his mother used to wake up screaming because in her sleep she was being strangled by a witch. 'Every night she screamed and it was a real problem for us,' he emphasized. He hung one of his brother's nappies at the door, hoping that might keep the witch away, but it didn't work.

Waking one morning he found a large cat in the house, peeping at his sleeping mother through a gap in a door. 'It was a big cat, this big, and I said "Cat, you are a witch. I am going to kill you".' The cat was trapped in a room, backed into a corner. 'I kicked it and it went back on its legs like this, it put its front paws out in front, and it disappeared. The image faded.'

After that the bad dreams stopped, but there were other

hauntings. During the spirit-infested season that follows the horse festival, in the spring month of Chaitra, it used to be necessary to eat more garlic, just to keep the ghosts away. Old people remember a large one that would block the passage into Nag Bahal, one of Patan's biggest squares, and refuse to let anyone pass. Around the corner, at the fountain by the Kumbeshwor temple, the slapping sound of a woman washing clothes was sometimes heard after midnight. If she caught you before you fled the square, you would die. And near the bridge between Patan and Kathmandu there was a rankebhoot – a 'lamp ghost', which may only have been the light of phosphorescent gases escaping from the rice fields. The children who lived down there enjoyed watching travellers running in the evening, to be within the safety of the city before night fell. It wasn't only the rankebhoot that frightened them. The kitchkandi under the bridge posed an even greater hazard.

'These things have been disappearing since electricity came,' said Sundar Man. 'Before, people used to terrify each other with stories.'

'They've all gone. They were all scared,' agreed his mother-in-law, Dhana Laksmi. She wore a hat and a hearing aid. Her eyes twinkled and she had one tooth left on top at the front. She poked it forward coquettishly to show when she was teasing. I wanted her to be my informant on the traditions of the city and I returned to her for advice frequently. She considered me pitifully ignorant of the realities of nature. Now she looked at me with concern. Did this interest in ghosts mean I was having trouble with them?

The only ghost Dhana Laksmi ever saw was in the yard outside her house, when she went to sweep before dawn one morning, decades ago. It looked like an old woman but it was smaller than a living person. When she asked it what it wanted it left without speaking to her. After that she never stepped out until first light. 'You'd be afraid too, if you saw it,' she pointed out.

The ghosts hadn't disappeared altogether. Kitchkandis are spectres that stalk beneath bridges, in the disguise of a beautiful woman. If she seduces a man then he will die, but he has a chance because her identity is betrayed by her feet, which point backwards. To keep kitchkandis at bay some taxi drivers hang a charm of women's bangles from their rear-view mirror. I asked them if they were afraid, and the young men mostly laughed, but one driver offered a subtle view. Since the fields around the city had been covered with housing there were fewer ghosts than there used to be, he said. However, although he wasn't a Newar himself, he believed that the old spirits still haunt those areas where many Newars live.

Sometimes when the electricity returns after a power cut, even if the lights, the kettle and the fan don't immediately come on, something almost imperceptible changes and you realize that the power is back. Everyone lives surrounded by wires, buried in their own walls and in the houses all around them. When a man and a boy came to install cable television they brought the line from a tangle on a pole somewhere, through a low passage and over a rooftop, looped it from the corner of one building to the next and arrived at my bedroom window, adding another strand to the complicated web of the city's wiring.

The air is a living vehicle of radio, text messages and wireless internet. The ground is scored and raised by a network of poorly repaired trenches, where extra pipes have been added to the water mains until the pressure is so low that, during the few hours a week when the water flows, people use pumps to get it out of the pipe and into the tanks beneath their houses. The ancient, buried conduits that supply the fountains are little understood. Sometimes a spout that had been dry for decades would flow again after an earthquake, before the depredations upon the aquifers and the deeper foundations of modern developments made half of them permanently derelict. Wells, tanker deliveries, rubber hoses and the copper jars carried on the hips of women complete the city's water system.

Another infrastructure, no less recognized and more slowly changing, runs through the old parts of the city. A grandmother spirit, who can be nasty, inflicting severe stomach cramps or worse if she is not properly invoked, resides at junctions in the chwasa stones. People bring objects that present a magical threat to their household to the chwasa: the clothes of the dead, a baby's umbilical cord, or the ashes of a torch that has been used in an exorcism.

Nasahdya, the god of sound, is represented by an empty space; a triangular hole in a wall that opens his passage through the buildings, because he can only travel in straight lines. Every neighbourhood has its guardians; its own full set of those gods (Nasahdya, Ganesh, Durga, Bhairab ...) that daily life requires. Apart from the empty space of Nasahdya, these guardians are uncarved, natural stones, which have never been moved from the place where the earth divulged them. They form a network of gods and goddesses, spirits and ancestors that underpins the city, its genii loci.

Many courtyards have another stone somewhere, which is Lukmahdya, the Hidden Shiva. The old lady Dhana Laksmi told me Lukmahdya's story on his feast day, wrinkling her nose and poking her tooth at me. The god entered the city after he'd given a demon the power to turn people into ash and, realizing that he needed somewhere to hide, he chose the garbage of the courtyards for his camouflage. 'You know that small yard?' she said. 'That's where we used to throw our rubbish. That's where he is.'

Even heaps of reeking trash were holy, if they were in the right place. Even the dogs in the street and the crows on the roof were gods, and had their annual festivals.

☀

> [I saw in Patan] a large number of destroyed houses, as the natives rarely repair a house: rather, anyone who regards himself as a man of distinction constructs himself a new house and lets that of his father decay.[1]
>
> – Prince Waldemar of Prussia (visited in 1845)

Hirakaji's son Sunil pointed out a house to me while we were walking together, a low brick building with tiny windows filled by wooden grilles, where as a boy he once paid a few rupees to watch a pornographic film. The same house had belonged to Gayahbajye, who was a famous priest and a powerful magician. His powers were so great that he transported gods from different parts of the Valley and placed them in the temples near his home. A room inside has been left empty since he vanished while meditating there hundreds of years ago.

The low wooden door was opened by a woman who introduced herself as Gayahbajye's daughter-in-law, by which she meant that she was married to his remote descendant. The lady was an amateur painter and she had decorated the small low rooms with her own watercolours, of birds and local monuments. She showed me the special room, with an electric lamp through a hole in the kitchen wall. It was dark, with a pile of timber in it. Some priests, and officials from the government's Department of Archaeology, had come to investigate the mystery, she said, but when they started digging the room began to fill with water and they abandoned the attempt. She spoke as if it was yesterday, but this happened fifty years ago, before she was born. Every morning she worshiped the wall outside with poinsettia flowers and rice.

Gayahbajye's house stood in a square of fine old buildings, until old houses on two sides were replaced with new ones in the early 1990s. Enclosing the square to the south was the imposing fifteenth-century shrine of a secret god, open only to initiates of Gayahbajye's lineage, until part of it was demolished in 1996. In 1997 half of Gayahbajye's house was torn down too.[2] Kathmandu people do not find the old houses picturesque. Sometimes a magnificent carved window, centuries old, is cut in half when a brother – inheriting his part of the ancestral property – rebuilds his side in brightly painted concrete. There is no charm in inertia; living in a small dark house in the shadow of your brother's lofty statement, your wife jealous of your brother's wife. In this way the city is constantly renewed by the ambition of pious family men.

The prayer for consecrating a new house begins:

> Oh well-born son! Any man in Nepal, whether he be a philanthropist or not, should build a house as follows: assemble carpenters and brick makers and other incarnations of Bisvakarma as necessary. Then, choosing an auspicious time, prepare and bake bricks. Have the auspiciously ordained foundation laying ceremony ... Then build a magnificent house with the proper auspicious marks and proportions. If a man does this, I call him great.[3]

The family priest will determine whether or not a proposed building site is auspicious or is, for example, already occupied by naga serpents. An astrologer will determine whether the venture is a wise investment, and the best time to start work.

Dhana Laksmi told me the story of a shopkeeper in Mangal Bazar, called Hem Narayan. He was advised that if he built where he intended then the nagas who lived there would have no outlet, and would bang their heads on his foundation. He took a cavalier attitude.

'If the nagas bang their heads who will suffer?' he asked.

'The oldest man in the family.'

'What about the kids, will they be affected?'

'No,' he was assured. 'The kids will be fine.'

'I might as well, then,' the old man reasoned. 'I'm going to die soon anyway.'

The foundation was laid but before the first storey was complete he and his brother fell ill. When the fever subsided, twenty-one days later, they found themselves preposterously stooped. Their heads bobbed in front of their shoulders like tortoises'. Their caste was Mahaju and people knew them from then on as the leaning Mahajus.

For as long as the streets and courtyards have lain where they do now a house has been about eighteen feet from front to back, with a wall in the middle, dictated by the nine-foot span of the floor beams. Wealthy families and kings built four blocks at one time to create a courtyard. For the rest that was achieved more gradually, until a space was enclosed by four houses and an extended family enjoyed their privacy and security within. This courtyard is a chowk, where children play, clothes are washed, grain is dried, men gamble at cards and the family eats feasts. The chowks are the basic unit of the old quarters. The height of the roofs' ridge beams, where they met each other end to end or at right angles, was roughly the same. The skyline was a hand-knitted pattern of clay-tiled slopes, with the pagoda-roofs of the temples rising above them.

> O client, many lucky signs must be present and many rules of proportion must be observed when a house is built ... First the smoke of the brick kiln goes up to heaven and the 330 million gods smell it and ask where it came from; the king of the gods, Indra, tells them that it is the smell of smoke made on earth by an ambitious man who is firing bricks to build a house to stay in; and the gods, hearing him, immediately give their blessing: 'Fortunate and upright man! May this house be well favoured; may it be durable; may it be without flaw; may it be a dwelling place of Laksmi; may the builder live long; may his heart's desire be fulfilled!'[4]

To stop the rain from washing away the mud between the bricks Kathmandu's builders invented a wedge-shaped brick, which covers the joints and gives the most prestigious buildings a smooth burnished lustre. These walls are prone to bulging under

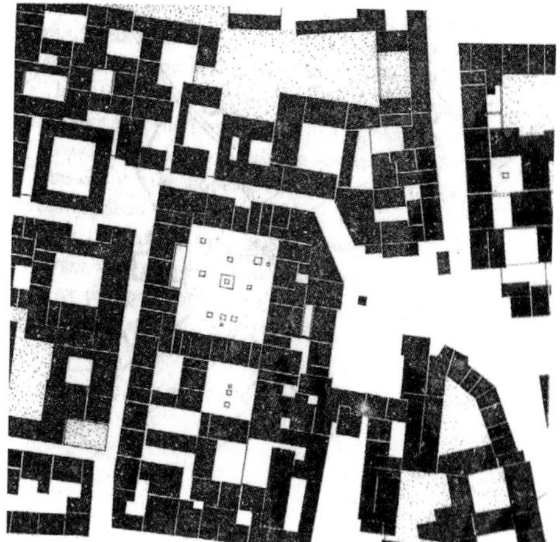

their own weight so a wooden frame is made to stiffen them, like the steel inside reinforced concrete but much more expensive. Where the timbers show on the surface they are decorated with carved serpents and the heads of animals.

The foundations are not deep so, in time, uneven settlement will cause the walls to crack. And, because the stones of the foundation do not rise above ground level, the base of the walls will be exposed to surface water, making the ground floor damp. At every stage of the construction, as the door jambs and lintels, window frames, floors, ridge beam and roof tiles are put in place, a puja is done and red and yellow powder is smeared on the unfinished building. In this way the gods run through the house like the wiring. There will be a few small gaps in the brickwork where the bamboo scaffolding was fixed. They will be overlooked when the builders leave and sparrows will nest there. No nails are used anywhere in the structure. If water seeps in and rots the pegs that hold the frame together an empty house can be ruined in a few monsoons.

The ground floor is a shop, storeroom or workshop. The sleeping and living quarters are in the middle and the purest and most private places, the kitchen and the puja room, are nearest to heaven.

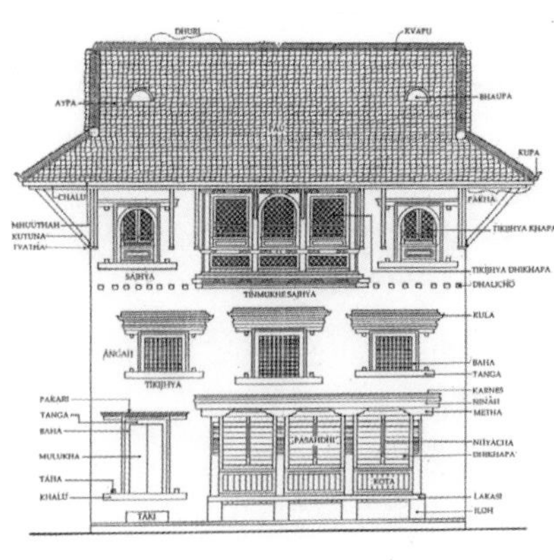

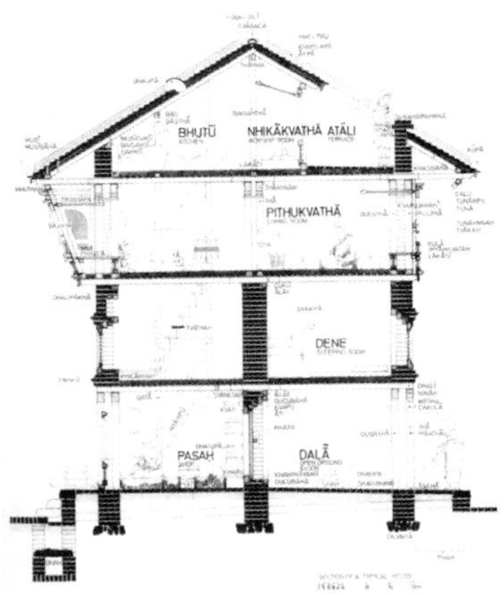

> O well-born, may the merit of your good deed help you to attain the four goals of life, the seven kinds of well-being, the eight kinds of property, and rid you of the eight terrors ... may you have good fortune and happiness in all ten directions and at all three times. Good luck to the whole world!

In the old parts of the city, when people refer to a house they often mean the site it stands on, and every structure that has ever stood on that site. It is a continuous family institution, of which the fabric (like the people in it) is continually replaced. When someone breaks down the beautiful old brick and timber house his ancestor made, and builds for his family in their ancient place a new concrete home (ugly inside and out, and cold in the winter) the new structure retains the centuries-old shape of the plot and the hierarchy between the storeys above it. Before he starts to build he digs a hole, does a puja in it, and fills it in. Then he digs the foundation.

Hirakaji and all of his neighbours, who were descended from the same ancestor, had each rebuilt their share of the ancestral site in concrete. The old house, before it was divided by inheritance, must have been large, with a passage through the centre into the chowk behind. One afternoon I was working at my desk, and I suppose I was unable to concentrate, because I wandered onto the roof to look out over the rooftops and the pinnacle of the Mahabuddha temple, and someone bolted the door from the inside. I was stuck up there, until a neighbour appeared on his roof. I stepped over the low wall and followed him down his stairs. The upper floors of his house were dark, the walls were unplastered and the windows were unglazed. We passed through rooms piled with the clay moulds of statues, and down unlit stairs, until we emerged not on the other side of the passage, as I expected, but into the chowk behind. The history of the family had made a labyrinth inside that group of buildings.

At its most local levels, of the neighbourhood, or the individual house, Kathmandu is ordered by religious concepts, either around holy stones, or divinely sanctioned carpentry and bricklaying techniques. The same is also true of the city as a whole.

In the sacred diagrams called mandala the principal god or goddess is worshipped in the centre, surrounded by a retinue of related deities, representing the different aspects of the governing spirit's nature, and their relationship to the power at the centre.[5] A mandala is something like an icon, which channels the power of the god it depicts, and therefore something like a prayer or a spell. I also read that each ancient city is a giant mandala, a diagram of the order of the universe, with the king's palace at the centre, surrounded at the margins by the temples of the Eight Mother Goddesses, by the twelve sacred bathing places and the eight cremation grounds.[6]

So I went to see a Buddhist priest of the Vajracharya caste – a gubhaju – because they are the ones with the power and the responsibility to master and mediate this side of life to the laity. I had a whole sheet of typed questions: What does the city's mandala mean? Does it belong to a particular god? What's the meaning of the festival of Matya? (I thought the tortuous route of that day-long procession might hold some secret.) Can one also think of a single house as a mandala? Would it be possible to draw a map of the city, which wasn't a map of chowks or streets but a map of gods? I was fascinated by the idea that the city had a secret design, but I couldn't understand what the nature or meaning of such a scheme could be, so I didn't know what to ask him.

The gubhaju lived in an upstairs room by the bus park at Lagankhel. The passage to his narrow stair was stacked with boxes of the same crockery and thermos flasks as were for sale on the pavement outside. The walls of his room were almost entirely covered by pictures of gods, and tableaux of traditional life, which seemed to have been cut from magazines or calendars. Especially prominent were several large pictures of himself in his robes, adopting special postures, with a bright sunburst inserted behind his head by the photo studio. On the windowsill there were two white doves in an iron cage. It was a bright fresh autumn day and the gubhaju had his windows open. On my recording of the interview there is a constant hubbub of the bus conductors and market traders outside.

The gubhaju was in his eighties, sitting cross-legged on the floor. He rifled through heaps of paper and handed me photocopied scraps: a mandala of the goddess Durga with a Sanskrit text beneath; a Newari text he'd composed himself on the faults of modern society, and the rituals that would correct them; a list of forty-nine holy places of the Valley that he had visited and their holy days; and a history of his most illustrious ancestor, a tantric who performed magic acts. He chuckled and pulled his legs tighter around himself as he talked. I asked him about the city's mandala.

'In ancient times,' the gubhaju said, 'the Kathmandu Valley was a lake and at that time it was a golden age. In the Age of Treta, the bodhisatva Manjushree cut the mountain and let the water flow out. Only then people started settling here.'

That much I knew. I asked him about the mandala again and he said, 'It *is* like a mandala. The centre is Gujeshwori. In whichever direction you go from there, east, west or whichever, is 7 kos [14 miles]. People celebrate the day Manjushree cut the mountain on the tenth day of the waning moon of Mangshir.' He took out his charts and showed me.

I pressed him again. 'Actually, we don't talk in detail about the mandala,' he admitted. 'It includes everything, birds, animals, human beings, everything, but we're not allowed to explain it. The first god that was created was Gujeshwori, who is both male and female and began creating the other creatures. All the other creatures came out of Gujeshwori.' I was following him more or less. I knew that at Gujeshwori there is a hole in the ground, fringed with stone petals, which is related to female power somehow. It does stand somewhere near the centre of the Valley. And I wasn't surprised by his secretiveness, because I had read that gubhajus reveal the real truth of their religion only to the initiated, and there would be no question of my ever receiving it.

We were interrupted by a woman who had come with her two children to consult him as a healer or magician. The children, she complained, were not doing well at school. He prescribed some rituals. She touched her head to his feet, and she paid him with a small plastic bag of what seemed to be flour. After they'd gone I tried another tack and asked him about the Eight Mother Goddesses, whose temples are in a ring around the city.

'The Eight Mothers are outside the city, not inside,' he said. 'We can explain it up to the Eight Mothers, but the mandala inside the circle of the Eight Mothers we cannot explain. Eight is a very significant number. They are for protecting people against disease, fire, water and so on. These goddesses are located in the eight directions.'

He talked about many things. I tried to hold him to what I saw as the point, and to work through my list of questions, but I might as well have been asking 'How many hamburgers make a Wednesday?' for all the sense my questions seemed to make to the gubhaju. I drew a diagram of concentric circles like I'd seen in a book, representing the location of the most important buildings in the centre of the city and the lowest on the outskirts, and I asked him about it.[7]

'In the past,' he said, 'when you are in high rank you go nearer to the centre and if you are poor and of low rank you have to move out of the city. The king, the palace, is in the centre and near the palace are the higher-ranked people.'

'Maybe it was to do with land prices?' I said.

He ignored it. 'In the centre are located the gods and goddesses. In the next yoni come ... how to explain it? ... they are just like spirits. Then comes the human yoni. Then comes the demon yoni, then the animal yoni. The furthest place is Narka. Narka is hell. Altogether there are six yonis,' he said, noticing that I had sketched only five. The gubhaju spread out a different mandala on the floor between us. 'This is simplified,' he assured me. 'A small number of gods are depicted – there are sixty-four gods here. The deeper you go the more gods there are.

'I don't know about Kathmandu but I know in detail about the Patan area,' he said. 'I have a dispute with the priests of

Kathmandu. They say I don't know about the things of Kathmandu, but when we have debates about religion I have defeated them many times, because I have done research on this mandala which they have not done.'

I left when the old man had talked for as long as he wanted to, and at the time I was disappointed I hadn't received a clearer explanation, perhaps resembling some kind of map. Now it seems he gave as clear an account as I could have hoped for. And for what it was worth I already had a book with a translation of the liturgy that gubhajus use, describing the Valley's mandala. So if he wouldn't discuss it with me, or if I couldn't understand his explanations, I could get some impression. When a gubhaju begins a ritual he recites in Sanskrit:

> OM, now in the period of the Attained One, Lion of the Sakyas [i.e. the Buddha] ... in the Kali world era ... in the Himalayas ... in the land of Nepal ... flowing with the four great rivers ... adorned with the twelve holy bathing places ... surrounded by the mountains ... the Eight Mothers, the Eight Bhairavas ... on the south bank of the Bagmati ... in the city of Lalitapattana [i.e. Patan], in the kingdom of Aryavalokitesvara [i.e. the red god Bungadya, who came down my street in his giant cart] ... [8]

Working from the inside out, it would go something like this: in the centre is the Buddhist god Cakrasamvara, surrounded by four goddesses and the four Kings of the Directions. Then there are three circles of lotuses, thunderbolts and flames. In life, the king's palace sits in the centre. He is not exactly a god, but anyone can incarnate aspects of the divine and in the king's case he incarnates aspects of the loftier lords in heaven. His palace is surrounded by the temples of the greatest Hindu gods. They receive pure, vegetarian, non-alcoholic offerings from Brahmin priests. Courtier families and priests live near the palace and the various other castes live among one another throughout the city. Each caste has its own affinities to different gods, according to its nature and occupation. In the middle ranks of the caste system, for example, Jyapu men (of the farming caste) have an affinity with Bhairab, Shiva in his wrathful aspect, who is also associated with beer. Jyapu women have an affinity with Hariti, the Buddhist goddess of smallpox, who has power over young children, so they act as midwives.

On the city's outskirts, the low castes, by performing unclean tasks such as butchery or drum making, or conducting death rituals, absorb pollution on behalf of the community, allowing the high castes to stay pure. The edges of the mandala, or the areas beyond the ordered life of the city, are the land of the dead. Butchers are permitted to live just inside the gates but the lowest, most impure people, the Pode sweepers' caste, who shovel shit, must live outside, where the demons and the witches also live, and where the ghosts are most numerous among the rice fields. They are the receptacles of all the bad omens, of all the pollution, degradation and filth of the city, and their affinities are with the lower and more dreadful spirits. The cremation grounds are near their homes, each associated with a Mother Goddess to whom the Pode act as priests. The goddesses receive blood sacrifices and offerings of alcohol. Just as the Brahmin priests of the high gods are themselves high and pure, so the untouchables can have great and frightening powers, like the blood-drinking divinities to whom they minister. In the wilds around the edge of the mandala there is a ring of skulls.

The mandala is more than a map of the city. It is a social and political ideology, a description of the order of the universe, which is repeated in a well-ordered city here on earth.

Beyond the Khumbeshwor temple, on the spirit-infested and shit-strewn edge of Patan, where the city wall once ran, lives a colony of butchers. The old woman Dhana Laksmi Shrestha was once young and living nearby, on the better side of the temple, in a neighbourhood of high-caste Shresthas, when there was an outbreak of caste-inflected killing in the late 1940s. It seemed to show something about how the different communities lived separately but together inside the mandala. I'd heard her refer to it.

'Did you see the people hanged?' I asked.

'Hang? I've seen so many people hang.'

'Who did they kill?'

'*Who*?' She squinted at me. She thought I was a moron. 'Why, they killed themselves!'

I tried to explain which particular tragedy I had in mind.

'There was a place for the men to shit and there were pigs there. We had another place the same,' she said. 'You know pigs?'

I offered a different word, the only one I knew for 'pig'.

'This kind is a black one. It eats shit and it has hair like this.' She stuck her fingers up to demonstrate a crest of bristles, wrinkling her nose and poking her front tooth at me. 'A pig's work is to eat what we shit. A man went to shit by the stream, a guy like you, and a pig came. If you touch a pig you have to take a bath, and the pig was coming to where that guy was shitting. He was afraid that it would touch him, so he hit the pig with a small brick. Now, sometimes you hit a pig with a brick and nothing happens. But that time just a small brick hit it on the head and the pig died. The pig man saw.'

The butchers owned the pigs. A generation later, Shrestha mothers who weren't born when it happened would tell their children about the enormity of the crime the butchers had then committed, so that they would not play with the children of the butchers' colony.

'The person who killed the pig was a [high-caste] Chhetri, but he was poor and lived in a small shed. He was so strong he could carry bags of salt. You know "safes"? He could carry a metal safe all by himself. His son sold ice cream.

'That butcher was one who had a lot of money. He could buy you and me together. His name was Dil Bahadur. He was big, the biggest butcher in Nepal! He was consumed by spite. He was waiting for an opportunity. He found the opportune time, he got all his friends together in the middle of the night and went to the Karki's [Chhetri's] shed. On that day there were five people in the family – one had gone out. He was working, he hadn't come home.' This was the lucky ice cream seller.

'Who killed him, how did they kill him? No one knows how they killed that strong man. Two hands would not be enough. But if one person is attacked by many people, if two hands have to defend against ten hands, then however strong you are it's not going to work,' Dhana Laksmi reflected. Her eyes sparkled. She was wrapped in blankets, sitting forward, taking her time over every relevant detail.

'There were three small children, two or three years old, in the Karki's house. They tied rope around the babies' necks then stuffed cloth and cotton down their throats. That's how the kids were killed. The wife was also killed. She had a rope around her neck and five knives in her bottom, where she pees.' Dhana Laksmi gestured to show me where she meant. 'In this way they were killed.

'In the morning, when the men were shitting together, these Karkis didn't come so people went to their hut and saw the bodies. They were frightened and they screamed. The police came and sat around. There were so many people it was like a jatra [festival]. The police brought the dead people out, including the three kids. I've never seen so many people, and then more police came. It was bigger than a jatra, it was like a mahajatra!

'The kids with the cloth stuffed in their mouths, even now the thought of it is difficult ... ' Dhana Laksmi turned to a description of investigative methods which still serve the Nepal Police. 'They took the people of all the houses. How many people! They took them all. Only the women were left. Everyone was separated and they started choosing people. There are some people who know who is guilty. There was a person who knew whether someone was guilty or not, sometimes just by looking at their face.'

'Who was this person?' I asked.

'It is a person within the police. He is called *inespector* or something,' she said, satisfied. 'Eventually five people were chosen. They were held for many days. They were questioned and three people came out guilty. They were the real culprits.'

I was reminded of the police chief of a western district who had told me, despite accusations of torture, that his men no longer used traditional methods of investigation. Dhana Laksmi was coming to the climax of her story and some aspects of legal procedure had changed since her young days. 'There used to be people who would come around announcing a hanging,' she said. 'They went through the streets with cymbals and drums and a huge crowd assembled. Outside the butcher's house a gallows was made from bamboo. It consisted of two A-frames with a pole fixed between them.'[9]

'The men were brought out. They were wearing only that thin yellow dhoti that Brahmins wear and they had shackles around their feet and hands, and around their necks, so even if they ran they wouldn't get away. They were on a platform with wheels and they were paraded around the city. There were so many people they looked like ants!'

The condemned men reached the lane where they lived, where the gallows stood. 'They took the rope, made the first one stand on a chair, they put the rope around his neck like this, and they removed the chair. So they were hung.'

I asked her where she was while this was going on.

'I was in a window right next to it! My daughter was very young, so I ran there leaving her with my mother. He went limp and he died. I didn't know how people were killed before that. They died very fast. They moved for a while then they died.

'When one man was dead they put another one there. They put the rope in the same place and he died. They had killed two, then they brought the main guy. Everyone shouted "They've brought Dil Bahadur!" They made him stand up there and they put the rope here.' She demonstrated how they placed the knot at the side of Dil Bahadur's jaw. 'If they put it here you don't die. You don't go quickly. He went *phir, phir, phir, phir, phir, phir, phir*. His whole body moved for a long time. Eventually he died.

'What kind of justice is that?' she exclaimed. 'He died pretty soon. If it was up to me I would have chopped off parts of his skin and put salt inside. Dil Bahadur's home was right there, and the people from his family had been taken to Nag Bahal and locked in a house. After everyone was dead they let them out and they came to the hanging place. They cried so loud that even the heavens could hear them! The police chased them back inside their house.'*

The cops dug a hole and threw the bodies in it and Dhana Laksmi moved on.

'That rope is so scarce and desirable, that the only way you can get one is by hanging yourself. There'd be no point in that, would there?' she speculated. 'The cops sold it to the medicine wallahs.

'Two snakes copulating. You don't see that very often, but I have seen it. They twist their bodies together. You are supposed to cover them with a piece of cloth and the seed will fall on that cloth. The cloth, plus the rope, the medicine wallah will burn them together, and he'll say a mantra. It's very expensive, that ash, and if you put it in your hair you can entice anybody. Even if a husband doesn't like his wife he'll fall in love with her. Or the other way around. Now the story is over. I need to eat.' But she wasn't quite finished. 'I think they may have used such a medicine on our neighbour's daughter,' she reflected, returning to the present. 'She eloped with the shopkeeper's son, and he beats her up every day.' She went for lunch.

---

* After this book was first published in India in 2014, I came into contact with the family of the man named here as Dil Bahadur, whose hanging Dhana Laksmi described. It appears she had confused the names - the victim was Dal Bahadur Karki, whereas the man convicted and executed as the principal murderer was Jit Bahadur Khadgi. The murders were discovered on 15 May 1945 and the executions took place at the beginning of 1947. According to Jit's nephew, Siddhi Bahadur, his uncle was innocent, maintaining his innocence to the end, and the murders were in fact committed by a man named Kajiman Tamang. According to the Khadgi family, a case was fabricated against Jit Bahadur, using Kajiman's false testimony, because the family's wealth and low caste status inspired the animosity of Narayan Shamsher Rana, the governor of Lalitpur. The case, which was famous throughout the Valley at the time, is described in a Nepali language biography of Siddhi Bahadur Khadgi, *Sangharshashil Siddhi Bahadur Khadgi Jiwan ra Byaktitwa*, by Hemang Raj Giri, published in 2015.

5

Mrs Hirakaji had had an operation of some kind. Her sari revealed the large scar on her stomach, and she was less willing to do house work than previously. So Hirakaji hired a child, not more than twelve years old, and stood over her in his gnomic way while she sulkily swept my floor.

I watched the family participate in the cycle of the festivals. At Matya, when the map of Patan is redrawn as an itinerary of every Buddhist chaitya in every chowk, Hirakaji took his place outside his shop, solemnly holding the rope that described the route across the street from one dark opening to another. The community ambled past on its procession around the hundreds of holy places. The old part of Patan is only a couple of miles across, but at Matya it takes ten hours or more to trace every tiny passage to every hidden chaitya in a mazy clockwise circuit that never crosses its own path.

A few months later Hirakaji dusted down the row of electric candles that lay year-round on the stairs and put them to blink on the window ledge, while the street filled with oil lamps like runway lights, and Mrs Hirakaji painted a track of red clay up the stairs, from the threshold to the puja room, to guide the goddess of wealth inside.

I wanted to know every grain of the city's texture. I noticed that in the autumn, in particular, the streets were littered with unlucky packs of cards. They'd been torn and scattered there by remorseful drunks. Or, for example, I heard about a woman, a friend's friend's wife, who threw a pot of piss out of her bedroom window at night, and was killed by electricity that leapt in from the cables outside. Oxyacetylene torches suddenly whitened

dark workshops. Monkeys crossed the road on overhead wires. Sometimes they also completed the circuit with a bang.

There were lovesick kids in the cyber cafés and broken-hearted grown-ups on the pavements. Sometimes I experienced a moment of pleasure, bordering on excitement, while sitting in the back of a taxi, stuck in traffic with the windows down, watching dusty Kathmandu grind past like a machine without oil. I heard a song playing on a tape in a taxi. It was new folk music for kids who'd moved from the villages to the city.

Sweetheart, I don't know if you're in the mountains or the plain
But I'm going to the cyber and we'll meet on the chat.
You're in a strange town but I'm in Kathmandu
And I'll meet you on the internet.
My sweetheart, we'll meet on the internet.

And painted on the back of a bus:

For beautiful girls a heart is not a heart but a toy
Those who fall in love with them will end up crying

And on the back of a truck on the Ring Road:

Driver's life is golden life,
One one turning one one wife

(It meant: for every turning, another woman.)Above the open cab door, where the fat moustachioed driver sat over his vast wheel, was painted:

'I'm so tired of love songs.'

Hirakaji's child-servant seemed a bit too young, and she didn't come often. So I hired someone of my own, a pretty girl in her late teens, not above five feet tall, named Sita. Her three brothers were labouring on building sites in Gulf emirates. She was saving to buy a job, wiping up piss and shit at an old folks' home in Israel. She came round a few times a week to clean my rooms and cook some food. I was too uncomfortable then with the idea of servants to make her do the laundry, which I took to a dhobi elsewhere. Since I only had two rooms, and I ate most of my meals out, there wasn't much for her to do.

I sang Sita a song that I'd heard in a taxi. She said she would find the CD for me, and came back with the video on a pirate disc. On it, a man and a woman made eyes at each other across the crowd at a village wedding, then performed a teasing duet.

I like my sister-in-law,
Well, she's beautiful,
But she's a little bit black.

I have a vain brother-in-law,
Although he's OK
He's a bit of a hooligan.[1]

I asked Sita what she thought of it. 'Of course he's a hooligan,' she said. 'He wants his sister-in-law.'

> 'Kings, serpents and tigers are never to be trusted: he who trusts any of them is soon ruined.'
>
> – the Wright chronicle[2]

Contemporary politics, which was a genuine matter of life and death, was playing as a farce of shameless, naked greed and short-sighted incompetence. Since parliamentary democracy was established in 1990 two political parties had dominated the stage. The Nepali Congress was the principal party of government. They were the epitome of democratic ideals and personal integrity until a decade in power corrupted that image. Now they stood exposed as flabby hypocrites, their leaders climbing over one another to get in bed with every power centre and business interest. The alternative was the Communist Party of Nepal–Unified Marxist Leninist, which was known as the UML. They had long since torn off their ideological pyjamas. The politicians wrestled bitterly on the bedroom floor. They demonstrated a painful series of contortions. Short-term advantage was everything. Cunning stratagems rebounded on their originator. When the Maoists launched their people's war in 1996 the politicians in Kathmandu hardly noticed. They more or less ignored the rebels, besides ordering some police atrocities. They became exposed as impotent men fighting over a courtesan, or bald men fighting over a comb. All the time the Maoists tightened their encirclement of the city.

The prime minister was said to be a drunk who fell off his chair at parties. Diplomats reported, amazed, that he drank two bottles of whisky in a night. In May 2002 he had dissolved parliament to extend the state of emergency, cleverly outwitting his colleagues, and split the Congress party in two! Unknown to him, the war in the hills was going worse than ever. The constitution required him to hold fresh elections by the autumn, but it belatedly emerged that that would not be possible. With five weeks to go before the deadline he went to the king to ask for another year. (He hoped that by acquiring helicopter gunships he could make the country safe for voting.) It was a true surprise when the king sacked him instead, citing incompetence. Anyone could see the Maoist threat to democracy, but this ambush from the royalist Right seemed to take the democrats off guard. They were almost united in denouncing the 'regression'.

King Gyanendra had come to the throne the previous year, after the royal massacre. (It was his misfortune that most people still believed he'd done it.) Throughout the year of official mourning he had made a display of rigid, scowling royal dignity. He was known to be conservative. He had never concealed his disapproval at the concessions his dead brother made twelve years earlier, when royal government made room for parliament. No doubt he found his views on democracy confirmed by the mess the kingdom had become. Clearly, he relished the opportunity to put the palace back at the centre of things. Clearly he thought that he could fix the Maoists, where the corrupt and incompetent politicians had failed.

The foreign supporters of the war effort were alarmed by the lack of political unity in Kathmandu, and they blamed the parties for it.[3] 'Nepal's house is on fire and the politicians are arguing about who gets to sleep in the master bedroom,' the American ambassador complained.[4] Britain was supplying troop-carrying helicopters. America was sending M-16 assault rifles and (secretly) military advisors. After the prime minister was sacked the ambassadors made their rounds of the democratic leaders, urging them to work constructively with the king.

When British ministers travel to obscure countries, I was told, the briefing pack they read on the plane contains a photocopy of the introductory section ('Facts about Nepal') from the Lonely Planet travel guide. By chance it happened that in the week after the king sacked the prime minister, while the kingdom's political personalities were trooping to the palace to offer their views on the formation of a new government, a junior British Foreign Office minister was in town. It was a year since the September 11 attacks on America and he was pushing one message above all: 'The terrorists must get this lesson very clearly, that the international community will not allow them to win ... No matter how much they kill people, murder people, victimize people, infringe their human rights, the international community will not allow terrorism to overtake Nepal.'[5]

When I interviewed him the minister told me, 'There are training elements here but I won't go into any more about deployments.'

I was invited to a dinner in his honour at the ambassador's residence. It was a handsome Victorian villa, decorated in the hall with old weapons and photographs of previous ambassadors, with feathers in their hats, sitting in carriages. The chief butler, figged out in pyjama-suit livery, was old enough to remember when the British used mirrors to signal between the embassy and the ambassador's weekend cottage, on a hill overlooking the Valley. ('Send more Marmite!' was the joke diplomats made when they told the story to new people.) That very day the king had appointed an elderly royalist as his new prime minister and a British delegation left halfway through the meal to meet him, returning to pronounce (to appreciative chuckles from the room at large) that the new old man was 'not exactly a bundle of energy'.

I was seated at the same table as a group of officials from London and I had an interesting evening. They were almost as young as I was and they were in high spirits, obviously finding the occasion as exotic as I did. They talked about the Nepali government's need to have better information on the enemy. At the end of the night the minister was swept away in a motorcade to the airport and Afghanistan, where Britain had a war, passing me in the street as I kick-started my motorbike. 'It becomes clear,' I wrote when I got home, 'that the military assistance that the minister did not want to be specific about is in setting up an intelligence capability.'

☀

Three months after that, the chief of the Armed Police Force, his wife and bodyguard were killed while they took their morning walk, as they did on the same section of the Ring Road, not far from Patan, at the same time every morning. One of the assassins shot himself in the leg with the gun in his pocket but the others escaped ('dressed in black, like ninjas', according to witnesses in the newspaper), leaving the police to round up 'scores of suspects from the adjacent locality.'[6]

I followed the cortège as the bodies were driven through the city. The route from the victims' home to the burning ghat at Pashupati was several miles. It was a parade of soldiers and policemen. The dead couple were in an open-backed truck, strewn with flowers and burning incense, accompanied by their grieving daughters. The streets were lined with thousands of onlookers, but how many of them were drawn by grief, or outrage, or curiosity it was impossible to tell. The daughters had rushed to Kathmandu the day their parents were murdered. Now they lit the pyres. I watched from a rooftop above the temple as the 'Last Post' was played and the white smoke rose, with ranks of armed police lined up at attention on the steep steps of the gorge above the holy river.

Three days later, at the end of January 2003, the government and the Maoists announced a ceasefire. It seemed that the rebel leaders holding secret talks with the palace had not kept the controller of the hit squad informed (but years afterwards some retired officials would claim that that murder was nothing like what it appeared to be).

☀

The Maoists opened a contact office in Kathmandu, in a small house behind Singha Durbar, the government secretariat. There was a hammer and sickle flag hanging from the balcony, stained green by the wet concrete. Some pictures of gods had recently been pasted above the door, with joss-stick ends and a garland of marigolds. Whenever I visited it was locked. All the curtains were closed.

There was an alternative method of making contact. I would text the number 4 to a mobile phone, the guy would call me back, and we would meet in the Hot Breads Bakery on the street outside the palace. To prove his bona fides he showed me the Maoist deputy leader's frequent-flier card. I was trying to organize another trip to meet the rebels in the hills but I found my contact frustrating. He told me wild stories that I didn't believe and which, if he believed, he seemed foolish to tell me. I didn't bother to write them down, except one. I'd asked him something about the Maoists' motivations and he became serious. 'You are high-quality person and I am low-quality person,' he told me, 'but I have a most beautiful wife and you say to me "On this night send your wife to me." So I send her, but I get angry and start the revolution.'[7] This was his description of the feudalism in the countryside.

The peace talks seemed unlikely to succeed almost from the moment they began. It took three months for the government to appoint a negotiating team, and then the king changed his prime minister and it started all over again. Both sides committed ceasefire violations. The Maoist demand was for an elected constituent assembly, which would write a new 'democratic' constitution shorn of the remaining vestiges of 'feudalism'. They claimed that all they wanted was to complete Nepal's 'bourgeois revolution'. They even hinted that they could live with a ceremonial monarchy.[8] Apparently, they wanted to nurture good relations with the private sector. Their enemies warned it was a trick. If the Maoists had their way it would be like the Khmers Rouges again. People in Kathmandu said the rebels were rearming, recruiting, not serious about the talks, just playing for time, and maybe they were. It took the king's people seven months just to put their position on the negotiating table, and the royal government was rearming too.[9]

I flew to the town of Nepalganj, a couple of hundred miles southwest of Kathmandu, to see the third round of talks begin there. Then I went into the hills to try to find some fighters. By now it was August 2003, and the monsoon again. The air was saturated with low cloud, the rivers were in spate, and where the hills needed to ease themselves fresh landslides had spilt across the road. I was with a Canadian academic called Petr, whom I had met at the peace talks, and he had hired the manager of his hotel as an interpreter. Two swollen fords made us walk the last part of the way into the Surkhet district headquarters. In the morning we set out on foot again. It was sunny at times but mostly we walked in the cloud. The lanky, twisted rhododendron trees, bearded with ferns and orchids, looked strange in the mist. In the forest we came into a clearing.

An old man was living there, in a hut of birch logs and turf, dressed in orange, with a cannabis tree at the hut's dark entrance. He was a widower, the former editor of a Surkhet local newspaper. He gave us tea. The editor had renounced any interest in whatever was going on. He had no news at all. Once he'd had money but he'd renounced that too, and now he was dedicating his last years to the enrichment of his soul. We completed our first day's walk in the dark.

That night we stayed in a farmhouse. In the stone kitchen, sitting on straw mats on the mud floor, by the light of the cooking fire, the family asked us questions. 'What caste are you?' 'In your country, where do you collect firewood to cook rice?' In the morning their boys showed us the way. The sky was blue and bright and the hills were very green. The family had given us small twists of cloth with salt inside, which we could moisten and use to remove leeches from our legs. We didn't need them. The boys beat a snake to death on the path and larked in the streams. We walked across steep terraces and through maize that stood above our heads. On the second night we stayed on a ridge with two dozen Maoists, in a captured police station where they were running a party school.

The largest room was decked with red flags and party slogans painted on banners. The Maoists taught scientific socialism, military science and the history of the communist party there. Their handsome young faces were dramatic in the candle light, with areas of red cloth and the hammers and sickles emerging from the darkness behind them. After sharing their food I squatted against the wall, writing in my notebook, while an eager rebel pressed me with questions.

'Excuse me, Sir. How would you solve the economic problem?'

He was seized by a sudden excitement. He started pointing behind me as if something was crawling up my back. I turned around. There was a large brown smear with a single chip in the concrete at the centre. A policeman had been shot there, crouching against this wall, in just the same way that I was.

The next day again we walked on, now with the Maoists. One of them carried my bag for me. They were leading us towards some kind of meeting (I didn't understand what kind), where they promised we could meet a senior leader, and find more fighters to photograph. It must have been on the long descent from the ridge that my knees began to hurt. In the bottom of the valley we forded the brisk, cold river at least twice. Each time I took my boots off and gingerly felt my way over the rocky bed. Then we walked on and on, to somewhere the rebels insisted was close by. With every step, and for each of the many days until we got out again, the pain in my knees grew worse.

When we eventually arrived in the village we'd been walking towards the Maoists were not ready to talk to us, and although there were people walking around and standing guard with guns we were not allowed to take any pictures.

They put us in the upstairs room of someone's house, with a wooden balcony outside the window, and made us wait there for a day. I lay on that balcony with its view of the pretty, sad little village – the neat arrangement of stone houses and rice fields in the flat valley bottom – and I smoked cigarettes endlessly, although the Maoists disapproved of smoking. Because it might annoy them it annoyed Petr too. I'd been away from England for a bit more than a year. Although I was increasingly absorbed in Nepal, my world in those days was still mostly the one I had recently left. University was the last important thing that had happened to me and I looked back to that. All of my most important friends were from there. Above all, the girl I still loved. She was American and her name was Maria. I thought about her lisping voice. Earlier that summer we'd been on holiday together. We went to Delhi, Jaipur, Fatehpur Sikri and the Taj Mahal; places that she wanted to see because she'd read about them in a novel. I thought she was reading novels about India because I was in Nepal, and there aren't many novels about Nepal. It wasn't the kind of thing she'd admit to. At that moment, she was on her way to live in Nashville, Tennessee. I thought about that. I wasn't expecting to see her again. Smoking cigarettes all day on that balcony, in a village full of unfriendly Maoists, I thought about those things deeply, or at least at great length, and repetitively, and regarded everything else with indifference.

I had to rouse myself and interview somebody. It might have been the next day. Comrade Prabin was a teenage kid, as they all were. He told me, 'The Maoist soldiers came to my village. I thought "They are just like me", I felt courageous and I joined.' That had been a year earlier. After fifteen days with the Maoists he deserted them and went to his brother, who was a member of the Armed Police. For four months he stayed in the police camp before his brother sent him away to try for army recruitment. He went home first, but he fought with his parents again, ran away a second time and rejoined the rebels.

'I don't want to hurt my brother and my friends,' he said, 'but I'll fight with anyone!' Then he started crying. 'If I go home my parents would just bother me and I would come away again.' Since he was a child he had wanted to be a soldier.

Sometime during those days Petr said, 'This is a children's crusade.' Most of the Maoists were teenage runaways. When I asked why they joined they mostly gave bland, ideological reasons. They were going to transform their society and reject the fatalism of their parents. A young woman said passionately, 'I don't believe your fate is written on your forehead!' At night they listened keenly to a radio programme about anti-virus software, by candlelight. After another day they gave us what we were waiting for.

A poor mother and her children were cowering in their hut without enough to eat. She played with great pathos how she had to bow and scrape to beg food from her neighbours. A group of soldiers appeared, dressed in looted army uniforms, armed with looted army guns. They accused the family of being Maoists, shouted, trashed the hut, smashed the kids with their rifle butts, shot the mother and threw the bodies in a lake. But a daughter survived to join the Maoists and take her revenge!

This was enacted on the grassy area outside the village's abandoned health post.[10] After the play, a revolutionary dance routine and a military parade, there was a speech by Comrade Sharpshooter. 'The government will take responsibility if the peace talks break, because we don't want war, we don't want killing,' Sharpshooter said.

Everyone knew the ceasefire was about to collapse. Before we set out from the district headquarters the police chief had complained to me that the Maoists had just kidnapped a cop. Now these Maoists claimed that the army had shot a Maoist boy and raped six Maoist girls; the cop was a hostage against two rape victims still in custody. Everything was like that: hard to confirm; cruel, and falling apart; worse than I could previously imagine, with worse to come. The road was still three long days' walk away. I was motivated through the steep, sweaty, painful trek, my mind going over every remark Maria had made, my knees giving searing pangs at every step, by an urgent need to get out of there, into a jeep, then into a twin-prop, and back to Kathmandu to write it up. And then I wanted to spend a lot of time with people who weren't Maoists.

6

> 'To be sure Hindus are far too little concerned with chronology to be in a position to claim that they introduce plausibility or logic into it, even when they invent it.'[1]
>
> – Sylvain Lévi

The next man to peel back a layer was Sylvain Lévi. He began studying Sanskrit in Paris in 1882 because Professor Abel Bergaigne did not have any other students. Six years later Bergaigne was dead and Lévi, aged 25, became the new professor of Sanskrit at the Ecole de Hautes Etudes. He set himself a daunting, lifelong task, to trace how India had shaped the cultures of Asia through the spread of Buddhism, which first flourished in India but had long since disappeared from there. He mastered Tibetan, Chinese, Japanese and various other languages he would need.

In 1898, on his first journey to the Orient, Lévi visited the Kathmandu Valley, because he believed it held a central place in Asian history. In this isolated country on India's border, Buddhism was preserved alongside Hinduism, perhaps in a similar way to how it had existed in India itself a thousand years earlier. He thought of the Nepal Valley as an historical laboratory that reproduced the phases of the Indian past on a miniature scale, where he could unpick 'the order and the plan hidden under the muddled mass of events'. He would discover how Kathmandu 'came to be populated, organized and policed' and trace how 'the cults, languages and institutions slowly changed'.[2] 'Nepal,' he declared, 'is India in the making.' In three months in Kathmandu Lévi gathered enough material to keep himself occupied in Paris for years. The first comprehensive history of the Kathmandu Valley appeared as *Le Nepal*, over three volumes between 1905–08. Some of his results are out of date now, but the framework that Lévi uncovered is still the basis for all modern histories of the city.

In Kathmandu the Maharaja provided an escort of two Gurkha sepoys to keep an eye on him and a 'pseudo-pundit' to assist his research, who was 'an abyss of ignorance' according to Lévi.[3] Indeed, he discovered that the entire population of the city was 'absolutely, totally, radically ignorant'.[4] Everywhere he went he was thronged by gormless and foul-smelling crowds. 'Justice must be given to the Newars,' he quipped. 'I have seen some of them wash themselves at least once in their lives!'[5]

His guards and even his coolie entered into his quest for antiquities, shaking stones and interrogating the inhabitants of the neighbourhoods they visited. As they passed through the city the guards went ahead, pushing the crowd apart with a stick. Then came Lévi on one of the Maharaja's horses, doffing his hat and bowing to the few natives who bowed. 'I feel I am becoming popular,' he wrote in his journal.[6] And the pundit sahib, who knew Sanskrit better than the native pundits, was an object of curiosity. At a temple the people shouted 'Jutta! Jutta!' at him. He had marched in with his shoes on. He turned, and lectured the astonished crowd in Sanskrit.[7]

At Tebahal in Kathmandu Lévi found a statue which his guide dismissed as a modern Newar work. Lévi showed him the ancient lettering and humiliated the man. 'Here you, Pandit, come read your Newar!' The guide fell silent.

A hostile crowd had gathered, unhappy to see the foreigner handling the god, and washing off the vermillion that caked the inscription. The guard challenged them: 'Who could dare to speak Sanskrit with the Sahib?' and the crowd was quietened too. Eventually the priest of the place appeared and Lévi informed him that his god had been made by King Manadeva, in the fifth century. Now the people were impressed, and they asked him, for some reason, 'Are you a German?'

'I repeated my eternal reply,' wrote Lévi. "I am French, France is a great country and Paris, my city, is as large as the Ayodhya of King Dasharatha."'[8]

☀

Lévi rediscovered Bendall's inscription at the end of my street, which had become buried in the fourteen years between their visits, and he began to despair that there was anything important left for him to be the first to find. Even before he reached Kathmandu he was intent on deciphering a particular inscription, which he knew lay half buried on a stone column inside the temple of Changu Narayan. The temple stands on a hilltop at the eastern edge of the Valley, a long half-day's ride from Kathmandu. Bendall had been interested in the same place, but someone gave him bad directions, he got lost and missed out. Lévi was not so easily deflected. The 'childish rancour' of the priest prevented him from entering the precinct, but he persuaded the Maharaja to provide four soldiers who excavated the buried portion of the column and took rubbings. The Sanskrit poem they delivered to Lévi is the most important text in Kathmandu's early history.

Dated AD 464, the inscription describes the immediate ancestors and the victorious battles of King Manadeva. Manadeva was beautiful, a world-class hero. He had soft skin like worked gold, and well-fleshed shoulders. He was 'love incarnate, a festival of flirtation for lovers'.[9] He was also skilled in the use of weapons of attack and defence, and he had 'received initiation in the fashion of the Kshatriyas, by combat and battle'. But especially, the poem praises Manadeva's mother, the beloved Queen Rajyavati. She conferred the crown on her son after his father's sudden death. She was 'of pure race', pious and loving, and so dedicated to her husband that Manadeva had to beg her not to commit suttee on his pyre. Instead, she completely purified herself, and gave all her fortune to the Brahmins to increase her dead husband's merit.

Yet Manadeva's inscription glosses over the death of his father, 'who went to paradise as if he had gone for a walk in the garden', in a way that some people find strangely glib, or even evasive. According to the Wright chronicle, Manadeva was the killer. The father was the old king who had offered himself in disguise as a sacrifice to end a drought, and Manadeva was the prince who raised the blade by the fountain of Narayanhiti. The spout turned its head away in disgust, and the water swarmed with clouds of worms when he tried to wash the blood from his hands.

Lévi dismissed the 'capricious memory of the annalists'. His interest was in a larger story, of how Indian civilization spread and the tribal peoples at the margins were brought inside the caste system. He constructed a chronology starting from the earliest authentic record of 'Nepal', which comes as a reference to a vassal state that traded with the plains, carved on a stone pillar at Allahabad in northern India in the fourth century AD. From Manadeva's pillar inscription in the mid-fifth century onwards, there are numerous inscriptions inside the Valley, exalting the lineage and piety and proclaiming the edicts and the tax system of the Licchavi dynasty, who prospered on a trans-Himalayan trade in wool, yaks' tails, musk, copper, and iron. By their Sanskrit language and their patronage of both the Hindu and Buddhist religions, Lévi realized that they must have come from northern India, seemingly in the early centuries of the first millennium. Yet the Licchavi inscriptions were fragmentary and difficult to interpret. The number of known examples grew only gradually from seventeen in Lévi's day to stand at around two hundred today.

How did these parvenu kings from the plains, with their pioneer spirit, manage to 'subdue, make malleable, frame and organise a barbarian multitude,' such as they must have found in this remote valley?[10] Lévi thought the process was based on Hinduism's capacity to assimilate contradictions. The Licchavi dynasty, as Manadeva's inscription showed, emphasized their status as Kshatriyas, the warrior caste known as Chhetris in modern Nepal. Manadeva was fit to rule because he had pure-blooded parents, and had proved himself in battle. The Brahmin priests were prime agents in this. They received generous offerings (such as Queen Rajyavati made after her husband's death). In return they provided the caste ideology that legitimized the kings' rule, and they discovered extraordinary genealogies for them. The process found its clearest expression in the genealogy of King Jayadeva II, inscribed at the Pashupati temple in 733. It traces the Licchavi dynasty through fifty kings (forty-eight of them unnamed), from Manadeva's known ancestors further back one thousand years to someone called King Licchavi and before him, through the royal god Rama, back to the Sun himself.

The Brahmins re-baptized the local gods ('divine plebs', Lévi called them) as Hindu gods, most often as forms of Shiva or his consort Parvati. The gods' former priests were replaced with Brahmins, and new legends were discovered to reveal their Hindu origin. Meanwhile, in their own interest and on the king's behalf, the Brahmins organized the tribal peoples into the lower castes. The people adopted Hindu values, against cow eating or the remarriage of widows, in favour of cremating the dead and so on, in exchange for higher caste status. This involved an element of speculation, but it fitted the evidence and in it Lévi anticipated the views of later scholars. 'The assimilative power of the Hindu life order,' wrote the sociologist Max Weber a decade later, '[is] due to its legitimating of social rank and, not to be forgotten, possible related economic advantages.'[11]

Eighty years after Lévi's visit another linguist and historian, the Kathmandu native K.P. Malla, argued that the tribal people whom the Licchavis ruled were his own ancestors, proto-Newars, speaking proto-Newari.[12] The language of the Licchavi inscriptions was Sanskrit, but the place names were in a completely different language. It would have been no surprise to Lévi that this 'linguistic archaeology' seems to show the Licchavis building their palaces and temples where population centres and cults already were. It's therefore possible, or even likely, that some of Kathmandu's oldest institutions predate the Licchavis and the beginning of recorded history. Perhaps Bungadya, the red god who came down my street in his giant cart, started life as the rain god of prehistoric rice farmers.[13] Maybe Lord Pashupati, Shiva in his form as the Lord of the Animals, Nepal's patron deity since Licchavi times, was the fertility god of ancient cowherds. And maybe the Eight Mothers, sometimes represented by a natural stone, occasionally as huge-breasted women in some of the Valley's earliest sculpture, maybe they were part of some fertility cult, too. For it's not only the Valley's traditional historians who like to discover that their subject is as old as possible.[14] Modern historians and anthropologists, like the genealogists, try to push the beginning as far back as they can in their search for a 'tribal sub-stratum' among the city's people. In the ingenious interpretations of scholars, Kathmandu's history stretches continuously back beyond where the written record began, beyond even archaeology, because very little digging has been done.

The Licchavi palace did stand for a while where the Wright chronicle says there was an ancient capital, near the Bhatbhetini supermarket. It dwindled into the village of Hadigaon, and when that was enveloped by concrete suburbs, tons of ancient pottery shards were exhumed from the foundations of the new bungalows and discarded. An exceptional royal statue of the second century AD was discovered, and transferred to the National Museum.[15] Two stone edicts of King Amsuvarma, dated AD 606 and 608, still stand at Hadigaon, in a quiet square of concrete buildings between a grocer's shop and a Saraswati temple. One of the stones describes payments to the palace servants, who must have once passed by: the runner, the bearer of the flywhisk, and the water mechanic. 'Favoured by the feet of Lord Pashupati … Amsurvarma in perfect health' the second inscription proclaims to the unheeding modern residents, 'the collection of taxes on houses and fields during the month of Shrawan … is regulated and it will henceforth be the practice for all to follow'.[16]

Some of the temples to which Amsurvarma's revenues flowed are still popular and rich, and others are now unknown. Kings of Nepal invoked Lord Pashupati as their patron from Amsuvarma in 605 until King Gyanendra in 2008. Whenever Gyanendra addressed the nation on television he would say, 'May Lord Pashupatinath protect us all,' but whenever he went on television there was always something wrong.

*

Friedrich Engels wrote:

> The stage of commodity production with which civilization begins is distinguished economically by the introduction of (1) metal money, and with it money capital, interest and usury; (2) merchants, as the class of intermediaries between the producers; (3) private ownership of land, and the mortgage system; (4) slave labor as the dominant form of production.[17]

He had ancient Athens in mind but it seems to have happened in a similar way in Licchavi Kathmandu. The first metal coins appeared in the fifth century, at the same time that the series of inscriptions begins with Manadeva's panegyric to himself and his mother. Ambassadors from China travelled repeatedly to Ni-po-lo in this period. By the seventh century, according to the annals of the T'ang dynasty, 'the merchants there, fixed and itinerant, are numerous' but 'cultivators rare'.[18] The inscriptions testify to a sophisticated administration of land ownership and the existence of slavery, although whether it was the 'dominant form of production' is not clear.

The extent of the Licchavi stone sculptures that are still lying about, and are still worshipped every day, shows that there were several villages a mile or two west of the palace at Hadigaon, on an area of higher ground above the east bank of the Bishnumati river. Two trade routes seem to have crossed there, leading between the Tibetan passes and India. Among the villages that lined the roads, the northerly one was called Koli in Sanskrit and Yambu in the Valley's native, 'proto-Newari' language. The village to the south was known as Dhaksinkoli, or Yangala. The Licchavi villages slowly fused together along the trade routes to create the city of Kathmandu, and the trade routes survive in the street plan.

I started in the south, where there is a modern bridge across the Bishnumati River. The old trade route passed an orphanage and climbed the slope to run diagonally across the city's heart.

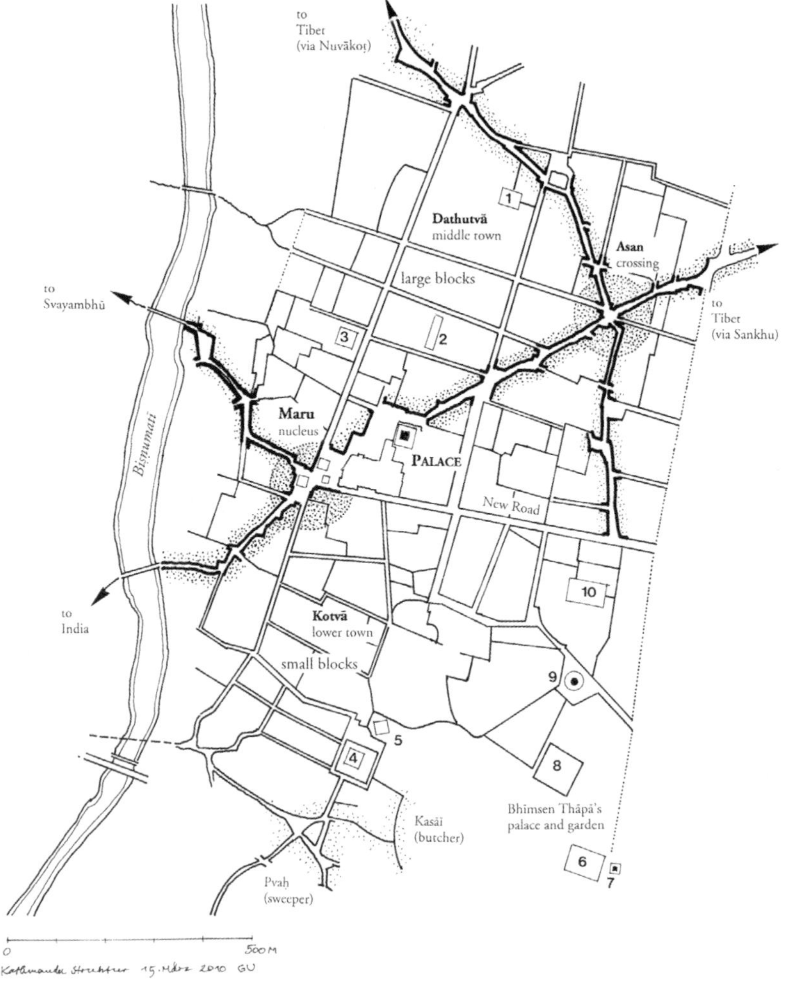

I planned to follow it, thinking I might notice something of the founding principles that remained unburied, but I was led off my course before I reached there because as I parked my bike at the riverside I saw a slum lane I'd paid no attention to before, and I walked inside. The low brick houses were decrepit, propped up with wooden beams or piles of bricks, patched with plastic sheets and wire. The wooden verandas on the first floor were sagging under heaps of whatever trash the people saw fit to store. There were women doing laundry in the street and the dirty water drained across the broken paving. Ducks were nosing around in it. There was a small collection of stone gods (all modern, besides one – perhaps) beneath a flight of steps, which led up to the higher ground the old city was built on.

As I climbed the steps an old man called out from a window, first in Newari, which I couldn't understand, then in Nepali, inviting me to come upstairs. I mumbled 'no no' and walked on, then thought better and walked back. I found him outside his house.

Taking Bangdel's *Inventory of Stone Sculptures of the Kathmandu Valley* from my bag, I asked him the name of the neighbourhood, flicked through and found it. There was no picture of the linga that had caught my eye but I showed him a similar one in the book.

'No, there's nothing like that here. All those gods are new,' he said, then added, by way of elaboration, 'People made them and put them there.'

It made sense to me, because this was clearly an outcaste neighbourhood, where no gods were previously allowed. A woman was listening from her doorstep. Clumsily, I asked them which caste they were and they answered together 'Newar'; pointedly, because if they had been high-caste Newars instead of sweepers, they would have said which Newar caste they belonged to. Hardly less crudely, I asked where the city gate had been. The old man agreed that we were standing outside it.

'And those gods down there, they're all new?' I repeated needlessly.

'The only god we have here is this one,' he said, and he led me to look at a carefully made hole in the concrete paving. The tip of a natural stone appeared from the ground. It had been worshipped that morning with marigold flowers.

'It's a grandmother,' he said.

'Which grandmother?'

'Chwasa Grandmother. When a person dies we take their clothes and put them here.' He tugged at his own shirt front to demonstrate 'clothes'.

'I understand.'

'What country are you from? *Amrika*?'

'Britain.'

'You could take me with you when you go,' he joked.

'I'm not going. I'm staying here.'

Now the penny seemed to drop: my interest in the age of the local sculpture, a book of photographs showing the finest pieces. 'What are you?' he said, 'A thief?'

'I'm a journalist,' I said, 'I write the news and send it.'

'You're staying in Nepal earning money? Earn it! Earn it!' he said good-naturedly.

'Sure, thanks, I will.'

'You're not a thief, you're a journalist!'

I said namaste to him and to the woman who was sitting on her step, and I carried on; walking around and down the slope again to where the old trade route comes in. Then I followed it. The road passed the pagoda temple of Bhimsen, the god of trade, with shops on the ground floor and the sanctuary upstairs. It would have been one of the last buildings merchants passed before they left the city for their dangerous journey to India, or the first they reached as they came in. Around the temple there were several kiosks of watch and clock menders, displaying pendulum clocks on their walls, with the dials of watches strewn across their dusty benches. Pieces of tiny clockwork were preserved beneath the pinnacled crystal domes of broken wine glasses.

Most of the shops, however, were selling cloth, clothes, and shoes. Commercial porters and men with handcarts laboured past, laden with goods for the traders, but the bazaar wasn't busy. Half of the shopkeepers had left their counters to chat or play chess with the others. As I approached the tiled pagoda roofs of the temples in the palace square I could see the white peaks of the Himalaya rising behind them, and it occurred to me that in the past people must have felt the abode of the gods was very close.

The old villages of Yambhu and Yangala spread to meet one another around the palace square, but although they've been joined since the fourteenth century the two halves of the city still feel different. Yangala, the southern part, is quieter, less commercial, less recently rebuilt or, if it is, rebuilt less high. Yambhu is consumed with trade. The streets have been remade as canyons and clogged with cars, motorcycles, rickshaws and porters, moving bales of cloth, refrigerators and TVs. The shops were selling gold; or shampoo and face cream; woollen blankets and shawls; copper plates; ironware; khukuris and horrendous curved swords; yak-tail flywhisks; saris and salwar kameez. Small alleys had been transformed into dripping caverns of bright plastic decorations, because the Tihar festival was approaching again, and stalls had appeared to sell the things that people would need for their puja.

The two trade routes cross at Ason. The temple at the junction belongs to Annapurna, the goddess of grain, and the traders were selling rice and vegetables, chillies and dried fish. The road I'd been walking continued north-east towards Boudha, the Kodari pass and Tibet, but I switched ways and took the other one, leading from Patan north-west to pass between the mountains at Rasuwa. As I approached the tourist district the shops began to sell sleeping bags and foam mats, until all the goldsmiths and tailors gave way to merchants of trekking gear, handicrafts, pirate CDs and pashminas and I was in Thamel. I found myself walking behind a white woman, whose backless dress showed a large tattoo, and I watched the shopkeepers watching her.

I went for a pizza. The restaurant was crowded with tourists at lunchtime, and I was disappointed to have to share a small table. Opposite me sat an elderly German man with a glass of wine. We apologized to one another for the way the table rocked when we moved. He asked me what was meant in English by 'green pepper', then explained that he seemed to have ordered the wrong thing. I made a show of settling down to read the newspaper, but as we were finishing our food I thought it would be safe to start a brief conversation, and he told me about the adventurous trek he'd just returned from, and the many other treks he'd made over the past fifteen years. 'Every time I come home, my wife says that was the last one,' he said. He was about to turn 71, he was a retired industrial chemist, and his flight home was that evening.

'My new hobby,' he said, 'is the art and architecture of Kathmandu.'

I took the *Inventory of Stone Sculpture* from my bag and showed it to him. 'Ah yes, I have it,' he said. 'I bought it on Amazon, it arrived and when I opened it, look! It was signed by Bangdel! Now I am correlating my own photographs, because his are all in black and white. I have over two metres of books, only about art and architecture.'

'Of Kathmandu?'

'Of the Valley, yes,' and before I could remark how lucky he was with the literature that is written in German, he started complaining about the price of a recent publication, and speculating whether it might not be cheaper to buy it anyway than to travel repeatedly from Stuttgart, where he lived, into Heidelberg, to read it in the university library there.

By the fourteenth century Yangala and Yambhu were joined and the elongated, sword-like shape of the old town was established. But the memory of the city's two halves survived in the annual festival of Kumar Sasthi, a 'vile custom of the Newars of Kathmandu', which was described in a book by the Scottish orientalist Francis Buchanan Hamilton, who visited in 1802–03.

> On the evening of the fifteenth day it becomes more serious. The opposing parties are drawn up in the broad, level, sandy bed of the river which runs between the city and Swayambhunath ... the only weapons used being stones ... The fight begins about an hour before sunset, and continues until darkness separate the combatants. In the one which we saw, four people were carried off much wounded, and almost every other year one or two men are killed: yet the combat is not instigated by hatred nor do the accidents that happen occasion any rancour. Formerly, however, a most cruel practice existed.

> If an unfortunate fellow was taken prisoner, he was immediately dragged to the top of a particular eminence in the rear of his conquerors, who put him to death with buffalo bones. In remembrance of this custom the bones are still brought to the field, but the barbarous use of them has for many years been abolished.[19]

The entire celebration was abolished completely in 1846 but the difference between Yangala and Yambhu is still retained in other civic festivals, which remain the sole property of one half or the other, or treat the two parts separately.

Patan was formed in a similar way. The ancient routes can still be traced in its street plan, and some neighbourhoods preserve the names of villages that were recorded before Patan, or Lalitapattana, or other such names for the city were thought of.[20] The process that joined the villages into cities continues merging the old cities into a conurbation; and many of the conurbation's primary facts were established by the Licchavis, stretching back in an unbroken thread over a millennium and a half. The principal Buddhist shrines – the great white domes at Swayambhu and Bouddha – were built by them, one on its hill to the west, and the other on the north-east trade route. They have been restored so many times they're layered like onions inside. The festivals are managed by hereditary trusts called guthis (from the Licchavi gosthi), and in Kathmandu the guthis divide along the invisible border between the two halves of the city. A common measure of volume is still the Licchavi mana, which is about a pint. I learnt to recognize the smooth, hemispheric dome of a stone Licchavi chaitya, and I was deeply gratified to find them throughout the old parts of the city.

7

The ceasefire had ended almost as soon as I returned from the countryside. The army said its soldiers were ambushed while walking through a hospital. The counter-claim, a day later, proved true. Seventeen rebels were arrested from a house in an eastern village called Doramba, where they had gathered uninvited. Along with their unwilling host and his son, their hands tied, they were marched for three hours to a forest and shot. It had happened on the same day of August 2003 that the final round of peace talks began.[1]

The Maoists ended their ceasefire ten days after the massacre, with a series of targeted attacks. In Kathmandu they shot two colonels on their way to work, killing one of them. The next day they shot and wounded a former minister in his car.[2] In Doramba they hacked the local nurse to death, in revenge for the massacre, calling her a spy. 'Bomb scare grips denizens of the capital,' was the headline in the *Kathmandu Post*.[3] Men walked into government offices, left bombs in the toilets, shouted warnings and fled. Near the prime minister's official residence a schoolboy was blown up when he went for a piss. Soldiers raided campuses and searched homes in the middle of the night. To discourage assassins, carrying passengers on motorcycles was banned.

A fertilizer bomb packed inside a pressure cooker will knock a wall out, and if it is exploded in a taxi (which may have defied a Maoist strike) it punches the roof into a pyramid as the blast erupts through the lid. Suspect-looking pressure cookers appeared on busy streets and these malign objects, a version of which everyone had in their kitchen, now loaded with the invisible menace of the rebellion, drew idle crowds of people to stare from what they supposed to be a safe distance. There were armoured vehicles on the city corners, and checkpoints with razor wire. The queues of motorcyclists waiting to be patted down were long, but those soldiers never caught a Maoist.

☀

Even while the peace talks had lasted an alliance of the parliamentary parties, led by the Nepali Congress and the UML, were on the streets protesting against the king. (They feared the palace would make peace with the rebels at their expense.) The palace saw no need to offer them concessions. Distrusting one another, the party leaders demanded that when the king met them he should meet them all together. The king, recognizing their opportunism and the cracks in their alliance, preferred to offer them assurances separately. The army was loyal to him. Strengthened with new recruits, foreign weapons and training, the generals believed that they could quickly win.[4] Blaming the Maoists for breaking the ceasefire, the army escalated the violence in the countryside. The international community gave the king support.[5] So he thought that he controlled the agenda now, and that power flowed from him.

That September of 2003, after the peace talks had failed, gatherings of more than five people were banned and the city blocks around the palace were cordoned off from protests. The political parties declared that they would lead a 'decisive' street movement to restore democracy. By November they were into the Tenth Phase of their Decisive Movement, which showed little sign of progress.

The democratic leaders, standing at the head of their student wings, tried to force their way through the police cordon and approach the palace. Scores of people were carted away in goods lorries. The steel roller-shutters of the shops in Bag Bazaar crashed down. When the police charged there was a thumping of thousands of feet, as the students maintained a tactical distance. The street was briefly empty, except for lost shoes, and red paper flags drifting in the gutter. Then the students would throw bricks. The police, advancing more slowly now and firing tear

gas, threw the bricks back. Tear gas wafted through the window of the Camford Computer Training Institute. There were sirens and booms. Inside the Padma Kanya Ladies' Campus the ladies were putting bricks in a pile, collecting bottles and ammunition for their catapults.

'In Nepal the police are a very dirty act. Very miserable condition,' a student told me while I wrote it down. 'I read Karl Marx and Lenin. Their theory is very important for Nepal.'[6] The king? 'He is a tyrannical thinker, a bourgeois thinker. We don't want to be slaves to him.'

The students chanted:

> 'Give back Singha Durbar or lose Narayanhiti.'[7]
> 'The queen looks like a Bombay hooker.'
> 'Hang hang King Gyanendra!'
> 'Gyanendra thief! Leave the country!'

'We'll beat them up if they say too much,' said a cop, standing in the first rank of cops.

It went on like that for months. I was struck by a brick only once, a painless direct hit on the plastic bottle in my back pocket.

While I was standing outside the Padma Kanya Ladies' Campus with my motorcycle helmet on, a fusillade of missiles coming over the wall, a policeman appeared beside me. 'Fun, yeah?' he said. He was called Suman and we became friends.

On the roof of the Police Club I drank beer with the men who led the riot squads. One of them had four stitches in his head. Another one had a foot injury. The officers talked about tours as UN police in Liberia or Sudan. Their radios reported a blast in the north of the city but they didn't move; they were watching a dance routine being filmed in the car park. A television maker had chosen the club's ridiculous pedimented façade as the backdrop of his production.

On nights when Suman was on duty we drove from bar to bar in police vans. Or we drank whisky at the club, and played with the hats that are exchanged by the world's police forces. (The extravagantly peaked caps of Eastern European security agencies, the fancy-dress helmet of the British copper, a French kepi.) If the police dropped me home after nine, which was common, Hirakaji would have barred the door from inside and I would ring the bell until he came down, bareheaded and grunting, to allow me to stagger inside, profusely offering to help him close the door.

It was with the police that I met a man who sang what he called the urban blues, accompanying himself on an acoustic guitar. 'My first son is as black as coal / And my second son has no penis,' he lamented, rhyming in Nepali. 'Don't go down to Tundhikhel / Or the soldiers will rape you.' In a cloud of hash smoke, in an upstairs room of the Police Club, we laughed like drains.

Kathmandu was besieged, infiltrated and ungovernable, but in its insular condition it celebrated. Weddings, dripping with jewels, went on for days. Chauffeur-driven cars, stacked with women in shining saris, lined up to unload at five-star hotels. Smart bars and new restaurants kept opening, and doing well. The taxi drivers waited outside. When the young and the cosmopolitan enjoyed a music festival, nodding their heads on the grass with beer and joints, they made sure it was relevant by calling it 'music for peace'. I went to a rock concert (I knew the band); then to the Miss Nepal pageant; then the opening of a nightclub in a five-star hotel. By the time I left I couldn't walk straight, but it was easier when I was sitting on my bike. I had an illegal pillion. We were driving after the curfew, so the roads were quiet. As we approached the roundabout at Maitighar I was shouting to her that if we hit it fast we could lean right over as we turned in, then flip to the other side as we came out.

After we crashed she shouted 'Tom Tom get up!' but I couldn't easily, because the bike was on my leg. Then we pushed it to the side of the road, sat on the kerb and lit a cigarette. Another drunk, who had watched us, came over and took one too. 'Tom!' said my friend. 'At last I've got some wooonds!'

I was glad she was taking it that way. As soon as she closed the door at her house I leant against the wall. I thought, 'I need a shit, but if I pass out on the bathroom floor …' The hallway flew away into a tiny speck, I slid downwards, and I fainted. After I came round we watched Annie Lennox on MTV.

It felt much worse in the morning. I went to get myself cleaned and bandaged. The dressing had to be pried off every day for a week. Every limb hurt every time I moved. I was deeply, desperately in love with a girl eleven time zones away; in Nashville, in Tennessee, of all the places. I tried to figure out what she thought. I lay on my bed hardly moving, sweaty, bearded, and wrapped in a sheet. I spent days in miserable inertia, passing hours in Trevor-Roper's obituaries on the internet.

April is reputed in Kathmandu as the month for street movements, when the weather is nice, before the protesters who are bussed in from the countryside have to return to plant their rice. It was in April 2004, about two years after I arrived and a full 18 months since the king sacked the prime minister, that the parties' Decisive Movement to restore democracy really got going.

They gathered in the alleys south of Bag Bazaar, with motorbikes pressing through the crowd like on any other day. The police were drawn up on the main street, where the protesters were expected to emerge. Then the protesters streamed out, and those who were standing there already produced flags and banners, revealing themselves. For a moment they mingled with the police, then the cops lashed out. There was a stampede. Bricks were thrown. The bazaar shutters clattered down. Doctors, university lecturers, and lawyers joined the movement. Hundreds of people were loaded into lorries and driven away, every day for weeks.

'What does the public say? The public wants a republic,' the students shouted. They wrote 'Welcome to the republican bazaar' on the road. 'What's the crown prince like? He's like a mad dog! What's his father like? Just like his son!'

A Nepali Congress politician told me, 'The NC is letting the republican element go ahead because the king is not giving in, but the Congress is not a republican party.' The shutters of the teashop crashed down as the street outside filled with chanting demonstrators. 'He could crack down and impose martial law,' the politician continued, assessing the king's options, 'but that's not going to solve the problem. Six months, one year down the line it's still going to be there.'

Inside the Padma Kanya Ladies' Campus barrows of bricks were being unloaded and the ladies were collecting pebbles for their catapults. The students emerged and were driven back by the brick-throwing cops. The residents of the bazaar watched from their upper windows and rooftops.

One day the police used so much tear gas they ran out of it. It wafted through the halls of Bir Hospital where protesters covered the floor, scored with laathi marks, and the doctors displayed x-rays of the buckshot in their patients. But as the movement escalated, and the parties seemed to be getting somewhere, they became less willing to compromise with one another. The leaders postponed contentious issues until their next meeting. Now, the Congress party president felt the time was right to make overtures to the palace.

MEDI PRO
Kodak

'We should not be afraid to talk with the king,' he announced.

Sensing a conspiracy, his allies warned, 'If any leader goes to the palace door like a dog and surrenders to the king he will be condemned!'

The prime minister (whom the king had appointed) resigned, and the king thwarted the political parties again, by reappointing the man he'd sacked in the first place. The prime minister who had dissolved parliament but couldn't hold elections, who was dismissed for incompetence less than two years earlier, whom his colleagues refused to deal with because he'd played into the king's hands, who was said to fall off his seat at parties, fell back into the prime minister's chair again. It looked like everyone was back where they first began, but now the prime minister relied entirely on the king for his position.

8

'I can't wait for the Chinese to finish the railway to Lhasa,' said Suman, the cop. 'Think of all that good counterfeit shit coming our way.'

The Chinese have filled Kathmandu's bazaars with phones, phoney iPods, pocket televisions, fake Levis, Raybans and Sony, cheap coats, warm blankets and rice cookers. A friend said, 'thanks to the Chinese, the poor can afford to wear clothes.' Sitting at home, at my desk, I asked Sita, my maid, to make some tea. When we were drinking it together I asked her if she liked it.

'Is so nice,' she said. 'What is it?'

'It's called lapsang souchong,' I told her. 'It's from China.'

'Everything is from China now,' said Sita.

There were shops selling plastic household goods or metal household goods; gents' tailoring or ladies' tailoring; silver vessels or gold jewellery. There were shops selling dry foods and cold drinks, with a swastika and the words 'auspicious profit' marked in vermillion on the fridge door. There were shops that sold schoolbooks, musical instruments, sports equipment and trophies; and another peculiar genre – found only in the city centre – which sold laboratory glassware, surgical instruments and small animals, eternalized in formaldehyde. There were photocopying shops and cyber cafes. There were many kilometres of Chinese clothes and electronics.

In folklore the god Bhimsen had no role until he took responsibility for the merchants. 'At least I can make one into two and two into four,' he said.[1]

Around the beginning of the age of Kali the gods foresaw a great increase in the human population and called a meeting, to discuss how man could deal with the pressure. Bhimsen was blasé. 'Man will develop the cunning to present himself as a saviour and friend to every fellow being, so that he can exploit everyone else,' he assured them.

> He will learn to trade and once the trading instinct is aroused, the profit motive will keep the world going. Wealth accumulates and breeds men without feeling. Man will profit from his woman and the master from his man. The big trader will profit from the small trader. The priest will profit from the layman. The king will profit from everyone else. Thus the species of man will survive the age of Kali.

The gods thought it sounded plausible and the meeting broke up somewhat reassured. The merchants of Kathmandu became devotees of Bhimsen.

It is a mystery why no coins minted between the eighth and twelfth centuries have ever been discovered. At the same time the stone inscriptions also fell silent. The last day of the Licchavi dynasty is conventionally put at 20 October 879, when a new calendar system was established, although no one knows why it was established or by whom. The few sources of history that exist are of limited use. Brief notes at the end of some religious manuscripts, mentioning the date and the name of the king at the time it was copied, have been used to reconstruct part of the chronology. Bendall pioneered the technique, Lévi also used it, and an Italian scholar named Luciano Petech more or less exhausted the study of these colophons. After painstaking research all that emerged was a 'dismal list' of names and dates.[2]

It doesn't help that whatever can be deciphered of the politics is extremely confusing. The Valley was divided into tiny fiefdoms. Lévi dismissed these dark ages as 'little kings killing and pillaging one another'. Later historians have called this time, between the decline of the Licchavis and the rise of the Malla dynasty, the 'Transitional Period', as if it were only a staging post the city occupied for a few hundred years, in between more complete states of being. What may have changed or stayed the same while the caterpillar was in the chrysalis is hard to say. Their inscriptions show that the Licchavis had Buddhist monasteries, and manuscripts from about the twelfth century onwards show that the oldest of today's monasteries were thriving by then. It's not clear if the same monasteries emerged from the darkness on old ground or if these were new foundations.

Was Uku Baha, the statue makers' monastery at the end of my street, really founded around the end of the seventh century, as tradition attests, or was it founded nearer to when it was first reliably recorded, perhaps in the eleventh century? There is quite a large Licchavi chaitya in front of the principal shrine, its stone dome sheathed in gilded repoussé work. But I found four other Licchavi chaityas within fifty yards, and there are one hundred more scattered across Patan, so that proves nothing.[3] The Corinthian half-columns on the courtyard walls date from a remodelling that followed an earthquake in 1934. The torana over the door is of 1820. But five of the struts that stand above it all, carrying the roof, are made from a tree that grew sometime between 690 and 890.[4] Each one shows a slightly different wood nymph in lovely detail, carved almost in the round, with a string of pearls in her coiled hair, her breasts unconcealed by the thin scarf around her shoulders, and a shift of embroidered gauze slung around her hips. With one hand above her head to hold the roof up, and the other at her shoulder, one knee slightly bent and her legs crossed at the ankle, with a glazed look on her face, each nymph juts her arse out abstractedly.

They've been casting statues of the gods in Patan, and around Uku Baha in particular, for a long time. The oldest known metal Buddha from the Valley is marked with a date which seems to mean AD 591. The story of this art is partly the story of whatever was going on during the Transitional Period, and also of the city's trade with the outside world. Indeed, the Buddha of 591 is now in a museum in Cleveland, Ohio.

The Chinese envoys of the seventh century recognized the quality of Nepali metal work and described it in exaggerated terms.[5] The early artistic influences flowed from the south; from the Gupta dynasty, which ruled the plains while the Licchavis ruled Nepal, and later from the Pala dynasty, which ruled Bengal. It is not well recorded, but in the first centuries of the second millennium many Buddhist monks and artists must have fled to the Valley from the Muslim invasions of the Pala lands.[6] Part of the pantheon of Buddhist gods and boddhisatvas that Nepali statues represent, and their style, derives from the Palas.

The Buddhist statue makers of Nepal were monks themselves, living in monasteries such as Uku Baha. From around the tenth century their work was much in demand in Tibet, which looked south to Nepal and India for the sources of Buddhism. By the thirteenth century Nepal's reputation was so great that twenty-four Newar artists were summoned to the court of Kublai Khan in Beijing, where their leader, Arniko, became the general director of bronze workers. Later, when Indian Buddhism had been destroyed and that of Tibet was flourishing, artistic influence flowed the other way, and Nepali statues developed the more slender waists, slanted eyes, hooked noses and thin lips of the schools to the north. By the early twentieth century, isolated from the world and ruled by orthodox Hindus, the Buddhist sculptors of Uku Baha were casting household pots and temple bells and there were only four god-makers left.

The statue is first modelled in sheets of wax. It is then coated with a fine mixture of clay and cow dung, to capture the fine details of the surface and purify the 'womb' from which the metal god will emerge. It is caked inside and out with layers of coarser clay mixed with rice husks, and pierced with nails to hold the sides apart after the wax is melted out. The hole in the mould, where the hot wax flows out and where the molten copper will be poured in, is called the vulva. There are tiny domestic foundries in blackened yards behind houses throughout the neighbourhood.

I went with Sunil to the house of his childhood friend Rajesh, to watch him cast a statue that was on order for the shop. Upstairs, Rajesh's wife was slapping wet clay onto moulds on the terrace outside the kitchen. The ground floor was crowded with pieces of wax gods. Exquisite heads and torsos were standing on a shelf. A corner of the floor was given to a forest of delicately expressive hands.

In the yard, where the furnaces were, the heat was so fierce that the walls were too hot to lean on. The two workers – when they could get a break – draped themselves panting across the cooler concrete inside. Rajesh, sweating like a man in a sauna, was feeding timbers into brick ovens and lifting corrugated tin sheets to peer at the glowing moulds. For three or four hours he roasted them.

When the heat was extreme he brought an ingot of zinc and began pounding it with a hammer. It cracked and he weighed enough to make an alloy of 5 per cent zinc with 150 kilograms of copper. The metal was melted in a crucible. The crucible was inside a brick-lined oil drum, fired with paraffin and an electric fan. The roar of the flames made shouting difficult. 'It's much easier than before,' Rajesh yelled, but the piece of technology the

Licchavis would have most envied seemed to be the fan, which replaced a hand bellows when Rajesh was a boy.

I was surprised to notice how thin a liquid copper becomes. By the time it was ready the flames in the kilns had died down and the men dismantled the bricks and stepped inside, hands wrapped in gloves and wet rags, to bring the moulds out. Where a piece had fallen off Rajesh gingerly repaired it, with wet clay on his bare hands. His assistant (wearing sandals, and a woollen hat to stop his hair from burning) dipped a small crucible in the larger one and began to pour the metal into the clay.

'If you pour metal on your foot you'll have a big problem,' Sunil remarked.

After the work was done I talked to Rajesh. We were watching his wife throw buckets of water on the steaming moulds. In the days of Pala influence the design of statues was described in texts, using ratios of bodily proportion, but those methods had been lost, perhaps during the decline of statue making a few generations earlier. Rajesh said he took his designs from photographs and examples he found in monasteries. By studying the old models the statue makers had rediscovered old details, such as the web of skin 'like a duck's' between a Buddha's fingers. In Rajesh's workshop there was an unfinished sculpture by his brother, which the artists called the Museum Buddha because it was copied from a twelfth-century design made newly popular by the posters for the Patan Museum. 'A new type of design like that will be more expensive,' said Rajesh. 'Most people can't afford it.' The Museum Buddha would cost five lakh when it was finished.

'Does that make you a rich man?'

He thought that was funny. 'My ambition is not to be a rich man. My ambition is in a spiritual way,' he said. He was watching as the moulds were smashed open to show the heads he had sculpted, a Lokeshwar and two Green Taras in iridescent newly cast copper. He said that his statues inspired people to contemplate religion, and that made people happy, but they were 'just idols'. His views were modern. Statues were not gods, he said, and religion was an interior experience. He experienced it when he completed a beautiful wax model.

Rajesh's grandfather cast household utensils. Statue making was rescued in his father's generation by the arrival of Western tourists in Kathmandu, but Western tourists have stopped buying statues like these, which cost hundreds of pounds, even for a small one, and which are mostly gold-plated, in divergence from Western tastes. Tibetan monks, however, are richly supported by Western admirers, as well as by wealthy devotees of their own community. Almost all of the Tibetan Buddhist statues made in the world today come from Uku Baha and a few other quarters of Patan, and when a new monastery is founded, in Kathmandu, Lhasa, the Hebrides, California or Bhutan, thousands of new statues are required. Meanwhile private customers buy in bulk on behalf of friends and relatives in the Tibetan diaspora. Nevertheless, trade is slow, because everyone is selling similar things, and Tibetans, unlike tourists, know how to bargain.

I asked who makes the most money on a statue, the shopkeeper or the artist. 'The shopkeeper,' 'The artist,' they answered.

'I heard that the Chinese are beginning to make statues like this now,' I said. Like Arniko, modern Newar metallurgists have travelled from the Valley to China to teach them.

'Yes, the Chinese are copying,' said Rajesh. 'Actually I don't care. My statues are still getting the same price.'

I asked, 'Who is the best statue maker in Patan now?'

'Nowadays he's dead. Siddhi Raj Shakya.'

'And after him?'

'After him …' There was a long pause. 'After him his brother, Bhodi Raj.'

'He's an old man?'

'He's dead.'

'So who is the best living statue maker?'

'Kalu Kumar. He is special at designing angry statues, tantric ones.' Nobody is able to make both angry and compassionate gods well, it seems. 'If I make an angry face,' Rajesh admitted, 'automatically it will give a little bit of a smile.' We went upstairs together to have a cup of tea. When we were sitting on the sofas in his sitting room, with white cups and saucers in our hands, Rajesh asked, 'Do you believe in rebirth?'

I admitted that I did not, so he tried to explain how what you do in one life determines the next. 'When you become angry your face becomes a little bit black. Some people are born black, some people are born white, some people in between, according to their karma. If you give something to others, in the next life you will be rich. Some people work hard but they hardly receive any money. Some people work one hour and they receive a lot of money, like Ronaldo. A person who doesn't know about this, that person will be jealous.

'You were born in England and I was born in Nepal. Why were you born in England and I was born in Nepal?' he asked.

'I must have been very generous.'

He agreed. Rajesh was about 50, although he looked younger, and his son was a teenager. To judge by the amount of time he spent on his computer, and his lack of interest in statues, Rajesh thought his boy might pursue a career in programming or something like that, and it was fine by him.

It seems to have been only politics that was in darkness during the Transitional Period. The sculptors and the manuscript copyists kept working. They produced works of exquisite refinement, but their products are the only clues they left of themselves, and they seem inscrutable now. The mystery of what was going on in the Valley only really lifts around the end of the fourteenth century.

In 1379 there was a great feast to celebrate the completion of a canal. Three buffaloes and 220 barrels of beer were consumed; 'everyone was fed to his entire satisfaction ... Everyone felt happy and gay.'[7] Three years later there was a royal wedding. This time, 'six buffaloes were killed. There was more than enough to eat.' It is lovely to realize that the anonymous chronicler was there enjoying himself, because it's clear from the rest of his record that life was full of misery. And, because he was there, the first eyewitness account of a Kathmandu party is a critical moment.

The chronicle is called the *Gopalarajavamshavali*. It was turned up by Bendall in the Maharaja's library, but he couldn't read the medieval Newari. It wasn't published in English and Nepali until 1985, by which time its contents had been lost to the city's memory for several centuries.[8] At the beginning the chronicler casts back long before he was born, but the accuracy of his astrological data seems to show that he copied his record from a good authority. So, when he says (giving details of the moon cycle) that on Monday, 7 June 1255 an earthquake killed the king and one third of the population it seems to be an authentic event. Many temples were destroyed and for a month the survivors lived outdoors. The chronicle reveals that coronations were still taking place at the old Licchavi centre of Devapatan, next to the Pashupati Temple, but the earthquakes seem to have finished it off. Another one killed another king there in 1344.

It was a constant round of calamity. The rains failed and half the people died. One coin bought only four manas of rice. The gods hardly intervened at all. There were freak snowfalls far too often, crops were destroyed by hailstones as big as mangoes and oranges, and there was catastrophic flooding. People were killed 'by plucking out their eyes'. There was pillage and arson, and the frequent 'cutting to death' of villagers. Raiders from outside the Valley became victorious 'by beheading a lot of people'. There was a confusing litany of raids, sieges, lootings, burnings and massacres covering decades, and the personalities, except one, are hard to follow. In 1371, after yet another raid, fifty-three prisoners were beheaded. One of Kathmandu's leading actors, King Jayasthiti Malla, who would lead the Valley out of the darkness, strode forward. He was pleased with his success, for which he rewarded his new astrologer.

9

In a pink-painted room decorated with streamers and bunting, beneath a scarlet canopy on scarlet cushions, I watched a middle-aged woman being possessed by one of the Mothers. She became a goddess named Kumari. Dressed in scarlet and gold, with spectacles on her nose, she looked like a fairy schoolteacher. She was so composed, as she alternately arranged her arms in a series of mudras then jangled them in her lap, chuntering unintelligibly, that I assumed she was still warming up. Her husband was sitting in front of her, occasionally garlanding her or scattering grains of rice. In his neat shirt and trousers he looked like a clerk.

The room was filled with people, most of them relatives. They were sitting attentively on the floor, or creating a low and respectful commotion as they greeted each other and tried to squeeze through the crowd at the door. There were about forty pairs of shoes at the bottom of the stairs and more people coming up all the time. Maya Laksmi was first possessed following a serious illness when she was young, just after she got married. Like many women whom the goddesses visit, she never had children. Now she was possessed every Saturday and on the first day of every month. This was a Friday and a special occasion, because it was the first time Maya Laksmi was being possessed in a dedicated room on the newly built first floor of her house. She was inaugurating it.[1]

After several hours, when the possession was over, everybody seemed well pleased. Maya Laksmi was beaming, covered with flowers, moving between rooms, helping to serve the feast and saying ‘hello’. Then she returned to her throne and kept chatting, giving tika to anyone who hadn’t already received it, and occasionally being briefly and pleasantly repossessed. In ways like this a few childless women have gained some importance. Their powers derive from Kathmandu's long and deep immersion in tantrism, but whether tantrism has really given women a good deal on balance is uncertain.

> This whole world, from Brahma to the worm, is held together by the union of male and female. How shall we think shame of this when God himself was constrained by his passion for a young girl to assume four faces [to look at her]?[2]

Siddhartha Gautama, the historical Buddha, was born just within Nepal's modern border with India in the middle of the first millennium BC. He taught that people can escape the suffering of the world by recognizing their own impermanence and rejecting worldly desire through a life of monkish meditation. Around the time of Christ a new school of Buddhism emerged called Mahayana (the Great Way), which encouraged followers to seek the liberation of all living beings by becoming buddhas, or bodhisattvas, themselves, through thousands of lifetimes of striving.

The pantheon of bodhisatvas expanded. Manjushree, who drained the primordial lake, is one; the beautiful and compassionate Tara is another; and the greatest is Avalokiteshvara, in whom Tibetans recognize the Dalai Lama. In Patan the people discovered him in Bungadya, the rain god, and so Bungadya seems to have been known for at least ten centuries by the Buddhist name Karunamaya.[3]

The two Ways were practised side by side. In both, monks and monasteries were essential. So the version of 'Buddhism without monks' which emerged in Kathmandu was a puzzle to some later visitors. A third wave of development was set off around the sixth century AD by a new set of scriptures known as Tantra, which emerged in Hinduism and Buddhism at around the same time. Tantrism emphasized the importance of female power, or shakti, in the universe. Kathmandu and Patan are rife with tantric manuscripts. The gods were depicted in a carnal embrace with their consorts, as if the universe was born from the thrashing of divine couples, and animated by shakti. Goddesses, especially the Eight Mothers, came into new significance. Tantrism emphasized the complete communion of the devotee with his deity. It offered the chance to attain enlightenment in a single lifetime, by using new ritual techniques, through the possession of secret mantras and the performance of taboo-breaking 'left-handed practices'. In Buddhism this was called the Diamond Way. To do like the gods did, tantric practitioners needed to find a consort, and get married.

The oldest known document in the Newari language is from the statue makers' monastery of Uku Baha. It is dated 1114 and prosaically sets out some financial regulations. The courtyard today (with Corinthian half-columns on the walls and almost naked wood nymphs in the eaves) is crowded before the shrine with a weird menagerie of metal sculpture, piously endowed by the statue makers. Inside the covered entrance-way a television set had been installed, and tuned to American serials on Star World. Some kids were listening to the English, speaking Nepali among themselves, and I heard them switch to Newari when a parent spoke to them.

'The donor has to furnish 170 pieces of shawls, clothes and betel nuts,' the document of 1114 reads. 'The shawls and garments are to be shared by the monks in attendance. As for the children and wives of the monks, give the shares according to their status and number.'[4]

The statue makers of Uku Baha, and the kids watching the telly, are the descendants of the married monks. The same thing happened in almost every quarter of the city. By the time the last celibate monk died in 1468 the monkhood had become a hereditary Buddhist caste, whose members are now called Shakya or Vajracarya. Many of the city's courtyards are invisible monasteries, which might look like ordinary squares, but in which the male descendants of the medieval tantrics form an invisible monkhood, living for most of the year as ordinary family men.[5] The boys of these communities are initiated as monks.

On important monastic occasions, such as these initiations, the older men bare their right shoulder, like a monk does in his robes. Offerings, such as a broom, represent the discipline of monastic life. And once a year every Shakya or Vajracarya man may receive alms, like a monk, at the festival of Pancadan. Only a few families in Uku Baha took the trouble.

'Most people don't bother with the small festivals any more,' Sunil said. The dozens of annual rites are time-consuming and expensive, and the unhusked rice that is given as alms is more trouble than it's worth.

Being initiated as a mere monk is not the same as initiation into the deeper tantric secrets of the Diamond Way. That requires long and arduous preparation, lifelong obligations, and is not for people who are easily discouraged. Who would want to eat the 'five nectars': excrement, urine, phlegm, blood, and semen? The most powerful and secret gods, who cannot be looked upon by the uninitiated, are fierce, with garlands of skulls, and many weapons in their many hands, eternally grinding inside their crazed female counterparts. The texts instruct disciples to worship them with offerings of the 'five lamps': the meat of a cow, a horse, an elephant, a dog, and a man.

These techniques aim at the liberation of the devotee by an inversion of conventional morality. Obviously, the public would never understand. So, as the great god Shiva instructed in one of the (Hindu) Tantra, 'all this must be kept secret – it must be kept secret – it must be kept secret at all costs.' He re-emphasized the point elsewhere: 'I shall reveal unto thee a supreme secret, which must be kept hidden like the yoni of thine own mother.'[6]

The *Saktisangama Tantra* teaches that:

> Woman is the creator of the universe, the universe is her form ... she is the true form of the body. There is no jewel rarer than woman, no condition superior to that of a woman ... There is not, nor has been, nor will be any destiny to equal

> that of a woman ... There is not, nor has been, nor will be any holy place like a woman ... [7]

The Tantra goes on to instruct the initiate to worship 'a girl of sixteen whom he loves, who is fair and fresh and seductive, who has the exalted spirit of youth, who has lively eyes, who is intoxicated by passion and always moved by desire ...' He must learn to contain himself though, because his illumination will only increase if he can draw his semen more deeply inside *himself*. In the course of the ceremony he should remain unmoved, even while he arouses 'agitation' in her. The *Prajnopayaviniscayasiddhi*, on the other hand, instructs the initiate of the Diamond Way to present his master with a girl in the bloom of youth, bright eyed and adorned with garlands and necklaces. The master accepts the offering and screws her.[8]

I read these excerpts in a book, which claimed: 'These are of course ambiguous expressions which were no doubt meant to be interpreted in a figurative and esoteric sense ...' but I had the feeling that they represented a long-ago cult leader's fantasy and its fulfilment.[9] 'The processes of speculative thought are directed towards the erection of fine-spun philosophical and mystical structures which transform the erotic and sexual element into a symbol of the stages of divine epiphany or into an object of meditation ...' I read.[10] But if anything about people remains the same, surely the emphasis was on the erection? It was puzzling, like the masturbating, humping couples and *ménages à trois* that are carved on the temple roof-struts are puzzling. Is it foolish to take this stuff literally, or more foolish not to?

It's easy to imagine that in the past the social order was better enforced, and sexual freedom more limited than it is today. Monks may have married, and people had their affairs, but it's hard to credit Kathmandu with any really extraordinary carnality. Surely the place was always uptight and hypocritical? But maybe that's wrong. Maybe the city in the past was more like the countryside is today, where it's an aphorism that 'you don't have to persuade your sister-in-law'. Or maybe an ideology of personal liberation enabled a select group of people to seek gratification. If the tantra weren't taken literally, why the emphasis on secrecy? Why the anxiety about abusing the powers that sexual rites bestow? Maybe the libidinous author of one Tantra did want his pupils to imagine the 'coupling of the master with the consort'?[11] But did he really intend them to take literally his injunction to imagine their own coupling with the master's consort?

At least, the Tantra that 'recommends a diet of human flesh, excrement and urine, menstrual blood and semen; advises the adept to kill all creatures and love all women without restraint; denounces as inferior beings those who follow the precepts of morality; and asserts that evil will befall those who worship the buddhas and bodhisattvas' was surely not meant nor taken literally?[12] Such left-handed practices (those who seem to know insist) are some sort of thought experiment. Tantric rituals do involve meat and alcohol, which are forbidden in more orthodox rites, but the five nectars and the five lamps are substituted for curds, milk, sugar, honey, and ghee. Bowls made of human skulls *are* used. But the high-caste couples who are initiated understand (don't they?) that the references to ritual sex should be interpreted figuratively somehow; just like when it is written in the Buddhist scriptures that differences of caste don't really exist it's not reasonable to take literally those teachings. The private tantric shrines of high-caste lineages are dotted across the old parts of the city, and the initiated occasionally come with their spouses at night. But it's easiest to imagine that the gods and goddesses possess them decorously. These are conservative people, who might blush at a Hindi film.

Maybe, over time, the tradition was sanitized by social and religious authorities, who said, 'This doesn't mean what it seems to mean; these are the values we defend'. Perhaps some of those people led a secret, tantric double life themselves. Possibly, beneath the surface, the original tradition continued to flow, like an underground river.[13]

☀

Not all of the tantras are concerned with esoteric liberation and spiritual bliss. Others deal with the use of magic (frequently in gaining the submission of a woman) or the preparation of aphrodisiacs (such as Dhana Laksmi's formula, with the snake semen and the hangman's rope), and with potions to delay ejaculation.

A newly popular sexual medicine was making its power felt over the Maoists' revolution. In the high mountains of Dolpa district, above 3,500 metres, above the tree line, a creature grew that was half caterpillar half mushroom. I went there for a holiday with two old friends; it was our spring break. We flew by a small plane, then again on a smaller plane, which squirmed and burrowed through the clouds and mountains, to bump down on the district's sloping grass airstrip. This place was so remote, we met an old man there who didn't know what a newspaper was.[14]

The erotic properties of the caterpillar fungus, which is called yarsagumba, had long been known to Tibetan medicine, which itself is derived from the Tantras.[15] Lately yarsagumba was much in demand in China, where it fetched a high price. The craze for collecting it in Dolpa was only a few years old, and it was like a gold rush. For the first time the region had – at least partly – a cash economy. People bought cigarettes and booze and dried food and clothes, which merchants carried across the passes from Tibet in caravans of yaks. In their tents, where their wives breastfed their babies among bales of merchandise, the traders weighed yarsagumba on their scales. It went at about fifty US cents for a single, tiny desiccated caterpillar (the parasitic mushroom rooted in its head), or two thousand dollars a kilo. The tax alone, on collectors and merchants, was worth tens of millions of rupees a season.

'You'll see a lot of guys in uniform with guns up there,' a police inspector at the airstrip said. 'But no Maoists.'

Every spring, thousands of people from neighbouring districts came to search for yarsagumba. It was almost impossible to see; like a dead blade of grass, or a dried-up stem, hidden among the other dried-up grass and dead stems on the high slopes. It grew in wide-open, exposed areas, where it was bitterly cold at night. The yarsagumba hunters burnt dung-fires and tried to sleep beneath plastic sheets. They emerged, clapping their hands and slapping themselves in the freezing dawn, to massive blue skies and grey rocky mountains. Because they came from the lower hills, and they were poor, poorly fed, poorly equipped and ignorant, a few hunters died every year of altitude sickness or falling off the cliffs. Our path climbed high along the side of a canyon, to reach a village called Dho in four days.

The houses of Dho had thick stone walls with no windows, and firewood stacked around the edge of their flat roofs. Women were scratching in the poor earth where the barley would be sown. At the monastery the prayer flags snapped in the wind, and when the sun was high the shadows of the clouds slid over the great pale landscape. Beside where we'd pitched our tent some yarsagumba hunters had made their bivouac. They had collected enough caterpillars to buy a sheep; it would be one of the few times they ate meat all year.

We were drawn out of our tent by a commotion. The sheep had escaped. With the agility of a goat, it was climbing rapidly on an almost vertical cliff face. It already had a good start when the men set off behind. Perhaps fifty yards up they overtook it, and climbed higher to stone it from above. When the sheep couldn't climb any more the men took hold of it, and threw it off the mountain. It rolled broken to the bottom. They swung themselves easily down. They were tough people.

We found some Maoists, or they found us. Comrades Jwalamukhi ('Volcano') and Leknath were a couple of hard-looking guys dressed in woolly hats and tracksuits. 'In Nepal,' they said, 'the main problem for people is money. We fully help the people to collect yarsagumba.'

We talked about the various levies they imposed. Last year's tantric sex-drug revenues had provided for their revolution a large amount of clothing and equipment from the Tibetan bazaars, they said; it had allowed them to set up an FM station in the district, and, they claimed, to build a number of trails and bridges for the benefit of the people. Two more rebels arrived, Comrades Sitar and Samanata ('Equality'). I asked them about the royal army, which was vying for control of the trade, and they gave a fair account of Mao's tactical doctrine. ('If they come in a big group it is necessary to save our life by running away … They follow us for two or three days, they get tired, and then we attack them.')

In this Tibetan cultural setting, as we watched horsemen with red threads in their hair canter by, it was obvious to ask about the activities of the communist party across the mountains. That bothered them, and they grew hostile. 'In the time of fighting many people are killed, and that is not a big problem. In Tibet, in the time of fighting, many people died. That is not a big problem,' Comrade Volcano said. 'The war in Nepal is taking a long time, and many people have died. But in the future, we will have the government.'

One of my friends asked them which country in the world had the political system they most admired. After conferring, the surly foursome chose Britain's constitutional monarchy. 'If you want to earn money, that's not a problem. We'll help you,' they assured us when we parted.

No one paid the government tax, as the government people wearily admitted. We did meet the uniformed men with guns, but they were all between the district headquarters and the yarsagumba grounds; whereas the Maoists were between the yarsagumba grounds and the Tibetan border, across which the entire trade flowed. Our walk made a circuit. We crossed two high passes. In places the trails, which were stacked like dry-stone-walls against the mountainside, were terrifying. At Ringmo there is a freezing lake, devoid of any life, which is famous for its extraordinary turquoise colour. A long time since we'd touched water, we bathed in its piercing shallows.

On the shore there was a Bon monastery. It was almost completely dark inside. The blackness was lanced by a single shaft of sunlight from the cupola, as distinctly formed as a beam of wood, which allowed us to see a section of the decaying frescos, and we could dimly perceive masks hanging on the roof-beams, demonic things, which the dancers wore at festivals.

Our walk down brought us by a clinic that dealt in herbal medicine. 'If you take yarsagumba every night for a month, with a glass of milk,' said a monk who worked there, 'then as soon as you've finished, you'll want to do it again.' The clinic was stacked with snakeskins and roots and bark and leaves and horns. On the walls there were photographs of medicinal plants with their Latin names beneath them, because this place had been funded by a global conservation charity to preserve biodiversity. The monks showed us fragments of human skull, which they ground and mixed with herbs, mostly, they said, as a cure for headache.

The rise of tantrism in medieval Kathmandu turned the city into a magical garden, if it wasn't one already. The Mother Goddesses, who in their earliest forms had huge breasts and round bellies, became fierce and well-armed, either young and beautiful or old and dreadful, but never pregnant. Strange occurrences seem to have been common. In the Wright chronicle, a sixteenth-century tantric travelled to Lhasa, the capital of Tibet, and was sitting there with the Grand Lama of Bhot (the Dalai Lama) when he noticed that his house in Kathmandu was on fire. He put it out, by pouring his tea on it.[16] This was the age when the ideology of the city as a mandala reached its greatest development. It was also the age of Gayahbajye, the great magician who disappeared from the room his daughter-in-law had shown me.

Gayahbajye started life as a real man, who lived in the fifteenth century. His legends describe how he gained his powers, in the sweeper neighbourhoods towards the river and at the cremation grounds; because although he was a Brahmin his guru was a member of the most skin-crawlingly revolting and horrifying caste; a sweeper. The guru therefore had an affinity with powerful magic and left-handed practices, which Gayahbajye forced him to impart. Gayahbajye completed his initiation by robbing a group of witches, who had gathered at a Mother temple with their skull-bowls after midnight. For the rest of his natural life he made a mockery of travelling conjurers. His wife startled people by blithely burning her own leg to cook rice. His pupils carried water home in baskets. The old man could turn himself into a buzzard. For acts such as these he has been loved for five hundred years.

I realized that the old lady Dhana Laksmi's beliefs must have been formed in Gayahbajye's day, or else his legends must have changed since, because many of the horrifying things that she had seen, at the Mother temples and by the burning ghat at Shankamul, bore a resemblance to Gayahbajye's world.

According to Dhana Laksmi, witches fly between the Mother temples after midnight and before three, lighting their way by burning their finger like a candle. They achieve their power by dancing naked at the cremation grounds. When she was young Dhana Laksmi didn't have a watch, so she would rise as soon as she woke without knowing what time it was. On her way down to the Mother temple by the river she once saw a witch in the distance.

'If you look at her, and she looks at you, and your sight meets, then you will die,' she said. She was fortunate to escape by hiding behind a wall.

She ran on into another story. Because she thought I was interested in hangings she told me about another one. A man (he was a drum maker) had killed his mother and was hanged from a tree by the road to Shankamul. Everybody knew about it, apart from her. In the early morning, when she went to do her prayers, she saw a man standing beneath the tree. Then she saw his face, which was twisted. Then she saw the rope. Then she got scared and screamed and ran into the temple of Chamundamai, the terrible form of Kali who represents the Eight Mothers there.

There were two policemen sitting inside. She told them, 'There's a person who has hung himself and you don't even know about it!'

'He was hanged yesterday,' they said. 'We're the guard, but we got scared and that's why we're sitting here.'

Dhana Laksmi moved straight to another story, which was related in her mind. It was sometime in the late 1950s. She was going to do puja at Shankamul again, before dawn. Outside the same temple of Chamundamai a man was lying on the ground, with a sword in his hand.

'Get up,' she told him. 'Why are you lying there? Get up! Who is this?'

She lit a match and saw that the man's head was lying apart from his body. 'He couldn't have killed himself,' she thought, 'because if you cut yourself you have to stop. Who would cut off their own head? I couldn't believe it. I saw the sword in his hand, the head at the foot of the goddess. I was so scared, where would I go? Oooooooeeeeee! Then I went flying! Because I was so scared, I went flying!'

She moved on again, making her own associations: This time there was a terrible drought, and to save the kingdom the king disguised himself in a sheet and offered himself as a sacrifice. His son took up a knife and cut the king's head off, and the stone spout of the Narayanhiti fountain, seeing what he had done, turned away and ran red with blood. When the prince went to wash his hands the water filled with clouds of worms. This was one I'd heard several times before, but Dhana Laksmi's not much of a reader and I didn't think she'd found it in a vamshavali. I didn't ask. Someone had told it to her, just like she was telling it to me. 'I am old,' she would say to explain her knowledge. 'You people don't know anything.'

I went down to the Shankamul ghats and the Mother temple of Chamundamai before dawn. There were a few fields left between Patan and the river. The sweepers were already out sweeping, and milk had been delivered to the shops, which weren't open yet.

I walked along the bank, in front of the quiet temples and the ashrams. There was a sadhu who appeared to be sleeping, cross-legged and more or less upright, with a blanket over his head. A woman walked past carrying a bucket, brushing her teeth as she went. Three cops ambled by, very slowly. New houses had come close to the river on the opposite bank. The concrete skeleton of a new block of flats loomed against the lightening sky. Cocks were crowing and two women were doing yoga beneath the footbridge.

I went into the Chamundamai temple, which stands before the bridge, a three-tiered pagoda in its own enclosure, surrounded by trees and smaller shrines. It was light now, but the electric bulbs still made it brighter inside the sanctuary and the caretaker's shed than it was outside. I took in the pair of Licchavi chaityas, whose stone hemispheres were burnished – made almost translucent – by fifteen centuries of rubbing. I puzzled over the names I could see written, and scrutinized the goddess inside. On the wall, behind her tiny brass statue, was an image of Kali in her headless form as Chinnamasta, strutting, lithe and naked, sword in one hand and her own head in the other, her shakti-giving blood spouting from her severed neck into the mouths of her naked devotees.

I asked the caretaker about her. 'Since I've known, Chamundamai has been stolen three times,' he said, referring to the idol inside. 'The good thing is that the original goddess is never in this temple. We keep her in our community.'

Like all the Mothers, Chamundamai is tended by a community of sweepers. Three times they've replaced the missing proxy in the shrine. I asked the caretaker if he had ever heard of a time, before he was born, when a headless corpse turned up here.

'On the day of the goddess's birthday we are not allowed to go into the temple,' he said. 'It was then that there was a sacrifice – a self-sacrifice. We know that it was a sacrifice. It was a woman. She sacrificed herself.' They found the body the next day when the temple reopened. He was a child at the time. He reckoned his age, how long ago he got married ... it must have happened in about 2037, which was 1970. 'She was not killed. She sacrificed herself,' he insisted. 'Before, this goddess was a very well-known goddess – as much as Bagalamukhi or Dakshinkali. But since that woman killed herself, this place has been very quiet. You hardly meet anyone.

'We don't know who she was,' he said. 'The only police station then was at Gahiti. In the morning, when the guy who was the caretaker came to the temple, he saw a person. The head was somewhere and the body was somewhere else, so he went to complain at Gahiti. We are not educated and it was not recorded in history. It happened when we sweepers did not get educated. Not only us, but most of the Newars did not get educated then.'

The Vajracarya priests, or gubhajus, are masters of the Diamond Way. As far as I could tell, the gubhaju I knew was quite eminent, although he had not been able to practise all the rituals since his wife had died. I went to see him again, because although I knew he wouldn't discuss the details, I hoped he might describe something of the powers that can be achieved or the terrible consequences if tantric secrecy is compromised and mantras fall into the wrong hands. I had read that conservative gubhajus are affronted by the public display of copulating, esoteric gods in the statue shop windows,[17] and that if a stranger should stumble into a family's private shrine he might be struck blind, or suffer an accident. The gubhaju declined to gratify me with the details and dismissed the issue. 'Those are just stories to frighten people.'

The doves in their cage had been moved from the window to the top of a cupboard. A small cabinet where he did his pujas was carefully strewn with magical bits and pieces. The old man sat bolt upright, occasionally reading without glasses and speaking rapidly. (Young people said they couldn't understand a word he spoke. I needed a fairly elderly interpreter.) 'In Mahayana,' he said, 'it is forbidden to harm another living being, but in the Diamond Way blood sacrifice is permitted.'

A man came in from the bus park, an ordinary-looking fat man of about 40, with pens in his shirt pocket, and a sore back. He held up his shirt and the gubhaju patted him with a broom of grass and peacock feathers. The man flicked through his money and selected a twenty, which the gubhaju tucked inside his waistcoat. The man went back outside. The consultation lasted about a minute.

Another man came in, a Newar, from Kathmandu proper rather than Patan, who had made the journey across the river to sit at the Diamond Master's feet. He touched his head to the old man's crossed legs, handed him a fifty, and sat down next to me. Like me he placed a recording machine on the floor. In his lap he was clutching a sheet of banalities, printed in English. '18,' I read. 'Crown. I choose to enjoy this journey. 19. Eyebrows. I choose to like who I am. 20. Corner of the eye. I choose to wake up every day in a positive mood ...'

'Emotional Freedom Technique,' the newcomer said. 'American. Gary Craig.' He was a student of healing: all forms of ancient mysticism and modern quackery intrigued him, except scientific medicine.

Between the interruptions, and however I tried to approach the subject, the gubhaju declined to be drawn on the tantric powers of his famous ancestor, nine generations ago, or on anything that seemed to relate to the secrets of the Diamond Way. That evening I met a man whose family priest was the same gubhaju. He was a retired senior government official, and an enthusiast for traditional culture. The man talked about a particular festival he loved, a masked dance called the Kartik nach, and how certain parts of it were performed in private.

'They do all these things, but they don't tell us about it,' he said. 'They won't talk about it to you.' When the masked dancers perform the parts of gods and demons, he said, the men inside the costumes are possessed. The spirits are not only represented, they are actually present in the streets and squares. When, at the touch of a monster, a dancer faints, he really faints – every year – and can only be revived by secret ritual.

I told him that I had consulted the gubhaju that morning. 'He wouldn't talk about anything but Mahayana.'

'Yes, they'll talk about Mahayana,' he said. 'Our whole culture is based on tantrism,' he continued, referring to the Newar culture of the old city, the symbolism of rituals and buildings, the strict distinction between the outward and the secret, the theories of the mandala, the popularity of gods and goddesses in their terrifying aspects, the healing powers of gubhajus and the terror of witches. 'They have wonderful pujas, which they will not talk about. There are five things that are important in the tantra: sex …'

'… meat, alcohol …' I offered. He agreed. The last two remained unremembered and the conversation moved on. I told him that my real interest in meeting the gubhaju again was to ask about left-handed practices.

'These tantrics do puja at midnight,' he said. 'They do puja through the night! Sometimes they cut off fingers and hands …'

'Their own fingers and hands or someone else's?'

'Someone else's,' he said, drolly, as if I'd asked whether people throw rubbish on their own doorstep.

In medieval Kathmandu the masked dancers sought human blood. In Wright's chronicle, a sixteenth-century king abolished a dance that demanded human sacrifice, but the practice evidently continued. Another king was attacked by a man in a jackal mask, for interfering in another such 'piece of cruelty'.[18]

The priests who perform the masked dances of the Harisiddhi goddess temple, a few miles south-east of Patan, on the full moon of the month of Falgun, are recognizable by the strange feminine dress they wear all year round. They are widely feared, or were, at least until the 1970s.[19] Every twelve years they bring their dance around the Valley, drinking copiously wherever they go, and it is, or was, believed that at this time they select, or used to select, a young girl, whom they keep hidden for a year, and train in secret rites, before they offer her to the goddess. Finally, her body is dried and powdered as a potent incense. It may be that the thrill of the crowd at many festivals, when the masked dancer lunges, trying to grab a child, is a faint memory of this old-fashioned way of doing things.

The fading terror was still there, in a story of my neighbour Amita. She was a beautiful woman, in her late twenties, with a son who was twelve or thirteen. She lived in a small, half-ruined house but a sprawling household; with her mother-in-law, her husband, his four brothers, and their wives and children. Besides her good looks, of which she was proud, Amita was notable for her naivety and the simplicity of her nature, which allowed the other women in her family to be unkind to her. One of her sisters-in-law came from a nearby village, with another famous goddess temple, a village called Khokana.

'I went to Khokana at Dasain with sister-in-law,' Amita said. 'There was a jatra.' It was full daylight and the crowd was large. 'The gods were brought in a line. They trembled and shivered.' She was talking about men in costumes who had actually become the gods they represented. Above their brightly coloured robes they wore round wooden masks, painted black and red and blue in the distinctive features of the different deities. 'Each one had a sword. In the middle there was a shrine and the gods stood around it in a half-circle. Everyone had to go and touch their feet. I was terrified! Their swords were held so straight! What if they decided to slaughter me?' She giggled with pleasure; almost shivered herself, at the thrill of it.

One goddess in particular occupied her imagination, and by coincidence it was the same one who had so gently possessed the medium Maya Laksmi. 'There was a Kumari mask,' Amita said, 'It stood in the middle of all the others and that mask was shivering vigorously.'

The masked figures withdrew to an upstairs room of the temple, but when it was time to sacrifice the buffaloes they came

back down again. The animals weren't decapitated, as they often are. Rather, their heads were dragged upwards and the arteries in their necks severed so they died slowly, spouting blood. 'When the slaughter happens, each god goes, lifts the mask and drinks the blood,' Amita said. It was proof of the strange power which was present there that later, when the meat was cooked, however long it boiled, it never became well done. 'There were two ducks slaughtered too,' Amita added, by way of giving a thorough account of the significant facts. 'They don't drink the blood of the ducks.

'The masks kept shivering. Then they went upstairs again. Opposite the house where the gods go up, there is a temple of Sikali. It is said that the goddess takes a human sacrifice every day. I was so scared, I didn't go there! People say the goddess calls the person who will be sacrificed, and the person doesn't feel a thing! I heard that there are women who come there all dressed up, and say, "I've come to eat dhaubaji."[20] The priests send her in and close the door. Then the goddess takes her.'

Amita's sister-in-law didn't miss the chance to have some fun. She cajoled the terrified girl to go inside the goddess's room. Amita resisted bravely. 'I was so afraid!' she said. And she smiled beautifully.

Remembering the mask that had frightened her the most, which stood in the middle of all the others and shivered most vigorously, she saw the connection, and she understood the identity of the goddess who takes the women. 'They say the statue looks like that of a Kumari,' she explained.

10

In the winter the early mornings were cold and misty, and the roofs of the pagodas in the palace square loomed up in shades of blue and grey. Women wrapped in shawls emerged from the whiteness, doing their rounds of the shrines with a tray of offerings and a burning wick. Others were buying vegetables for the morning meal. The women who sold the vegetables, spread on plastic sheets at the roadside, were bundled up in shawls as well, gripping a filterless cigarette between two knuckles.

The bureaucracy shortened its working hours from nine-to-five to ten-to-four and the officials spent half the day sitting in the delicious winter sun, drinking tea. In the evening, shopkeepers gathered to crouch around small fires of paper rubbish and plastic bags in the gutter. Couples walked down the deserted lanes on chilly winter nights arm in arm, in their party clothes. This was the busiest of the wedding seasons. A groom's janti, led by a red-coated wedding band, would half-block most streets, and it took a long time to press past with a car or a motorcycle. At the centre of the crush, in a racket of drums and trumpets, the women's cashmere shawls and chiffon saris, woven or embroidered with gold and sequins, were picked out in the headlights. The wedding car would be covered with flowers. The vehicles pressing to come the other way would have blocked the street on both sides. I spent three Kathmandu winters in Hirakaji's bleak concrete rooms, without a heater, wrapped in a blanket while I sat eating my dreadful food at the kitchen table.

☀

'The genealogy of Jayasthiti Malla,' wrote Sylvain Lévi, with his concern for Hindu history making, 'has been systematically falsified by his descendants.' Jayasthiti was the late fourteenth-century king who rewarded his astrologer in the *Gopalarajya-vamshavali*, who led the Valley out of the confusion and obscurity that followed the first transitional period into a second golden age. It seems that kingship came to him through marriage to a princess. He was probably a noble from the Mithila kingdom (straddling the border between modern Nepal and the Indian state of Bihar), whose royal family had already intermarried with the obscure early Malla kings of the Nepal Valley. Later histories, such as Wright's, remember Jayasthiti as a law-giver, who brought order by codifying the caste system. 'He definitively organized society on the Brahmanic type, assisted by Hindu Pandits he fixed the different castes and classes,' Lévi wrote. His name itself – sthiti – relates to concepts of law and social order. But he got his name before he got his reputation, and of the thirty-three documents that survive from his reign none mentions the legal innovations for which he is remembered.[1] Perhaps, like his ancestors, that achievement was given to him later, when it made sense to do so.

Under Jayasthiti the various fiefdoms of the Valley were united for the first time since the decline of the Licchavis. Under his successors there was a multiplication of trade and an extraordinary artistic flourishing. For three generations the kingdom remained united, until a king divided it among his heirs and the Valley was carved into three rival city states. There was Bhaktapur in the east, then Kathmandu and Patan, facing each other (or with their backs turned) on opposite sides of the Bagmati River. The cousin-kings attended one another's birth rituals, weddings, coronations, and funerals. The rest of the time they were at each other's throats with insults and war, and they competed in the architectural glory of their capitals.

In each city centre stood the palace. On their exterior, the palaces were decorated like temples, with stone lions at the door and gods and goddesses on the timbers. The kings filled the plazas beyond the palace wall with temples of the high, pure

Hindu gods who rule in heaven. Within, they built towering shrines to their private goddess Taleju, whose secret worship offered them power in this world. More palace courtyards spread out to accommodate her priests. Her secret mantra was passed from father to son on the king's deathbed, to validate the succession and to give the new ruler control of her power. So, a forest of pagoda roofs was raised over the centres of Patan, Kathmandu and Bhaktapur. Masterpieces of timber and fired earth accumulated through the joint proceeds of jealousy, trade, and debasing the coinage.

Silver coins were rare in South Asia before the sixteenth century, when European traders introduced them, made from silver from the Spanish Americas. By the second half of the century silver coins appeared in Kathmandu, derived from the trade running through the Valley between India and Tibet. Taxes, levied on each porter-load of goods, had to be paid in local currency, so merchants took their Indian coins to the mints to be restruck. The industry expanded after 1640, when wars elsewhere in the Himalaya closed alternative routes, and Kathmandu signed a treaty with Tibet allowing thirty-two Newar trading houses to be established in Lhasa, tax free. Most importantly, the agreement provided that Nepal would mint Tibet's coins from silver ingots supplied by Tibet. Nepal-made coins were the sole currency in Tibet for more than a century, during which time the silver content declined from about 95 per cent to less than 50, while the three cities of the Valley swelled with splendid palaces, temples and the tantric god-houses of merchant families.

They have been turned into jails now, but there were still several mints in the city when the old woman Dhana Laksmi Shrestha was a girl. They had channels of water and big wheels to drive the machines. 'An idiot got into the water to see what would happen,' she said. 'He was pulverized. An idiot means someone who won't listen to others and doesn't even have enough brains for himself. He was one of those.' She looked me over, squinting, wrinkling her nose and sticking her tooth out like a finger. 'You don't seem to be like that,' she said.

Dhana Laksmi visited the mint at Naku when she was about fourteen and she had a good time. 'When you went there they would check your pockets, so people would bring a banana or some khuwa [a kind of sweet] with them and eat money that way. The 25 paisa was the biggest, only a fully grown man could swallow those, but even a small person could eat the 12 paisas. I ate some money and when I got home I shat it out on a tray.' She half-gestured a squat, to show me how she'd done it.

How much did you eat? I asked her, and she answered by exclaiming, 'How much did I eat!' and making an expansive gesture, adding, 'Money's all made of paper these days.'

King Pratap Malla, who was the ruler of Kathmandu from 1641 to 1674, when the three cities were at their pomp, invited merchants from Kashmir to establish trading houses there. Branches of their families ran depots in Benares and Lhasa and they helped to enlarge the trans-Himalayan trade. Before becoming Kashmiri, the merchant clans had their origin in Baghdad, so the area of the city where they settled, and where some still live, is sometimes called the Raki Bazaar.

On the last day of August 2004 twelve Nepali workers were murdered in Iraq and a video of their deaths immediately circulated in Kathmandu. The next day angry mobs ruled the city. They attacked a small pharmacy called 'Saudi-Nepal', presumably because it had a Muslim-sounding name (perhaps the owner had saved the money to build it by labouring in Saudi Arabia). There were restless crowds standing around to watch tyres burn everywhere, raising columns of black smoke across the horizon. The police were looking on.

Nepal's principal export is labourers, who struggle on the building sites, and in the kitchens and laundries of Gulf emirates and the factories of more dynamic Asian nations. It seemed that the twelve men in Iraq had been conned, sent there illegally somehow. They may have been told they were going to Kuwait. The crowds directed their anger at the 'manpower agencies' that send workers abroad. At Moonlight Manpower all the windows were smashed. At Gallivant Manpower the furniture and paperwork was burning in the street. The students who had done it crowded round me.

'Because of the manpowers' carelessness, these people were murdered! If there had been staff here, there would have been a bad result,' they warned.

'We're going to another manpower and we will do the same!'

'Horrible murders. Very cruel death.'

A policeman came over and protested. 'All the records are burnt,' he said. 'What will happen to the people who paid money to the manpower?' It seemed from the singed documents that they had been due to go to Malaysia.

'We are angry and we are shocked,' the students insisted. One of them asked me, 'Sir, in your view, have we done right or wrong?'

They were angry all the way across town. The offices of Middle Eastern airlines were burning. A man tried to make off up the street with a looted computer but the crowd made him smash it. The guards at the Egyptian embassy shot a man who was trying to climb over the wall.

'Our government was weak so they were killed,' I scrawled in my notebook and, outside the ruins of Pinnacle Manpower, 'All manpower are thieves. They are butchers.' The students were throwing the furniture out of the fourth-floor windows of Pinnacle. There was a big cheer when the filing cabinets went on the fire in the street. The students pried open a steel cupboard and found 363 passports inside, which they took away to their campus. The burning paperwork said that each passport holder had paid between one and three-and-a-half lakhs to work abroad. Some policemen arrived, but they were hopelessly outnumbered and left again. 'They've gone because nothing wrong is happening,' the students said.

The fax machines and telephones coming from the windows caught on the overhead wires, making small explosions and sending blue sparks around the area. The crowd fled and I stumbled, on my hands and knees, in a puddle, my heart beating like a disco.

It was hard for me to reach the Kashmiri mosque because of police firing tear gas, but a couple of hundred rioters had had the run of it before the police arrived. The ground was scattered with charred pages of Arabic; the prayer room was blackened; there were smashed plant pots and broken glass; a blackened tomb; water tanks knocked off the roof and split. The police were wandering around, spitting on the ground and poking things with their lathis. The Imam had been beaten up, then locked in a room for his safety. I wrote in my notebook: 'The sensitive students said "Don't touch him", the others said "Kill him! Kill him!"' He was still locked in, quaking in the corner, surrounded by broken glass, visible through the broken window in the door.

In the afternoon the government declared a curfew, which was not lifted for four days. Helicopters flew low over the now empty streets, and no one swept up the glass. The newspapers identified a conspiracy. Who organized these crowds, and why did the authorities fail to respond? Among the first targets had been newspaper offices, yet there was no response to the journalists' emergency calls. It was strange. The Congress party president said that the army and the palace hoped to weaken the democratic forces by sowing chaos. A Muslim leader detected complex planning, perhaps by Hindu fundamentalists: 'The way in which they opened the gate and entered the Mosque showed they used to visit,' he reasoned.[2] Journalists thought it was an attack on the freedom of the press, perhaps by the army. The manpower agencies, which were undoubtedly engaged in various conspiracies to cheat and endanger their clients, were associated with the political class and escaped further attention. Pakistan blamed India's RAW intelligence agency and some people thought they might have a point. 'The mayhem is hatched by foreign element to sabotage Nepal's burgeoning sectors like foreign employment business, tourism and the economy,' claimed a nationalist lawyer, noting that the destruction was so meticulously achieved it must have been planned for years. Years later, when I was thinking about those riots again, I mentioned it to a friend, a political junky with diverse and impressive sources of gossip.

'Oh, it was the Congress party trying to discredit the government,' she said. 'Remember, in those days Congress still had its grass roots organization.'

It was years later, when all the mess was cleared up and the losses were reckoned, that I met a leader of the Kashmiri community. He was distinguished-looking, with hair hennaed orange and a tweed waistcoat, sitting behind a vast desk in the offices of his son's company. The family had kept up with the times. The old man's father was a contractor on Nepal's first roads; the old man opened the first bus company; the son had gone into manpower.

'We have some family papers from 367 years ago,' he said. 'The king was Pratap Malla. We came from Saudi Arabia to Baghdad and from Iraq to Samarkand and Bokhara, then Afghanistan to Kashmir and Kashmir to India, Nepal and Tibet. Pratap asked us to stay here and do business.' He adopted the voice of Pratap Malla, '"I will give facilities, customs duty free, for the Kashmiri Muslims."' He still had cousins in Lhasa, who came to visit from time to time.

He picked up the phone on his desk and spoke in Urdu. A while later someone came in with a sheaf of papers, which he handed to me. It was a university thesis, written thirty years ago by a member of the community, about the community. 'Read this and give it back,' he said.

There were four families of Kashmiris; first came Syed, then Joo, then Sheik, then Khan, the old man explained. He was from Syed. Now the four families fill 200 households in the city, a total of around 1,000 people. Later other Muslims came, but they are not the same. 'In 1857 when the Indians were ...' he trailed off searching for the word.

'The Mutiny?' I suggested.

He found the *mot juste* in Urdu then continued in English, '... fighting for their independence, many Muslims came here from India; from Bihar, UP and Punjab. The Kashmiri families gave them ten per cent of our land and property, so we have various types of Muslims here but our Kashmiri system is different.' The tomb of the Begum of Lucknow, who led the resistance against the British in 1857, is inside the Kashmiri mosque in Kathmandu, he said. After the uprising failed she fled to the Nepal Valley and left her bones there. He asked if I'd ever visited the mosque.

'Only once,' I said.

He was the chairman of the mosque during the riot in 2004 and he was inside when it was attacked. 'We lost 4 crore 25 lakhs near about, and in our own property, in this office, I lost 2 lakhs near about,' he said. All the labourers' passports they'd been holding were destroyed.

'You must have been terrified,' I said.

'Even today we are frightened,' the old man said calmly. An Indian court was due to rule on the disputed holy site at Ayodhya, in India. The previous day representatives of the community had met the prime minister and the chief of police to ask for protection if right-wing Hindus rioted in Kathmandu.

'There was no protection in 2004,' I said.

'No government was there,' he confirmed. 'I made so many calls. The prime minister at that time was my best friend, but they could not do anything.'

'Why?'

'Direct instructions from the palace,' he said.

These kinds of things didn't happen in Malla Kathmandu. The system of government created an illusion of timeless stability based on strictly segregated diversity, and upon so many and such elaborate rituals that the city was absorbed in a continuous pageant. Anthropologists have called it a theatre state.[3] The Malla kings literally wrote plays for their subjects to act in, dramatizing stories of the gods and the recently discovered myths of the Valley's creation; for the stories of the ancient lake (and so on) do not in fact date from the earliest times, as they purport to, but from the intense and elaborate cultural production of the Malla period. The founding legends starring Manjushree and Shiva, with which every telling of the story begins, first appeared in medieval texts that were fraudulently pre-dated, like the genealogies of kings had always been, to give a divine provenance to the flourishing civilization of the Mallas.[4] The idea that Kathmandu had been founded in the shape of a sword could only come after the Licchavi villages had fused into a long, thin city.

The parts in the plays were acted by the different castes, according to their role in life. For example, the worship of the rain god Bungadya, who had been identified by Buddhists as the bodhisattva Karunamaya for many centuries, was ancient, but his procession in a giant cart around Patan can be traced only to around the seventeenth century, when the Malla city state was at its height.[5] When the great festival wound its way around the streets the responsibilities of building this, or providing that, pulling the ropes or playing a certain drum, keeping the god's decorative regalia or making the sacrifice, were given to the different castes and lineages, as they still are, according to their intrinsic character. So the productions and processions tied the quarters of Patan and all of their constituent communities together, even while the population was divided into dozens of exclusive categories. As Hindus themselves, and to give their Hindu subjects a part in the drama, the Malla kings seem to have added a Hindu identity (that of the saint Matsyendranath) to Bungadya's already multiple character, and it is as Matsyendranath that the god is best known today. The result of this complexity and elaboration was an extremely stable society. Any conflicts that might have arisen had their outlet in other festivals, which ritualized social rivalry in an annual tug-of-war, or a brick-throwing match between different neighbourhoods.

While I was driving late at night I ran into dense crowds. Three dipankar buddhas were standing among the people, beneath electric lights at the side of the road. Each of the gods was at least a foot taller than the tallest man, with a serene and shining golden face, wearing bright silk robes over the bamboo cage of his body. A little further on I drew up at the side as two more giant figures danced slowly past. Every few yards the buddhas settled to the ground, to allow the man inside to rest, then they danced on. Figures such as these, affectingly beautiful, and appearing only when the stars and planets were powerfully aligned, must have made a powerful impression on the city's people.

The Kartik dance, which fills Patan's palace square with crowds and peanut sellers every night for a week in the autumn, was another such piece of state theatre.

'Here, now, in a moment ...' the drunk announcer was slurring over the PA system. No one listened and nothing happened. 'Sit down so others can see. It's for your own good, sit down ...' Everybody was milling about, talking, eating nuts and fiddling with their phones. Four dancers with golden headdresses stepped out of the crowd and performed a series of elaborate hand movements, before alternately shuffling from side to side and pirouetting with their swords held above their heads. Behind the closed door of the palace the lion-headed god Narsimha was preparing for his dramatic entry in a secret puja.

According to the theory of the theatre state, the Malla regimes didn't so much administer power as dramatize it. The castes and the festivals in which everyone played their part recreated on the city's stage a model of the Hindu universe. The theatre state presented a world that was complete and eternal. Within this natural order any amount of intrigue and petty warfare carried on, but that was natural too.

When King Pratap Malla of Kathmandu became jealous of his cousin, the king of Patan, he chose the day that Patan's spectacular new temple would be consecrated to attack the town. Spoiling the ceremony won only disgrace for the Kathmandu raja. He made amends to heaven by building his own Krishna temple, in his own palace square. Later, Pratap Malla went raiding Bhaktapur, and carried off two stone lions and a golden serpent to decorate his palace. So it went, in an endless round. Bilateral treaties of friendship, negotiated by two of the cousin kings to exclude the third, were written and put aside at a rate of two or three a year during periods of special rancour.

In 1721 a Jesuit named Ippolito Desideri passed through the Valley on a journey from Tibet to India, and described the state of Kathmandu warfare:

> When two armies meet they launch every sort of abuse at one another, and if a few shots are fired, and no one is hurt, the attacked army retires to a fortress, of which there are many, resembling our country dovecots. But if a man is killed or wounded, the army which suffered begs for peace, and sends a dishevelled and half-clothed woman who weeps, beats her breast and implores mercy, the cession of such carnage, and such shedding of human blood.

The decadent Malla states had little defence against external aggression. Like Nepali politicians in later ages, they were incapable of uniting against a common enemy, and by the mid-eighteenth century there was a gathering threat in the hills, from the prince of a tiny state one hundred miles away, a ruthless and determined man named Prithvi Narayan Shah of Gorkha. In the brief memoir he dictated at the end of his life, Prithvi Narayan recalled standing on a hilltop as a young man, sometime around 1740, surveying the three cities of the Valley. 'Which is Nepal?' he asked and his attendants pointed out Patan, Kathmandu and Bhaktapur.

'Oh King, your heart is melting with desire,' crooned the astrologers.

'I was struck with wonder,' Prithvi Narayan recalled. 'How did they know my innermost thoughts and so speak to me?'

The astrologers answered him: 'At the moment your gaze rested on Nepal you stroked your moustache and in your heart you longed to be king of Nepal, as it seemed to us ... You, O Prince, have held at all times great respect for cows, Brahmins, guests, holy men, the gods and goddesses. Also, in our hands lies the blessing of Saraswati. You will one day be king of Nepal.'[6]

He began conquering the tiny kingdoms that surrounded the Valley and encroaching on the Tibetan trade routes. The kings of the Valley began concluding treaties with their common enemy against one another. Prithvi Narayan held them in contempt. 'Three citied Nepal is a cold stone,' he wrote, 'great only in intrigue … [having only] empty pomp and pleasure.' City people were soft: 'With one who drinks water from cisterns, there is no wisdom; nor is there courage.'[7] He and his men were hard. They drank water from streams.

☀

In his manual for protracted guerrilla war Mao Tse-tung wrote:

> Our operations may be extended to include cities and lines of communication not strongly held. We may hold these at least for temporary (if not for permanent) periods. All these are our duties in offensive strategy. Their object is to lengthen the period that the enemy must remain on the defensive.[8]

The Maoist rebels implemented blockades of Kathmandu repeatedly in 2004 and 2005. From a sandbagged emplacement where the road passes out of the Valley, a soldier showed me the empty road through his binoculars; the single ribbon that carried almost all the city's supplies twisting away through the hills. The Maoists would burn a dozen trucks when they issued their threats, and that was enough to cut the traffic of goods vehicles from thousands to a dozen a day, and make the blockade last a week. The few trucks that passed careered recklessly, in terror of the jungles beside the road. Half of the Royal Nepal Army was committed to securing the capital. The sole major entry point for its food and fuel had only children herding goats, women collecting firewood, and soldiers bartering for fruit in the shade. Inside the city there were accusations of hoarding, and prices quickly rose.

'Cause uproar in the east and strike in the west,' Mao wrote. 'Appear now here and now there, using false banners and making empty demonstrations, propagate rumours about one's own strength in order to shatter the enemy's morale and create in him a boundless terror.'[9] Army patrols along the empty highway did not run into any Maoists at all.

Prithvi Narayan Shah also blockaded Kathmandu. His siege was described by an Italian missionary who lived in Patan, named Father Giuseppe:

> Every person who was found in the road, with only a little salt or cotton about him, was hung upon a tree; and he caused all the inhabitants of a neighbouring village to be put to death in a most cruel manner (even the women and children did not escape) for having supplied a little cotton to the inhabitants of *Nepal* … it was a most horrid spectacle to behold so many people hanging on the trees in the road. However, the king of *Gorc'ha* being also disappointed in his expectations of gaining his end by this project fomented dissentions among the nobles of the three kingdoms of *Nepal*, and attached to his party many of the principal ones, by holding forth to them liberal and enticing promises; for which purpose he had about 2000 *Brahmens* in his service.[10]

In 1766, after a long siege, Prithvi Narayan took the hilltop town of Kirtipur, dominating the entrance to the Valley, by treachery, offering an amnesty to its exhausted people. Afterwards, as Father Giuseppe recorded, he issued an order

> to put to death all the principal inhabitants of the town, and to cut off the noses and lips of everyone, even infants who were not found in the arms of their mothers … none escaping but those who could play wind instruments… it was most shocking to see so many living people with their teeth and noses resembling the skulls of the deceased.[11]

According to Wright's chronicle, the heap of noses and lips weighed eighty pounds. The kingdoms of Kathmandu, Patan and Bhaktapur (which had failed to come to Kirtipur's support) still held out.

☀

Indra Jatra is the great civic festival of Kathmandu, when the chariots of the gods are hauled through the city; around the southern quarters that were the village of Yangala one day, around the northern quarters that used to be Yambu the next. On the fourth day of Indra Jatra families who have lost a member in the previous year walk the course of the old city wall.[12]

At first I didn't notice the mourners, because I was expecting more of a parade. Except for widowed women, and sons who had lost a parent, they were not wearing white, so they didn't look very different from the people who were making their way in other directions. Where neighbourhoods had arranged displays of offerings for Indra Jatra tourists were taking pictures, but they might not have noticed that they were in the midst of a procession, that there were slightly more people walking one way than another, occasionally pausing to judge the route. More women than usual were sitting on their steps watching the people.

From the midpoint of the sword-shaped city we walked north along the western edge, on top of the sloping ground between old Kathmandu and the Bishnumati River. It was no less urban on one side than the other, but this had been the line between the fields and the houses when many of these people were born. We looped out to take in the Mother temple by the cremation ground on the riverbank.

The route led down the eastern edge of the city through bazaars I'd rarely visited; a concrete canyon of gaudy children's clothes from China, a stretch of sewing machine sales and repairs, then more familiar quarters of anonymous hotels, and showrooms of electric light fittings. Again, at the southern tip, we walked along the top of a slope, with a row of low-caste houses facing out and the warren of the old town within. The procession had quickly become a steady flow and eventually it filled the lanes, partly sombre and partly festive. There were decorations and recorded music. Musicians joined the crowd after dark, and the lamps that people lit were pretty. But the families walked, talked and were pressed together quietly. A taxi driver called out to the middle-aged man beside me, 'Uncle, whose is it?'

'My daughter,' he said, not looking. 'My little daughter.'

Indra Jatra lasts for eight days. The castes of the different neighbourhoods take their different roles. The gardeners and the painters dance behind the masks of different gods. The oil-pressers are responsible for the giant pole erected in the palace square. The Jyapu farmers have an affinity with Bhairab – Shiva in his destructive aspect – who during the festival is the god of beer. Two men of the cowherd caste dress as an elephant and crash around the streets, scattering the crowds.

A long series of black cars with blinking lights arrived at the Malla palace. The modern state pageantry provided pick-up trucks, bristling with rifles, and jeeps crammed with plain-clothes security officials, hanging out of the windows. They swerved up to the palace gate. The government celebrities and foreign ambassadors assembled on the balcony. I recognized a

senior official who I thought was involved in an international adoption racket.

The square was crowded. The men in the elephant costume were causing an uproar. A masked dancer made a break, leading a crowd of excited spectators through the security cordon in front of the palace. Fleeing in front of the mask was a child, decked with bells, glancing terrified at the monster on his heels. 'He's called the dragonfly,' said the man beside me. 'His job is to annoy the mask.' The senior cops on their radios looked rattled. The bigwigs on the balcony looked on indulgently like kings. The king himself, Gyanendra Shah, was standing in the middle.

The living incarnation of the Malla kings' private goddess Taleju was brought out; a small girl surrounded by attendants, treading on a white cloth laid in front of her. She was installed on her chariot, then drawn past the king and the ambassadors, and off around the city. A military band, wearing something like British regimental dress, struck up a march.

That night the chariots of the gods were still being hauled through the streets. People threw water from their windows onto the teams pulling them. There were groups singing hymns, and masked dancers. Beer spouted from the horrifying face of

the White Bhairab in the palace wall. Young men sitting on their friends' shoulders charged into the throng, clambered over each other and captured the jet in their mouths for as long as they could, before being thrust aside. I met Suman the cop round the corner for a drink and we talked about work. I told him about my interview with the prime minister and he told me about meetings with foreign donors trying to reform the police.

'These guys meet the bosses. I know what both sides are thinking before they think it. I understand them both; they don't understand each other at all. They leave so confused!' Then he started telling me about Haiti, where he'd been on a UN police mission. 'I went to church, I've never seen anything like it.'

'People falling around and jabbering?'

'Much worse. People banging their heads, trying to climb the walls, ripping their clothes off, tearing themselves … '

'Did you see any voodoo?' I asked. 'Do they kill chickens and stuff?'

'Crazier,' said Suman. 'Lizards in a box, that kind of thing. Mind you,' he reflected, 'coming from Kathmandu, with all these terrifying gods everywhere, it doesn't seem so strange.' The noise outside had risen as the chariots were manoeuvred through the exultant crowd. 'What a commotion,' Suman said indifferently. He was a Chhetri, it wasn't his culture.

A series of musket shots announced that some stage had been completed, but the celebrations went on. It was on this night, when all of Kathmandu was drunk, that Prithvi Narayan Shah and his army entered the city. He marched into the horrified crowd in the palace square and he installed himself as the new king, at the centre of the old festivals, and the time was up for the Newar rule of Kathmandu.

PART TWO

The Revolutions

11

Every year on the festival day of Shiva, Nepal's patron deity, on the parade ground in the centre of Kathmandu's one-way system, the army drilled before the king, members of the government, diplomatic corps and press. The unemployed pressed idly around the railings to watch, as they had already been doing during days of rehearsals, and the drivers circling outside them craned to watch too, as if there was any chance of seeing through the crowd.

A friend of mine, a diplomat, was there. He described the inefficient arrangements, the faintly slapstick air of the Nepali army on parade. There were displays of bomb-disposal equipment, a dog team jumping through burning hoops, cannon were fired and armoured cars trundled past. High above the city a plane circled, somewhere to the west, towards Swayambhu, and released the parachutists. The appalled audience watched as the canopies opened above the black specks and they drifted in to land before the grandstand. Above all except one, as he plummeted unassisted towards the wrong part of Kathmandu and disappeared into the jagged roofscape.

The next year I went to the Directorate of Public Relations and asked to be invited to Army Day. Everything was as my friend had said. Bands marched, the king took the salute. Squads charged with their drawn khukuris. The wind was in a different direction and the parachutists were released to the east. They soon settled into three categories. The largest group was doing fine and presently began landing in front of us. A second group, of two parachutists, was clearly falling short. They landed somewhere near Singha Durbar. The greatest interest attached to the final category, a group of one, who it seemed would fall

somewhere between. The audience gave him all of their attention. As the soldier drifted closer we could see him working on his lines. He seemed to have less height than horizontal distance left to cover. There were buildings below him, the awkward terrain of the Tourism Board roof. He sank over – but cleared – its compound. He still had a busy four-lane road to go. The drivers would have been riveted. There was a new railing around the parade ground, about ten feet high. At that point a small tree grew beside it. The tree was too much for the parachutist. A couple of men jogged over to see how badly broken he might be. Satisfied with the result, the dignitaries' attention and mine returned to the armoured cars in front of us.

The army was the same institution that Prithvi Narayan Shah had built in three decades of war, when he forged the men of the tiny kingdom of Gorkha into the force that captured Kathmandu. Its oldest units traced their names to his time. During his campaign, and in the decades after his death, the army swept dozens of tiny kingdoms in the hills to create the modern state of Nepal. The army's loyalty was still to Prithvi Narayan's descendant, Gyanendra Shah. Its officers were the descendants of Prithvi Narayan's officers; the most qualified among them could reel off the names of every ancestor who stood between themselves and one of the first king's lieutenants. The other ranks were recruited from the ethnic groups and castes recognized since his time as most suitable for fighting.[1]

The vigorous new rulers were different from the Newars who lived in Kathmandu, like they were different from many of the other people inside their new empire, but they didn't transform the appearance of the city straight away. Prithvi Narayan Shah's additions to the Malla kings' palace were on an imperial scale but they were in the same Newar style. The new lords built their mansions inside the old city, perhaps with a frieze of soldiers marching across the façade. They were Chhetris, the caste of high-born warriors, and they had a militaristic, aristocratic spirit. The rest of the country became subject to their social, cultural and political supremacy, and over time Kathmandu developed physically to reflect their values. In the generations that followed the city spread to include dozens of new palaces. In a similar way, much later, new suburbs would cover the sites of those palaces, to express again changed social and governing principles.

In his deathbed testament, the *Dibya Upadesh,* Prithvi Narayan warned that if his followers became 'pleasure seekers' they would lose their edge, and his 'little, painfully acquired kingdom' would run wild as 'a garden of every sort of people'.

> But if everyone is alert, this will be a true Hindustan of the four castes, with the thirty-six sub-castes. Do not leave your ancient religion. Don't forsake the salt of the king. Do not take the chamberlain's post from Kalu's family. Do not take the care of the foreign policy for Tibet from Kalu Pande's family. In giving the kazi's post to the Pandes, Basnyets, Panthas, and Magars, give it to them each in turn ... Even if they should commit some crime deserving death do not kill them yourself. Instead ... send them into battle. If they come back alive, it is well. If they are killed, it is well.[2]

It was a Chhetri ideology. The lords were served by Brahmin priests, who also held an exalted status. The other castes had their proper places as traders, infantrymen, farmers, serfs, artisans and slaves, and this hierarchy was the basis of national strength, unity and order. Even after 250 years, especially in the minds of those near the top, some version of this scheme is still embedded in what it means to be Nepali. For example, 'King first, country second' was how some people characterized the army's ethos during the Maoist insurgency, and officers could acknowledge that as a description of their patriotism. In this way a glossy hardback produced by the Directorate of Public Relations could say, 'the history of Nepal is largely the history of the Nepalese Army'.[3]

On a Saturday night at the end of March 2004 the Maoists attacked a town called Beni, in the hills 100 miles west of Kathmandu, and retreated after it got light on Sunday. On Monday morning I arrived at Pokhara, the nearest airport, and paid a taxi driver double to take me there. Army families were waiting at the airport gate, either for news or for the bodies of their sons and husbands. There were army men in civilian clothes checking vehicles outside Pokhara. At the driver's village we stopped for him to leave behind the camouflage jacket he was wearing, then we carried on north in his old Toyota. It had holes in the floor and the seats were sprung, so with arse low and knees high I could see the tarmac flooding between my feet. It was a sunny day and hot. The steep, jungle-clad hills were bright green and huge. Several cars of distraught tourists passed us going the other way. We had the windows down and the driver seemed relaxed. I wondered if I could have got him for less.

The rebels had felled trees across the road, which were being cleared ahead of us, and they had tried to blast a bridge. There was the hole, the size of a dinner plate, which the pressure-cooker bomb had punched through the tarmac deck.

At Beni I sent the driver home. I didn't know what the rest of the day would hold, which later seemed a good reason to have kept him. At the time I was worried about getting him in trouble, and I didn't want him following me around, complaining that it was time to leave. A man had been shot in the bazaar two hours earlier, after he punched a soldier. The townspeople were standing around, morbidly curious, upset and febrile. They were holding cloths over their faces. The stench of the bodies in the street was something I'd never smelt before; so rotten it was sweet, stomach-turning, and completely unlike the smell of other animals rotting. The bodies mostly looked like teenagers. Someone lifted the cloth that covered one to show me the exit wound at the base of a dead boy's throat.

All the shops were shuttered and there were helicopters overhead. 'Bombs and bodies littering street' was the first thing I wrote in my notebook. 'M's bag of biscuits.' That must have been a reference to one of the dead Maoists carrying a snack. Two young men led me to see the charred corpses of a man and a woman in a burnt-out hotel. To them it was the most exciting of all the horrors. Apparently the Maoists had given a warning before they set fire to the building and the others inside had fled. These two preferred to hide.[4]

Beni lies inside the junction of two valleys. The Maoists occupied the hills around, and started to infiltrate the streets after they became quiet at night. The attack started at eleven, with gunshots and a bombardment of mortars upon the army camp. The assault teams were formed up in advanced positions. These young men and women, armed with socket bombs, digging tools and wire cutters, would fight their way through the minefields and barbed-wire obstacles, covered by machine-gun fire, which guarded the army camp and other government buildings. Videos captured after other battles show them, waiting in silence 'with the light of battle in their eyes'.[5] They would take the greatest casualties. After the opening salvo they were ordered in. They used pressure-cooker bombs as assault charges, placed against the perimeter with long bamboo poles, to blast their way into the police station. Waves of assault troops were followed by waves of other fighters, armed with rifles, and behind them the stretcher teams.

'They were here, all along here, all night,' said the warden at a boarding school, indicating the lane below the dormitory. 'The children were also watching, most of them. Boys this side, girls that side.' Half an hour after the battle started the lane was full of Maoists, passing bombs one way and casualties the other. The school children were afraid at first, but later they enjoyed watching the rebels coming and going; they were eating noodles, and drinking water which they took from the houses along the lane. They used a messenger on a bicycle, and they stayed until half past ten in the morning. In the morning, the children watched a dozen policemen being led away with their hands tied.

'Even when it was light they were walking here like they were coming home from a movie. Singing, joking, showing no fear,' said the warden. 'They were saying, "We achieved our aim", and "Whatever we wanted to do, we did it".' The Chief District Officer had been kidnapped. The jail had been opened. The police station was taken. Two lakhs were removed from the vault of the finance company. The government buildings were still smoking when I arrived. The army, however, had resisted the onslaught.

I went to the army camp and found the colonel, now in his third day without sleep. He wore a thick moustache and the soft sack of his gut hanging over the belt of his camouflage trousers. A mortar had exploded near his office. The desk was covered with broken glass and empty magazines from his rifle. 'Eleven hour, continuous, non-stop battle. Intense. High pressure, tremendous pressure,' he said.

The army had no warning that a force of several thousand Maoists had entered the hills above the town until the shooting started. The colonel said, 'They came like sea waves, one after another, one after another. More than fifty per cent women. That's what I saw when I was shooting, and many, many child soldiers, below fourteen.' He had fourteen men dead, fifty wounded, two taken prisoner, and the cops had lost more.

I asked him about the hostages. 'That's a big question mark,' he said.[6]

In the days before the attack the Maoists had imposed a blockade on the town, which was the kind of thing they did from time to time. 'The main cause of this incident, I think, was the blockade,' said the colonel. 'The villagers were not allowed to move so no information came.

'The main thing is lack of information. We can reach every part of the country but we have no information and with no information there is no point in going there.

'No indication. No indication,' he confirmed again, and after a while he said, 'This is a big, big victory for us.'

The colonel walked me round the camp. The whitewashed walls and tin roofs, the smart military flowerbeds and canteen, were wrecked by mortar fire and bullet holes. The ground was half-covered with brass cartridges. There were six dead Maoists in the vegetable garden. 'They are all young, all children,' the colonel said. 'This one's a girl.' Then he left me to examine the things the Maoists had left behind.

I looked at the Maoists' photo albums. The pictures showed young people on holiday, posing by the lake at Pokhara, and families celebrating festivals in village homes. There were groups of Maoists posing with guns, wearing assorted pieces of uniform.

In one shot a girl sat on a step, facing straight into the camera, holding a bunch of plastic flowers. She looked happy and bold. On the facing page was a photo of a boy with 'I love you' written on it in English.

I looked at the captured guns and pressure-cooker bombs and the spools of wire used to detonate them. I saw that they used a camera flashgun to discharge the conclusive current down the line. I turned to a printed booklet, which seemed to be a bomb-making manual, and started photographing the pages. A soldier was watching me.

'What do you think about the Maoists?' he asked.

I said I thought it was a discredited ideology.

'They made China great,' he said, as if it was a question.

I left the baffled soldier and went down to the spit of land where the rivers meet, where the helicopters were landing. The green ones were picking up and dropping off commandos, who were on cordon and search operations in the hills to the west, where the main Maoist force had retreated. The civilian charters were being loaded with the bodies of dead cops, which were still being carried down to the landing ground. The choppers whipped up burning storms of grit when they came in to land and the people on the ground turned their backs and crouched at the edges of the field, then came forward when the rotors slowed to begin loading. There were several of us who wanted a lift to Pokhara and not much space. Several helicopters left without me.

The last helicopter had a pilot I recognized. He recognized me, picked me out, and rejected the other passengers. The inside of his helicopter was arranged like a car, with two front seats and a long back seat that flipped up, like a seat in a cinema. Three police corpses were piled beneath it. Their limbs were standing out in the positions they had set in, beneath a bulging grey blanket. The bodies were stiff and rotting, hard and soft at once, and the seat did not go down properly over them. I was invited to climb in, but I was out again, retching, before I could find a way to sit. The people standing around laughed at that. I sprayed deodorant on a woollen jumper, tied it round my face, and climbed back inside. We took off.

When we were up the pilot handed me the second headset. He had the Grateful Dead on the stereo, I think, a long bluegrass banjo solo which lasted most of the flight, maybe ten or twenty minutes, occasionally broken by a snatch of radio traffic. We floated like a bubble towards – and then over – range after range of hills, two guys in the front and me awkwardly perched on the corpses in the back. Then lower, over the lake and the temple on the island in it, into Pokhara airport. There was still a group of women wailing by the gate. I said thanks to the pilot, and went to file my story to the *Telegraph* and get drunk.

A few weeks later I was back in Pokhara, trying to persuade the army to take me on a patrol. I was with a friend, an American photographer called Tomas, who wanted the same thing. The army's regional headquarters for western Nepal was in Pokhara and the general had agreed. He told us to wait; he would have someone call us when the right opportunity came. So Tomas and I hung about in the tourist strip by the lakeside, deserted at the beginning of the monsoon, and spent the nights in a futile search of the empty bars for pretty tourists to talk to.

At the divisional headquarters the army showed us a video they had found in a camera after the battle at Beni. It showed long columns of rebels on their march across the barren high land that lies to the north-west of the town. Somewhere up there they had cut a sand-map into the ground; an extraordinarily accurate model of Beni, at the junction of two valleys, with the details made on it as meticulously as on a model railway. The Maoists assembled around it and the famous commander known as Pasang stepped forward. He seemed about 40, with a weathered, handsome face; the very image of a communist partisan, wearing a satchel by a strap across his shoulder. He told them he was addressing an army of eight thousand. This plan, he said, has been made by the Central Committee, and he read a speech by the Supreme Commander, Comrade Prachanda, the Fierce One.

'The Party has taken the historic decision to decentralize education,' an army colonel translated for us. I stopped taking notes for a while. 'We will bear up to 85 per cent casualties. If there are 100 soldiers we will fight until there are only 15 … We are always for a constituent assembly. This is our demand and we will not compromise.' A new constitution was what they would die for. A detailed briefing began, using the model. There would be six frontal charges and the assault teams would take heavy losses. 'You must be willing to sacrifice your life, and those who die we must give respect,' Pasang told them. They stood for a minute's silence. Further down the trail they held a farewell programme with revolutionary music.

We sat with General Basnyat in his office. He had maps on the walls decorated with pins and arrows. His name showed that he belonged to one of the aristocratic clans that led Prithvi Narayan Shah's army two and a half centuries earlier. He spoke English a bit like an Englishman and he talked cheerfully about Ferdinand and Isabella and Napoleon Bonaparte, but he took a pessimistic view of his own war. 'It looks, yes, that they are in virtual control of the countryside,' he admitted, 'but that control is through fear.'

I asked if his soldiers should not be on patrols, protecting the public.

'Of course their job is to fight, but I don't want to send them into an ambush. Even if we get through one way, then coming back …' he trailed off.

During those days in Pokhara, of waiting to go on a patrol, there was a double killing. A man and a woman, supposedly Maoists, were arrested from their home by the army and driven to another place in a pick-up truck. People living nearby heard the engine. It stopped. After a moment there were shots. I saw the bullet marks on the trees. The army said the couple were trying to escape. A local newspaper covered the story, called it a human rights abuse, and a delivery man got beaten up by a soldier.

In our meeting the general had said: 'If you are playing a game with a set of rules and someone starts playing foul, will you tolerate it, like Mr Buddha? You get frustrated, then you get these people talking about human rights. What human rights?' Meanwhile the army faced three shortages: 'Communications, helicopters, intelligence,' he said. 'If I had two or three helicopters I could take care of them easily.'

These were the kind of things Western governments were interested in then. Tony Blair had appointed a special representative to Nepal; Britain had recently added two short take-off and landing (STOL) surveillance planes to the helicopters it had already given.[7] The British embassy had a growing contingent of spooks and military experts. There were vague reports in the newspapers of American military advisers, and controversy over a shipment of Belgian machine guns. The international community would not allow the Maoist terrorists to win. I asked: could they win? 'Who knows,' said the general pleasantly. 'If things keep going on like this, maybe.'

He said his son was an American citizen. If things in Nepal didn't work out, he might settle down over there himself. 'Mr Prachanda is very confident that he will be entering the Kathmandu Valley in three to four years,' the general said, and he didn't seem to disagree. 'Prachanda seems to be a good leader, or he wouldn't have been able to raise that organization from scratch.' My patrol with the army never happened. And it took Prachanda only two more years to enter Kathmandu.

Prithvi Narayan Shah's conquest of Kathmandu was of concern to the great powers of his day, which meant the British East India Company in Calcutta. They were upset by his disruption of the trans-Himalayan trade routes, and concerned that the growing Gorkhali power in the hills could bump up against their own, even faster expansion in northern India. Yet to begin with they were not quite sure where Kathmandu was.

When King Jayaprakash Malla of Kathamandu asked the British to support his besieged city in 1767 they sent a force of 2,500. Its leader, Captain Kinloch, was obliged to put his trust

Son Yun's Map No. 2

in an unreliable guide, and in a map which was 'neither a Plan, Perspective, or Profile, and altogether out of proportion'.[8] He never knew how close he was to Kathmandu when – already defeated by starvation and incessant rain, and mad with fever – his invasion was finally halted by a mutiny. Kinloch succeeded only in confirming the Gorkhas' deep suspicion of the British. From then on Nepali and British writers predicted another war between the two empires. Military events and foreign knowledge of the country advanced together. A chance to penetrate the terra incognita arrived in 1792 when the Gorkhas invaded Tibet and the British government in Calcutta began receiving angry letters from China. A young British officer, named Captain William Kirkpatrick, described it:

> The court of Pekin, resenting certain encroachments which had been made by the Government of Nepaul upon the rights of the Lama of Tibet, whom the Emperor of China had, for some time past, taken under his protection, or, in other words, had subjected to the Chinese yoke, came to the resolution of chastising the aggressor, or *the Robber*, as the Rajah of Nepal was contemptuously styled in the Chinese dispatches.[9]

A Chinese army drove the Gorkhali army from Tibet, crossed the border and reached within two or three days' march of Kathmandu. Now the Nepalis desperately appealed for British support, and Captain Kirkpatrick was the man appointed to capitalize on the situation. In the preface to the book he wrote,

Kirkpatrick describes how a treaty between China and Nepal was hastily concluded before he had a chance to set off. The Nepalis once again had more to fear from British interference than from China, and withdrew his invitation. But the British argued that this was very rude – they insisted – and after a few months' delay Kirkpatrick started out in February 1793, with four fellow countrymen and two companies of sepoys, to establish trading relations with the Company's northern neighbour.

The party took great pains over making their map, which was the more difficult because they must not be seen taking compass readings. In such mountainous country the only way to measure distances was by timing each day's march, and each night the British officers met to discuss the condition of the route and the speed they had made. They often reckoned their progress at just two miles an hour. They gauged their altitude with a barometer, and although they had a quadrant to measure latitude they didn't understand how to use it and didn't trust their readings.

From the Indian border the way ran through thick jungle, where malaria was so virulent the route was impassable for half the year. After leaving the seasonal trading post of Hettowra the road entered the narrow valley of the Rapti River, 'strewn with huge fragments of rocks, rent from the craggy precipices', where the numerous fords were slippery and the porters fell about beneath their loads. They were surrounded by a 'wild and picturesque scenery' of immense hills clothed in beautiful trees. At Bhimphedi the path turned steeply uphill and ran 'close to the brink of frightful precipices'. The footing was made insecure by loose fragments of rock, which were dislodged and fell on the rear of the party on the path below.

Finally, Kirkpatrick reached the fort guarding the pass. 'The perpendicular height of Cheesapany fort above Bheem-phede is about five hundred and thirty yards,' he reckoned, 'which it took me very near an hour and a half to ascend in my hammock.'[10] He offered a disparaging assessment of the fort's defensive capability. The true summit lay a mile further on.

> The mountains of the Himma-leh suddenly burst upon the view, rearing their numerous and magnificent peaks, eternally covered with snow, to a sublime height; and so arresting the eye as to render it for some time inattentive to the beautiful landscape immediately below it.[11]

He took a barometer reading. Now the road went down again and although it followed the edge of an 'immense abyss' it was wide enough to spare the captain in his hammock much fright. They passed through an area where he was told that violent winds sometimes whipped up blizzards of small stones, which 'render it a very unpleasant stage for travellers', then crossed the face of a mountain that provided 'the most alarming, if not the most dangerous passage' of the whole journey:

> The breadth of it [the path] no where exceeds two feet, and it is in some places not so much. On one hand is the side of the hill, which ... is here quite bare, affording neither shrub nor stone capable of sustaining the stumbling traveller, on whose other hand is a perpendicular precipice some hundred feet deep, at the bottom of which the Markhoo-kola rushes impetuously over its rocky bed.[12]

I am also afraid of heights. Today Kirkpatrick's route is a narrow back road, but his discomfort is still available to travellers whenever two vehicles edge past one another at the side of the precipice.[13] Kirkpatrick was rewarded a day later when he stood on the peak of Chandragiri and looked down upon

> ... the valley of Nepaul, beautifully and thickly dotted with villages and abundantly chequered with rice fields fertilized by numerous meandering streams ... the scenery gradually rising in an amphitheatre and successively exhibiting to the delighted view the cities and numberless temples of the valley below; the stupendous mountain of Sheoopoori; the still super-towering Jibjibia,[14] clothed to its snow clothed peak with pendulous forests; and finally, the gigantic Himma-leh,

> forming the majestic background of this wonderful and sublime picture.[15]

The king was away from the city so Kirkpatrick continued north to meet him, and did not enter Kathmandu until a month later. By then, in March 1793, the weather had changed. Like on my own first day the hills were hidden by haze and it was hard for him to take bearings. He made his camp at the bottom of the Swayambhu hill, at the west of the Valley, and it was from that perspective that the expedition produced a diagram. It is more like a mandala than a map, or more like the drawing of an ashtray than of Kathmandu.

He was the first tourist. Everything was a discovery. 'Nepaul in general is remarkable for the excellence of its bricks and tiles,' he observed, a page before noting 'a remarkable number of noseless men' among his porters.[16] 'The singularity of the circumstance leading us to enquire into the cause of it,' he learned that they were from Kirtipur, barbarously mutilated when the town fell to Prithvi Narayan Shah a quarter century earlier. It was Kirkpatrick who coined the cliché of the guidebooks that 'there are nearly as many temples as houses, and as many idols as inhabitants'.[17]

Kirkpatrick's official interest was especially in the currency, commerce, natural resources, and military capabilities of the 'Nepaulians'. But he also peered into the vamshavalis; into the buildings; the form of the government; the administration of justice; the customs and manners of the people; their arts, languages and learning. He was only in the Valley for a week. The wonder isn't that he misunderstood some things, but the huge amount he was able to discover. The currency alone, inconsistently divided by various denominators and minted in alloys of different values, was impossibly complicated. Commerce, he found, showed scope for improvement, under proper regulations. Potential commodities included elephants, shawl goats (whose wool is now known as pashmina or cashmere), yak tails, coarse blankets, salt, and marijuana. 'Their cutlery (as swords, daggers, &c.) is by no means contemptible'.[18]

Near his camp, at the foot of the steps that climb the Swayambhu hill, he saw a colossal stone image of the god Boudh. At the top he found a cylindrical machine, around which 'was curiously wrapped either some leaves, or a complete copy, I could not ascertain which, of the Bhootia [Tibetan] scriptures.'

> Upon my signifying a desire to be informed of the title of the book, I repeatedly received for answer, Mani; but whether

> this is the proper name of its author, or no more than a general denomination by which they discriminate sacred from profane writings, I am unable to determine. I observed that as often as those who entered the temple approached and touched the holy volume (which was always accompanied by gestures denoting profound respect), either the priest who attended, or the worshipper himself put the machine in motion, every revolution of which occasioned a bell to strike.[19]

Some scholars in those days believed that Boudh was the law-giver of the Tibetans (though Kirkpatrick doubted that), others said he was the same as the Chinese god Fo. Perhaps, as it appeared to Kirkpatrick, this idolatry was an apostasy of Hinduism. He was shrewd and clever but he couldn't understand what he saw at Swayambhu, just as he didn't know that the Himalaya are the highest mountains in the world; so while he delighted at the romantic scenery, Kirkpatrick wondered that the snow-capped giant he called Jibjibia 'cannot be supposed to be less elevated than the Peak of Teneriffe.' He occupies a high place in Kathmandu's history because he wrote the first modern book about the place. The Scottish soldier is like the Chinese ambassadors of the seventh century, and the Italian monk Father Giuseppe, because he's given a fixed point to hang the city's shifting story on. But in its objective of opening Nepal to British trade, Kirkpatrick's mission was a failure. He left and the country was closed again for a decade, until another security crisis in Kathmandu gave the British another opening.

12

I went back to Surkhet, the district in the mid-western hills that I had visited at the end of the ceasefire. I took the same translator, Manoj, from the hotel where he worked. We travelled on a crowded bus from the district headquarters through police and army checkpoints. After those there was an unattended Maoist checkpoint, which marked the beginning of their territory. We got off at a village called Badichour, where a Maoist boy was checking passengers.

Badichour was just two rows of wooden houses, up either side of the broken track the bus used, on a flat strip of land with the hills above and the river in the valley below. High, hardwood sal trees partly shaded it. Most of the people who were wandering around, listening to FM radios, seemed to have some sort of status in the Maoist party: Assistant Area Committee Member, and such like. Another bus arrived and delivered a gang of teenagers. One of them wore a pistol slung under his arm.

We found a 19-year-old correspondent for *Janadesh*, the rebels' weekly newspaper, or probably he found us. He was just the kind of naïve, earnest kid I'd come to associate with the Maoists. He gleefully reported that there used to be a police post, a village government office and a bee-keeping project in Badichour. They had all been driven out. (The bee keepers were apparently imposing inferior bees.) A Chinese road-building project had been burnt down too. The only thing left was the health post, which had no staff or medicine. This village was dismal and small. Manoj, the translator, was told that in the morning we could take the bus further into Maoist territory, but in the morning we were asked to wait another day while permission was sought from higher up.

Every day two buses passed twice along the track, once in each direction. We watched them come and go. They were mostly filled with young Maoist men in civilian dress. There was a young man on the roof of one bus figged out in full, brand-new battle dress, with a shining black helmet that made his outfit look like a child's costume. His friends enjoyed trying the hat on. They were transferring piglets between sacks. I was desperately bored. After the buses had gone we watched two rebels play on a stolen motorbike. They were running it on paraffin, which they'd taken without paying from the village shop. The bike spluttered and banged, streaming white smoke as they ragged it up and down the strip. There was a village idiot too, wandering about. It was said that he'd gone mad after his wife left him. In the evening we were encouraged to believe that the first bus in the morning would bring our permission to move on, but in the morning no message came.

We climbed down the forested, fifty-yard slope to wash in the river. The water was cold, despite the heat of the day, running fast over boulders. Then I interviewed the young woman whom the Maoists had put in charge of promoting women's rights. Like many of the rest she was deeply sincere, and innocent-seeming despite the life she had. She was also very pretty, but so austere I was afraid to smile at her in case she was morally shocked. 'The government didn't give rights to women and I knew that if we asked for them they wouldn't fulfil them, so I joined the Party,' she said. She wanted to end caste discrimination, and discrimination against widows. 'Very committed, very lovely, very futile,' I scrawled in my notebook. 'We are fighting with our minds,' she said, 'and the government is fighting with weapons. If I go in front of them they will kill me, and I am afraid of that.' Her activities seemed to consist mostly of organizing women's meetings, and putting pressure on families to withdraw their sons from the army and police.

I also interviewed the man, with an almost empty ledger under his arm, charged with recording land holdings and implementing 'scientific land reform'. So far he had redistributed land to seven families. And we attended a village gathering, on the patch of grass in front of the burnt-out road-building project. It was a farewell ceremony for the Maoists' Village-in-Charge, who was leaving to become a fighter in the PLA.

The departing rebel asked the nervous, silent villagers for their suggestions on taking the revolution forward. Did they have any advice on combating imperialism? He was lacing his speech with English words, such as 'metaphysical' and 'dialectically'. The people are the mirror of politics, he said, in which he could see his face. They stared back at him. Either they couldn't think of anything to say or they weren't willing to risk it. I had some tobacco in my mouth, which I'd taken from Manoj. The tobacco was slipping down my throat, choking me. My eyes were watering. Already under scrutiny, I was reluctant to try retching it out at this special function of tobacco-hating zealots. The villagers remained awkwardly silent, until someone had an idea that worked. He offered praise and thanks for all that the young leader had done for them. Others began to chime in. At last the meeting broke up.

That evening, in the tea shop below the room where we were sleeping, the *Janadesh* reporter bombarded me with questions. 'Sing a song in English ... Is the rice more delicious in your country or in Nepal? ... Are you afraid?'

'No.'

'What about when the bullet goes in your head?'

'Why would a bullet go in my head?'

The kid was annoying. He slept that night on one of the beds in our room. Before he went to sleep he rubbed his face with half a lime because he was worried about pimples.

At seven we were woken by two PLA men, who came in and offered to be interviewed. One of them had a fragmentation grenade, captured from the army, which he was anxious to show off. 'Is it good?' he wanted to know.

The other man, a former primary school teacher, was a PLA journalist. Sometimes he carried a gun in battle, but more often just his tape recorder, because there weren't enough guns to go round. Now that we were awake, and everyone was sitting on the beds, he played us a tape he'd made six months earlier in the battle at Beni. He made it while lying on the ground, holding his machine in the air; sometimes running; sometimes helping to capture ammunition. Sometimes the voices babbled cheerfully, sometimes they were urgent, but they never seemed to panic. Often the Maoist voices were women's. There was a burst of gunfire and the voice of a government soldier, very close. 'Mother, I am dead,' he said. The PLA man liked that.

Those two came with us when we were finally allowed to move on that day. It was probably only an hour on the bus to the next village, which was a strip of pretty cottages, with a Maoist checkpoint at the bottom of the hill next to the People's Village Government office and the militia barrack room. A one-armed Maoist took us to a woman's house and ordered her to put us up. After he'd gone the woman said he'd told her that we'd be staying for three days. We decided to leave in the morning. Clearly the Maoists were stalling, or had no idea what to do with us.

It was navami, the day before Nepal's greatest festival, Dasain, the year 2004, and there were no festivities. 'How can people celebrate when the country is weeping?' Manoj asked. My decision to go looking for Maoists at Dasain, when there was nothing else going on, had cost him his own celebrations. But that evening, while we were sitting upstairs overlooking the dark street, four or five men came by, cheerfully, like revellers going home. One of them was carrying over his shoulder the body of another man, who seemed to have passed out. A group of hushed women gathered in the shadows when they'd gone.

'They've been beating him on the road and now he's going to die,' they told Manoj. Forty minutes later intermittent screaming began at the bottom of the hill, where the militia barrack room was. It lasted for a quarter of an hour.

In the misty early morning, when we went to tell the Maoists that we'd had enough and we were leaving, we met Comrade Pratik smiling broadly. He was the same commander we'd met last time in Surkhet. I noticed his bodyguard's M-16 before I recognized him. Now he commanded a whole brigade. 'Someone was drunk, causing a nuisance,' he said. 'We dealt with it.' I felt truly sick of it. There were no buses on a holiday. Through the hot morning Manoj and I tramped back along the red-dirt track we'd driven a day earlier. The surface had been ribbed by rain and then baked hard, making it arduous to walk on. We were thirsty and sore-footed.

At length we came to a house and asked for water. That night we slept again in Badichour and in the morning we met two men, who seemed particularly stupid, who wanted their picture taken with their pressure-cooker bomb. They were going the same way as us, into the district headquarters to blow something up, but I don't think they took the same bus. There was a Maoist among the passengers though; who we knew was carrying a large amount of cash. I worried what would happen to him if he was picked out at the checkpoints, but of course he wasn't. It would have been with relief to all the passengers that we passed through the army's security without a problem, and back into the area of what was called government control.

When I first arrived in Kathmandu I'd told Hirakaji that I wanted his rooms for a year. I'd stayed for more than three, and now he wanted them back.

Sita helped me pack. My belongings, which once fitted into a rucksack and a suitcase, had grown enormous. There was a gas bottle, two cooking rings and a small fridge; framed black and white photographs showing historic scenes, and my own shots of modern fighters with guns; trekking gear; and several yards of books. We piled it all with the cane furniture in the lane outside. Mr and Mrs Hirakaji came to say goodbye. 'Thomas. If I have done anything wrong, please say,' Hirakaji told me with formal courtesy.

Suman the cop sent a couple of his boys round, off-duty police in a rented pick-up truck. We loaded the stuff and I followed them on my motorbike, across the river to a district near the bridge called Thapathali. It was central, a smart neighbourhood of detached bungalows in walled compounds. The rent was much more than Hirakaji's, but it was still cheap, I thought, for a modern villa with hot water and a garden. Ministerial and army staff cars sometimes drove through the area, and at times of particular political activity my street was parked-up with dark-glassed SUVs and the limousines of Asian ambassadors, dining with the old man over the road, who was believed to have special insight or influence. Like in Patan, most of my neighbours were related, but they came from a different sort of family. Their ancestors had been prominent at the Shah court two centuries ago. This was a ruling-class neighbourhood. It belonged to the phase of Kathmandu's development that occurred under the Gorkhalis.

Like many foreigners working in Nepal, I was probably already more familiar with high society than with any other strata. Many of my friends at the police club were from important Gorkhali families. They were not all police officers; they were also the cousins and classmates of police officers, and the cousins and classmates of their classmates and cousins. They hung out at the police club because, if you were entitled to, you could smoke dope and behave like you owned the place. They were Ranas, Thapas, Pandes and Basnyats and they were married to other Thapas, Ranas, Basnyats and Pandes, like their parents also were. Their fathers and uncles had senior jobs in the army and police. The younger generation mostly worked for banks, the United Nations or Western donor agencies. Their ancestors' personal weapons were exhibited in glass cases at the national museum. Their family vamshavalis described their loyalty and complex family ties.

Within a generation of Prithvi Narayan Shah's death, his descendants and the families that rose with him were locked in a blood-drenched struggle. They coveted one another's mansions and offices and they put one another's eyes out. They butchered each other when the tension spilt over at late-night meetings of the court, because it appears that whenever inflammatory accusations were being flung around the court always gathered in the middle of the night. The losers were hacked up, and in the days that followed their allies received the same; or they were drowned; trampled by elephants; impaled on iron spikes; skinned; buried to their neck with their hair coated in wax, and set on fire. According to Baburam Acharya, who was the 'historian laureate' of these sorts of things, their motives were always the simplest – of revenge, and jealousy, and self-aggrandisement – yet half the time they believed one another's lies. The greatest surprise is that the young country and its institutions proved so durable amid these antics, as it remains, despite all the fuckery that goes on today.

The third Shah king, Rana Bahadur Shah, who was born in 1775, stands out not because he was murderous, or mentally unsound, or especially libidinous (which many of his ancestors and descendants also were), but for the very unacceptable way in which he bore those traits. He fell in love with a Maithili Brahmin widow and though he could have kept her as a concubine he made her into one of his queens. The mixed-caste couple had a son and when the boy was two years old, in 1799, Rana Bahadur Shah abdicated in his favour. According to British reports he did it for two reasons. His beautiful, unsuitable queen had contracted tuberculosis, and Rana Bahadur Shah would commit himself to religious austerities to save her. Secondly, the king's horoscope foretold that he would die young. Their son would be a defenceless orphan, the object of whatever malice people had borne his parents' love, unless (as the queen convinced him) he abdicated and had the child secure on the throne in his own lifetime. Rana Bahadur Shah made the lords sign an oath of loyalty to the infant king. Then he cared for his dying wife, and made offerings to the gods and the Brahmins to save her.

When she died he lost his mind. He threatened to burn himself on her pyre. He attacked the deities who had failed to save her, tearing out statues and discarding them at the cremation ground, smashing others, offering the Hariti at Swayambu incense made from human shit, and smearing more shit on the linga at Kumbheshwar. The queen's Brahmin doctors were made to lose their caste. Their hands crushed in oil presses, or blinded with cactus milk, they were driven from the country and their wives were given to the tailors. Rana Bahadur had the commander of the army flogged, for following orders too slowly. He paraded another lord in public, dressed in his wife's clothes. Lords were hung on walls. It was too much, everyone feared for themselves. The lords told Rana Bahadur Shah that he wasn't the king anymore, anyway. The army rallied to them and he was forced to flee.

Rana Bahadur Shah went to Benares, in British territory, and the Company used the leverage his presence gave them to reopen the trade issue. A commercial treaty had been ratified in 1792 (around the time of Kirkpatrick's visit), but it wasn't implemented by the Nepalis. Now, in 1801, a second treaty, stipulating the implementation of the first, and giving the British the right to have a permanent resident in Kathmandu, was written and ratified. Captain Knox, who had been one of Kirkpatrick's companions, set off for Kathmandu in 1802 to take up residence. The unwanted foreigners stayed for a year this time, during which they were rarely allowed to leave the home the Nepalis had selected for them, in an unhealthy and ghost-infested bog just north of the city.

Nevertheless, the enterprise produced two achievements. The officer in charge of the sepoy escort was a young man named Charles Crawford, who later became the Surveyor General of India. He drew the first accurate map of Kathmandu, 'constructed trigonometrically with great exactness and immense labour', for which he won a prize of three thousand rupees.[1] Crawford's map shows how the city was and remained, largely unchanged, until the urban sprawl that began in the twentieth century. And the intelligence work of the mission's surgeon, Francis Buchanan, produced another book.

Buchanan was a formidable man, and apparently also a sour one. He suffered pain for most of his life from a leg wound, picked up in his young days as a ship's surgeon during a naval

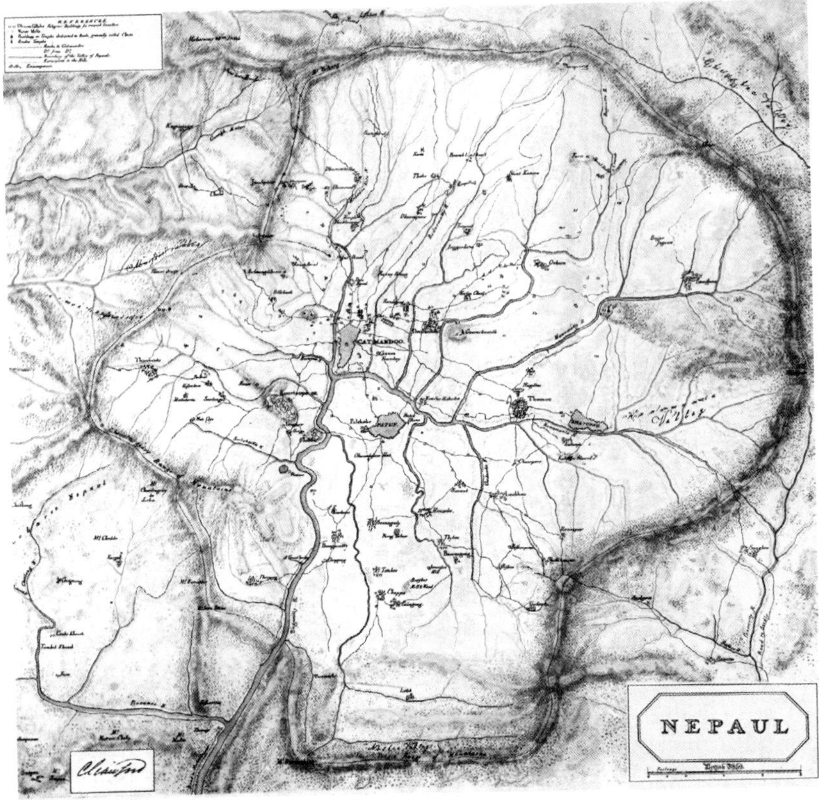

battle in the West Indies. After entering the East India Company's service, as the surgeon on a British embassy to the Burmese court at Ava, he first witnessed Buddhism being practised, and that experience helped him to understand what he saw at Kathmandu better than Kirkpatrick could. (Later, he would make pioneering discoveries of Buddhism's lost archaeology in northern India.)

Buchanan's remarkable accomplishments ran the distance from archaeology, ethnology and Asian religions to the taxonomy of the fish species of the Ganges, botany (his one true love), and military intelligence. War between the British and the Gorkhalis was still over a decade in the future when he lived in Kathmandu, but it was already visible on the horizon. He would have seen the country as a likely future British possession. So he described everything he could, took note of the Nepali army, the quality of its men and officers, sketched their fortifications, and described where an invading force could find water. During his wretched year in the city Buchanan was mostly confined inside the ill-situated British residency, so he employed a pandit to obtain as much information as he prudently could, without alarming the 'jealous government' or annoying his own leader, Captain Knox, who was struggling to establish stable relations.

To Buchanan, the 'Mountain Hindus' appeared a 'deceitful and treacherous people'; 'cruel and arrogant' towards those in their power, but abjectly fawning upon their superiors. 'Their men of rank, even of the sacred order, pass their nights in the company of male and female dancers and musicians, and, by an excessive indulgence in pleasure, are soon exhausted. Their mornings are passed in sleep … they are, in general drunkards, which, joined to a temper uncommonly suspicious, and to a consciousness of having neglected their conjugal duties, works up in them a fury of jealousy that frequently produces assassination.'[2]

The few observations of Kathmandu society that Buchanan was able to make seemed to me almost touchingly close to today's city in some respects; even as other descriptions would appal people now, or else make them rueful and nostalgic. 'In my grandfather's day,' a friend said, 'they had a servant to undo the string on their pyjamas. He'd hold their dick while they pissed, shake the drops off and put it back for them.'

'In Nepal most of the domestic servants are slaves,' Buchanan discovered.

> A male slave is called a Keta, and costs about thirty Mohurs. A female is called Keti, and costs about the same price; but, if young and handsome, she will bring ten Mohurs additional … Most of the slaves, it must be observed, have been born free. A few have been degraded, and sold by the Raja on account of crimes alleged against them: but by far the greatest part have been sold by necessitous parents … The masters in general do not give their slave girls any other allowance than

> a small quantity of rice ... The poor creatures are therefore required to sacrifice their chastity ... The Ketis of the court, indeed, are allowed some privileges ... In the day time they attend the Maha Rani or queen; and when she goes out, some of them with swords follow her on horseback and form her bodyguard ... They are allowed to carry on intrigues with any person of good birth: but the young Rajputs of the guard are their usual favourites. Some Brahmans and Bankers from the low country, induced by the beauty of these girls, have formed connexions with them; but they in general paid dearly for their indulgence. Fidelity to one mistress is not a virtue among such men, and the Ketis of the court think the whole corps bound to punish any infidelity against one of their number, nor will the police interfere to prevent them from plundering the delinquent of his entire property. The slaves of private persons are not only ill fed, but are hardly wrought. The common duties imposed on them are to wash, to bring firewood from the mountains, to clean the cooking utensils and the house, and to carry the umbrella.[3]

The Amazons of the court sound extremely exotic by today's standards, like nothing in modern Kathmandu's bourgeois values. But the origin can be discerned, in the practice of private households, of the domestic servitude that still feels so normal behind compound walls throughout the city; where the daughters of necessitous parents are hardly wrought, and fed broken rice by abusive masters and contemptuous mistresses.

After the British mission failed, and Buchanan was gratefully allowed to leave, he spent another two years compiling intelligence on the frontier by interviewing fallen aristocrats, judges, scribes, priests, and slaves fleeing the Gorkhali court. Many interesting accounts that shed light on the earlier history of the city, such as of the annual battles between Yambhu and Yangala, the northern and southern halves of Kathmandu, come from his *Account of the Kingdom of Nepal*.[4] When war between the Company and the Gorkhalis came a decade later he was urgently consulted by the British authorities. And Captain Crawford, the map-maker, by then the Surveyor General, answered the Commander-in-Chief's questions on the practicality of launching an invasion force directly at Kathmandu.

☀

While Francis Buchanan was in Kathmandu, the mad king Rana Bahadur Shah was in exile in Benares, and the commander of his bodyguard was a gifted and a complicated young man named Bhimsen Thapa. In posterity Bhimsen has been a hero to everyone, from Karl Marx to the propagandists of the British Empire; and in his lifetime, also, he had a quality that made his friends and enemies unsure which category they belonged to.

Rana Bahadur Shah's exile lasted four years. He returned to Kathmandu in 1804, and was assassinated there in 1806. Bhimsen quickly took control. He beheaded scores of noblemen, their sons and grandsons, daughters and daughters-in-law, in the palace garden and on the river bank, where their corpses were left to the jackals and vultures. The wives and daughters of others were given to the sweepers. Sixteen of Rana Bahadur's queens were forced to become suttees. The regency passed to the sole survivor, a junior queen (who may have been Bhimsen's relative) named Lalita Tripura Sundari. As Queen Regent she enabled Bhimsen's absolute rule. He made himself the darling of the army, pursuing fresh conquests in the west, disputing lands with the British to the south, and casting new cannon. Patrols were ordered to arrest anyone found on the streets at night. Bhimsen's Kathmandu was the seat of a military dictatorship. For a militarist regime it is useful to have antagonistic relations with one's neighbours, as a way of consolidating nationalist support, and it worked – up to a point – for Bhimsen Thapa.[5] The long imminent war broke out in 1814.

There were complex, overlapping land rights on the border, and attempts to reconcile them satisfied neither side. The British sent police to occupy disputed areas. The Nepalis sent soldiers to attack them, and the policemen they captured were cruelly killed. The Council of Bengal prepared a 'secret letter', with 84 attachments describing planning and intelligence, and sent it to the Company's Directors in London.

Intelligence indicated that Gorkhali troops were formidable. They slept without tents, ate rice in the morning and then marched all day without another meal. They were liable to attack at night. And they had brass cannon, cast at Lagan Tole in Kathmandu and bored by a water-driven machine, erected by a Frenchman. 'The Frenchman was murdered for endeavouring to escape out of the country.'[6] The Nepali capital was surrounded by a brick wall three feet thick.

The Nepalis believed that Europeans could not bear the fatigue of travelling in the mountains. The British ordered four thousand pairs of special shoes and hoped that 'British enterprise and skill' and a few days' rapid advance would dishearten the enemy.[7] They drafted in advance the punitive treaty they intended to impose, shrinking the Gorkhalis' territory, exacting repartitions, and reinstalling a permanent British resident at the court in Kathmandu.

After months of preparation the attack was launched at five points along the frontier and immediately ran into trouble. A British general was picked off in the first action of the war, attempting to storm the fort at Nalapani.[8] The attackers were repelled by matchlocks, muskets and a blizzard of stones, spears and arrows. A battering train was called in from Delhi, but even when the wall was smashed the British couldn't cross it; several officers and dozens of men died in the breach. When the remaining defenders fled, after three more days of heavy bombardment, the invaders found the ruins 'crowded with dead'. The dispatches praised the *Goorkas*' 'conspicuous bravery'.[9]

On another front the British general deserted. On a third the general was so cowed by an early setback that he spent the rest of the war marching up and down the frontier. The campaign dragged on for months. Only in the Gorkhalis' most recently conquered territories, in the far west, did the Company find a weakness. The invading general there was the Massachusetts-born David Ochterlony, British resident at the Mughal court in Delhi.

Ochterlony understood how to move his men and artillery through the hills, slowly dismantling the Gorkhalis' defensive network one outpost at a time. And he realized that high taxes had made the conquered people rebellious. He could read for himself how isolated the defenders had become after he discovered that the Gorkhalis were using messengers disguised as holy men, carrying letters inside their bamboo staffs. 'My authority in the country no longer exists. The call for funds is urgent ... The enemy are upon us ...' a commander wrote in one of the first intercepts. Another message revealed, 'The whole country have joined the enemy, and are prepared to destroy us.' The translator of a third rendered it partly in summary:

> the people have betrayed us ... send one thousand five hundred firelocks to this place, otherwise it is all over with us ... We are ready to lay down our lives but cannot war against the decrees of Providence ... Send men and magazines. Fail not! fail not! fail not! (repeated seven times). The rest of the letter states their personal wants, and recommends their families to the care and protection of the Minister and Commander-in-Chief.

Today Nepalis mostly remember the Anglo-Nepal War as a heroic defence of their independence, against overwhelming odds. The vain, bloody resistance at Nalapani, with which the war began, is a staple of school textbooks.[10] They also remember it for the loss of territory, and the imposition of enduring interference by the power to the south in their internal affairs.[11] If the British remember it at all it is in a peculiarly Victorian light, as a good fight in which they came to appreciate their worthy opponents; the plucky, loyal 'Gurkhas'.[12] In May 1815, with the rainy season approaching, Ochterlony accepted the Nepali surrender on the far western front. Fighting stopped. In June the Council in Calcutta wrote to the Directors in London, proclaiming their success and promising a speedy and beneficial resolution. In December the Directors wrote back welcoming the victory, complaining about the expense, recalling the time it had taken, and asking to receive the full accounts as expeditiously as possible. It was only the following year, in early 1816, after another brief British invasion, that the Gorkhalis finally ratified the peace. The Sugauli treaty remains a byword, in daily use in Nepali politics, for the country's compromised sovereignty.[13] Recriminations on the British side were less enduring: the war had been unnecessary; it was wastefully conducted; the treaty was too lenient; the revenues of the Company had been injured; because of the war it was forced to pay a higher rate of interest; its debts had increased.

The Gorkhali army had taken a heavy beating. They'd lost one third of their lands. From now on they must suffer the presence of a British resident in Kathmandu. The minister and commander in chief, Bhimsen Thapa, who had wanted this disastrous war, looked briefly vulnerable, but survived.

13

I woke at about ten to ten on a Tuesday morning, the first of February 2005, and found that the telephones and the internet weren't working. It was slightly unusual, but not very strange, for things like that not to work. I noticed the two armoured cars on the road to the bridge, and near Bhotahiti there was a group of soldiers buying a large number of plastic jerry cans, but during the war the army was often seen on the streets. It was only at the first place I stopped that I learned there'd been a coup.[1] It was a particularly auspicious day, astrologically speaking. Many weddings were disrupted.

It was later said that the king had rewritten the coup-makers' manual by cutting off the phones and the internet like that, and he certainly made it very hard to know what was going on. I spent most of the first day finding a way to file my stories. Then I drove all over town looking for my contacts at home or in their offices. Most of them were out.

Nokia, Ericsson, Motorola, Samsung...we pay 20 rupees per kilo.

The king said in his speech that he was saving democracy and the nation from corrupt, fractious politicians and communist rebels. 'Even when bloodshed, violence and devastation have pushed the country to the brink of destruction, those engaged in politics ... continue to shut their eyes to the people's welfare.' The Shah dynasty would not stand by while its people suffered. I saw a motorcycle rally of about fifty royalists, sounding their horns, but only a few people applauded them. So uniform was their appearance, and so quickly had they each found a flag to carry, that I wondered if they were soldiers in civil dress. A few candles appeared around the statue of Prithvi Narayan Shah, and the statue of the king's father in front of the palace.

While the king was on television the army signals corps visited the internet service providers. Other soldiers went to radio stations and television newsrooms. The prime minister was detained inside his official residence and dozens, or scores, or possibly hundreds of politicians and lawyers, academics and journalists were arrested. No one was sure how many, because no one was at home, and no one was on the phone, but there was talk of lists with hundreds of names on and prominent people were naturally afraid that their name might be among them. This was enough for my first story, which I read down the telephone from the reception of the British embassy. But Nepal was the top story in the world, and by the second day there was little to add to those bare facts. So I was grateful when a friend at the embassy briefed me off the record that Britain was suspending military aid to the regime, and that line led my day-two coup story for the *Telegraph*.[2]

On the second evening the landlines were briefly reconnected for local calls (perhaps the coup makers needed to talk to each other) and rumours were urgently exchanged. A helicopter had fired on protesting students in Pokhara. On the third day I filed on the helicopter to one of my strings, the *South China Morning Post*, glad to have something to meet their early deadline. Then I pulled it before it was published after discrepancies emerged. The helicopter story made international news elsewhere, but it turned out not to be true. By the end of the week we were still without phones, still getting a grip on what had happened days earlier. I was sitting in the National Human Rights Commission, telling a commissioner that the story he'd given me didn't check out. (There *had* been shooting, and it seemed there was a helicopter somewhere nearby, but ...) 'I don't even know where my younger brother is,' he shouted. 'Here I am, sitting in the National Human Rights Commission, and even I don't have any information.'

For a few days there was pressure to find new story lines, then I was surprised at how quickly interest moved on. It was a relief.

A week after the coup I went with a Dutch journalist to the king's ancestral home, a hundred miles away. The old Gorkha durbar stood on top of its hill with the old bazar below it, the modern concrete bazar below that and the road curling away through a broad valley to the highway. Maarten and I had been there together before. Now the student who had been our translator refused to work with us, claiming he'd be shot. We tried the British Gurkha Welfare Centre, where they paid pensions to old British soldiers, thinking that two foreigners wouldn't look out of place there, and that they might give us an assessment of the situation in town. They gave us a glass of whisky but they didn't want to talk.

Since the coup the army had been firing from their camp at night, what were interpreted as warning shots against the Maoists. It heightened people's anxiety. Local journalists and human rights activists had stopped working; local politicians and student leaders had 'gone underground'. A waiter at the hotel offered himself as our ally. In the evening he brought us a bag of grass to smoke, and Maarten and I settled down on the roof with it, to wait for the shooting to start.

The waiter was quickly back again. 'The army's here. They are going to ask you some questions.' We decided to represent ourselves as development workers, then we changed our minds. We sat on the roof trying to look relaxed while a soldier watched us, and the rest of them went through the rooms downstairs. They were keeping us dangling. We were nervous, paranoid. Then they left without asking us anything.

The next day a banner-bomb appeared, strung across the road to the highway. 'Preparation is on for strategic counter-attack,' it proclaimed. 'Let's celebrate the 9th anniversary of our great revolution.' Attached to the bottom of the red cloth was a package wrapped in black plastic, with wires protruding. Bus passengers stooped below it to board other vehicles waiting on the other side. The army, fearing an ambush, was nowhere around.

The waiter brought student activists and local politicians who had 'gone underground' to our room. The authorities had raided the university campus and seized the membership records of the student unions. The police had been calling at their homes while they slept elsewhere. Maarten and I discovered our story at the Gorkha durbar. 'Every time the king does something strange he comes here,' one of the fugitive politicians said. 'He just wanted the blessing of his god to make his plan a reality.'

Eleven Brahmins began making one and a quarter lakh of rotis a week before the coup, while eleven more prayed for the peace of Nepal and the prosperity of the monarchy. A goat was sacrificed every day. The durbar shrines were spattered with blood. The jogis were sitting about smoking chillums. Eleven of them had participated. As the rotis were cooked they had been distributed in the town, and some were taken by road to Kathmandu, but this unusual occurrence did not alert anyone to the coming event. The king attended the first day of the ritual and he came back with the queen at eleven o'clock on the eleventh day, four days after his coup, for the finale. The priest was satisfied. 'The king told us, "Don't worry, Nepal is going to be peaceful, I love all Nepali people",' he confirmed.

But obviously it made no sense any more. People need to think that a regime knows better than its own propaganda, that it takes seriously what's really going on, or repression won't work. It's the necessity of being a plausible authoritarian. The king seemed to believe in bonds of nature that tied the monarchy to the people as the actual basis of his government. ('He's like a deaf and blind elephant walking in the jungle,' is a typical assessment recorded in my notebook.) So it was obvious that he would fail, but it also seemed that he would cause a great deal of harm in the process.

I felt the period of his direct rule as a time of real alarm, that the country was being led into bloody oblivion.

It was well known that the army 'disappeared' people. That's what gave the palace press secretary's remarks their impact when he told unhappy newspaper editors in the week of the coup, 'The army is totally in charge. You'd better be careful. They might "disappear" you in a couple of hours.'[3] There were secret arrests at the brick factories in the east of the Valley, because the men and women who worked there came from the same poor villages that a Maoist might come from. God knows what happened to them.

The tyrant in Kathmandu in the early nineteenth century was Bhimsen Thapa. After the Anglo-Nepal War the British residency was re-established on the same inauspicious, spirit-riddled ground that it had briefly occupied in Buchanan's time. It was a huge site. After Indian independence in 1947 the British gave most of it to India for its embassy, but they retained enough for a spacious compound of their own, with a cul-de-sac of detached modern homes like an English suburb. There is still a British cemetery behind the embassy, tended by a Christian gardener, but the Gothic residency building shown in a drawing of 1835 is long gone. Bhimsen's lethal adversary lived there, a sickly Englishman named Brian Houghton Hodgson. They seem to have enjoyed each other's company, sometimes, as people engrossed in political conspiracies sometimes must. The complexity of Bhimsen's nature is suggested by Hodgson's shifting feelings towards him.

Hodgson studied under the economist Thomas Malthus at the East India Company's training college at Haileybury in Hertfordshire, and it was Malthus who gained the credit for having 'turned him from a young aristocrat in social feelings and sympathies' into 'an advanced liberal in politics'.[4] He passed out at the top of his year with prizes in Bengali, classics and economics and, in 1818, moved to Calcutta to continue his studies in Persian and Sanskrit. In Bengal a bout of fever nearly killed him, and meant that he must be posted to the hills if he would survive in India at all. So at the age of 19 Brian Hodgson received his first junior posting in Kathmandu, where he would eventually spend twenty-one years, living in the Gothic residency with his Nepali Muslim wife, Begum Meharunnisha, and their two children, Henry and Sarah.

At the residency Hodgson pursued pioneering studies. For his ethnological work he collected 'one hundred carefully verified skulls', and for his botanical, zoological and bibliographical research he kept a staff of illustrators and scribes, toiling at his own expense to draw or copy whatever he found that appealed to his vast interests. He discovered 39 new mammals and 150 bird species. He introduced the ancient literature of Mahayana Buddhism to Europe, where it inspired Richard Wagner's fantasies of the Orient.[5] And here I found a connection. Hodgson's Buddhist collaborator was a learned pandit named Amrit Ananda, who lived at Mahabuddha in Patan, on my old street. Hodgson must have gone there on his horse sometimes.

Hodgson was there about forty years before Wright followed him to the same house, to find his chronicle. Wright's collaborator, Gunananda, must have been Amrit Ananda's son. Or

grandson? The Wright chronicle ends with the rule of Bhimsen Thapa. It blends genuinely ancient material with ideas of more recent origin. It seemed possible, likely even, that it was compiled in Bhimsen's time. Hodgson would have asked his pandit friend about the history of Nepal. Could Amrit Ananda have written the ancient chronicle Wright discovered? Did Hodgson commission it? Or is the Wright chronicle, describing the ancient origins of everything, a Newar plea to the Gorkhalis, to respect the rights and customs of a conquered people? To Amrit Ananda, Patan under the rule of Bhimsen Thapa must have felt like a city under military occupation.[6]

The slender white tower Bhimsen built still dominates Kathmandu. It looks like a Muslim minaret, because it was inspired by the architecture of the Muslim court at Lucknow, in northern India, which was then the greatest native power in the region. To Bhimsen it would have stood for massive, modern prestige; many times higher than almost any other structure. Even now,

increasingly hemmed in by shopping malls, its stands clear of the other buildings when you look out across the rooftops from anywhere in the city. I paid my admission and walked in misery through the Gothic enclosure towards the foot of the stairs. *Did the scourge of the British copy the exotic feringhi style of Hodgson's residency, for the wall around his pseudo-Islamic monument to native independence?* I had wondered before whether the view from the top might reveal the ancient trade routes engraved in the street plan, in a way that I could photograph. The viewing platform swayed 50 metres above me, a narrow cage on iron brackets, running around the outside of the dead minister's monstrous penis extension.

The other people climbing the tower were a mixture of young types in T-shirts and tourists from the countryside; the men in white cotton pyjamas, the women with gold rings around the edges of their ears. The portholes in the wall soon showed that we were above most of the other buildings. I attended to the dials on my camera, making sure they were where I would need them. Then I reached the light coming through the door. People were standing around casually, draping themselves against the cage and linking their fingers through it. I could see the open ground of Tundikhel below me, which was used to parade the army long before it became Bhimsen's showpiece. Its worn patches were resolved from this altitude into a pattern of use. I edged away from the door to look north, where the old trade routes ran, but all I could see was the irregular jagged effect of the concrete houses, stretching without interruption to the hills. Without pitched, tiled roofs it was impossible to understand their arrangement. The streets and chowks were invisible. I turned to face the smooth white wall. Embracing it humiliatingly, I edged back around until my fingers found the edge of the doorway. I stepped back onto the stairs.

I started down, but now I could hear people saying that there was a temple at the top. I wouldn't be coming back again so I turned and went one more flight up. There was a small stone lingam there, covered with vermilion powder, and a small group of women (a crowd in that small space) were offering money to it. Above us, where the space ran out, there was a star of iron-work which kept the top of the tower in shape, and here at least, where there was no horrible emptiness to look out through, even though we were enclosed, people seemed to feel our position above the city was exposed, and they moved around each other gingerly, as if there was a danger of knocking someone off.

I climbed down and started walking to the place where I thought Bhimsen used to live. On my side of the road there were kiosks selling long-distance bus tickets, Chinese watches (displayed in a basin of water to show they were waterproof), and slices of cucumber. The traffic fumes were filthy. On the other side was the army headquarters, surrounded by coils of razor wire. I sometimes met the colonel from the Directorate of Public Relations on the sofas in the weird lobby of the officers' club, surrounded by antique weapons and new murals of old wars. Today soldiers were hunched at intervals on the grass outside, sitting an exam. Opposite the army's gate was the alley that led to Club Babylon. Two concrete sphinxes painted black and gold guarded the entrance to the hall, where drunk officers watched girls dance under a shower. I walked through alleys of anonymous concrete hotels, frequented by Nepali and Indian commercial travellers, suitable for sex, criminality and revolutionary intrigue. After the hotels there were more interesting alleys of mixed Newar-style, Shah period and new buildings, crumbling, butchered and unsuitably built, with new stuff going up all the time. There were small printing presses and motorcycle workshops. Deliveries were being made. Text was everywhere, on signs and posters and graffiti and banners. After ten or fifteen minutes I reached Lagan Tole.

The neighbourhood centred on a large square, occupied by women selling vegetables. There was a file of stationary traffic around one side, waiting to leave through the alley I had entered by, where a huge white SUV painted with the blue letters UN had blocked the road. In that corner, where the traffic was pressing to leave, there was a high wall topped with barbed wire, surrounding a dilapidated mansion. This, I thought, but was not sure, had been Bhimsen Thapa's house.[7]

There are many European-style palaces in Kathmandu and by its glass windows and white stucco façade this looked similar to those. But it was cruder in execution, and the niches in the walls, with cusped and pointed arches, were in the north Indian Muslim style of Lucknow. Most of the rooms seemed unoccupied. The windows were hanging open; the small glass panes were missing or opaque with dust. The gate was painted green and closed. Above the wall beside it, standing on a platform inside, there was an armed soldier in battle dress. He watched me as I waited and I ignored him, slowly reading the notices posted there. The gate opened to give a glimpse of green army laundry on the line. A man stepped out.

'Whose house was this?'

He looked at me, a foreigner holding a camera. 'Bhimsen Thapa's,' he said, and walked away.

I knew that getting inside would be difficult. When I asked the Directorate of Public Relations for permission they denied it had been Bhimsen's house at all. I visited a young officer I knew, who I knew was also interested in history, to ask his advice. I told him I thought I'd found Bhimsen's house, described the location, and explained that it was full of soldiers.

'*Still?*' he said, as if they'd somehow been forgotten there for two hundred years.[8]

To secure his place after the disaster of the Anglo-Nepal war, Bhimsen 'played both ends against the middle',[9] presenting himself in Nepal as the enemy of the British, and to the British as their only check against unrestrained Gorkhali militarism. For Brian Hodgson in the residency this situation could be uncomfortable, being forced to witness and hear the constant drilling and parades, the threats, and to suffer the limitations and affronts that 'the Minister' concocted for him. These were partly mind games. When Bhimsen incited the peasantry to disrupt Hodgson's shooting trips Hodgson gave his gun dogs to the Minister's son. But as the Minister's enemies became stronger during the 1830s Hodgson began to worry. What if the army had its grip on Bhimsen, not the other way round? In a jumpy letter of 1837, personally handwritten in case there were spies in the residency, he warned:

> ... in the 20 years that we have been here since the war, we have seen nothing but drills and parades, heard nothing but the clink of the hammer in the arsenal and magazine ... They have neither arts nor literature, nor commerce, nor a rich soil to draw off their attention from arms; and they have that lusty hardihood of character and contempt of drudgery which make war especially congenial. [10]

Nepal covered the Company's soft northern flank. Maybe Bhimsen's enemies would make better neighbours?

For years Hodgson had advocated two strategies to deflect Gorkhali aggression and avoid another war. Nepal's surplus military manpower should be recruited on a large scale into the British Indian army. In a typical report of 1832 he lauded Nepali troops as biddable and gallant. Secondly, he was an ardent champion of that earlier British goal, the increase of Himalayan trade. Commerce, he hoped, would bind the warlike highlanders to peaceful coexistence, but his goal was hampered by cases in the Kathmandu courts, which Indian merchants always lost.

Hodgson's description of a trial by water to settle a civil dispute suggests something of the spirit of the city. 'The names of the respective parties are inscribed on two pieces of paper, which are rolled up into balls, and then have puja done to them.'[11] The papers were attached to reeds and two sergeants from the palace carried them, in the company of various other officials, to the water tank called Rani Pokhari. The sergeants set the reeds in the water, two members of the leather-working caste waded in, stood beside them, and at a signal submerged themselves. Whichever surfaced first, the reed next to him was destroyed, the other paper was opened and the man named on it declared the winner. 'Several public and private taxes are then paid and the Court registers the decision.' A later imperial writer believed that 'the obvious even chances of a rightful verdict appeal perhaps more to those accustomed to Oriental justice than to ourselves', but he seems to have ignored the obvious scope for cheating.[12]

The crumpled pieces of paper that Hodgson carried to the execution grounds beyond the city, where the sweepers mutilated offenders, contain a trace of the sex life of the early nineteenth century.

> JAIL DELIVERY OF DASAHARA [Dasain festival]. 5TH SEPT, [1826]. TOTAL 27 SOULS.
> *4 capitally punished* 4 executed by decapitation and hanging – males as follows:
> 1st, a soldier for sexual commerce with a Chamarni [female sweeper] knowing her to be such and against her advice. (In cases where such unlawful commerce with outcaste females results from fraudulent concealment of female her nose cut off and turned out of country – and man scot free.)
> 2nd, a hill-man for killing a cow by a violent blow.
> 3rd, a Magar – for sexual commerce with niece.
> 4th (was hanged) for incest with mother-in-law – a young wife

> of dead father. Woman unharmed because she long resisted the seduction – the man a Parbattiah
> *6 maimed* Six mutilated as follows
> 1st, a Keta [slave boy] – nose cut off for seducing a Keti (female slave) from his master's house and running away with her.
> 2nd, Both hands cut off for stealing from a Brahman – was his servant and stole jewels etc. Ordered for execution but reprieved on disclosing where property might be found.
> ....
> *3 banished* Three expelled the country with every circumstance of ignominy – being Religionists and incapable of being put to death – as follows:
> 1st, a Brahman for seducing another Brahman's wife – woman degraded from caste.
> 2nd dto. for theft.
> 3rd, a Sunyasi [religious mendicant]: for sexual commerce with a Chamarni.[13]

And so on. The jail delivery of Dasahara 1829 included seven decapitated: one for killing a cow, one for killing a man, one for having sex with a Brahmin woman, two for having sex with their mothers-in-law and two for crimes unknown. Two people lost a hand each and one lost an ear for theft, two women had their noses cut off for adultery and two men had their penises removed for sex with outcastes.

Neither of Hodgson's projects bore fruit. His recommendation of large-scale British recruitment of Gorkhali soldiers was not taken up during his career, and trade remained embroiled in legal disputes involving Indian merchants. Attempts to agree to a common code for settling complaints failed over the insistence that a Nepali man had the right to behead any British subject caught in adultery with his wife. 'The incompatibility of this clause with our ideas of retributive justice suspended for a time the negotiation,' a residency memo stated.[14]

Bhimsen was fortunate as minister in that he presided over the regencies of two child kings. Girvan Yuddha Shah (the son of Rana Bahadur Shah and his Brahmin queen) conveniently died in 1816, when Bhimsen was briefly vulnerable after the war. His teenage wife expired one month later. Their son, the new King Rajendra, was only three years old, allowing Bhimsen to enjoy another royal generation of unchallenged ministerial authority. During their long minorities, he deliberately raised his kings to be unfit to rule, debauched and half mad with premature vices. For twenty-six years he presided over the emasculated court with scarcely a hitch, his position assured by the support of the Queen Regent Lalita Sundhari. But in 1832 the Queen Regent died and Bhimsen's system was shaken.

King Rajendra turned 18 the same year. Hodgson described the dangerous new equation in a secret letter, which he wrote out himself, 'for obvious reasons', and asked that it not be handled in Calcutta by 'clerks and office people':[15]

> The Raja [King Rajendra] is hemmed into his palace, beyond which he cannot stir unaccompanied by the Minister, and then only to the extent of a short ride or drive ... The Raja has been purposely so trained so as to possess little energy of body or mind ... and rendered a mere idol for occasional exposure to the worship of the multitude.

What is more, Hodgson reckoned, this weak and decrepit youth would probably have been 'spirited into his grave as soon as he begot a successor', had it not been for the fact that his senior queen was 'spirited and clever', and (as the mother of the next in line) would be a nuisance as queen regent. As it was, the senior queen was working hard to make Rajendra feel 'indignant' that he was a 'political nonentity'. To his wife's disgust the king was moving slowly to assert himself, so slowly that she threatened to take over the kingdom herself, but whether it was caution or 'habitual dependence' holding Rajendra back, Hodgson couldn't be sure. Habitual dependence seemed more likely, but if it was caution then that would be wise.

SHAH DYNASTY

First six kings

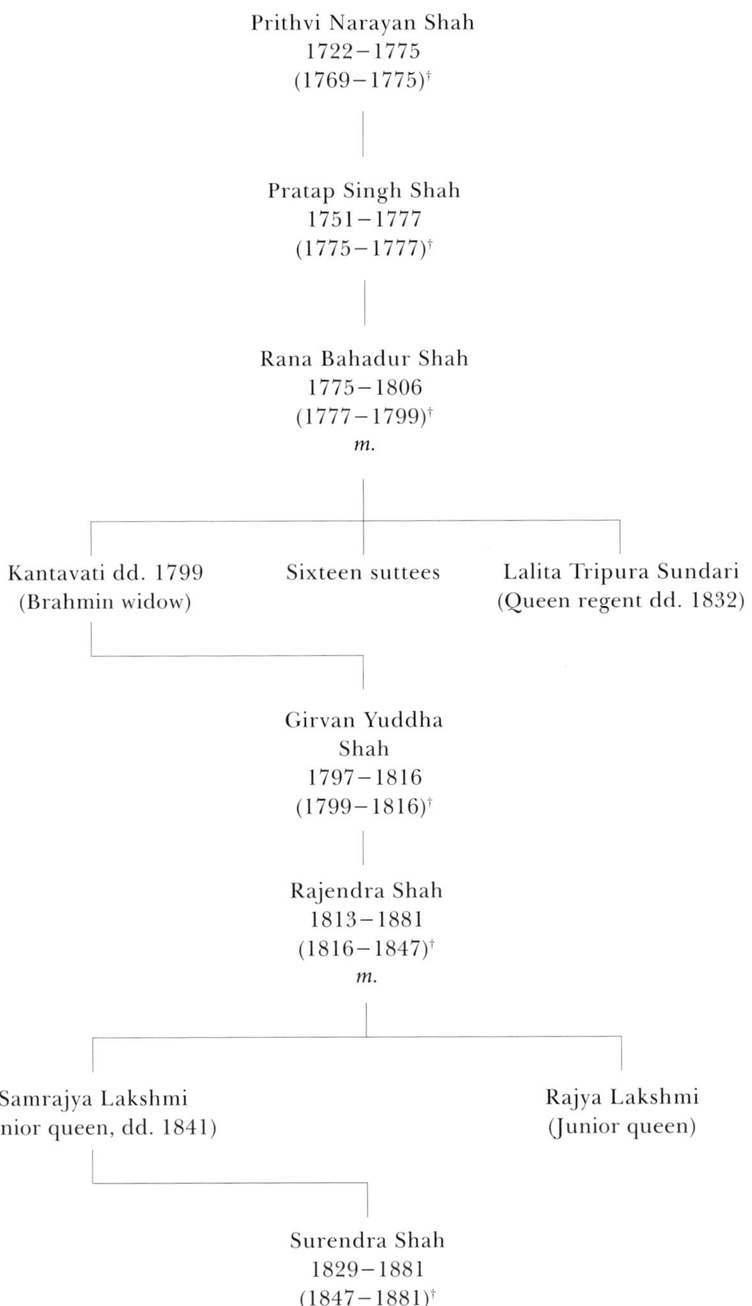

†Regnal years

> The spirit of the Royal and Ministerial parties may be conceived from the fact that the Raja, having fallen ill last rains, resolutely and against all possible exertions of influence refused to employ the Court physician, from an avowed fear of being poisoned or otherwise made away with, as he said his father and grandfather had been, by Bhim Sen's procurement ... I am sorry to say the general opinion was that the Raja's allegation was true in all its parts both as respected himself and his father. The physician is a creature of the Minister's and has now held the position of Raj Vaidya [royal doctor] for thirty years.

Hodgson seemed to believe the rumours himself, at least sometimes. Why not? 'The vegetable poisons of Nepaul are quick and deadly and to this day no antidote has been found for them,' wrote Captain Thomas Smith, who was his assistant in the 1840s.[16]

In case Bhimsen's spies were intercepting his communications, Hodgson gave the principals code names. King Rajendra was 'Willow', perhaps because he blew with the wind. The senior queen was 'Termagant', because she was overbearing and turbulent. There was also a junior queen, and Hodgson called her 'Bella' because she was beautiful. It was natural that he should worry his letters were being opened. He had his own spies in the palace's office for confidential correspondence. By the end of 1833 he knew that the Nepalis had opened channels to Britain's enemies in Tehran and Lahore, emboldened by rumours that Russia was preparing to invade India. His ability to neutralize Gorkhali agression was critical to the Company's security. At the height of the tensions, the city was a pressure cooker and the fate of northern India seemed to hang by a slender thread of intrigue.

Bhimsen's enemies aligned themselves with the senior queen, so 'Bella' became Bhimsen's ally and the hatred between the two women partly shaped politics for a decade to come. Courtiers switched sides all the time, as the balance of power shifted or as their enemies, friends and relatives realigned themselves. The factions put placards around town denouncing their rivals. In one telling I counted seven factions, in another there were basically just two; pro-Bhimsen and anti- (but with complicated sub-factions within them). The parallels to contemporary statecraft were inescapable; in the number of players, the scope of the game, the style of play. Then, as now, the practice of politics was short-term cunning. Governance was only about distributing state appointments and the resources they controlled.

To gain British support both factions were whispering in Hodgson's ear, while publicly denouncing the other for selling the kingdom out to the feringhis. Faced with the riddle of whether Bhimsen was the problem or the solution, Hodgson vacillated. In the first faction-riven summer of 1833 he wrote to the Governor General in Calcutta that 'at the bottom of Bhimsen's profound character I have at last discerned as I conceive, an intense hatred of us'. Two months later he reported that all would stay well as long as Bhimsen remained in charge, and praised his vigorous, just and pacific administration. By the autumn Bhimsen was the villain again.

On 24 July 1837 the senior queen's youngest child was unwell. The royal doctor prescribed a remedy that the queen should drink, to be passed to the patient through her milk. (It was a well-known preparation including a small amount of marijuana, commonly given as a digestive or to help children sleep.) Fearing poison, the queen refused to drink it, but she did give it to her baby. Some people later said that the potion seemed a strange colour. Anyway, the death of the child was evidence enough and Bhimsen was arrested. When the king asked Hodgson whether he should release the fallen minister Hodgson advised him not to, and even hinted that the British had foiled a Thapa plot to depose him. Bhimsen was released, but his enemies controlled the government. Two years later in 1839 Bhimsen was arrested again for the baby's murder, and the extra charges of poisoning the previous king and queen, back in 1816, were also added. Some of the royal doctors killed themselves to avoid interrogation and they were wise to do so.

> The Court physician, who attended the child (a Brahmin, and whose life was therefore sacred), was burnt on the forehead and cheeks till his brain and jaws were exposed. The under-physician, a Niwar, was impaled alive and had his heart extracted while he was yet living.[17]

From the place where he was held Bhimsen appealed for Hodgson's help, but the resident claimed he was powerless to intervene. He did write to Calcutta, asking permission to mediate on behalf of his 'old personal friend', but nothing came of it.[18] Bhimsen's cell was described as a filthy drain, but his jailers allowed him to keep his khukuri. When they told him that his wife had been paraded naked through the city he used it to cut his own throat. His living body was dumped on the river bank, where he'd dumped his victims thirty years earlier. The wound killed him nine days later.

The messengers who brought the news of Bhimsen's death to Hodgson said that he wept on hearing it. Now he wrote to Calcutta in his best style: 'Thus has perished the great and able statesman who … ruled this kingdom with more than regal sway'.[19] They had known each other for twenty years. 'He was a man born to exercise dominion over his fellows, alike by means of command and persuasion.' He may never have poisoned anyone. The residency's own best information was that Rajendra's father, King Girvan Yuddha, had died of smallpox, and his wife of a miscarriage one month later.

Hodgson had another reason to mourn his old adversary, because it turned out that Bhimsen had been a moderating influence after all. The senior queen's faction which now rose in his place, was much worse, and Hodgson faced his great emergency.

In the last year of his life Bhimsen had revealed to Hodgson that the senior queen's faction was involved in secret exchanges to form an anti-British alliance, with the Burmese court at Ava, with the Indian states of Udaipur, Jodhpur, Scindia, Hyderabad and the Marathas, as well as with China and Afghanistan. In 1839 the British invaded Afghanistan and the Nepalis knew that they were overstretched. In Kathmandu they started casting more cannon. Someone at the court was spreading Brahminical prophecies, foretelling the end of British power. 'A rash and violent woman governs the Durbar,' Hodgson warned, 'and all men of experience anticipate the worst that can happen unless renewed dread of the Company should speedily recall the Raja to safer counsels.'[20]

The Company wasn't in a position to strike dread into anyone. The war in Afghanistan meant the Governor General couldn't deploy substantial forces on the Nepali frontier, where the Gorkhalis seized two hundred square miles of British territory in 1840. Kathmandu was one of the most sensitive diplomatic posts in Asia, and the senior queen was plotting to destroy the resident.

On 20 June 1840 Hodgson was called to the palace and detained the whole night in a tedious audience. As he was making his way home at dawn disturbances were already breaking out in the Kathmandu garrison. Later he learned the senior queen had lied to the army, claiming he'd spent all night at the palace persuading the king to cut their pay. The two hundred Indian sepoys of his guard were posted on the roof of the residency, but they were hopelessly outnumbered as the mutineers advanced. Quick-thinking, Hodgson stopped his men from firing. They couldn't have held out for long. And the mutineers hesitated. They decided they needed written orders from the palace. Thank God Hodgson was at the top of his game. He told the king that he had already sent two messengers (by different routes) to India, with the news that if anything happened to him the palace was to blame. Both messengers, he said, had already got clear. The mutineers attacked the houses of five prominent noblemen instead.

Anyway, that was the account he recorded in his old age, which appeared in his Victorian biography and in many other tellings that are based on it, of the Kathmandu mutiny of 1840.[21] But modern historians have shown it can't be right.[22] Certainly, there was an anti-British element to the events. In the months after the scare Hodgson's spies obtained copies of messages sent between the palace and the mutineers, discussing their pay and grievances.

> I have arms and ammunition in plenty, but no money, and just now the marriages of my sons are costing me more than I know where to get. This is the reason I have reduced your pay. I want treasure to fight the English … when I have completed the marriages and got money in hand, I will throw off the mask and indulge you with a war.

So the king wrote to the mutineers, two days after the trouble at the residency. They wrote back:

> True, the English Government is great; but what care the wild dogs how large is the herd? They attack! They are sure to fill their bellies. You want no money for making war … We will plunder Lucknow or Patna; but first we must be rid of the Resident.[23]

These letters don't disprove Hodgson's recollection, but they are not consistent with it either. And in his report to Calcutta, written just days after the mutiny, he gave another version. He said that the trouble broke out in the afternoon of the 21st, not at dawn. There were groups of disorderly soldiers at the Tundikhel parade ground, and there were reports of threatening language directed towards the residency. The day developed into a rainy evening. Until almost midnight Hodgson was sending scouts in disguise towards the city, where they saw the mutineers attack five noblemen's houses, shouting slogans:

'Woe to those who live in luxury themselves while they advise the starving of the poor soldiers'

'Down with the feringhis'

'We will be chiefs ourselves.'[24]

When he wrote this report Hodgson thought that only a small group of mutineers had threatened the residency, according to their 'natural prejudices' rather than as part of any plan. Days later, still 'the City was resounding with coarse and ominous threats', but, he wrote, 'after comparing and tracing back numberless rumours ... I acquit the Durbar of any direct knowledge or instigation.'[25] He didn't even mention spending the night at the palace.

Did an old man's memory conflate the day of the mutiny with an all-night audience at the palace, which the records show did take place a month earlier? Did later information cause him to re-evaluate the mutiny? Did the need to vindicate his record come into it? I knew the traditional account before I read the revised version. It reminded me of the anti-Muslim riots I saw, when the manpower agencies were ransacked and the Kashmiri mosque was attacked. What had happened? Who did it? The people who were pulling the strings that day didn't leave any tangible trace. The more complicated you recognize the scene to be, the more numerous and devious the conspiracies become. Those noblemen whose houses were attacked – which factions did they belong to? Why was nothing stolen from their ransacked homes, nor their women molested? If you don't know who has done what to whom it's as if nothing really happened at all.

In the midst of these scares, Hodgson turned towards a policy of direct interference in Nepali politics. In a bluff of military strength he persuaded the authorities in Calcutta to bring whatever troops they could spare towards the frontier. Then he was able to form a pro-British faction in the palace and engineer an administration known as 'the British Ministry'. For the two years that it lasted the British resident was closely involved in the Nepali government. (The Indian embassy, operating from the same ground, would attempt something similar 160 years later, with similar results.)

During the British ministry the senior queen died. 'That remarkable woman,' Hodgson called her in tribute, 'imperious queen'.[26]

Before her death she seems to have been living at the edge of reason. She feared her surviving children would be murdered, and the junior queen's children installed in their place. Agonizingly, the poison that she believed had killed her baby had been given by her own hand! She demanded to travel to Benares in India to do rites for its soul, but Hodgson refused to give her a visa. Without one she set off anyway, and in the southern jungles she caught the fever that weakened her. A final, blazing row with the king finished her off. Rumours appeared in the Calcutta press that she'd been poisoned too.

When the king heard of the stories in the newspapers he went to the residency with the young crown prince, demanding condign punishment of whomsoever had spread the slander. 'Tell the Governor General,' the Maharaja raged, 'that he must and shall give him up! I will have him and flay him alive and rub him with salt and lemon until he die. Further, tell the Governor General that if this infamous culminator is not delivered up, there shall be war between us!' The residency's record of the encounter continues: 'Upon this the heir-apparent stopped his father with insulting epithets and blows, striking him again and again ... [soon] the hot fit passed off and the Raja made a humble apology to the British Resident.'[27] The royal pair climbed back onto the backs of the noblemen who had carried them there, and trotted away.

With Kathmandu's kind of leaders in charge, there was a case against getting too closely involved. In 1842 a new Governor General, Lord Ellenborough, reverted to a policy of neutrality in Nepali politics and ordered Hodgson to disengage. The disaster in Afghanistan was complete, so the British could again rely on simple military deterrence to contain the Gorkhalis. The British suffered no setback when their puppet government fell and Hodgson's successor, Sir Henry Lawrence, resumed the old policy of non-engagement. Lawrence even shut down Hodgson's spy networks. He thought they gave away more about the workings of the residency than they discovered.

The Nepalis organized an extravagant farewell for Hodgson, paid him lavish compliments in open court and escorted him in pomp to the edge of the Valley. They thought he'd preserved their independence by averting a second war. He wrote emotionally to Lord Ellenborough, paying tribute to 'my kind and honest-hearted mountaineers – for such they are, apart from their detestable politics'. He never returned to Kathmandu. The authorities in Calcutta forbade him from living there in a private capacity. Within a decade of his departure his wife the Begum Meharunnisha died there without him. His children left the city, but they died too. Perhaps his greatest legacy to Kathmandu was that, after he left, the political factions remained obsessed with whom the British were backing, even when they backed no one. The obsession runs strong today, when independent India has inherited the Company's role in guiding the fruitless struggles.

14

> The country is small and poor, and there are many and hungry chiefs, squabbling for power and pelf, it is therefore their destiny to quarrel.
>
> – Henry Lawrence, British resident, 1844

Each of the prime ministers who followed Bhimsen Thapa was murdered sooner or later, either in office or after leaving it, shot down in public or mysteriously picked off through his window while he was at his prayers.[1] The defeat of a court faction meant death to its leaders. Condemned politicians went to their end bringing the khukuri that would kill them, to be sure that it was sharp enough. The families that lost worst were obliterated, so their descendants are missing from the modern wedding circuit. Only the lineages of the victors may swill whisky and chatter, and eat buffets, in a whirl of sequined saris and jewels, in the ballrooms of five-star hotels.

'Why don't you speak to the Jang family?' Suman the cop suggested. 'And you know Sanjiv is descended from Vijay Raj Pandey?'

The ruling class were still living this history. The families that survived preserve gossip of the old conspiracies, which may not be recorded elsewhere; or else may be written into books as the authentic record, whether it's true or not. Intriguing scraps can be placed alongside the other sources. 'In the light of family legends,' the learned analysis might run, 'it must have been so-and-so's ancestor who told such-and-such this lie, which is how it ended up in one of Hodgson's letters.'

In recent times powerful men have realized that it is unnecessarily risky and destructive for them to seriously go after one another, so they duke it out with the poor as proxies and the top people always give each other another chance. In the past the lives of the rulers were dangerously unpredictable, and nerves must have been especially strained by 1846. Court politics had been a bloodbath since Bhimsen's suicide seven years earlier. At around 10 p.m. on 14 September that year, the latest prime minister was praying inside his house when someone shot him through the window. The surviving queen, 'Bella', was the dead man's lover.

As soon as she heard of his murder she went to him with Ganga water, gold and sacred basil leaves and placed them in his mouth. Then, with dishevelled hair and weeping aloud, she took a drawn sword from her attendant. She raged. The entire court must be assembled in the palace building called the Kot. She swore that until the inquest was held and the killer put to death she would neither eat nor drink a thing.

The lords began to gather and a few brought their soldiers with them. An elderly noble was already in chains before the growing assembly, with the queen shrieking for his blood, when the king left, apparently looking for someone who hadn't yet arrived.

Poor, weak Rajendra went to the British residency, where a young captain named George Ottley had been left in charge as acting resident. It was two in the morning and either Ottley was drunk or he was wary, because he sent a servant out with the message that he was having a 'rheumatic attack' and couldn't come downstairs. The king returned to the Kot. When he reached there he saw blood running in the gutter of the street outside. At seven in the morning Ottley received 'the following astounding intelligence': twenty or thirty of the leading nobles had been killed. Scores of others were being rounded up and sent into exile. Guns had been placed at the city gates. The streets were filled with troops. 'Rumours of every kind are rife, and the tales of bloodshed like water are fearful ...'[2] Ottley fired off three hasty letters to Calcutta that day, describing the conflicting rumours. In his excitement he forgot to enclose an attachment he referred to, listing the dead.

It took him about two days to recover his cool. Then he began to provide measured reports of the rumours that were being sown in the city. So many lies and interested accounts were recorded at the time that it's not possible now to reconstruct with certainty how the massacre began. Everyone there was armed. All of them would have feared all the others. Clearly someone was going to have to die that night. It was already getting very late.

Most of the killing was done by soldiers loyal to a promising young general called Jang Bahadur Kunwar. He was well known for feats of courage involving wild elephants, and for leaping from great heights, and he had already shown himself willing to murder his elders when the situation required. Now, while Jang Bahadur's soldiers poured fire into the courtyard from their double-barrelled guns, and his six brothers swung their swords, Jang Bahadur was upstairs with the queen, who was still crying for vengeance while she signed the papers to make him the next prime minister.

Two days after the massacre Jang Bahadur and his brothers, with a large, well-armed escort, visited the British residency in an 'English carriage'. Jang announced to Ottley his own appointment as commander-in-chief and 'sole minister'. Ottley offered his congratulations and regrets at the bloodshed. Jang cut him short (he'd come to address the Governor General). On the night of the massacre, Jang explained, there had been mutual recrimination and uproar. In the confusion, the killing somehow started.

Over the coming months Jang made his rule secure. One more massacre was necessary. Thousands of the relatives of the victims were exiled to India. The king and queen, Rajendra and 'Bella', soon followed them there. The child crown prince was under Jang's control and Jang made him king in his father's place. He changed his own last name to Rana, which had a royal ring to it. The Rana family held the Shah kings prisoner (much like Bhimsen had), made themselves hereditary prime ministers, and ruled for a hundred years.

☀

Jang Bahadur Rana was charismatic, ruthless and physically brave. He continued Bhimsen's practice of building in the north Indian Lucknavi style, with cusped and pointed arches, fluted pilasters and refined, Islamic, acanthus capitals. He was intellectually sophisticated for a man who was barely literate but, unlike the well lettered, he was attractively undeceived by his own bullshit. Jang Bahadur was a serious piece of work. To a personality like his, Kathmandu – once he had it – must have seemed small and easy.

Three years after his coup Jang became the first Hindu prince to visit Britain, where he went to the opera, watched the Epsom Derby, and attended parties hosted by the queen and members of the aristocracy. He captivated society, the women in particular, with his exotic looks and costumes. His English conversational skills, described at the time, were exciting. 'How do you do?' – 'Very well, thank you.' – 'Will you sit down?' – 'You are very pretty.'[3] A portrait of the handsome Gorkhali prince hung in the British foreign secretary's office until 2000, when the foreign secretary decided it was time to move on.[4]

At home, Jang Bahadur's British journey provoked complaints: that he had lost caste by crossing the Black Water, even (though he denied it) that he had lost caste by dining with foreigners. He was obliged to put down a coup attempt as soon as he got home, and the British admired the moderation of his response. Despite calls for their death, or blinding, the conspirators were merely jailed, besides one, who was subjected to the 'disgusting ceremony' of caste degradation. Before an audience, two drum-makers pissed in his mouth.[5]

Nepal's ruler seemed to be a pragmatic and open-minded liberal. He reduced the use of mutilation as a punishment. To the dissatisfaction of the Brahmins he also restricted the practice of widow burning, and he mocked the law against inter-caste sex by appearing in public with a Muslim dancing girl. The Governor General worried that 'the chief practical result of [Jang's] civilization will be that he will get his throat cut some time before that event would otherwise have occurred in the common course of nature in Nepal.'[6]

Jang further endeared himself to the British by coming to their rescue when Indian sepoys mutinied in 1857, and much of northern India rose up to drive the feringhis into the sea. Indian men turned on their British officers, white women and babies suffered enormities at black hands. The native rulers of the plains saw an opportunity to save their kingdoms, and their world, from the Company's remorseless expansion and they joined the rebellion. But Jang had seen Britain, and he thought the British would win. He defied the sympathies of his court and sided with the Company. He sent three Gorkhali detachments to help suppress the uprising. Then he rode from the hills in person at the head of an army of eight thousand to join the British siege of Lucknow, where the rebels had made their stand.

Lucknow was a great city. Its architecture, and its independence from the British, had inspired the architecture of Kathmandu for decades. When it fell, after the *Goorkhas* had over-indulged themselves on its people, wine and treasure, Jang Bahadur cited the hardships of the hot weather and took his army home. The loot they brought with them filled 4,300 carts in a baggage train 16 miles long, escorted to the border by British cavalry. While the British unleashed pitiless retribution on the plains, Jang became a Knight Grand Cross of the Order of the Bath. He was rewarded again with a portion of the land on the south-western border that had been forfeited after the Anglo-Nepal war, thirty years earlier. Those lands, in the area around Bardiya, became the private, tax-free property of the Rana family. Over generations, land was distributed to allied families. During the Maoist insurgency, the army collected the harvest from the peasantry on behalf of absentee landlords.[7]

Perhaps out of pride, or sympathy for the other side, or exuberance and an excess of talent, Jang Bahadur didn't give the British everything they wanted; but by saying one thing and doing another, by showing them letters that pleased them, but which he never sent, he did manage to keep them happy. Lucknow's rebel queen, the Begum Hazrat Mahal, whose lovely city he'd helped despoil, fled India and found asylum in Kathmandu, where he gave her a big house to live in, and where she was later buried in the Kashmiri mosque.[8]

☀

Jang Bahadur's pseudo-Lucknavi palace at Thapathali had long since given way to the suburb where I lived. When I finally met the important old man over the road, whose guests blocked the street with their limousines, it was to ask him about the Thapathali durbar. Himalaya Shamsher Jang Bahadur Rana (his full name) suggested that we meet at a French restaurant. As he remembered the palace, over coffee and a crème brûlée, he seemed to make a strong effort to visualize the current ruins as they'd once been, narrowing his eyes and sometimes lowering his head, putting his fingertips to his temples.

'In my childhood there was a connecting network of balconies and you could walk all the way from Lower Thapathali to Upper Thapathali,' he said – a distance of several hundred yards. The different parts of the palace were occupied by different branches of the Rana family, but even then the place was in decline.

'There was a very large drawing room. There is an account by Sylvain Lévi, and Lévi said it was very well furnished ...' Lévi visited in 1898 and found the audience chamber 'forty or fifty metres long ... filled with the necessary bric-a-brac of sofas, chairs, armchairs, chandeliers, gilded mirrors on the walls, portraits painted by English artists ...'[9] By the time Himalaya Shamsher was born, in the mid-1920s, his branch of the family had suffered a setback and other Ranas had stripped the great hall bare. 'It was the custom to loot everything,' he explained, 'so in our time it was a hall and there was a screen, where ladies would watch when there was some entertainment. I was born in the room next to that hall.'

The walls were two feet thick, so Himalaya Shamsher's family didn't need the woollen winter coats that other people wore, despite the fact that Kathmandu was much colder in those days. Nor did they feel the summer heat so much (which was, besides, milder than it is now). And there were servants who carried his elderly relatives on their backs to the kitchen, where meals were eaten sitting on the floor. There were no toilets as such, but a room with brass pans that were carried away by the cleaning people. Somewhere in the palace there were still fragments of the library of Himalaya's great grandfather, a maharaja who ruled Nepal briefly before he was born, and those books proved that he had been an educated man.

I asked what had happened to the books. Himalaya Shamsher screwed up his face and pointed upwards with a twist of both hands. 'Gone, gone. But I remember Hans Andersen's book. I was fascinated by it.'

A few days after that meeting Himalaya Shamsher passed me a message, that he wanted to show me where the palace had stood. We sat together in the back of his enormous car. I ventured to mention the enormous cars that jammed the street whenever the newspapers filled with speculation about the government. He ignored that. Then we drove out onto the main road beside our little colony and turned in again on the street that now led to the maternity hospital. 'There used to be a big gate here,' he said as we made the turn, 'but it was gone before my time. And there was a guardhouse, which was sold to some sweet makers.' The famous Ram Bhandar sweet shop was still there, now split into two rival factions (the Unified Ram Bhandar Party – Revolutionary and Ram Bhandar Party – Democratic, as it were), both offering the same thing.

As we drove around the area between where we lived and the maternity hospital, Himalaya Shamsher pointed out where the old boundaries lay. A few fragments of palace remained, glimpsed through the gates of modern compounds. By the white-washed temple of Ram, which had been a storey higher when it was part of the palace, he said, 'Here the soldiers used to parade and people used to park their horses when they came to see Jang Bahadur.' Soldiers still drilled, and horses were still tied there, in Himalaya Shamsher's young days.[10]

The driver took the huge car up narrow and crooked tracks, so that the position of some former wall could be pointed out, then ground out a difficult manoeuvre to take us out again. This area had been atrociously planned, or rather it hadn't been planned at all. The land was divided between brothers and cousins then sold off by them. The new owners arranged the access to their property as best they could. To get from the old Lower- to Upper-Thapathali we had to make a wide circuit.

There was a larger fragment of palace up there, with Lucknow-style cusps in the stucco above the windows, in disrepair but still occupied by distant relatives. I noticed the brick-made base of a European classical column beneath a bush. We got out of the car and climbed a flight of steps up the side of a house, to see what could be understood of the neighbourhood's layout, but it was only an arrangement of small compounds packed in ad hoc. A man emerged from a doorway. He was strong and lean, with a grey beard and bald scalp, dressed only in his sacred thread and cut-off jeans, and a rudraksha rosary around his neck. I'd met him more than once before, at parties. He was another Rana. He greeted us warmly; he looked as happy and healthy, standing half naked on his sunny step, as if he'd given up everything to live on a river bank.

On an assignment I had a driver who had been for many years in the army. At night we sat in a highway hotel room drinking (I had whisky from the shop, he had some raksi his wife had packed for him) and he told me a story about his first night's leave after he was married. It was decades ago. His wife was having her period so they lay down on separate beds. In fact her period had finished, he clarified (perhaps untruthfully), but she was still within the five days when she remained polluted by it. Eventually the couple relented, got in together, had sex, then returned to their different beds.

'If a menstruating woman uses a glass it has to be purified by touching it with gold, for example touching it to a ring in your ear, before you can even water a plant with it,' he told me, raising his glass of moonshine to his ear. The driver was perhaps slightly more superstitious than most, but I doubted it. He wore a lucky ring on his finger, made from the iron shoe that fell off a black horse on a Thursday. Certainly his views on pollution were mainstream. There is a short list of materials that cause pollution: blood, saliva, shit, the soles of the feet, leather, dogs and pigs (which both eat shit), and so on. The need to avoid pollution by contact with these things gives rise to an elaborate set of precautions.

Because of contamination by saliva anything that has been touched by a person who is eating is deemed polluted (the hand having already touched the mouth). Because you use your left hand to clean your arse the right hand is generally preferred for other purposes, but once you have begun to eat with the right the left must be used for passing dishes or touching unpolluted objects until the right has been purified with water at the end of the meal. Plates and drinking vessels cannot be shared, obviously, unless you throw the food into your mouth and pour water in without touching the pot to your lips. Further, a serving spoon must not make contact with the dining plate (which is contaminated by whoever is eating from it) after the meal has begun. Ideally, the food being served should not be in contact with the plate and the spoon at the same time: you have to dollop it on from a height. In fact, since your food is polluted once you start eating it, and your plate rests on the table, it is no great stretch to realize that the table must be polluted too, which is why people traditionally eat sitting on the kitchen floor. The floor is purified by spreading cow shit on it. It's confusing and there are many refinements. Children dread to visit elderly relatives, fearing what unsuspected clause of the pollution rules they might violate this time.

People themselves can be polluting. So you must not touch a recently delivered mother (because of the blood), nor a bereaved son or a widow during thirteen days of death rituals. Their pollution is only temporary, but the pollution of impure castes, and below them the downright untouchable, is permanent.

India had been polluted by the Muslim conquests and then by the British. Only Nepal retained its purity as a Hindu kingdom, until it was declared a secular republic in 2008. It was the ruler's sacred duty to uphold the law and the social order, as the Licchavis had done and as Jayasthiti Malla apparently did with his caste laws. So, a few years after taking power, Jang Bahadur

Rana began preparing a new 'law of the land', or Muluki Ain. To emphasize their credentials as pious rulers, successive Rana prime ministers each published a new edition of the Muluki Ain on the day that they took over. It remained Nepal's only law until 1963. '[Nepal is] a Hindu kingdom the law of whose court maintains that killing of cows, women and Brahmins shall not be allowed,' the Ain proclaimed. '[It is] a sacred land ... of the holy shrines ... dedicated to the radiant phallus of Pashupati and Gujeshwori ... It is the only Hindu kingdom in the age of Kali.'[11]

Pollution could spread easily and it was the duty of the government to stop it. There were people walking around Kathmandu branded on the face with letters to show the caste they had been reduced to by pollution. If a woman had sex with a lower-caste man, then slept with her husband and cooked for her family, all of them would lose their caste. It was a crime against the state, and so a husband had the right to kill his wife's seducer and cut off her nose. Fines were levied for sharing food and water. The punishments were graded finely, depending on the relative purity of the receiver and the giver of the pollution or, for lovers, of the woman and of the man. Because cooked rice transmits pollution more easily than anything else, a man might be allowed to marry a woman of slightly lower caste, and sleep with her every night, but not to accept the food she cooked because it was polluted.

Fitting Nepal's ethnic diversity into a single hierarchy wasn't straightforward. The caste Hindus of the hills, such as the Gorkhalis, had their hierarchy of Brahmins, Chhetris and Untouchables. The Newars had a similar, but separate, hierarchy among themselves, and so did the people of the plains bordering India. Then there were the assorted ethnic groups of the hills and mountains; some being slowly Hinduized, and others still culturally oriented towards Tibet and not Hindu at all. The high-caste Hindu values of purity and impurity were the organizing principle. The Gorkhalis' Brahmin priests belonged at the top, then the Chhetri lords and a few priestly Newars. Beneath them were 'non-enslaveable alcohol drinkers', a category that included many Newars and other hill ethnic groups, followed by 'enslaveable alcohol drinkers', comprised of less esteemed hill peoples. All of these castes were pure: water that they had handled was acceptable to drink. Further below them were the 'water unacceptable' castes under two headings: touchable (Newar artisans, Muslims and Europeans) and untouchable.

To work it all out Jang's researchers studied millennia-old scriptures (the dharmashastras), but they also recognized contemporary practice. A caste's purity was determined by whether it worked with filthy things, but especially by whose food and water it shared. The lowest of all, the sweepers or scavengers, accepted the leftover food of all the castes above them and absorbed all of their pollution. Above them came the skinners, executioners, metal workers, leather workers and drum makers, and the Badi, whose women practised prostitution. Each could receive water from those above but not from those below them, yet to those higher up they were all outcastes. Jang Bahadur's jurists recognized that, although impure, washermen were not quite untouchable, because despite dealing with dirt they were allowed as far as the first floor of purer people's homes.

Meanwhile, at the other end of the scale, Jang's priest helped him discover the origins of his newly renamed Rana family. As it turned out, the Ranas went all the way back to the same Indian princely lineage that the Shah family claimed to originate from, before they became hill ruffians from Gorkha. It was a lunar dynasty, descended from the moon. Equipped with this genealogy Jang was the equal, or nearly the equal, of the king himself. He married his daughter to the king's son.

A similar process had been going on since the beginning of recorded time. The Licchavis and their priests spread Hindu values to tribal peoples and discovered the genealogy of their solar race. Religious texts of the Malla period retooled the history of Kathmandu to prove that it was a sacred land of holy shrines and power-places. The Malla kings then turned the stories into plays, and their cities into a stage for the cosmic drama. The Shahs and Ranas, in their quest for political legitimacy, upheld the ancient law of caste and reinvented their own family origins. They also sanctified the Valley's rivers, emulating in Kathmandu the holy city of Benares. The first temple to be built on the banks of the Bagmati where it passes nearest to Kathmandu was made in 1782, then another in 1813: sixty years later the ashrams and temples stretched a mile and a half along the ghats.[12]

Now the holy Bagmati is degraded and polluted. The extraction of water near the source, to supply the booming conurbation, has shrunk the once broad stream. The extraction of sand from the riverbed to make concrete has canalized it. Drifts of plastic trash have formed floating islands. Where the black surface is still hundreds of bubbles rise and lie on it, like on a swamp. In other places there are swathes that are unreflective, as if made from a different liquid. Where the black river runs over a small weir it churns up a soapy white froth. The era of the Bagmati temples was relatively brief.

I went to witness the remains, beginning where the Bishnumati flows in. The holy confluence was marked by a temple, built by the junior queen-mother of a Rana maharaja. There were some men wading in the black water with shovels, searching for something. They had dug a hole in the riverbed to create

a pool and were sifting the black objects and slimy ribbons it contained. I asked two teenagers on the bank what the men were looking for, but they made a joke – or at least they laughed at me, and I doubted the diggers were searching for a water filter. In Wright's chronicle huge kites sometimes gave portents. Now the great birds scavenged in their hundreds on the river-banks. One of them glided low up the Bishnumati, passing a perfect bird-shaped shadow for a moment across the group in the stream.

The river had retreated fifty yards from the stone steps of the ghat, but the cremation places still stood where the river used to be. There were sets of six-foot girders set up in parallel, like train-tracks, to support the logs of the pyre. The ashes were still warm at one of them and I took a photograph of a black, shirtless man crouching to light his cigarette. The impure Newar castes had their separate burning places here – leatherworkers, blacksmiths, butchers, sweepers – and there were timber yards stacked with logs to fuel them. I took a diversion to check out the Sewerage and Solid Waste Management Board, built with German aid in the 1970s. It wasn't an actual sewage works. I wasn't sure the city had one.

The neighbourhood was a chequerboard alternating temple complexes with yards where scrap and garbage was recycled. A two-storey heap of empty plastic bottles; then a decaying temple shaded by trees. There were fragments of statuary everywhere. I checked out the important Panchali Bhairab temple, where there is an arse-shaped stone reckoned to be the god's buttock, then reached the bridge at Kalopul, where scavengers live in bivouacs of trash. A little further on there were two new apartment blocks, for modern middle-class nuclear families. Several had understandably chosen to glaze in their small balcony. Near the far bank three boys were playing in the black water, thrashing up a white foam, submerging themselves, and calling to have their picture taken.

☀

In 1853 (seven years after Jang's coup) the surgeon then posted at the residency, Dr Henry Ambrose Oldfield, witnessed an execution on the bank of the Bishnumati River. Executions often happened at the same place, where the slope of the land formed 'an amphitheatre' and a suitable site to watch the spectacle.[13] The official in charge had been notified of Oldfield's interest, and had asked him to select a time convenient to himself for the execution to take place, which made the surgeon feel uncomfortable. But he chose a time, and ended up waiting on the riverbank for two hours anyway, because the executioners and their prisoner were late. They came with a crowd of three hundred, which they had accumulated as they paraded through the town.

The victim was made to kneel on the ground among the bones of other criminals. He 'seemed indifferent to all about him', although he had 'a sulky, scowling look'. He was naked, besides a rag around his loins, his arms were tied behind him above the elbow, and his hair was in a knot on top of his head. Two or three executioners examined his position and moved his head about 'according to their respective fancies, evidently looking at it in a professional light'.

Oldfield now expected the man to be put out of his misery and suspense, but an important omission had occurred. Of the twenty executioners present none had brought a blade, and none of the spectators was willing to lend theirs. When two or three khukuris were eventually pressed from the crowd there was a debate as to whether any of them was sharp enough. The principal executioner selected one, declared that he could 'make it do', and began grinding it on a stone, occasionally testing the edge with his thumb and joking. The crowd began to complain that it would soon be too dark for them to see, and shouted their disgust when at length the khukuri was rejected and the authorities began searching for another one. Oldfield wrote:

> At last one of the Gorkha sepoys in attendance upon me volunteered his 'talwar' amid loud applause for this disinterested offer. The talwar was handed to the executioner, who, feeling its edge in the most artistic style, pronounced it a first rate one; and with an air of pride, like a child with a new toy, at using so superior an instrument, he went to the side of the poor wretch, who was kneeling bound, and had been so for at least a quarter of an hour.

His head was severed (which Oldfield described in surgical detail). The crowd applauded the executioner's skill ('Wah! Wah!'). The sword was cleaned and returned to the sepoy, who refused to part with it, because it was a very good one, and very sharp, and he had inherited it from his father, who had used it much in the late war with the British.

I made another trip to the river, arriving on the banks of the Bishnumati at about four in the morning to see the slaughter. It was dark and mostly deserted. The stink of the stream was so high that when I parked and drank some of the water I'd brought from home the bottle tasted cheesy and revolting. I'd seen a man driving three buffalo along the black river bank. Now I found the truck from which the beasts were being unloaded, and the man I approached said he would take me to the killing place. We stepped through a gate into an area where a little light was escaping. There was a pick-up truck parked in an inch of bloody slurry; a pile of bones and horns and hooves waist-high; and another pile next to it, of undercooked buffalo shit. A man slit open a wobbling white sack, and another cubic foot of muck slid out beside it. There was open ground to the left, where I could see buffaloes tethered in the dark, and a shed in front where the lights were on inside.

I slipped through the door. It was a long space, bright with the blue-whiteness of fluorescent lamps. The floor was slick and red. A dozen people in slimy clothes were each working over the separate remains of a half-butchered buffalo; a heap of parts on a spread-out hide. *Perfect* I thought, as I exchanged a few friendly questions with the people nearest the door and started taking out my camera, looking at the dials and thinking about how to use it.

They wouldn't let me take any pictures without the owner there. He wouldn't come until six. So I went home and ate a bowl of noodles, and when I returned I found the owner's son was sullen and rude. He thought that if I took a photograph it might appear on television, and he wouldn't accept my assurances. Go somewhere else, he said, and in daylight now I realized

that there were many slaughterhouses. Other life was stirring too, in the rows of low-caste housing. Kids in school uniforms. Women in saris. Open doors revealing small shops inside. People smoking cigarettes.

At the third slaughterhouse they offered me tea but I didn't fancy it. The glasses weren't kept very separate from the gore. Meat was being weighed into boxes and taken away on rickshaws and butchers' motorbikes. The workers were hacking skulls apart, which seemed to be the last part of it, but they said they'd kill one more buffalo that morning so I stuck around. The animals were tied up in a yard outside, and to be slaughtered the victim must be led in through a sump of old blood that the abattoir floor drained into.

The creature was partly resistant, but seemed less alarmed than a buffalo can be when a vehicle passes it on a country road. I expected a sword, like at a sacrifice. A boy stepped forward, swung, and struck the brute on its head with a sledgehammer. It fell to its knees. He hit it again and it went down, hardly twitching, as they immediately began to carve it up. In minutes the buffalo was skinned and divided.

People who live in Kathmandu have few occasions to develop the type of innocence that's become common in the West. In Kathmandu the sleek butcher's dog still lies down to sleep with the goats tethered at the counter. While walking with someone senior and respected you might both notice a street dog, tenderly licking the bloody uterus hanging from her fur coat. (Was it just for me the decorum was shattered?) At a funeral, the mourners seem not to notice the grotesque sight of two monkeys fucking on the wall beside the pyre.

Somehow Kathmandu achieves honest recognition. Prejudice is open. Unpleasant realities are a common occasion. Nature can't be denied. Shameless, blatant self-serving deceit is ordinary; and people represent their personalities more freely than in England. Despite the layers of obscure belief and custom, the hypocrisy and lies, I sometimes felt that Kathmandu people had a better grip on reality than my own deluded countrymen. The impression was crystallized, in a way, by a friend.

'What isn't in Kathmandu?' she said. 'Everything is here!' She meant the things you could find in the shops now, like babies' nappies or decent coffee, but by the pleasure with which she said it (although I didn't think she cared about shopping) she seemed to refer to *everything*. The surgeon Henry Oldfield's book describes some dark deeds with relish, but I found him affectionate. He seems to have loved Kathmandu. He produced scores of meticulous watercolours, five large boxes of which are kept at the Royal Geographical Society in London. There are careful studies of the ridgeline of the still uncharted snowy range, as seen from high points around the Valley. He made detailed studies of the city's picturesque, seemingly terminal decay. And he carefully recorded stone sculptures of the gods in grey shades, then boldly daubed the red tika on.

Oldfield became a personal friend of Jang Bahadur Rana, and for that the gothic shade in his humour must have helped. When Jang started a war with Tibet in 1855 he took a pair of criminals from the jail and dressed them in soldiers' uniforms. Then he strung them up by the roadside at Balaju, and declared they were deserters *pour encourager les autres*. The corpses hanging from the tree looked more like British sepoys than Nepalis. 'The coats in which they were hanged were the same old uniform jackets of the residency sepoys, which must have been bought second hand in the city,' Oldfield remarked, with what I thought was a flicker of amusement.[14] But he wasn't joking when he described Jang's medical vocation. 'Jang has great faith in European surgical skill, and is, indeed, very fond of surgery, at which he often does a little himself,' Oldfield wrote. 'I remember him excising a small fatty tumour from a man's neck very successfully ... [he] occasionally amused himself by vaccinating patients, but rarely succeeded with them.'[15]

Oldfield's friendship with Jang, and their common medical interests, gave him the opportunity to see something of Rana family life which was denied to other British officials. In 1851 he was summoned to the house of Jang's brother, whose youngest wife had given birth to a live child that morning, but who was in a dangerous condition. When Oldfield reached there he found Jang and three of his brothers waiting outside. The Raj Guru (royal priest) appeared and pronounced that there was no objection, as a matter of caste, to the foreigner treating the lady, 'if she herself had no scruples'. Jang went up to where the women were, and explained that if the girl did not receive treatment then she would die.

> The patient, however, said she felt sure she should die if nothing were done; but she did not fear death, and would much sooner die than allow me to see and treat her, as, should she do so, all the other women would point at and taunt her ... She was supported strongly in these views by her mother-in-law and the other ladies. All Jang's persuasions failed, and on his pressing the matter he got well abused by the ladies for his pains.[16]

According to Oldfield's footnote the patient died, untreated, eight days later. The following year he was summoned to the Thapathali durbar to treat a 'lady of rank' who turned out to be the king's sister. Every Nepali doctor had given up on her. Jang told Oldfield that if he could cure the princess he would receive fifteen thousand rupees, but if he treated her and she died then he would 'get the credit for having killed her'. He was led through a series of small rooms in private apartments to a passage-like space where the patient lay on a mattress on the floor, covered with cashmere shawls.

> She made no objection to my seeing or speaking to her. She sat up in bed and answered the few questions I put to her willingly, showed me her tongue and held out her arm for me to feel her pulse ... Poor girl, her case was evidently hopeless, as she was in the later stages of consumption, besides other local affections. She was striking in appearance and singularly like her brother the King ... I made a salaam to her, and retired.[17]

Outside, Oldfield told Jang that the princess was going to die and he would have nothing to do with her.

> He said I was quite right, and then hurried me into the garden to see a wild boar fight with some Nipal hunting dogs ... Next day a large piece of [piggy's] loin, covered with a layer of fat nearly two inches thick, was sent to me. I had it dressed, and its flavour was most delicious, the flesh white in colour, and tender.[18]

A footnote records that the princess died four months later.

Sometime in the first decade of the twenty-first century an acquaintance of mine was driving on his motorbike in one of the smaller towns of the Valley, after dark. As he rattled down a brick-paved lane he realized that his headlight was exposing women who were squatting in the gutter with their skirts up. One of them, looming by his front wheel, spat at him in Newari, 'Aren't you ashamed!' The mild-mannered web designer admitted later that he did feel a bit abashed, and he drove down the rest of that street with his light off. This practice had become rare by then but it used to be standard, reinforced by the understanding, intuitive really, that it's unclean to shit inside your own house.

Successive foreign accounts from the nineteenth century made similar observations about the city's appearance. It was normal to remark on the fine brick buildings, with elaborate and grotesque carvings in the timberwork. The streets were 'narrow, crooked, and dirty'.[19] Each chowk might be crowded with twenty or more families, and full of filth; 'doubtless often a fertile source of fever and disease', Oldfield thought.[20] Stagnant gutters did the duty of sewers.

Oldfield's paintings show the temples and houses falling down. He found Patan even more dilapidated than Kathmandu proper. Its inhabitants were 'crushed by the loss of their independence

... stricken with a sort of apathy which prevents their attempting even to check the progress of further decay'. After their conquest of the Valley, the Hindu Gorkhas had seized the landed endowments of Patan's Buddhist monasteries, and the fabric they supported was 'broken into ruins or overgrown with jungle'.[21]

Oldfield left in 1863, and a few years later another British surgeon, Dr Daniel Wright, finally arrived. Like others before him and since, he had difficulty (more difficulty than he knew) in pinning the facts down. In the 'Introductory Sketch' he published with his chronicle, he commented on the problem of collecting information in a country where 'Baron Münchausen himself would be considered a marvel of accuracy and truthfulness!'[22] Wright described how some parts of Jang Bahadur's palace at Thapathali were permanently deserted, after a kite once marked them as inauspicious by settling on the roof. He described the oil paintings, chandeliers and pianos that furnished the great hall. And he offered this, tucked away in a footnote, about the strange suicides that occurred before the great black god in the palace square.

> The suicide always takes place at night, and the body is found in the morning, with its throat cut from ear to ear, and its limbs decorously arranged, lying on one of the steps![23]

15

A friend's niece or nephew was half a year old and to mark the ceremony of his or her first meal of rice there was a party at a five-star hotel. Someone led me from the ballroom to the foyer to meet an elderly Rana, a distant relative of the baby, with the promise that I would find him amusing and a fund of stories about the old days. The old man was smoking and drinking whisky with another Rana, who was the king's ambassador to London. Introductions were made and I was left with them. 'Oh God, not you,' the ambassador said. My articles in the *Telegraph* were a frequent pain in his arse. In those days members of the ruling class were quite open in their impatience at naïve foreign prattle on democracy and human rights, which they felt was at odds with the practical reality of their country. They were battling Maoist rebels and they expected more understanding from old friends like Britain. My exposure as an equivocating Western liberal didn't bother the older man.

Baikuntha Shamsher Rana was overweight and short of breath. He was also charming and candid and, not surprisingly, quite a near neighbour of mine. I became an occasional visitor at his house, where he hosted a conservative political salon and card games. I met royalist politicians and retired army officers there, and when I saw government ministers being driven through our neighbourhood I sometimes guessed they were coming from his house. I don't remember any substantial information I obtained, or in fact any proof that these men really had the confidence of the king or his circle. But I enjoyed meeting them, and especially I enjoyed Baikuntha's company, and I went there to listen to him.

The small garden was half wild. Inside the door was a sign that said 'Aum sweet Aum'. Baikuntha lived almost entirely in a single room. There were four Chinese illustrations on the walls that seemed to be made of gold leaf, providing a residue of grandeur to the ashtrays and whisky bottles, and the old-people's clutter of thermos flasks and Tupperware and emergency lights. On the other side of the room a small group was playing marriage for five rupees a point. 'If you want to move in high society you have to learn this game,' Baikuntha said. 'The queen is a player and the king is also very keen.' Casino chips were being counted in and out of a biscuit tin and scores marked with a pencil stub.

I asked him what had happened to all the furniture and pictures the old palaces were stuffed with. He answered after a long pause, speaking slowly. 'When you are left with a legacy of great days and you do not have the money to carry on, what do you do? First jewellery goes, then property goes, then you start selling furniture, you sell even the beams.'

'You sell the beams then the house falls down?'

'Exactly ...,' he said. The second word was lost in coughing. 'And on till the last. You don't let it show. It is a principle of aristocracy anywhere in the world. Don't show your weakness, don't show that you do not have money.

'I'm making a grand error by drinking this,' he remarked, referring to the cheap bottle between us.

Baikuntha's current furniture was fairly modern but unfashionable. He had kept most of his possessions on his estate in the plains, where the Maoists had destroyed everything they could and stolen the rest. He apologized for the glasses we were using; the Maoists had thrown all his crockery and glassware into his empty swimming pool. 'Most unpleasant people,' he said with feeling.

The palace where he was born was a hotel now. 'My bedroom they have made into three rooms. Three rooms and a bathroom. Most other big palaces have been broken. New buildings have come up. It is,' he paused, and continued almost inaudibly, 'it's rather savage.'

I'd recently been in Singha Durbar, the government secretariat, to interview an official of the Ministry of Women, Children and

Social Welfare, who had told me that the building that housed his ministry was previously the Rana harem. 'Does that sound about right? Does it sound possible?' I asked.

'No, no,' Baikuntha spluttered chestily. 'We didn't call it that. My father had nine wives, and what do you call it? More than a couple of wives, does it become a harem? My grandfather also had many. (They had nothing but parties,' he added, more to himself than me.) 'These were women who were given titles because they bore children, these nine wives of my father's. But then he also took care of all the others. There was competition between him and my elder brothers for every maid in the house.

'My house had about eighty-five maids, and about the same number of male servants,' Baikuntha said. 'Mind you, only a few of the men were allowed inside. They were all outside, just so that their so-called harem, you can call it anything you like ...' he chose his own term, ... their hunting ground would not be, would not be ...'

'Disturbed by the footman?' I suggested. He nodded.

From the card table a retired colonel called over to me. 'So, you are from Geordie land?'

'That's right,' I said 'Exactly.'

There was a fit of coughing around the room.

'Newcastle upon Tyne,' said the Colonel. 'When I was there, there were a lot of Asians. The population is mixed but predominantly Indian.'

'Most of the Asians are Bangladeshi,' I said.

'Indians also?'

'I think they're mostly Bangladeshi.'

'Uhu. Yes.'

'But I guess it's pretty white by the standards of a British city.'

I turned back to Baikuntha. 'Were there elephants at your house?'

'Horses.'

'And cars?'

'Cars, yes, but very few,' he said and described how every car in Kathmandu had to be carried over the trails into the Valley by teams of porters. Then he talked about his childhood home again. 'Outside the house were all sorts of male servants and army personnel, because my father was also in the army. And inside were all those females. I saw everything inside that house. *Everything was there*. It is nice to be born in a place that has four swimming pools.'

In Baikuntha's house now there was one servant, a dishevelled woman who, like her employer, probably looked older than she was. He summoned her now to order his dinner: some salami, some tomato, egg, bacon, and a bowl of soup. They discussed how this dish should ideally be prepared, and how in fact it would be. From the card table the colonel suggested it would be healthier to microwave than to fry it.

'Have pity,' Baikuntha told him, and, turning to me, he said, 'The Ranas are, believe me, cruel people. Especially if they have king's blood in them. His grandmother was King Tribhuwan's sister.'

'But through a concubine,' the colonel clarified modestly.

'See!' Baikuntha declared, unreasonably. 'The mean character shows.'

I thought I'd try out an implausible story of Jang Bahadur, which another Rana had told me. Apparently he'd died by beheading, according to his own law, killed by a villager whom he'd cuckolded while hunting in the plains. 'What *is* the true story of how Jang Bahadur died?' I said.

'There's no intrigue in that,' said Baikuntha. 'No intrigue whatsoever. He had gone for shikar in the Tarai …' Then he turned to the card table and asked my question in Nepali. It provoked a long and animated story from his wife, the gist of which was that Jang had been snatched off an elephant's back by a tiger. Baikuntha turned back to me. 'It is the first time I'm hearing this,' he said. I offered my cuckolding story, which was dismissed out of hand. If the Tharu people, who live in those parts, weren't so extremely tolerant of people sleeping with their women, Baikuntha claimed, he'd have been beheaded many times himself.

They were wearing their coats and shawls indoors. The colonel was smoking and Baikuntha's wife was drinking large measures of Indian Bagpiper whisky, topped to the brim with water. The lights went out, and there was prolonged fumbling in the dark to turn the back-up on. Baikuntha said, 'You know what a guinea is? It used to have a value of twenty-one shillings. When I was studying in England I was paying eight guineas for a house I had taken in Shepherd's Bush. Shepherd's Bush was not the Little India of today. I was the only black man there.'

'Brown,' said the colonel.

'Brown, brown,' Baikuntha agreed.

'Of foreign origin,' the colonel said, pronouncing the phrase with exaggeration as if it was in inverted commas.

'All my neighbours were white. Tom, I liked your country when it was your own. Now I do not like your country. It is a Commonwealth country.'

'That's not what I object to,' I said. For a while I'd been trying to fix in my mind what I'd come to see as some kind of naivety in the West. My country couldn't understand the rest of the world in the way the rest of the world could understand it. England seemed denatured and provincial, full of people who'd never know how relative their judgements were. What I came out with was, 'I think it's become sterile and separated from reality. A British child might eat a burger – it's made from chicken – but he has no idea what it means to kill a chicken. For example,' I added.

'I was taken by the police,' said Baikuntha. 'Have I told you this? I was a Nepali and there was an Iranian pasha, the oil minister's son. There was an American, Richard. The bugger was thrown out of university because he was caught sleeping with the dean's daughter, who was underage. That is why he came to England to study. Anyway there were four of us altogether. We decided to have a whole lamb in London. I was driving. We went 150 miles away, caught a bloody sheep ...'

'You stole it?'

'No no, we bought it, brought it to my Shepherd's Bush house. Forty women were called to eat that lamb. Can you imagine? Harem! You talk about a harem in Nepal, I had a harem there. The language tuition centre in Tottenham Square!' He was bright now, in the dim glow of the emergency lighting, and he'd stopped wheezing mostly.

'We killed the lamb, the pasha did it the halal way. In comes the police. All four of us in custody! I did not know, how could I know that it has to go through a process of slaughter-houses and this and that? I had to ring up my embassy. And my uncle in the embassy said, "Babu, why did you have to slaughter a bloody sheep? You can't buy meat?"

'All four of us, we were well known in our own countries,' he said. 'In our own countries we had connections. As far as England was concerned we were hooligans who had slaughtered a sheep. My forty women were hungry. The sheep was taken by the cops and they ate it. By the time I was let out it was six o'clock in the evening. So what we did, we went to Marble Arch. All those people to feed and the sheep had been taken by the police. There was a thing called a transistor, and with that blaring we danced in Hyde Park.'

Baikuntha's great-great-uncle, Jang Bahadur Rana, fell ill on a hunting expedition in the southern plains in 1877. The same messenger who brought the news of his illness to Kathmandu probably also bore another, secret, message to his eldest surviving brother, Ranadip Singh Rana. The maharaja wasn't just sick – he was already dead. Ranadip staged a bloodless coup.

Jang Bahadur had six full brothers and they had been instrumental in his rise and in his thirty-year rule. The brothers had many sons. He had therefore arranged his legacy such that some of his powers and titles would pass by an unusual process horizontally across the generations of the Rana family; first to his own brothers, then in order of seniority between the cousins of the second generation – his own sons and his brothers' sons. Other titles would be inherited directly by his own sons and run vertically through his direct line. The division of powers that Jang's arrangements implied was complicated and ill defined, but the important point was obvious: in that huge family not

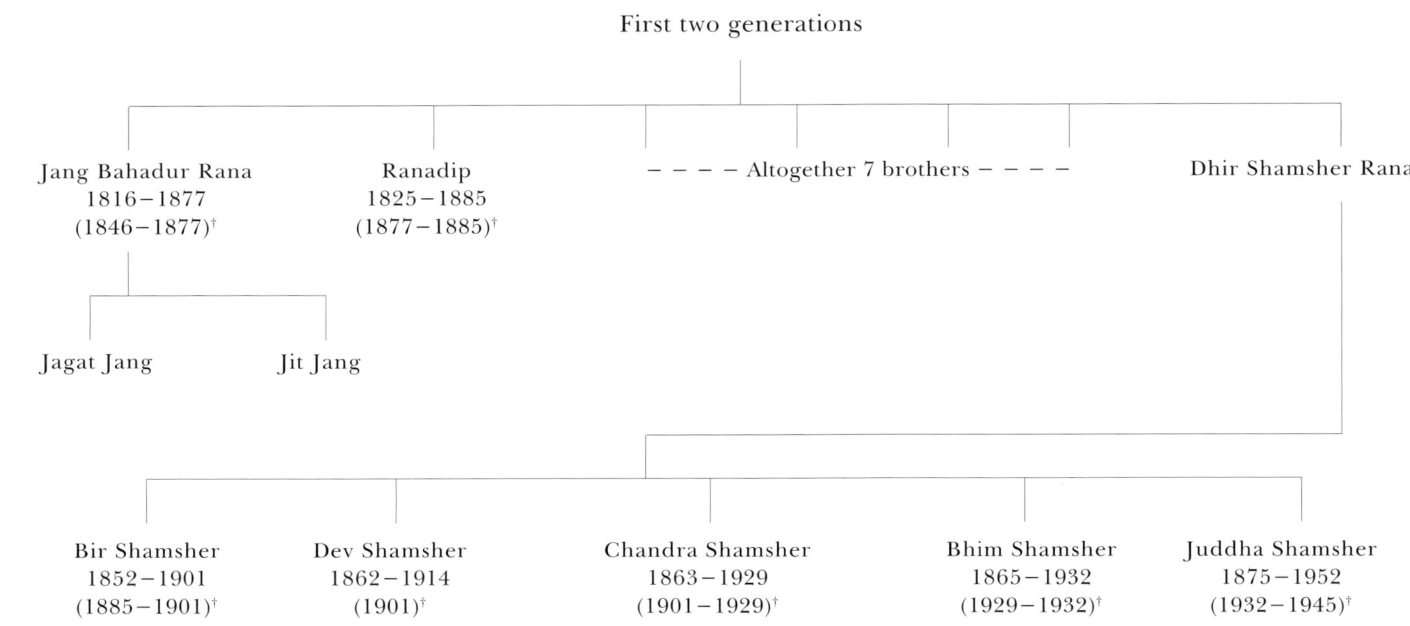
THE RANA FAMILY
First two generations
Jang Bahadur Rana
1816–1877
(1846–1877)†
Ranadip
1825–1885
(1877–1885)†
– – – – Altogether 7 brothers – – – –
Dhir Shamsher Rana
Jagat Jang
Jit Jang
Bir Shamsher
1852–1901
(1885–1901)†
Dev Shamsher
1862–1914
(1901)†
Chandra Shamsher
1863–1929
(1901–1929)†
Bhim Shamsher
1865–1932
(1929–1932)†
Juddha Shamsher
1875–1952
(1932–1945)†
†Years as prime minister

everyone would get their turn. By his coup Ranadip consolidated this inheritance for himself.

The rivalry of Jang Bahadur's sons against his brothers and their sons was not settled so easily. Jagat Jang plotted against Ranadip and was removed from the order of succession. That suited the seventeen sons of Jang's youngest brother, Dhir Shamsher Rana. But by 1885 the Shamshers had become worried that Jagat Jang would make a comeback, and that he'd use his restored powers to attack them.

On the night of 22 November 1885, Prime Minister Ranadip Singh Rana received a visit from a group of his Shamsher nephews. They drew their guns and shot their uncle dead. That night they managed to catch their cousin, Jagat Jang, and kill him too. So the eldest of the coup-makers, Bir Shamsher Rana, was the first to make himself prime minister in the second generation. Jang's surviving sons fled to India, where they had reason to expect that the British would support the dispossessed heirs of their old friend. The resident, Mr C. Girdlestone (who had recently been Cecil Bendall's ambivalent host), was seen as sympathetic.

While I was wandering on the riverbanks I was looking for a particular photograph. The shot I had in mind would be square, with the black river in the centre of the bottom half and a grey sky above, finely grained, conveying the detailed texture of every piece of trash. The black crows and white egrets that forage there would be rising in a cloud. I took my films to be developed at the shop where the Ranas got their photos done. Nothing that came back matched my imagination.

The darkroom belonged to a man of the picture-making caste. His grandfather had made religious paintings and, as a court painter, portraits and decorations for the Ranas, before he became a court photographer in 1908. His son became a court photographer after him. In the third generation the shop belonged to Kiran, the chief news cameraman of Nepal TV. I

saw him at receptions (where he was also a guest), and occasionally at news events, but rarely at his shop where the technician ran things. The technician was an anxious, obliging man. I asked if I could join him in the darkroom, and sometime after I left my next set of films he called to say 'come tomorrow'.

The technician led me upstairs, closed the door, plugged in and placed a pan of water on the electric ring on the floor. Then he mixed the warm water with the developer and cold water from the tap, took its temperature, picked up a can-opener and the first of my films and turned off the light. To make conversation in the pure blackness I asked him a question I knew the answer to.

'This is the last darkroom in Kathmandu?'

'The first and the last,' he said.[1]

I offered a question I dearly wanted the answer to. 'Where can you get black and white film?'

'Getting film is difficult now,' he said, and added the clarification, 'It's not available.'

When the lights were on again and the timer was ticking on the wall the technician showed me around. It was a grey, concrete room in which the counters and sinks were also made of concrete. The room was a strange shape, partly corresponding to the strange shape of the high narrow house. There were three enlargers standing like big birds on the counter, covered by black hoods. 'This is the oldest,' he said, and demonstrated where the glass negatives were inserted. Then he lifted the hoods off the other two and showed me those.

'We've almost finished the last of the chemicals. Sometimes when someone comes from America or Europe they bring some more.' It was the difficulty of obtaining paper that accounted for the extreme expense. He unwrapped and showed me his own old negatives – white and black images of his family visiting temples or attending feasts, with garlands around their necks and flowers behind their ears. Now he'd switched to digital. He suggested I do the same. As I was leaving I ran into Kiran, the owner.

'What's going to happen to our country?' he said.

'I thought you might know.'

We each asked the other how he was. He was looking pretty perky. He said he was OK. 'What film have you got?' he said. 'Ilford? Can you give me a few rolls?'

'I only have six or seven left,' I lied, knowing I couldn't hide my riches from him. 'Why?'

'I want to take my father's negatives, my grandfather's negatives, and take photographs from the exact same angle.' He picked up my contact sheets and stepped into better light to look at them without comment before sliding them back in the envelope. While he did it he was talking about the clashing agendas of the great powers in Nepal: America, India, China … the EU. 'This will become another Beirut,' he foretold.

I said we mightn't have to wait too long to find out. I was getting my helmet ready.

'Oh well,' he said, 'If you give me only one roll that will be enough,' and he bounded away through the back of his shop. I got on my bike, turned it around, and as I drove away I wondered how many other people he was hitting up for film. I wondered if I might give him one or two, anyway. I'd sell them dearly. I was spending about a quarter of my income in his lousy shop.

☀

The photographs in Kiran's collection are the best-known visual record of Rana Kathmandu. He has a picture of the temples and ashrams along the ghats at Thapathali, the wide and pristine Bagmati flowing in the foreground through sandy shallows. There's one (which must pre-date the family business) showing Jang Bahadur, seated but still formidable in middle age, with one of his wives standing stoutly beside him. Perhaps she was among those who went to her death on his pyre? There's a photograph of the fat and uncouth-looking Ranadip, seated between his disinherited nephews, surrounded by a host of unknown men in plumed crowns. Indeed there are endless groups of Rana men in their plumed crowns and uniforms, with their many wives in heavy saris, sitting rigidly through the interminable exposure that was necessary when the film speed was just 5 ISO.

This second generation of Ranas effected the greatest physical changes that Kathmandu had seen in many centuries, as they covered the fields around the city with three dozen stucco palaces.[2] The palaces were immense, with imperial Ionic and Corinthian orders, festooned with swags and balustrades and broken pediments. High Rana-style occupied the area between baroque architecture and wedding cake design. Among Kiran's photographs there is a view from the top of Bhimsen's tower across the wide, park-like expanse of the Tundikhel parade ground toward Singha Durbar – the Lion Palace – the greatest Rana edifice of them all. It was said to have 1,700 rooms and 7 courtyards, modelled on Versailles. In the photograph, taken before it was mutilated by fire and earthquake, Singha Durbar did look faintly like Versailles.

There was another picture, of Singha Durbar's builder, dressed up like a musketeer in cape and breeches with ostrich feathers in his cap. He had just received a British knighthood. Another generation later here was Louis Mountbatten, the last viceroy of India, with the eighth, and second-to-last Rana prime minister.[3] The English ladies were pretty in white dresses. The men were trussed up in their uniforms, almost completely covered with preposterous medals. After the British left India there wasn't much time left for the Ranas.

☀

The English word 'Gurkha' is a mispronunciation of 'Gorkha', the place that Prithvi Narayan Shah came from. The first British Gurkha units had been raised by General Ochterlony during the Anglo-Nepal war from Gorkhali deserters and prisoners, and from the men of the hill tracts ceded to the British by the Gorkhalis. In the first decades after the war some British officials doubted the loyalty of Gurkha troops in the event of another war with their own country. Others, like Brian Hodgson, argued strenuously but in vain for greater recruitment. Anyway, the Kathmandu durbar opposed its subjects joining the British Indian army. Nepalis working as British recruiting agents were arrested. Recruits were threatened with the loss of their property. Jang Bahadur decreed that if a British Gurkha's wife took a lover then the soldier had no right to cut his head off, and would be treated as a murderer if he did.

By the 1870s the British commanded only around 4,600 Gurkhas, the same number as sixty years earlier. To maintain that strength they needed around 325 new recruits a year, which they were obliged to lure out of the hills by 'illegal' means, sending secret recruiters in defiance of the Nepali government. The experience of the 1857 'mutiny', in which sepoys from the Indian plains had rebelled, made soldiers from the hills more valuable in British eyes. What's more, as the century progressed the British became increasingly concerned about the threat of a Russian invasion of India. Gurkhas were in urgent demand. The power struggles after Jang Bahadur's death made the rulers in Kathmandu insecure, so the British bartered their endorsement of each new prime minister for a supply of fighting men.

In 1878 Ranadip Singh Rana lifted restrictions on men volunteering. In 1884 Mr Girdlestone swapped the promise of more Gurkhas for permission to import precision rifles through British territory, which Nepal needed for its latest confrontation with Tibet. That deal foundered on improved Nepal–Tibet relations, but the following year Girdlestone was able to exchange better access for British recruiters for a gift of rifles, permission to import materials to make cartridges, a knighthood for Ranadip and the right to a nineteen-gun salute. Unfortunately, Ranadip was assassinated by his nephews before the agreement could be implemented.

Girdlestone was on leave when the Shamshers made their move and the acting resident, Colonel Berkeley, recommended that Calcutta recognize the coup. The policy paid off handsomely. The presence of Jang Bahadur's sons in India gave the British extra leverage over the Kathmandu regime. Bir Shamsher Rana not only allowed recruiters in, he sent his own teams to persuade men to join the British army, and gave the resident weekly reports of their progress. Within six months of the coup over two thousand recruits were provided, although the British rejected many of them as belonging to the wrong castes.[4]

In their eagerness to supply the British with recruits, the Nepali government sometimes told villagers that their army wage would be double what it actually would be, or they resorted to other, less subtle expedients. In 1887 Girdleston wrote:

> The coercion to which it [the Nepali government] freely resorted last winter in order to obtain recruits for us is one, though not the most influential, of the causes of the great unpopularity of the present administration ... Their rule is founded on terrorism ... except by undue pressure they are apparently unable to gain recruits.[5]

Girdlestone recommended that coercion should cease, to reduce the rate at which Gurkhas were deserting. His deputy seems to have been more realistic. In a letter to Calcutta of the same year Colonel Berkeley wrote:

> the present minister and his family are as bad as they can be; but they had already rendered us service and it is conceivable they might be able to do as much for us as Jang Bahadur did.[6]

Bir Shamsher died in 1901. He'd built six giant, mock-European palaces in his fourteen-year reign. His successor, the relatively liberal Dev Shamsher Rana, was forced out at gunpoint by his younger brothers a few months later. The new prime minister was another usurper, with his victim once again exiled to India. Chandra Shamsher Rana made himself even more obliging to the British than Bir Shamsher had been.

The descendants of the deposed prime minister, Dev Shamsher, preserve stories of how Chandra kept their branch of the family weak, by plying them with drugs, alcohol, and gonorrhoea-infected courtesans. Certainly, for a couple of generations after the coup, the men of Dev's family died young of vice and alcoholism. Chandra immediately began work on the greatest palace of all, his Singha Durbar. It cost five million rupees of tax revenue to build; then he sold it back to the nation, so the people paid for it twice. With the proceeds he built at least seven more palaces for his sons. When the First World War broke out, Chandra declared that 'the whole military resources of Nepal are at His Majesty's disposal'. Between 1914 and 1918, 55,000 Nepali villagers were sent to fight for Britain. Chandra even sent the prisoners from his jails. In 1920 he was rewarded for his 'unswerving loyalty' with an annual pension of one million rupees. Chandra Shamsher Rana ruled Nepal for almost thirty years.

Rising anti-British sentiment in India after the First World War (including within the Indian Army) made Gurkha soldiers, and therefore the Ranas, more valuable to the British than ever. More honours and flattering diplomatic protocols were bestowed. When the Second World War began the prime minister at the time, Juddha Shamsher Rana, appointed his eldest son Supreme Recruiting Officer. While the Quit India Movement put many of Britain's Indian subjects in opposition to the war effort, Nepal consistently exceeded recruitment demands. Juddha Shamsher gave money for the victims of the blitz in London, and his junior queens raised a fund to buy ambulances. Over 2,00,000 Nepalis fought for the British in the Second World War. Even a few Newars and other such unwarlike castes were accepted.

☀

Some palaces have disappeared more or less completely. Singha Durbar became the government secretariat, with most of the ministries inside. The palace's theatre, where private entertainments had been staged, became the national parliament. Several other palaces became government departments. Now shrubs grew in the guttering. Stone-paved corridors, sometimes smelling of piss, ran behind identical, high-ceilinged offices. (It was difficult to imagine how they used to live in all of those identical rooms.) The offices were mostly deserted. Sometimes they were partitioned into ply-board cubicles. They were furnished with steel shelves stacked with ledgers and bundles of files. They were littered with well-read newspapers. The bare desks, with empty tea-glasses on them, were marked with small wet rings. At the end of the corridor there would be a waiting room with the minister's office through a door beyond. Inside, sofas under white covers would be arranged around the walls. There would be a Nepali flag on the paperless desk, beside a telephone and a bell for the minister to ring his peon. There would be a calendar hanging on a nail in the wall, showing the king attending some public function, counting down the weeks and months before the inevitable fall of the old order's latest iteration.

The palace called Laksmi Niwas, by the main road that runs north from the city centre, became the headquarters of the army's elite 10th brigade. It was closed to all comers, but I could see the classical façade through the arch of the gateway, which was wrapped with barbed wire and high nets, erected against grenade attack.

Around the time that the Maoists made an elected constituent assembly their main demand in the peace talks, a journalist called Bhaikaji Ghimire called for the same thing in his newspaper. 'By 2003,' he said, 'only a few newspapers had dared to raise the question of a constituent assembly.'[7] He was arrested by the army and accused of being a Maoist. The army took him to Laksmi Niwas and began torturing him two days later. He was beaten with bamboos and polythene pipes and given electric shocks. He was suspended by his feet above a drum of water, wearing nothing but a blindfold, and dipped in it until he was nearly drowned; then they beat him again and repeated the process. At first the soldiers wanted him to admit he was a Maoist, then to reveal who his Maoist contacts were. 'Give us at least one Maoist and you will have your freedom,' they said. He lost consciousness and woke to find himself on a saline drip. A week later he was interrogated and tortured again.

Bhaikaji Ghimire remained continuously blindfolded for over a year. He wasn't formally interrogated any more but his abuse continued. The prisoners were only allowed to shit before eight in the morning and they were given no water to wash themselves afterwards. While they were shitting other prisoners would be led, blindfolded, to piss in the same place. Every time the prisoners used the toilet they would be given four strokes, and four strokes again afterwards. They learnt to distinguish the footfall of the more or less cruel guards. When they wanted to drink water (their hands were continuously tied behind their backs) the soldiers would pour it over their faces, so their clothes were always wet. (Their shirts were also soaked with blood from the beatings.) Bhaikaji Ghimire was able to wash and brush his teeth for the first time three months after his arrest, when a major came to inspect the prisoners and complained about the stench.

After many months Bhaikaji was loaded into a truck, 'the same way vendors load sacks into a truck', and taken to an army base just north of the city in the forest at Shivapuri. His feet were cut by being marched in shoeless, his wrists were too swollen to fit the cuffs (they were bound with rope instead). He was underdressed and freezing. Three days later the prisoners regained hope that they would live when their clothes were returned to them.

He was held prisoner for twenty-one months altogether. Towards the end he was transferred to another barrack, in Patan, where he got decent food for the first time and was allowed to keep clean, although he was still bound and blindfolded. While he was there he was photographed with his name on a board around his neck, holding a homemade gun and five bullets.

Eventually he was taken to a civilian jail and driven to court in a police van. When I met him in 2005 his physical recovery was going quite well. He took daily exercise and no longer walked with a limp, but he said he still suffered from back pain and the welts on his back were still visible.

A few months later the United Nations published a report which showed that scores of people had been treated in the same way at the 10th Brigade's headquarters in Laksmi Niwas. At least forty-nine prisoners who were loaded into trucks and taken to the forest at Shivapuri were never seen again. It appears that similar things happened in most of the army camps in the country.

Of all the horrifying facts – for example, the way the prisoners were revived between their tortures by medical staff – one detail affected me in particular. A prisoner described to the UN investigators how he'd peeped beneath his blindfold and seen the red neon sign of the Himalaya Bank shining on the busy main road outside.[8] You can't think about Kathmandu seriously without thinking about the torture camps and the secret executions. What were they done to protect, and how were they forgotten so easily?

16

I was at a party to celebrate some kind of cultural event, a book launch or an exhibition. A notable Rana socialite was there and I was talking to her. She didn't normally drink, she told me, and giggled, but tonight she was having a glass of wine. I told her about my historical interests, and how my elderly friend had described his father and his brothers competing to bed their maids.

'I *know*,' she said. 'Isn't it terrible?' She laughed again. 'Did you ever hear about So-and-so Shamsher?' she asked, giving a name I didn't recognize. He had been old when she was young and she wasn't young any more, although, as I'd noticed before and was aware now, she was attractive. I said I hadn't heard of him.

'It's a pity you weren't here before,' she said, 'you would have heard so many stories. He thought he was Krishna.'

'You mean he was mad?'

She twirled her glass and smirked. 'Well, what were they called now? Gopis? Krishna had one thousand and eight of them, didn't he? And So-and-so Shamsher, he also wanted to have one thousand and eight.'

'Did he manage it?'

'A very dirty old man,' she said. 'He had his last child when he was eighty-two so she was called Bayassi, which means eighty-two.'

We each took another drink from the servant's tray, and somehow started talking about jewellery. She used to enjoy making it, she said, so I remarked that besides the diamonds in her ears she wasn't wearing any. She leant forward and whispered, 'Yess! But they're worth more than all the rest!'

It must have been an exaggeration, but they were enormous. I felt myself experiencing a growing attraction towards her.

The long relationship between the Ranas and the British left a mark on both parties. Although they espoused conservative Hinduism (and needed to be purified if they touched a European) the Ranas' architecture and their material culture was inspired by Britain. British observers in the nineteenth century complained that the Nepali ruling class was too lazy to walk even a short distance (they rode on the backs of their servants instead), but during the second generation the Ranas acquired something of the British love of playing games, to go with their existing love of drinking. Even, or perhaps especially, after the British left India and the Ranas lost their formal power, they adopted a version of British manners and spoke in an anglicized way.

In 2005 some Ranas and other such types felt let down by the British suspension of military aid that followed the royal coup, and they disliked the diplomatic rhetoric of human rights and democracy, but they still had a social affinity. So it made sense that British embassy functions such as the Queen's Birthday Party were stuffed with socialites denouncing the demand for land reform, and in a country where there's a class war going on that stands for something. Perhaps the association helped both sides see themselves as they liked to, with a little stardust of grandeur and superiority.

I bumped into a Rana, whom I'd met a few times at receptions, on the street outside his house. He was driving out of his gate in his enormous SUV, and he stopped across the pavement when he saw me coming, to run down his window and complain about my articles criticizing the king's human rights record. *'After everything we've done for England, this is how you repay us?'* He was referring to the fact that his ancestors supplied Britain with Gurkhas. He had a big diamond in his ear, too.

In the summer of 2005 I crossed the land border from India into Nepal, after spending a week in Calcutta. I was with three British friends. We'd visited St John's Church, and the Park Street cemetery, and Curzon's Victoria Memorial. At the famous shrine of Kali we were told that the British had banned human sacrifices there. My friend put on an exaggerated accent. '*Have you* seen *what they're doing down at the temple?*' But we spent half our days in a hotel room, drinking and watching cricket on television. For the English, that summer was one of the greatest in the history of the game.

We were in the immigration office at Karkarbhitta, in the very south-eastern corner of Nepal, when shooting started. The officials who were examining our passports parted the curtains and peered outside. 'What was that?' I went into the street, where people were asking the same question. Almost immediately there was a loud explosion behind the police station.

Karkarbhitta was a drowsy little place, with hardly a vehicle on the road. People seemed unsure whether to take cover or stand and stare, but there was nothing to see. For a moment even the police were at a loss. A few of them, with rifles, ran down the road into the trees behind the station.

There was a burst of automatic gunfire, much louder than the original shots. Other policemen commandeered a man with a rickshaw, rushing him out of sight. Everything was quiet now. There was a low, speculative murmur in the street. A cigarette seller packed her basket and got ready to leave. The police reappeared, in a group around the rickshaw. The rickshaw wallah was toiling over the pedals. Lying across his vehicle was a bloody and unconscious member of the armed police. Shouting and waving, they went off down the road, trying to hail a public jeep. Another car sped away, with a bloodied man in the back seat, slumped on the shoulder of a colleague.

Ten minutes after the attack a silent crowd was standing in the street, gazing in the direction of the shooting. They were holding hands, or had their arms around friends' shoulders. Some of them wore odd grins, apparently still feeling the adrenalin of the event. While it was taking place my friends were 200

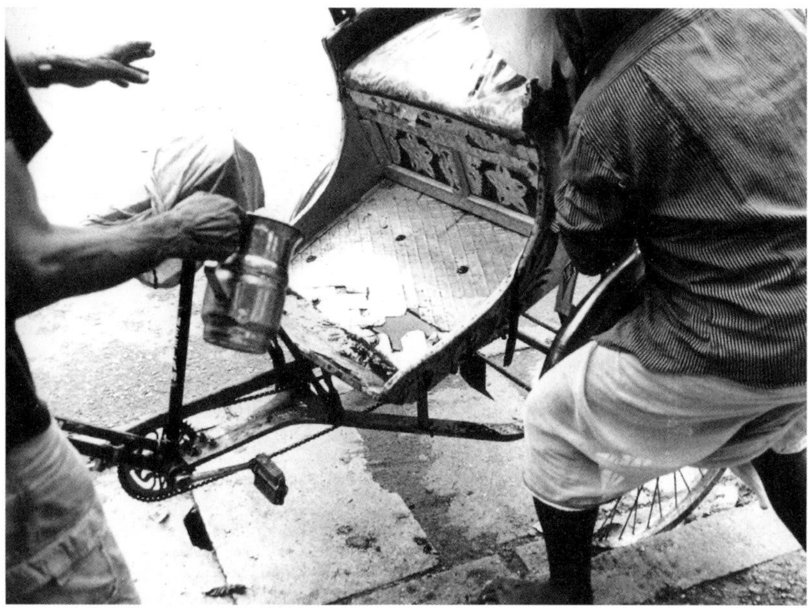

yards from the killing zone, in the immigration office arranging their visas. The commotion didn't distract the officials from extracting a five-hundred-rupee bribe to process their request.

We drove on, leaving the rickshaw wallah rinsing the blood from his rickshaw. The cigarette seller had unpacked her basket again. The attack may have been intended to disrupt a visit by the king to that district that day, because now we found hundreds of soldiers and police slouched by the roadside as we went, providing security. The army base at Itahari was surrounded by barbed wire and high netting. As we drove past it two helicopters rose from the compound and wheeled around. They beat away across the emerald paddy fields and palm trees of the lovely eastern plains. This incident showed something important: whatever the circumstances (and whether through graft or rent seeking), all that the administration is interested in is extracting resources. That's what it's for; that's all it's about.

In the early Shah state control of the land, with the right to collect rents and taxes, was linked to service in the administration and especially the army. The state functioned as a kind of revenue-farming-military complex, which drove the Gorkhalis' imperial expansion through the demand for more land to pay their followers. It was the Ranas, first under Jang Bahadur and then in a series of refinements by his successors, who gradually created a salaried civil administration. In 1910 Chandra Shamsher fixed salaries in cash terms rather than as a share of the harvest (albeit that payment was still often taken in commodities rather than coin).

Exactly what proportion of a peasant's produce was collected in taxes it's not possible to say.[1] Rice-growing land was taxed at between a third and a half of the crop, but there were also three additional annual levies, plus a tax on homesteads. Various other charges, based on caste, ethnicity or occupation, were effectively open-ended. Fines were treated as part of the landlord's income and levied in advance of any law being broken. Peasants were also expected to provision troops and feed visiting grandees. Then there were extensive forced-labour obligations, and the extortionate interest rates of the landlord and the moneylender. Thousands of people fled starvation and indebtedness in the hills to establish the Nepali diasporas in India, Bhutan, and Burma. Meanwhile, the financial surplus from cash crops (including cotton, indigo, opium, sugar cane and cardamom in the hills and tobacco in the plains) was extracted through a system of state trading monopolies. The proceeds helped build the Shamshers' forty palaces and stuff them with European curiosities.

Government servants, soldiers and supporters were paid in land grants known as jagirs, with the right to levy rents, collect taxes, demand unpaid labour and impose fines. Jagirs were formally re-awarded every year, so that then, as now, the enrichment of the governing class was based more on clientage and control of the administration than on any productive activity. (A government job is still colloquially known as a 'jagir'.) There was another form of land holding, known as birta, which was hereditary and tax-free (as far as the landlord was concerned, although not of course for his peasants). By 1950, the last year of Rana rule, one-third of all Nepal's cultivated land was held as birta by members of the ruling family. In these ways most of the nation's wealth accrued to unproductive lords while the peasants were stripped of capital. There was no investment or technological improvement in agriculture. The sole purpose of administration was transferring resources from the ruled to the rulers. Economic stagnation was the consequence, almost the design, of the entire political economy. Meanwhile, education was purposely made unavailable, for fear of awakening a political consciousness inside the country. On the mornings after the Ranas had gathered to gamble, wagons would trundle between their palaces, delivering vast amounts of coin from the losers to the winners.[2]

☀

> 'It is difficult to overlook the fact that the purchase and sale of human beings is prevalent in the hills.'
>
> – Chandra Shamsher Rana, 1925

There are no records to show how often, or how rarely, widow burning was practised in early twentieth-century Kathmandu. It was mostly discouraged by the authorities. Successive editions of the Muluki Ain placed ever-broader restrictions on who would be allowed to mount her husband's pyre – no mothers of teenage boys or infant girls, for example. The law eventually imposed the same penalties as for murder upon anyone who coerced a widow into the flames through force or intoxication – especially if they were her own sons, who stood to inherit her property.

In 1920, despite some opposition, Chandra Shamsher finally abolished suttee altogether. At the Pashupati temple, opposite the burning ghat on the bank of the Bagmati River, he blocked the top of the steps leading down to the 'suttee's gate', through which women had passed to the pyre. The steps are very steep, I noticed, almost like a stone ladder. If a woman had leapt, or been pushed down there, I realized, she'd have been half dead before she reached the fire.

Four years later Chandra proposed another reform. In an English-language booklet, printed in Bombay, he laid out his vision with the wisdom and gravity of a statesman. Like a modern development policy, his style suggests a foreign author, leading from behind. 'Gentlemen,' the anonymous writer had the dictator address his imaginary audience, 'To-day we meet to consider a delicate and difficult question.

'The world progresses and with it there is change, not only in our mode of living … and many things besides but in our domestic arrangements too. Our country and our people have now come much more to the fore than ever before. That alone should be an incentive to retain untarnished our reputation as a brave people, as a just people, as a humane people; in short as the fit progeny of our forefathers, the heroes of a hundred battles, ever the champions of the weak and oppressed … Let us look at it from the point of view of the slaves …'[3]

Over the next fifty pages the pamphlet lays out the case against slavery. There is the historical argument that in most of the world slavery is 'as extinct as the palaeozoic animals'. There is the economic argument, that slaves are less efficient than paid labour ('a Bani [hired] female servant would be found thrice as efficient and industrious as a female slave who, even if plain featured, will pass most of her time in flirting with the men slaves of the household or the neighbourhood'). There is the moral argument, that sending female slaves to the beds of male labourers so that the master can sell her children is tantamount to prostitution. ('If selling slave children, parting them from their mothers at a tender age, is reprehensible, this way of breeding them is more so … Not only that: often the master seduces the girls and then to hide his shame makes them over to others.')

A survey had found that there were 534 slave owners and 1,400 slaves in the Kathmandu Valley (and 51,419 slaves in total around the country). Chandra's government bought and freed them all, at the rate of Rs 120 for a young woman – the most valuable kind. There was a photograph in Kiran's collection of Chandra Shamsher emancipating the slaves. A great throng of men dressed in plain cottons, with white topis on their heads, was gathered at Tundikhel. On the platform Chandra Shamsher and the king were sitting on deckchairs beneath a parasol.

I wondered where all the slave-girls were that day. They weren't in the photograph. And where did the men go home to, when the ceremony was over? The new site that was given for them to live in the plains (called Amlekhganj, meaning 'Freetown') was unhealthy and few settled there.

The policy must have counted for something, but it seems to have been intended mostly for foreign consumption. For lack of alternatives, many slaves remained with their owners. Later editions of the Muluki Ain continued to describe the inheritance and sale of slaves.[4] Anyway, the institution of hereditary debt bondage, amounting to slavery, retained legal force in parts of the countryside at least until 2000, and is carried on in practice today.[5] Young girls are still taken from their indebted parents to work as unpaid maids in the Kathmandu homes of landowning families.

The old woman Dhana Laksmi Shrestha was born in the year the slaves were freed. She contrasted today's permissiveness with the society of her youth.

'Nowadays, the kitchen is open to everyone,' she remarked. 'Before, if you sold meat on an aunsi [new moon] you would be penalized, but now that there is no government nobody penalizes people for selling meat on an aunsi,' she reflected, seemingly apropos of nothing. 'I think I was about ten when I was sitting on my grandmother's lap and my mother was sitting next to me. My mother said, "Let's go to the Bagmati". I wasn't sure what to do because my grandmother wanted me to stay and my mother wanted me to go with her. It was in the year 1990 [AD 1934].'

'That was the year of the earthquake,' I said.

'I had heard – everyone knew – that something was going to happen that day but nobody knew exactly what.'

'How did they know?'

'The astrologers had said. The nine planets were going to fight that day, they were coming towards the same place. The astrologers had said. We were wondering if the entire Valley would be flooded with water,' said Dhana Laksmi. 'So my mother and I went around all the temples and we ended up at Tabahal, where the gatekeeper was my mother's friend, and she said "Panju, what's going to happen today?"

'The panju said, "Anything could happen, I don't know what's going to happen."

'We walked up to Kumbheshwar. There's a small pati where they used to sell meat. I was leaning against it. They sell meat there to this day. My mother's friend came and she also asked, "What's going to happen today?" and my mother said, "*I* don't know. Everyone says something's going to happen ..." and as I was leaning against that pati something pushed me and I went flying!'

As she was sitting in front of me Dhana Laksmi pitched violently forward, with alarming force for such an old woman.

'Then something pulled me ...'

She threw herself backwards as if she'd been shot in the chest.

'... and I went BANG against the pati!

'I said, "Mother, Mother, look!" The whole temple, the top, it swayed down and touched the ground then it went back up again. The whole earth twisted! It felt like it was twisting! The whole temple came all the way down again – then suddenly there was no road. But the pati didn't fall and that's how I survived.

'To go back home there was no road. How to go? What had happened to our house? The house where my grandmother lived had collapsed. And my grandmother had asked me to stay back! Many people died!'

After the earthquake there were mass cremations at Shankamul.

'I thought about the *Mahabharat* and all the people that died, and the river of blood that flowed. People died like that! There were so many dead that all the men could do was carry the bodies and throw them at the cremation ground,' Dhana Laksmi said. 'How many people? How many! In every house one or two. If I had stayed with my grandmother I would have died, but because it was not my time I was pulled away from the scene.

'It was on an aunsi that it happened, so you must not have meat on an aunsi.'

I checked the date in the moon charts. The great earthquake did happen on an aunsi. The deep lakebed clays of the Valley floor were liquefied by the 8.1 magnitude shock. Some people heard a gurgling from the earth, which ran under the city in stormy waves. Houses imploded block by block into heaps of bricks and broken timber. Fountains of dust turned the day black. Tides rose in still ponds. Trees bent like in a hurricane. Within a minute many thousands of people were crushed to death.

On the other side of the river the young Himalaya Shamsher Rana was playing carom with his cousin in a room near where he was born, beside the great hall of the Thapathali Durbar. The first thing he noticed was that the striker did not run straight.

'The ladies were shouting "Ram! Ram!" and we ran outside to see the ground going like this,' he told me, and he waved his arms from side to side. 'Just near there Khadka Shamsher had built his Gul Baitak [a circular palace building] and it collapsed, just collapsed, and there was a cloud of dust like an atom bomb.'

That night Himalaya Shamsher's family camped in one of the palace gardens. Two weeks later they built wooden cottages there. They never moved back into the palace. The garden was divided between his father and his uncle and later it was further divided. Thapathali began to become the neighbourhood of bungalows that it was when I lived there. 'I was so terrified of earthquakes, of being buried alive,' said Himalaya Shamsher, 'that even years later if I felt tremors I would flee the building, even leaving my wife and children inside. When I built the house I have now I made it earthquake-resistant.' That awful January of 1934 the Tundikhel parade ground became a refugee camp for people fleeing the ruins of their homes. They must have been poorly dressed, and everyone agrees that Kathmandu was colder in those days than it is now.

The prime minister, Juddha Shamsher, built the street called New Road (Juddha Road, he called it) through the wreckage of eastern Kathmandu, to open a European boulevard into the Malla durbar square. The new shops that lined New Road had elaborate classical façades and he placed his own statue in the classical plaza at the end, between the earthquake memorial park and the theatre, which later became the first cinema hall,[6] where the Bishal Bazar shopping centre now stands.

It was after the earthquake that residential areas began to spread in earnest beyond the boundries of the old Malla cities. 'A lot of damage was done to the houses in the very tightly packed city, you see,' said Himalaya Shamsher. 'So then they started moving out.'

'To places like Maiti Devi, Naya Bazar, Putalisadak?'

'Yes. And the roads were not there. You needed roads to move. So the roads were constructed by Juddha Shamsher.'

The orientation towards streets instead of squares was a novelty in Kathmandu's planning. The houses along the new roads were built on the traditional scale, using the old structural methods of brick and timber. But they had stucco pediments with cherubs above the windows, string courses and cornices between the floors, and quoins and pilasters at the corners, in imitation of the fashion for European classicism introduced by the palaces of the Ranas.

Someone told me that the early glass windows were glazed with photographic negatives. I imagined how the ghostly images of the rulers, of the festive scenes, of the architectural studies that the early photographers made, would have shifted across the city when the windows were opened. Perhaps they could have projected a ghostly negative image into the room inside, and maybe that did happen sometimes. But it seems that the photographers usually washed their used glass in acid and used it again. The glass negatives I saw didn't fit the size of the panes. Nothing else that guy told me checked out, either. I was reluctantly forced to drop the idea.

Life for most of the Valley's people was still untouched by modern change. The Newar Jyapu farmers, who lived in the cities and tilled the fields outside, paid almost all the rice they grew in rent to their landlords, then exchanged whatever was left for the wheat flour which, mixed with water, salt and turmeric, formed their diet.

They measured their days and seasons by the moon. After a life of ceaseless, gruelling labour, a middle-aged person might one day feel cold, or unusually tired, lie down and die shortly afterwards. The young were threatened by accidents, while tunnelling for the lakebed sediments they needed to fertilize their fields; or they might slice off their fingers 'in the delirium of hard work'.[7] The Jyapus were obliged to clean the homes and wash the clothes of the landlord's family, oil and massage the women, and carry his children on their shoulders when the family made journeys. If a member of the landlord's family died then the tenants would be in attendance, providing their services during the many days of mourning rituals. Despite these obligations, tenants were liable to be thrown off the land on a whim, with no redress.

The extraordinary thing is that despite their hardship and exploitation, oral histories describe a sense of injustice arriving like an epiphany only in the 1940s, when the peasants began to tentatively form their first, semi-political, farmers' associations.[8] A few years later, communist politics would flourish among them. Nepali communism, with its roots in peasant misery, has almost always emphasized class exploitation and 'land to the tiller', eschewed collectivization, and been moderate or ambiguous in its atheism, if it is atheist at all.

Among the elite, the first stirrings of a modern political consciousness had occurred earlier. In the mid-1930s a kind of proto-political party called the Praja Parishad (People's Council) was formed in secret. It managed to make contact with King Tribhuvan, the latest Shah king to be held a virtual prisoner by the Ranas, who was naturally resentful at the royal family's treatment. Another underground group was the ominously named Raktapat Kommittee (Bloodshed Committee), which began sending threatening letters to senior officials. And in 1937 a man named Shukra Raj Shastri was arrested for preaching an egalitarian interpretation of the Bhagavad Gita. This type of subversion had its constituency among members of the leading families, some of whom had been educated in India, including among disenchanted members of the Rana family itself.[9]

In 1940 a letter from the Bloodshed Committee was delivered to at least forty-one important men in Kathmandu. It presented a strange mixture of communism, conservative Hinduism, and blood-curdling threats. 'The people have always remained mute-dumb,' the author observed.

> Now this underground committee will describe in a few words about this Prime Minister who not only cruelly exploits us, but is also noted for his dirty designs, prostitution and above all his incestuous relations with his daughter-in-law ... This country has been experiencing disturbances, diseases and recurrent earthquakes every year since the reign of administration fell into the hands of this sinner ... who captures the beautiful budding Brahman damsels to be his concubines.[10]

Like later oppositional political movements in Nepal, the Bloodshed Committee objected to the service of Gurkha soldiers in foreign armies as being against 'the national honour', as well as on the humanitarian grounds that 'this is the age of the machine-gun ... if the Nepalese troops enter into the battlefield, we will not even be able to locate their bones.' The pamphlet continued in bloodthirsty fashion:

> The relation of this revolutionary Committee is also very intimate with the politburo of Lenin's Party in the Soviet Union. When our president briefed them about the atrocities of the Rana rule in Nepal they could hardly stop shedding tears. Their help is also assured. We have enough friends among us who can bring disaster to thousands, but what we lack is a few revolutionary conspirators ... brothers come and gird up your loins. If we can feed the vultures and the jackals upon his [Prime Minister Juddha Shamsher's] flesh then the valour of their deeds will be sung by Nepalese ever after ...
> Well Wisher
> J.B. Malla
> Permanent Secretary, Bloodshed Committee

The copy of this tract that is preserved in the government archive is the same one that was delivered to the prime minister himself, and perhaps it was in his mind when, the same month, the Praja Parishad used a smuggled duplicating machine to print and distribute leaflets calling for an uprising in Kathmandu. The Parishad members' identities were betrayed and they were arrested. Many of them were Brahmins and could not be executed (they were jailed instead). Three did not have that protection. They were hanged or shot at different locations around the city in January 1941, along with Shukra Raj Shastri, the luckless preacher of the Gita, who was taken from his prison cell to join them.

It is for this enormity that Juddha Shamsher is best remembered. Within days of the executions a blood-soaked sari was draped on his New Road statue. The statue stands there still, but three of the streets that radiate from it have been renamed for the martyrs he made. They are also memorialized by busts on the marble Martyrs' Gate in the middle of the city.

'To be a dictator,' the old roué Baikuntha Shamsher had told me of his ancestors, 'there are some norms of a dictator which have to be done. Which they did.'

After what Juddha did to the martyrs, the focus of anti-Rana activism was ever more firmly in India. A variety of groups were formed by idealistic young exiles, many of whom were also involved in the Indian independence movement. Some of them were the sons of land-owning families, which in the aftermath of the Second World War had seen incomes fall due to a shortage of the Indian coins in which rents were paid in the plains. They were joined by disenchanted Ranas, who had no position on the roll of succession. The opposition in exile was therefore founded on relatively privileged and educated sections of society, who nevertheless lacked access to the massive spoils of the state, which were shared among a very few. Added to them were returning Gurkha soldiers, 200,000 of whom had served abroad during the war and become aware of the modern world. At the end of the 1940s some of those groups coalesced to form the Nepali Congress party, which was modelled on the Indian National

Congress. The Communist Party of Nepal was also formed in India, in Calcutta, in 1949. The first Nepali translation of the *Communist Manifesto* was published at its first meeting.

Baikuntha Shamsher was a small boy growing up in a palace at the time. He recalled a society gripped by the fear that 'the Congress were coming'. 'At one time I have heard it with my own ears, a curse.' he said. '"Let the Congress enter your house!" It was a curse and it was a vile curse, because they were such hated people. I was taught how to use a revolver, which I could hardly hold.'

Meanwhile Himalaya Shamsher, who was older, had been educated in India, and who stood a distant thirty-eighth on the roll of succession, had his sympathies with the other side. He smuggled a Nepali typewriter into Kathmandu on behalf of the revolutionaries.

A strange phenomenon occurred in 1949, which was witnessed by a peasant in the east of the Valley:

> Our grandfathers and grandmothers were engaged in conversation when one of them spotted a strange figure flying diagonally across the sky. Everyone looked up at it. The figure looked like a fish carrying a cross-bar. We, the children of the locality, ran and jumped from terrace to terrace to follow it ... The same year it appeared again in the sky. As it flew over the god shrine people of the older generation were visibly upset. Then someone commented, 'we will have to bear the shit falling on our heads'.[11]

Things started to change quickly after that. In 1950 King Tribhuvan escaped his minders and took refuge in the embassy of recently independent India. India was no friend of the Ranas, who had been allied with the British. Nepali anti-Rana revolutionaries in India had been jailed by the British for also supporting Indian independence. The most notable of the young exiled leaders was the leader of the Nepali Congress, a charismatic writer and intellectual, a Nehruvian socialist and freedom fighter named B.P. Koirala. The government of Jawaharlal Nehru was already allowing the Nepali Congress to build a 'People's Liberation Army', which would invade Nepal and topple the Ranas when King Tribhuvan was allowed to go into exile in India. Another of the flying fish appeared, showering leaflets on Kathmandu. 'The liberation army forces have moved in at nine points in the country to resurrect the people, the nation and the king,' the leaflets declared. 'Their [the Ranas'] days are over now.'[12]

For three months the Congress alternated military gains with reverses along the southern border. The eastern hills – a traditional area of Gurkha recruitment – fell to a peasant uprising, which captured the weapons of government forces (like the Maoists later would) and swept right up to the ramparts of the Kathmandu Valley. Independent India slipped into imperial Britain's old role as kingmaker. Nehru was anxious to have a stable government on his sensitive frontier with China (China having 'liberated' Tibet earlier in 1950). He pressed the Ranas to accept reforms and allow King Tribhuvan to return. At the same time he kept the Congress in check, allowing them only limited scope to conduct their insurgency. (Britain, which now had little say in the matter, continued to support the Ranas, because the Congress party opposed Gurkha recruitment.)

In January 1951 the Ranas accepted the 'Delhi compromise' Nehru offered them. Nehru then handed the deal to the Congress as a fait accompli. In February another aeroplane arrived in Kathmandu, carrying the triumphant King Tribhuvan back to his capital. The century of Rana control over the Shah family and their kingdom was over. 'Hereafter,' King Tribhuwan promised, 'our subjects shall be governed by a democratic constitution to be framed by a constituent assembly elected by the people.'[13] The Congress Party formed a temporary joint administration with the Ranas to prepare for elections. There would be land reform. The ban on foreign visitors was relaxed. The modern age stepped inside and began to unpack its bags.

17

If you set off on an aborted journey you must not return to the same house that day. It was the king who brought that one to my attention, when he left for the airport on a trip that was cancelled and had to spend the night at one of his other palaces. There are many such rules, drawn from ideas of purity and pollution; health and hygiene, especially ayurvedic medicine; and from traditions which (sometimes) vary between castes or communities. They have the force of religion and social obligation.

In ayurveda the body should be a balance of different humours. To preserve the balance a Newar feast includes all of the 'six tastes': sweet, bitter, sour, salty, spicy, and astringent. Everybody understands at least a little about the body's humours, so no one who is competent to look after themselves would eat 'cold' food, such as fruit, when they have a cold, nor give small children cold drinks, which would be unloving and careless. During the winter, sales of Coca-Cola fall off a cliff, and only foreigners drink beer from the fridge. Naturally, childbirth and child rearing have their own extensive category of rules. Eating ice cream while breastfeeding is irresponsible enough to attract public comment.

'Most children die of pneumonia,' it is said. So a nursing mother can drink milk but not eat yogurt, because it is 'sour' (even if sweetened). Eating vegetables is forbidden because they are 'cold' (even when served hot). Eggs are 'hot' but they're forbidden too, because they stop you from healing. Mother and child are confined to the house for months, rubbed daily with mustard oil for weeks, and not allowed to wash for the first ten days after delivery. It takes courage to defy the rules. 'There was a woman in Konti,' I was told, 'who had three daughters and then she had a son. She took the baby all around, to show people that she had a son. The baby died – it was pneumonia, I think.'

I made terrible mistakes. I shovelled food onto my plate from the outside edge of a spoon, with a gesture like a back-handed tennis shot, but spoons are only used that way in death rituals. I picked up a baby with two arms beneath it, like the tines of a forklift, but you only hold dead babies that way! A woman scolded me while I was taking notes in an interview. I had chewed my pen and then put the polluted thing to the paper, and my notebook embodied Saraswati, the goddess of learning.

Social change, and the inconvenience the rules involve, has led to them being relaxed in recent decades (although not to the extent of obviating those mentioned here). And as the rules are gradually abandoned the city's gods desert its people. The body's balance is being destroyed by modern living in concrete houses, and by the pollution of the rivers. Traditional foods have declined and people eat anything, anywhere, giving rise to an epidemic of weakness, fatness and diabetes.

Kathmandu in the mid-twentieth century was an extraordinary relic of a traditional society. In 1951 there were essentially just two classes of people in the city; the enormously wealthy rulers and the mass of poor urban commoners who were farmers or artisans, with a small number of bureaucrats and wealthy traders in between. Now freedom of expression arrived. Social change was on the agenda. There would be land reform! A very few politically conscious people began to flout caste rules, or at least to speak, or boast, of doing so.[1] The king had promised that an elected assembly would write a new constitution.[2] There were political parties, and street protests, which were sometimes disorderly. (At first the revolutionary forces of the Congress party – the People's Liberation Army – were the only ones capable of keeping order in Kathmandu; later they were integrated into the police.)

The beginnings of a modern bureaucracy were hastily established in Singha Durbar, with the help of foreign experts who arrived as soon as the revolution was over, with money, technical advice and development projects. Foreign scholars came to study Nepal's unknown and miraculously preserved history and ethnography. A motorable road connected Kathmandu to the world. Aeroplanes kept landing. Shortly, the very first, pioneering tourists showed up. As the pace of change quickened a pattern emerged that would describe the following decades in a tightening spiral of repetition, but in the beginning the new ways made little impact on most people's lives.

In his 1950s psychodrama of stifling social confinement, *The Window of the House Opposite*, Govinda Bahadur Malla 'Gothale' describes a young woman called Misri from a high-caste Newar family. Misri has taken a month's break from the domestic duties of her husband's house to stay with her parents. The family belongs to a nascent middle class, with electricity, and a few family photographs on the walls of their otherwise traditional home. On the roof, her mother spends all morning doing puja. Her father sits downstairs in his room. In the smoky kitchen her brother's wife sweeps the floor and lights the fire and cooks the rice while two small children cry for her attention. Misri doesn't want to go back to her husband's house, and she can postpone it, but the thought keeps appearing in her head: 'I have a husband. There is my husband's house.'[3] In her agitation she goes from room to room. Eventually, she always finds herself confronted by her bedroom window.

Every day a fashionable 'man about town' comes to visit Misri's neighbour. The two men sit together, joking and playing carom or cards in a room of the house opposite. From the window his smiling eyes search for Misri, sitting at her own window. 'That man is a hoodlum, a trouble maker!' she tells herself. She wants to tell him, 'Who do you think you are, to look at me as if you would gobble me up!'

Her sister-in-law says, 'That man is always looking at this house. He looks as if he's thinking, "What can I get there?"'

But however she resists it, Misri keeps finding herself at the window. The hoodlum in the house opposite keeps seeing her there. He shamelessly beckons her. Misri is breathless with fear.

'Sister-in-law knows!' she thinks, and asks herself, 'But what have I done wrong?'

As the days pass Misri becomes disorientated and frantic. 'Does that hoodlum, that gangster, have the right to keep watching us? He is watching us!' she blurts out to her baffled mother. 'Do you think I'm a whore?' she accuses her sister-in-law, who is terrified that Misri will invent some pretext to punish her.

The hoodlum starts using neighbourhood children to send Misri notes which say, 'I love you. Do you love me or not? Send me your reply.'

Misri's husband has a good job in the bureaucracy. He feels as complacently assured of his wife's love as he does of his mother's, and because no one else has ever loved him he's pathetically grateful for it. He's kind to Misri. Because she must bow to his feet every morning before she can eat, he does not forget to let her do it before he goes to work, so she won't be hungry. But he's weak, and when he lays his head in her lap she sees in his face something pitiable and defeated. Unsatisfied as she is, Misri is relieved when the child servant from her husband's house appears to summon her back from her parents'. She tries to pick a fight with her husband, thinking that his strong emotions will make her feel calm, but he's only puzzled by her attempted provocations.

Again she sees 'that hoodlum' in the street. He has followed her to her husband's house and he's smiling at her, not just with his face but with his whole body. 'He's about to eat me up!' she thinks.

One evening there is a commotion.

> The noise of a demonstration rose in the distance. Gradually the words 'Long live…! Long live …!' were distinguishable. People had come out of the houses into the lane and were asking, 'What's the demonstration about?' … Misri watched from the window, and saw flags and placards going up and down on the main street.

She wonders if the hoodlum, whom she has begun to think of by his real name, which is Hiraman, might have been arrested. She asks her husband, 'Do they arrest the demonstrators and take them away?'

'We have democracy. Why would they arrest them?' her husband answers.

The author, who is concerned about women's status, mentions that Misri has her period, so for five days she can't cook the family's food. Still Hiraman's letters come. She wants to tell him, 'Please don't follow me. Don't give me a bad reputation. Don't push me into hell. What have I done to you?' But she doesn't do anything. Instead, she misses several opportunities to reject him.

Hiraman bribes a servant to show him into the house when no one else is there. He takes Misri by the arm and she feels his hot breath on her cheek. 'You didn't answer my letter,' he says passionately. 'Will you go with me or not?' Misri is terrified that they'll be discovered. 'I'll go! I'll go!' she says. 'Just let go of me!'

Afterwards, when he's gone and she has partly recovered, she's slow to realize that she really did say those words. Over the days that follow the servant continues to cajole Misri. Misri tells her, 'I'll go with him.' She means she'll go with her husband, or so she later decides, but the servant misunderstood. A date is set. Hiraman will wait with his car at the corner. Misri stares at the clothes in her trunk, wondering what to pack. Colourful printed shawls, printed dotted blouses, mercerized dhotis, georgette saris. She slowly combs her hair. Then she allows herself to be led out of the house.

It's a peculiar story. Misri's fatalism, her lack of either resistance or the ability to consciously choose Hiraman, seems astonishing, in fact exasperating, and is tragic. She's stupid and impressionable. (When her sister-in-law observes that a woman's reputation is fragile, and that one can't stop people from gossiping, Misri is surprised: she 'hadn't realized that her sister-in-law had such thoughtful opinions'.) But she is also believable and sympathetically drawn.

Misri's brother Ramesh can be manipulated too, but he articulates the values of an educated young man when he resists his mother's attempt to arrange his marriage. 'Should I consult the astrological signs?' he scoffs. 'I don't care about caste. I don't care about lineage or family … I want an educated beautiful wife who will understand my mind.' Those views would have been radical in the fifties. They would be upsetting to many parents today. Even more than today, the Kathmandu of *The Window of the House Opposite* was a place of stifling conformity. In blind fear of shame, and because she unconsciously wants Hiraman, Misri can't describe the threat she is under to anybody. She experiences a potentially simple situation as a form of unbearable pressure. Nobody is concerned to notice or has the wit to guess what is overwhelming her, or, if they do, their own status is too low for them to count.

Yet despite its portrait of a restricted city, straining, half-mad and confused in its limits and contradictions, the story suggests that the thing that is forbidden is also the thing which is done. And anyway, however conventional its residents were, the Kathmandu of the 1950s was also the city that produced this provocative modern book.

The new democratic politicians of the 1950s were drawn from the tiny educated elite, lacking any popular base.[4] They were anxious for personal advancement, which they sought through patronage, especially royal patronage. They had some policy differences (they had few policies), but they were not amenable to compromise. Conspiracy and betrayal were their tactics. Their parties were divided by factional rivalry and they went through a bewildering series of splits. They resorted to any expedient to pull down the government, and once in power they attempted to suppress their opponents however they could. Between 1951 and 1959 there were ten changes of government in eight years.[5]

King Tribhuwan turned out not to be so attracted to egalitarian reform after all. He alternately patronized rivals to deepen their divisions, until in 1954 he could declare that 'the supreme power in every sphere now rests solely in us.'[6] King Mahendra succeeded his father in 1955. The palace played the conservative and communist political extremes against the moderate Kangressi centre.

An election was finally held in 1959, and to the surprise of many the Congress party, led by the hero of the revolution, the multi-talented B.P. Koirala, won a sweeping majority. Social reform, especially land reform, seemed to be back on the agenda. But there were reports from the countryside of open conflict breaking out between peasants and landlords. Landlords were calling for the king to intervene and restore order. In 1960 King Mahendra did intervene, launching a coup that was the template for his son Gyanendra's coup forty-five years later. Claiming emergency powers, and relying on the loyalty of the army, he arrested B.P. Koirala and his cabinet and threw them in jail, where they remained for many years, killing themselves with cigarettes. Political parties were banned, for undermining national unity. Expression was curtailed. Mahendra's sayings appeared above newspaper editorials and on billboards around town, like his son's did after his coup, demanding discipline, unity and progress.

> A strong and resolute administration is essential for a small country like ours …
>
> – King Mahendra[7]

> Neither is there any limit to terrorism, nor does it respect human values.
>
> – King Gyanendra[8]

So, just under ten years after the Ranas were toppled, the aristocracy returned to power in an absolute monarchy presided over by a Shah king. The Congress party was reduced to launching guerrilla raids from India. They might have had some effect (along with economic pressure), except that China attacked India in 1962 and Delhi needed to make friends with King Mahendra.

The new royal government had an ideology of nationalism, modernization and development, based on a supposedly indigenous form of 'guided democracy' in village councils called panchayats. In reality village power lay with landlords and national power inside the palace.[9] The palace sought to minimize Nepal's ethnic and caste diversity. 'Social harmony' was stressed, under the slogan of 'one language, one costume, one country'. The norms of high-caste Hindus from the hills were constitutionally defined as national traits, and made compulsory by law. According to the demands of national unity, for instance, the German architect Wolfgang Korn couldn't refer to 'Newar architecture' when he published his book *Traditional Architecture of the Kathmandu Valley* in 1976.[10] Teaching or broadcasting in languages besides Nepali (such as Newari in Kathmandu, or Hindi in the plains) was banned.

The Panchayat was a strange time for me to get a feeling for, because the city's state of mind was changing but the radical changes of more recent decades weren't imagined yet. The regime was both traditionalist (in its Gorkhali prejudices) and modern (in its statism). At the beginning of 1962 there were rumours that a devastating earthquake would level Kathmandu. Thousands slept outdoors for weeks, and the temples were crowded with people making offerings. When no earthquake happened the power of the gods was vindicated. The Panchayat constitution was promulgated the same year. Every morning the rising class of bureaucrats, in their national dress of white cotton jodhpurs and tunic, walked or cycled out of the crowded heart of the city and crossed Tundikhel to their offices in Singha Durbar, radically unprepared for the challenges of the future. In the evening they walked or cycled home again, to eat rice served by wives such as Misri and her sister-in-law.

During the 1950s a new suburb began to emerge to the west of the city. The USAID[11] mission had rented for their office a palace belonging to Prince Himalaya, King Mahendra's younger brother. At first, American families adapted apartments inside the palace; then they moved out into houses nearby, which the prince built and rented to them.[12]

They were a pioneering, small community; living by dim, flickering light bulbs and heating their bathwater on a paraffin stove. 'Practically everything had to be imported from abroad,' since almost the only groceries available in the Kathmandu bazaar were 'eggs, chicken, goat meat and rice'. Even the occasional bunch of bananas was brought from India. One American housewife advised a newcomer that there were over 300 household items she should bring; 'We cook and bake and keep house much as our grandmothers and great-grandmothers did,' she wrote.[13]

Social life, by contrast, was a whirl of bridge evenings, embassy parties and formal receptions. There were eight to ten luncheons, teas and dinners to attend in a week, in the estimation of an education expert from Oregon who was resident for a decade through to 1962. 'I used my tuxedo more in the Nepal years than in all the other years of my life,' he wrote.[14] 'This may be pure gossip,' a visiting Indian academic recorded in his diary in May 1960, agog at Kathmandu's cocktail circuit. 'American ladies usually fall for "macho" Rana generals while their male companions seek suitable diversion in the company of their women folk.'[15] It probably was pure gossip, but the observation does seem to show that, since the beginning, the international community has been thrilled by the Nepali social elite.

The modern nation would need schools and a national history. A National Education Planning Commission was established with American money and advice in 1954, to recommend a system that would forge a common Nepali identity.[16] The process was completed after Mahendra's coup. Nepal's history became a parade of Shah kings. ('The stupidest ones they always said were brave,' a friend who went to school in the eighties told me.) Military feats such as the vain, heroic defence of Nalapani at the beginning of the Anglo-Nepal War were celebrated. But previously popular stories involving Gurkhas fighting for the British were dropped, because poor Nepalis spilling their blood for money, in another people's cause, were an embarrassment to a country that was building its modern self on a fable of courage and independence.[17]

By 1958 an elected constituent assembly had fallen off the agenda. Instead, a committee guided by a foreign consultant would draft Nepal's modern democratic constitution. Sir Ivor Jennings was the master of Trinity College, Cambridge and Britain's greatest expert in post-colonial constitution writing. The British Foreign Office and the Kathmandu durbar spent two years attempting to secure his services. When, at length, he accepted the job, his mandate was to produce a charter that would provide political stability.[18] During a stay of a few weeks in Kathmandu he presented drafts to a constitution drafting committee, and was surprised and gladdened at how meekly his Nepali counterparts accepted them. In a confidential note to the Foreign Office, Jennings observed that a democratic constitution in Nepal meant a document 'designed to vest power in the middle class, usually English-speaking oligarchy which was to pay attention to the needs of the hoi polloi because they have the vote … The difficulty in Nepal was to find the oligarchy'.[19] Instead he identified the Shah monarchy as the basis of stability, and designed an ostensibly Westminster-style system in which all authority and discretion resided finally in the king, not the cabinet. Mahendra made his coup in 1960, and elements of Jennings' 1959 constitution would resurface in the monarchist constitution of 1962 (as well as the multi-party constitution of 1990).

Nepal's stance as a non-aligned country, on the Himalayan frontier of Mao's China, ensured a ready supply of aid from Washington, Delhi, Moscow and Beijing. The early American aid work was part of a strategy to contain communism.[20] Jennings' mission was also a piece of cold war diplomacy. King Mahendra was adept at playing both sides for cash, and after his coup the West was pleased to accept his rule. Britain was among the first to endorse it; the British defence secretary (presumably anxious to secure the supply of Gurkhas) arrived in Kathmandu just one month later. Queen Elizabeth II paid a state visit in 1961, the same year that British financial assistance began.[21]

My chowk is on a narrow street.
What do I lack? Everything is here.

There was a communist poet lurching through the courtyards and passages of the old town. He'd discovered radical politics while studying in India in the early fifties. He and his friends wore long hair and unusual clothes. He went about drinking heavily and smoking, frequenting expensive bars and cheap dives; staying at friends' houses in the narrow lanes and courtyards; and having sexual affairs, although he already had a wife and children. His father was a millionaire. It occurred to me that as a young man in the late fifties Bhupi Sherchan might have seemed a bit like the hoodlum Hiraman in *The Window of the House Opposite*. The striking, pessimistic images of his anthology *A Blind Man in a Revolving Chair* still speak strongly to a broad public more than twenty years after he drank himself to

death. Someone showed me his poetry not long after I arrived in Kathmandu and I never forgot one bleak phrase in particular:

It's a cold ashtray,
This valley of four passes.[22]

Bhupi Sherchan was born into an important merchant family in the western mountains in 1935. His horoscope foretold that he would cause the death of his parents, so he was nursed outside the family home, until another eminent astrologer gave a second opinion. According to this new interpretation the child was destined to harm someone else. So Bhupi came home, but his mother died when he was five and the curse was remembered. Later in life Sherchan claimed that he became a poet because he was raised without affection.

In the late fifties, when the anti-Rana revolution was falling apart, Sherchan frequented a house in Kathmandu that was reached through a series of narrow passages, where his communist friends felt safe because they would be warned if the police approached. They called it the Red Fort. When I first read the poem he wrote about it I didn't know it was the artefact of a radical meeting place, I only read it as an indictment, and also a picturesque description, of the city's jaded, decaying state.

My chowk is in a narrow street.
What do I lack? Everything is here.
There are god-made men
And man-made gods,
Here there's a home for them both,
But both are dejected, both are without hope:
The men because they are bitten
By fleas all night, by rupees all day,
The gods because no-one worships them here,
No-one bows down at their feet.
So here in my chowk,
Men and gods are cursing each other,
Banging their heads together.

My chowk is on a narrow street.
What do I lack? Everything is here.[23]

The slums of the medieval city were a maze of slimy passages, derelict houses and green drains. Beautifully carved timbers were rotting away. The symmetry of the old buildings was dissolving into decay and random rebuilding. Inside the dark rooms a framed photograph, or the picture of a god, might hang from a nail in a beam. Radios played Hindu hymns and sentimental film songs. Brick walls were dressed with tattered Hindi film posters.[24] The city was gripped by false shortages and cartels. Was someone manipulating the price of sugar? Were people high up in the government conspiring to supply adulterated ghee? Ancient sculptures in the temples were going missing in the night.

In a society like Panchayat Kathmandu, where expression is curtailed, it's obvious that people aren't telling the truth. What they mean must be different from what they appear to have said. Is praise ironic? Does silence indicate dissent? By raising a possibility only to dismiss it, has the king just signalled what is really

on his mind? People's motives are a matter of conjecture; their actions are clearly at odds with their words. Something must explain the gap between the statistics in the newspaper and the hungry farmers, between the rhetoric of development and the enduring squalor, and between the official engagements on the radio news and the hole in the shrine where the god used to be. Rumours circulated. The rumours showed what people were prepared to believe, what offended them, and what they couldn't accept. So the royal family was said to be making money where legal impunity offered monopoly profits: in drug trafficking and art theft. Bhupi Sherchan wrote in a poem that is still quoted every day, up to and beyond breaking point:

So this is a land of hearsay and rumour,
A country standing on hearsay and rumour,
A country that has risen up on hearsay and rumour,
This is a land of hearsay and rumour.[25]

The worse things became, the more rumours gained credence.

☀

Following an international competition, King Mahendra commissioned an American architect to build a modern palace. The pagoda roof of the throne room rises on a bold pink tower pierced by a cathedral window above a blank brick façade. With interior details by Asprey of London (but the rooms named after the districts of the kingdom), an emergency suite in the basement, an operating theatre, and four staircases in the private quarters alone (so the king could slide discreetly and securely around the place), it represented a futuristic national vision of sorts. Construction began in 1964, after waiting almost a year for an auspicious date to lay the foundation. A Rana palace was pulled down and the bricks were re-used in the Shah replacement. Where the old palace had stood a broad new avenue called Durbar Marg was opened, on the axis of the new Narayanhiti Palace gates.

Today Durbar Marg is lined with five-star hotels, fast-food chains, boutiques and at least two Authorized Apple Resellers.[26] King Mahendra's statue guards the entrance. Back in the fifties, when it all began, 'money was still considered the latest innovation.'[27] The shift from the use of agricultural produce to coins in the payment of taxes, rents, and salaries was still in progress. The foreign donor agencies brought more cash into the city. The schoolteachers and the rapidly multiplying bureaucrats earned money.[28] So did the people who served the tourists. Gradually new categories of clerical staff and professionals emerged to work in the government offices, development organizations and travel agencies. Cash, and salaried employment, created a middle class for the first time.

Caste is not the same as class. (High-caste people are often poor, and low-caste people may occasionally be rich.) But the two systems are entwined, and the class system, which would increasingly shape Kathmandu in the later twentieth century, had its roots in the old caste society. Among Newars, members of the higher castes such as Shrestha were among the first to make the shift from the use of Newari to the Nepali language, giving themselves access to advancement in Panchayat Nepal. In the countryside, land was controlled by the rulers and their high-caste servants and functionaries. Groups with lower ritual status were often beholden to their landlords: they weren't only treated in degrading ways from a ritual point of view; in class terms they were exploited, indebted, and powerless. Landowning and priestly families gained access to education and moved to the city. Within a generation, the sons and daughters of the families that governed the countryside were entering a rising urban middle class. The grandchildren of the serfs were more likely to become Maoist rebels; or else factory workers, labourers, and pump attendants in East Asian factories, Arabian building sites, and gas stations.

As class joined caste as a moral and economic force in the city, status would be established by your new house, your ownership of a motorcycle, your choice of school for your children, and your ability to speak English. Land prices quadrupled between the mid-sixties and mid-seventies. Middle-class suburbs spread east, to create New Baneshwar. To the north, on land that belonged to a branch of the Rana family, the wealthy district of Maharajganj was built. In 1970 it was said that a new house was going up every day. The suburbs were spreading as far as Hadigaon, where Licchavi archaeology was dug up from the new foundations and discarded. By the 1980s intellectuals were lamenting a 'crisis of values'.[29]

18

There is a 1969 film called *Les Chemins de Katmandou*, released in English as *The Pleasure Pit*. In it (apparently) a French drifter called Olivier, disgusted by the bourgeois values of home, heads east and falls in love with an English flower-child called Jane (played by Jane Birkin), whom he meets under a tree on the road to Kathmandu. Once they arrive, in a milieu of drugs and free love, Olivier raises cash by pretending to be an anthropologist while stealing art from temples. He enters a scheme with an older rogue called Ted (played by Serge Gainsbourg) to saw off a particularly precious wooden Buddha's head and split the profits. It all unravels when Olivier realizes that Ted has set him up to get his hands on Jane. He tosses the severed head in the fire just as the police arrive, and Jane (hallucinating on heroin) falls to her death from a window. The film seems to be an interesting document, but it's unobtainable. I wrote to Jane Birkin's agent and he couldn't find it either.

Of all the foreigners who came to Kathmandu, the hippies made the greatest impression on the minds of their own people. They remain the favourite cliché of newspaper foreign editors grappling to locate the significance of the place, but, although they exalted in creativity the freaks seem to have left almost no trace of themselves in the city. Some were escaping the draft, others (especially the heroin addicts) had already been to Vietnam. Some were fleeing the reaction against the counterculture that was gathering in the West; still others (like my parents, who sadly didn't make it any closer than Benares) were on holiday, before going home to begin their careers. Kathmandu was cleaner and cooler than India, without the hassle and the sexual harassment. Drugs were legal, the locals seemed tolerant, and the foreigners were grateful to be left alone. They formed insular communities. The men greatly outnumbered the women, who were generally in relationships, so the free love thing may have been largely hypothetical.[1] They smoked a prodigious amount of dope.

The psychedelic theorist Michael Hollingshead flew in on 16 July 1969.[2] He was thirty-eight years old, on his first visit to Asia, carrying a typewriter, a thousand dollars, and a few hundred trips of California sunshine acid. He attached significance to the fact that he touched down on the same day the Apollo 11 moon rocket blasted off from Florida.

His romantic notions were killed off instantly, by the stifling taxi ride from the airport, and he was ready to turn tail for an air-cooled Manhattan bar before he reached his hotel. There he 'took a bath, changed into a Tibetan shirt and Indian *dhoti* – a sort of bin cloth you wrap around yourself – smoked a couple of chillums of good Afghani dope; and nearly fainted in [a] dream of dreams.' From his window he could see the paddy fields, and, rising in the distance, the peaks of the snowy range. 'The spell of the Himalayas was upon me … I had traveled halfway across the world to find in Kathmandu what I sought in vain throughout my wanderings in the West.' It was still as hot as hell outside but he set forth anyway to score some local hash, into 'the maze of dusty streets and alleyways, all somewhat reminiscent of the imaginary Baghdad of *The Arabian Nights* … There were temples and delicate *stupas*, huge sculptured statues, beautifully proportioned by some anonymous race of master artists.'

Hollingshead was briefly diverted by dreamy reflections on a stone Vishnu, but he still had to buy some dope, and he wanted to get rid of his shoes. Someone had recommended a particular teashop, so he went there. It was 'dustbin dirty and smelling of cow shit and urine …'

> There was pop music on twin speakers, very loud, and … perhaps fifteen young Westerners, silent, smoking chillums, and oblivious. They were dressed in a gay medley of Indian, Tibetan and Nepalese costumes, bedecked with beads and

> beards. One of them looked up, smiled, and handed me a chillum, which I smoked. The effect was instantaneous – I almost passed out, and had to sit down. I don't know how long I remained seated at the table, perhaps an hour, perhaps two.

From time to time the proprietor came over to ask Hollingshead if he wanted a cup of tea or a bowl of porridge. The most he could do was shake his head. Eventually he was able to stand and buy a tola of hashish. In the morning he telephoned the palace. He had a connection with the crown prince's private secretary, whom he'd met in Cambridge, Massachusetts, the previous year, while the prince was at Harvard. Hollingshead needed some help to obtain a one-year visa. He also intended to redouble his efforts, begun in Cambridge, to interest the Nepali monarchy in the hippie project. Perhaps the crown prince would be the patron of a new foundation? And he wanted to launch a poetry magazine, entitled *FLOW*, and for that he would need a licence from the government.

For the following year Hollingshead pursued radical interior experiences. He attained 'radiant visions' in 'charmed circles' of silent, stoned Westerners. ('It was considered a "downer" – bad form – to use words, but communication was no less intense for all that.') At the 'Bakery Ashram' near Swayambhu, where the hippies had their 'five-feet Sony speakers' turned up so loud that 'it was like sitting on stage with the Stones', the 'sound of the music eclipsed all cognitive function' and he was plunged into a river: 'hours – maybe even days – passed in an instant. Time ceased to exist … and it was with this insight that I was born into a new world.'

The local attitude to the hippies was more ambivalent than one might expect. They were filthy for sure, but they were mostly peaceful, and they had an admirable simplicity and freedom of lifestyle. Some people made reference to Hindu sadhus in order to make sense of the holy tourists. It was hard to understand why they took photographs of meaningless things, such as children playing or chillies drying. People watched their strange antics with amusement: the way they behaved with money, the clothes they wore, the way they played music and sang.

The hippies also caused problems: by pretending they'd had things stolen so they could make insurance claims; by stealing things themselves; by overdosing and dying in their rooms. They made public displays of affection at a time when Nepali women didn't show an ankle, and when young husbands and wives were too shy to appear together in the street. They stayed out late, although Newars in those days were still too afraid of ghosts to leave their homes after dark. Nepalis weren't as tolerant as the hippies supposed. Old people muttered Newari curses as they passed. When the hippies lay in the street all night, chanting and smoking and playing music, people threw water on them, like they throw water on a barking street dog.

'Perhaps the thing that disturbed local people the most,' Michael Hollingshead reckoned, 'was that, on average, one girl a month would flip out on acid and insist on walking through the centre of the city completely naked. I think the Nepalese were terribly shocked by this, for often the girl would be extremely beautiful.

'Throwing off your clothes is an act of liberation,' according to Hollingshead, 'or so someone once told the young Californian girl whom I saw briefly just before she was put on the plane to India.' In fact things could get a bit dicey for Hollingshead himself, because 'although I was not held directly responsible in the case of the American girl, it had not escaped the notice of the authorities that I was somehow involved with the LSD-cult, as they called it. At first it had seemed innocent enough … but this thing about girls taking off their clothes every now and then had them worried.' The worst that could happen would be for Mahendra to stumble into such a spectacle, 'for the king had a habit of cruising the streets at odd hours behind the wheel of his Ferrari'.

To get his publishing licence Hollingshead must see the prime minister. He bought in the bazaar what he was assured to be an

example of Nepali dress, suitable for a formal occasion: a pair of silver jodhpurs and some sort of long coat. He spent the night nervously preparing, and took a taxi to Singha Durbar in the morning. A companion guided him through the maze of corridors to a pair of huge mahogany doors with shining brass handles.

> The Prime Minister sat at a desk at the far end of a palatial room. He was wearing a white open-necked shirt with the sleeves rolled up. When he stood up to greet us, I noticed that he was wearing ordinary Western-style navy blue trousers and a belt ... By the time we reached his desk he was almost uncontrollably shaking with suppressed laughter ... Tears streamed down the Prime Minister's face as he took the form ... He hardly glanced at it, and signing it with a flourish, managed to say between giggles, 'I hope you don't write anything bad about Nepal'.

Only one task remained. Hollingshead descended to the basements where, in a cell-like room stacked with bundles and envelopes, a short-sighted man – the Chief Censor – removed his

wire spectacles to examine the document with a magnifying glass before he affixed his stamp.

Bhupi Sherchan wrote:

Her brassiere's baskets uplifting the stale fruits of her youth,
A flower-baby hippy walks down New Road,
In the arms of her prince, engrossed in a 'trip',
Half-naked in a saffron blouse,
Fixing every eye on New Road to her navel,
And the young men round the pipal tree
Stand thinking lewd thoughts deep inside.[3]

His Kathmandu was not a place of freedom, or intoxicating cultural exotica. It was disillusionment and suppressed sexual turmoil, boredom and petty squalor; where the sun always set in an empty raksi glass; where the chowks were steeped in hunger; where his wife was always serving satire on his plate; and if you dug down and looked, you'd find nothing. The hopes of the revolution, the almost holy sacrifice of the martyrs Juddha Shamsher had made, had been betrayed, and to scrape a living mothers' sons fought in foreign armies.

The newspapers (clucking like egg-laying hens, as Sherchan thought) were curious about the hippies (even commissioning a strange, rambling article from Hollingshead), and also dismayed:

> In this confused anatomy of Kathmandu's Hindu society run arteries of alien blood which provoke the prodigal Hindu youth to dress tighter and tighter, wear shorter and shorter skirt, dance to wilder and wilder beats of the brass, and drink more and more exotic cocktails. The transistor-carrying, picnic-minded, twist-obsessed, Hollywood-sinister gangs of Kathmandu's youth eat a crazy salad in expensive restaurants and every midnight fly past the dark alleys of Kathmandu at a record speed ... every two patrician and priestly Hindu families breed a dozen hippies who swing to the twang of the beat melody.[4]

A small cohort of city boys (and perhaps as few as one or two girls) came to Freak Street for Frank Zappa and Pink Floyd, blue jeans, sunglasses and guitars. The foreigners, who thought they'd shed their trappings, were the bearers of global youth culture. The Nepali kids traded their cotton pyjamas, and were even prepared to pay several hundred rupees for a pair of Levis. So both sides had something the other wanted, and in this way Kathmandu participated in a moment that swept the world from Tokyo to San Francisco.

Hollingshead's notion to make the crown prince hip didn't fly. After he became king in 1972 Birendra showed what he'd learnt at Harvard, by trying to clean up Nepal's tourism brand. With American encouragement, dope was banned. The government tightened the visa rules and kicked a bunch of hippies out when the city was scrubbed down for the coronation in 1975. Anyway, the age of the Boeing 747 had arrived, and the new generation of 'adventure tourists' had more money and less time. They weren't like the hippies, and they didn't like them either.

A new tourist district began to develop at Thamel, on the northern edge of the city, and Freak Street went into decline.[5] I thought the freaks' only legacy was a type of Kathmandu man, now entering old age, with a taste for the blues and psychedelic rock. But actually Kathmandu is a rock music town. Standing on any street in Thamel at the weekend you can hear three bands at once; mostly playing for their friends, since foreigners aren't much attracted by Hendrix and Janis Joplin covers now. You could trace the musical ancestry, through the older players whom the young ones venerate, to the kids who hung out with the hippies.[6] Now there's an annual jazz festival with international acts, a blues festival, a death metal festival, and a black music festival called Black History Month. At the end of the night when the crowd stands up it's for a local band playing blues rock.

19

> I have been asked what could there be to interest us in Nepal, and I replied: whenever there is one man, only one, there we are too; and where there is a memory of the past there we shall find fresh forms of the same illusions, fresh evidence, different but not discordant, of the basic patterns of the human spirit.
>
> – Giuseppe Tucci, *Nepal: The Discovery of the Malla* (1962)

I thought that tracking down the *Physical Development Plan for the Kathmandu Valley*, published by His Majesty's Government in 1969, would be an important part of my research; not so much for its record of Kathmandu's physical development, but to see the changing spirit that governed it. I found that massive hardback volume, too big to be allowed on a photocopier, in the British Library.

The frontispiece showed King Mahendra, poring over papers at his desk. It was the first such development plan in the country, apparently; assessing the pressures of population, land use and transport, which were 'certain to become more serious and complex in the future'. There were several pages of jargon that seemed to say nothing at all; whole paragraphs enlarging on the meaning of the title, or the desirability of the optimum allocation of resources. I read:

> Solutions proposed by the Plan take the form of spatially allocated sectoral programmes and projects (circulation and utilities, public services and institutions, production and employment, tourism and recreation, etc.) as well as

PRESENT TREND:
Fingers of a central urban octopus growing to endanger agricultural land and historic settlements

cross-sectoral programmes and policies (population distribution, land use, and urbanisation and housing). These then, form the short term and long term components of the comprehensive physical development plan and are key factors defining the optimum combination of coordinated and integrated socio-economic activities which is so vital to the efficient utilisation of the Valley's scarce resources.[1]

The *Plan* lamented the lack of active cooperation (including an almost complete lack of data) that its authors felt from the government.[2] Nevertheless, they offered forty pages of recommendations, which must have sounded pretty good:

– 'A more direct link to the Tarai via the Bagmati gorge'.
– 'The densely populated core areas must be controlled to inhibit further overcrowding and deterioration of their environmental quality.'
– 'Urban power supplies must be normalised and the increase in demand anticipated and provided for.'
– 'Sewerage systems are urgently needed …'
– 'The location and design of houses should be improved … making better use of and provision for natural elements such as sun, wind and rain.'
– '… bring about the harmonisation of new construction with traditional styles and materials.'[3]

And so on, much of it is so vague as to be almost meaningless. Very little of this was ever done. The point, to me, wasn't that the donors and experts couldn't save Kathmandu from its modern environmental disaster; from the overcrowding, the planning failures, the power and water shortages, the shit in the river and the destruction of the historic city. How could they? But the *Plan* was not, as it claimed, quite the first plan for Kathmandu. By one count it was the second of eight,[4] and that's not counting any scheme devised after 1997, nor numberless other documents promising better water supplies, garbage disposal, public transport, traffic management, heritage conservation, sewage treatment, or (the latest thing) earthquake preparedness. Each rotation of experts relived the illusions of its predecessors. Failures weren't accounted for. Broken promises were repeated, perhaps unwittingly. The ambitious proposals, the dubious statistics and constructively upbeat internal evaluations all served to keep the money-go-round of consultancies, conferences and workshops spinning. Few of them are remembered. Most aren't worth a thing. If anything, rather, the aid economy, of unproductive elite employment and booming land values, helped to make Kathmandu what it is today.[5]

Six years after the *Physical Development Plan for the Kathmandu Valley* appeared, the United Nations and His Majesty's Government jointly published a follow-up. Kathmandu in 1975 was still 'a refuge of beauty and spiritual repose'. To keep it that way would require action across 'the whole spectrum of physical, social and economic planning'[6] because 'the capital already serves as the major growth pole in its own development corridor'.[7] That didn't happen either, so *Kathmandu Valley, the Preservation of Physical Environment and Cultural Heritage: A Protective Inventory* stands today as a precious and moving record of what's been lost. Photographs show the old city centres largely without modern buildings. Country temples were surrounded by lovely rice fields, with a sandy track snaking away to the next village. There was a pair of stone lions; some fine wood carving in a group of buildings which dated from the eighteenth century; the cast metal statue of a mother goddess, who was visited by a procession of tantric Buddhists on the second day of each new year: 'The site is to be surrounded by a protecting greenbelt, and its informal approach path ... by a traditional wooden bridge is to be seen as part of the whole assemblage,' the *Inventory* decided, and moved on.[8] There were ancient sculptures in shrines everywhere; forest sanctuaries, pools and fountains; sacred caves and hilltops; stone steps leading down to a stream; wonderful places I never knew existed, which their names identify as a shit-hole by the Ring Road; a filthy bus park; a slum; a trash-strewn market place; a sewage-filled canal; an exhaust-blackened concrete mess.

When I was trying to understand the myths and vamshavalis I sometimes went to Theodore Riccardi Jnr, Emeritus Professor of Indology at Columbia University, Professor Riccardi was getting old, with a white beard and white hair, in a sprawling bungalow on the way to Swayambhu. He first came to the city as a researcher in 1965.

This time I told him I was interested in the early foreigners, who came in the decades after the place opened up; in what they found, and in their role in things; the scholars and the foreign officials. 'I'm thinking of steering clear of the hippies, more or less,' I told him.

'I know how you feel,' he said.

I asked him to describe the diplomats and foreign experts who arrived to help the place develop and Professor Riccardi hunched forward in his seat, then leant back and looked at a corner of the ceiling. 'You know, you don't realize it until later,' he said. 'The atmosphere of this country, politically, during the Panchayat, was a disaster. No one said what was really true. If you said something that was off-colour politically, like "King Mahendra should have his head examined", you'd get fearful giggles, nervous twittering, and, "My, my, but you're pretty radical, don't say such things". It was a time of cowardice.' This was a description of the foreigners. Then he compared Mahendra's rule and ideology to the strong men of the Arab world, and wondered how these rulers were able to stay in power for so long, stealing everything they could lay their hands on. 'It's almost a definable stage in history, the strong man,' he said.

I said, 'Sometimes people think of the Panchayat as having a developmentalist ideology that was partly sincere. There were these plans, roads were built, change happened. Mahendra sat at his desk with the *Development Plan for the Kathmandu Valley*, full of coloured maps, produced by Western experts.'

'This was what the Westerners wanted,' said the professor. 'This was prepared with malice, *filled* with malice, to take as much money out of the international till as it could. That may be an extreme statement but I believe it.'

'*The Kathmandu Valley Development Plan*?' I was a little surprised. It hadn't seemed so dramatic.

'Not *that*,' he said. 'But all the stuff on Mahendra reading this, Mahendra reading that. And all these blueprints for the future being handed to him, or handed to somebody. This was all a way of making the West think that Nepal, or countries like Nepal, would do what they wanted them to do.'

'You think it's as consciously cynical as that?'

'Yeah, I do. It was probably the need of the international community to sponsor development and it was their duty to take it. The deceit comes in that they were deceitful with each other. If you look at this place from the point of view of what it was thirty to forty years ago, except in one or two important fields, the place is a disaster. The Panchayat did nothing for this country. The Panchayat was a fraud. The programme was so … so … what shall we say? *Inelegant*. So clearly meant to keep power in the hands of those who already had it, and the most outrageous thing is that from the time of the victory of Prithvi Narayan Shah over this country to King Mahendra the government did nothing, nothing, to change the lives of these people. Nothing!'

He'd been speaking in a normal voice, but now more quietly he said, 'I think the experience of my first five years here was a profound sense of difference, difference from everything else that I had known. I was affected from the very beginning by the feeling that development, *as I saw it*, at that time, wouldn't lead this country to the best place, and I think that's been borne out. We love the motorcycles maybe, or we don't love the motorcycles. But this could have been done better. It wasn't. It's a failure.'

I wondered, given the unprepared state in which Nepal entered the modern world, could it really have been done better?

'I'll put it another way,' he said. 'Where were these aid givers coming from? What the hell did they know about this place when they got here? *Nothing*. They could speak *not one word* of the language. They thought that they were right on everything. I don't know if there's a real critique anywhere of what's wrong with this.'[9]

I'd been thinking about critiques of the aid business too. I said, 'The difficulty is that anyone who's in a position to write one is already on the gravy train.'

'That's right,' he said.

We both warmed to the subject of ignorance, failure and dishonesty in the development sector. I'd just written an article on a current, two-hundred-million-dollar case in point.[10] The professor went to another room and brought out a file of typewritten sheets, which was a diary he'd kept in the nineties. We'd begun to refer to development aid in general, and I think he felt that the passages he read aloud applied somewhat to the sixties as well as to the nineties, and the present day.

> Like their colonial predecessors the new colonial managers work and live almost totally apart from the people they are supposed to help. Their only contact with the poor is through their domestic servants although in many instances even these are hired through local contractors. Otherwise they meet almost solely with the English-speaking elite of the country … no matter how different the local elites are from the foreign bureaucracy they unconsciously emulate one another and take on each other's sympathies.

'Well, this goes without saying,' he interrupted himself, and flicked on through the pages. He came to a meeting with an ambassador.

> We talk, or rather she asks questions and we answer the way people usually answer ambassadors, the way one answers an elementary school principal. The ambassador turns to me. I can tell by the way she stares at me that she is preparing a question suitable for an academic. 'One of the things that bothers my staff,' she begins, 'is all the sacrifices. My people are really offended by the killing of animals …'

Then he received another visitor, so I never heard what the great Sanskritist said to that.

☀

After Bendall and Lévi, historical studies in Kathmandu fell dormant. The next steps were taken only after the end of the Rana regime, when a new generation of foreign researchers arrived. Kathmandu was confusing. Vast amounts of evidence needed to be skimmed and sifted, but it wasn't clear what the scholars should be looking for. Sitting on his sofa, in his airy, bare sitting room, Professor Riccardi tried to summon the feeling of those times.

'Being one of the first people working on this stuff … I think back to how confused you were, or how confused you could become. I think everybody was looking for keys. What had really gone on here in the past? It looked very different from anything else. The other thing was the materials. Coins were for sale, everything was for sale. You could buy silver coins for two or three rupees a piece. Beautiful things. And you could justify buying them on the grounds that you could use them to make chronologies. So everything was open.'

Priceless documents were floating around. One evening, in the year he arrived, a man named Basnyet offered to sell Riccardi what was purportedly the original manuscript of Prithvi Narayan Shah's deathbed testament, the *Dibya Upadesh*. He declined to buy it. He didn't want the responsibility of owning something like that.

'You are walking along a dark street and someone who has said he wants to meet you *meets you*, and says that he has a copy of the *Dibya Upadesh* that he wants to sell for thirty-two hundred rupees. That's a long sentence,' he said. 'And what do you do? Do you buy it, or do you forget about it? I chose in general not to *buy* things. I didn't want to take it out. I didn't want to own it. I couldn't protect the art, I could only take it. There were more people like me than like the others.

'It wasn't history, but anthropology, that became the glamour science,' Riccardi said. 'They were every two feet for a while in the 1970s; there was another anthropologist coming in to study another tribe, just discovered, or another caste formation, just discovered, or whatever.' A unique and intricate society's inevitable obliteration lent drama to anthropology and gave it moral purpose. History was shrouded in a kind of obscurantism, entrenched by the Sanskrit language, which few foreigners knew and which remained a priestly mystery among Nepalis. What was significant in the past appeared superficially identical to what was not.

Among the historians was the blind old man Baburam Acharya, 'an old-fashioned but accurate scholar', who revered the achievements of the great king Prithvi Narayan Shah. There was the Italian Luciano Petech, who produced a chronology of the confusing transitional period and the early Malla kings using the colophons of manuscripts. 'Petech was a Western scholar of the best kind, whatever you think of Western scholarship,' Professor Riccardi said. 'Petech knew Chinese, Japanese, he could read French, German this goes without saying. He knew some Arabic, he knew some Hebrew ...' There was a circle of Sanskritists who published a journal called *Purnima*, meaning 'full moon'. Their mission was to 'purify' Nepali history. ('When you hear the word purify,' said Professor Riccardi, 'you'd better look out.') There was Father Ludwig Stiller, the prickly historian of the Ranas and Shahs ('a Jesuit, so something's got to give'); and there was the great economic historian Mahesh Chandra Regmi. Professor Riccardi knew them and he offered entertaining assessments.

He remembered a man who sat in one of the city's busiest bazaars, the area called Ason Tol. 'The house is still there, I think, with the frieze of soldiers.' (I said I knew it.) 'Next to that house is a step. A little, a short man used to sit there with a box and he had books like, what's it called, *itihas prakash ma samdhipatra,* "Documents with relation to the history of Nepal". It is one of my favourites. It's a huge book, this thick,' the professor gestured with his fingers, 'with all kinds of documents. Copper plate inscriptions, gold-plate inscriptions, put together by the Yogi Naraharinath, who was a yogi who lived at Pashupati.

'The yogi loved Nepalese history and supplied everything he found in different temples as he walked, or ran, through the country. What you get when you get that book is probably close to one hundred and fifty, maybe more, documents. Nobody has even put them in alphabetical order, I think.

'Mahesh Chandra Regmi made a point, well taken,' the professor said, turning to Nepal's great economic historian. 'One time we were talking and he said, "You know, if you want to publish documents I can publish sixty thousand documents that I have in my library. But", he said, "I'm not interested in that. I'm interested in what you do when you read those documents, and you make generalizations and you create history." Mahesh Chandra's point was: you have to do the next step yourself. Otherwise, it's what? It's a little man sitting on a step in Ason Tol with a big thick book in his hands.'

I said, a bit stupidly, 'You know, when the Europeans invented the encyclopaedia it said something about European thought. This project of putting everything in alphabetical order. I suppose it says something about Nepali thought that this guy did what he did?'

Professor Riccardi reflected on the yogi. 'Well, this guy was a very attractive character in his way. He was the fastest thing on two feet. He was very sincere about his conservative Hinduism. He was a politician, he ran for office.[11] There may not be very much to *say* about the yogi because he was very elusive, *and I have no idea what he knew*.'[12]

So much art went missing from Kathmandu between the 1950s and 1980s that it seemed nothing would be left. The treasure was just lying around in all the holy places. It had rarely been stolen or traded in before. People were pious. There had been no market, so at first there were no laws governing antiquities. The art trade got started after the road to India opened. I heard about a Swiss woman and (separately) an American aid official who simply drove truckloads of art-works to the border during the fities, before anyone in Nepal understood the cash value. Most of these objects have no provenance; their history was lost when they were taken, but according to any normal understanding most of them must have belonged to religious institutions or public shrines. They were no one's to sell and therefore necessarily stolen. After a law was enacted in 1956 prohibiting the export of anything over a hundred years old they were necessarily smuggled as well.[13]

Among the few expatriates who remember those days, and knew the scene a little, it seemed as if an oath of silence had been taken. But I heard the names of dealers whispered, and sometimes the same names came up. Some pieces were probably lifted from their shrines by their caretakers; others were smashed out of the masonry by hired gangs. Some 'semi-hippies' were involved. There was a character known as 'Smuggler Jim' who is said to have been a 'loveable rogue'. Other foreign criminals are still feared in Kathmandu even as they enter old age somewhere else, such as on a beach in Thailand. They made a lot of money and no one wants to cross them.

I arranged to meet a retired official of the government's Department of Archaeology, in a café overlooking the temples of Patan's durbar square. 'There are four professions in which you can never trace the real culprit,' he said. 'One is he who sells girls: human trafficking. Next is weapons. Third is drugs. Fourth is icons.' The old man picked up a teacup from the table between us and turned it in his fingers as if it was a treasure. 'If I am a scholar I would see this with much interest,' he said. 'And I will love it more than you love it, because you just see it in the street. Even the worshippers, they just worship it and then go. But I know how it is made. It affects me more.

'We have a saying,' he said, and I expected some elliptical piece of folk wisdom. 'Art historians ultimately become the art lifter.'

The eminent scholar Dr Mary Shepherd Slusser first came to Kathmandu in 1965 with her husband, who was an American aid official, and fell deeply in love with the place. She has spent the rest of her life studying Kathmandu's art and architecture, and she has written frankly about how one group of paintings found their way out.[14]

> Aside from a few progressive merchants along New Road … who dealt clandestinely in Himalayan fine arts, there were, to my knowledge, no sophisticated dealerships. Typically, one sought art and antiques in the numerous funky, dusty 'curio' shops in the nearby town of Patan. … [which] dealt in a variety of 'collectibles' – ethnic objects, manuscripts or parts of them, paintings and sculptures old and new, good and bad, and in fact almost anything for which there was thought to be a market … Priceless Nepalese and Tibetan paintings hung draped in haphazard heaps over roughly-hewn sawhorses to be pawed through at will as in a second-hand clothes shop. Sometimes, if you were judged trustworthy, the shopkeeper would offer to lead you to an upper floor by way of dark, steep, ladder-like stairs to see something hidden away from the general public, it being illegal (theoretically) to export genuine antiquities. The proprietors of these shops also made 'house calls' to members of the foreign community who were customers, as was I in the role of an unpaid field assistant collecting ethnic objects for the Smithsonian Institution.

Items that would be unobtainable today went for about 50 US cents. One day a dealer came to Dr Slusser's house with a painting of the Buddhist goddess Vajravarahi. Dr Slusser knew it had been altered because there was a piece at the top that should not have been there. But its quality was so obvious 'that I knew I had to possess it, not for the Smithsonian's ethnographic collection of course, but for myself '. She beat the price down by half, to $300 plus an old camera. It seemed a frighteningly large sum at the time, when she was still 'too naïve' to recognize it as an investment.

Encouraged by this, the dealer (whom she discreetly names only as 'Mr T') returned with more paintings and fragments in

his coat pocket, which she bought every time. ('After the usual haggling it became mine.') They became items 429, 430, 431, 432 and 449 in her private collection. Mr T, 'realizing that there was a market even for scraps', kept coming back. It was clear that the pieces had been messed around a good deal (she begged him to stop tampering with them), but she recognized quality. Eventually she was pleased to discover that the scraps she'd bought could be partly assembled into the original paintings from which Mr T had recomposed them – fine works of the fourteenth and fifteenth centuries. It even turned out that a sixth painting had been glued to the back of another, which would have been 'one of the paramount Nepalese paintings of the time,' had it survived.

She sold two of the paintings to another collector during the 1980s. 'Despite the barbaric treatment suffered in Nepal,' they ended up in a 'deservedly honored place' at the Virginia Museum of Fine Arts. Some of the works underwent 'sophisticated restorations', although she admits that in one case 'extensive in-painting now confounds the fourteenth century with the twentieth'.

At the end of her article Dr Slusser describes buying yet another painting, which a man was hawking around town on the back of his bicycle. This time it was too expensive to buy for herself ('ah!

but that I had had a crystal ball!' she rues), so she was acting on behalf of an American diplomat. And this time she knew where it had been stolen from, because she'd seen it there: Mishra's old monastery in Patan, 'where it must have been since its consecration in 1565'. (This painting, a unique sixteenth-century diagram of the Valley's Buddhist holy places, was also later donated to the Virginia Museum.)[15] The poor condition from which it was delivered 'is perhaps the most cogent argument in support of collectors and collecting'. The other paintings, she surmises, must have been stolen from monasteries too, or possibly from other types of shrine. 'Had it not been for the intervention of the art market,' she believes, such paintings were destined 'for an ignominious end in someone's dustbin ... One shudders to think of the countless masterpieces of Nepali painting that have met a similar end. It is the world's good fortune that so many, including the ones discussed here, have been spared this fate.'

How does one evaluate that argument?

The paintings were mostly taken from monasteries. They used to be displayed for public worship once a year in a tradition that has largely died out. The illustrated manuscripts and manuscript covers, and the wooden and copper statues, were also lifted from monasteries and other shrines. More sculpture was pried from the panels called toranas that hang above temple doorways, until there's hardly an antique bronze left in the country. The thieves turned to the elaborately sculpted wooden struts that held the temple roofs up. The roofs collapsed. In the final phase, the desecration especially targeted stone sculpture. There was little else left to take. These were the gods from the sanctuaries of shrines and the walls of public fountains. They had been worshipped by the communities that owned them from the day they were consecrated until the night they disappeared, often for more than a thousand years.

Sometimes I would take my work to the offices of the Kathmandu Valley Preservation Trust, where there were a couple of yards of books and a large oval table in a room overlooking Patan's durbar square. In that small library there were a few American museum catalogues, auction house sales catalogues and the catalogues of other exhibitions. It was macabre viewing. There's a ninth-century stone relief of Shiva, with his bare-breasted wife lying at his side. It was pried from the place where it was worshipped, scrubbed clean and carefully lit in the Los Angeles County Museum of Art.[16] There's a Buddhist priest's crown attributed to the twelfth century, presumably taken from a monastery where people still wore it.[17] There's an entire wooden torana almost a yard across, elaborately carved with gods and serpents, taken from above the doorway of a Shiva temple.[18] A sculpted roof strut.[19] There's a thousand-year-old copper sculpture of Shiva sitting in LA. What seems to be the other half of the piece, his lovely wife, ended up in Cleveland, Ohio somehow.[20]

It seemed to me as I read these books that very little attention was given to the context in which the objects had recently belonged. Who preserved them for centuries and how were they used? Whose were they? Weren't those necessary questions? But whether through a narrow approach to art history, or for some other reason, the art lovers seem not to have been very interested. The texts were mostly concerned with the tenuous attribution of dates, enumerating the iconography and marvelling at the beauty of the forms.[21] There was an exception. In the catalogue of an exhibition at the Art Institute of Chicago in 2003 a painting was shown that had been made in 1704, which the book's text identified with Itum Bahal in Kathmandu.[22] The staff at the Trust remembered the case. The people of Itum Bahal had registered the theft with the police at the time it went missing, and now that it'd turned up in Chicago they wanted it back. The anonymous New York collector refused to return it.

The catalogues didn't say very much about Kathmandu, but it was possible to glean something of the buyers. There were a small number of really big private collectors, notably in the New York area but also elsewhere in America and in Europe and Japan. There were also other, lesser, collectors (who weren't multi-millionaires), and a small number of dealers, art historians and museum curators, many of them based in America, many of whom performed several of those roles at once. It was a small world. They traded art among themselves, gave advice and assistance in building one another's collections, and published a slew of glossy books celebrating them.

The biggest curator on the scene was Dr Pratapaditya Pal, who built the collection at the Los Angeles County Museum into the largest in the world. In the preface of a book celebrating what was probably the largest private collection, the Zimmerman collection, Dr Pal offered a brief and vague history of the market. Nepali art was a rarity in the West until the 1950s, he wrote. 'Soon thereafter, America rushed in with aid, and Nepali art began to flow out of the country. When I first visited Nepal in 1959, old metal statues were still being sold in the bazaars by weight rather than as objects of art.'[23] If the second sentence was intended to suggest that the works the Zimmermans bought weren't valued in Nepal then it seems a little disingenuous. They had been preserved for many centuries, many were gilded and covered with semi-precious stones, or the red powder of worshipers. 'Much vermilion powder (often thrown at images during worship) still adheres to this sculpture,' the catalogue notes on page 56. 'These accretions add to the attractiveness of the gilt bronze.'

In 1964 Nepali art was exhibited in America for the first time at the Asia House Gallery on New York's 64th street. Jack Zimmerman (a local tycoon) and his wife Muriel, who happened to have heard of Nepal for the first time two weeks earlier, were walking past, noticed the country's name on the exhibition's banner, and decided to step inside. Mr Zimmerman was so affected by what he saw that he decided to build his own collection. 'As far as the arts of Nepal and Tibet are concerned, the name Zimmerman has become synonymous with quality,' Dr Pal unctuously assures us.[24]

> As the Zimmermans will be the first to admit, for them the golden age of collecting was the late sixties. Mr Zimmerman still recalls how he bought three paintings literally off the street: 'I remember once walking down Madison Avenue and meeting a hippie. He had three Tibetan paintings rolled up under his arm. We unrolled them on the street, I asked the price, and we struck a bargain.' ... By the mid-seventies, however, some of the so-called hippies had become more business minded and had begun asking Madison Avenue prices.[25]

In the space of a few decades most of what was moveable of Kathmandu's artistic heritage was transferred to Western collections.

In 1988 Dr Pal, who was still in charge at the LA County Museum, told a reporter about the limits of responsibility. 'You create a collection by buying what is available,' he said. 'If by chance something comes on the market, and we think it's relatively clean, and we can afford it, we buy it.'[26] Nothing that came from a known monument would be entertained. 'Before buying anything, we expect the dealer to guarantee that it's not a stolen object,' he explained. 'That's the only precaution we can take.' And if a tax-savvy philanthropist wants to give something to the museum? 'Where they get the work is their business.'

'I would prefer that things stay in their countries of origin,' Dr Pal explained. 'I would expect, however, that the governments of these countries would have a sensible policy for protecting the work. But if the heads of the governments themselves are not interested in it, then fine, let it go! What are you going to do?'

The pattern of thefts seemed to match Western tastes. The lithe female forms of Saraswati, Tara and Uma-Maheswar were plundered. Lokeshvara and Vishnu sculptures depict beautiful male bodies, and were also in demand. Inevitably, Buddhas were sought after. Yet the elephant-headed Ganesh, whose statues are most numerous of all in Kathmandu, were rarely stolen and are little seen in foreign collections. Likewise pug-faced Bhairab, and the monkey-god Hanuman. The thieves had a sure eye for the oldest and the best. If they failed to pry a sculpture out at the first attempt they'd return for it, many times if necessary.

Sometimes, if they failed, they'd smash it in anger. The same magazine article that quoted Dr Pal on the limits of responsibility also quoted a photographer, who claimed to have worked for Western smugglers. She described thieves and middlemen in a regular exchange of photographs with dealers and 'museum reps'. 'A piece can be stolen either at random or based on information about what a particular dealer or museum is looking for,' she said.[27]

I thought of a conversation I'd had with Professor Riccardi. 'This was a bunch of Americans, British and God-knows-what, jumping into a big, big apple pie, and feeling it all over themselves and swallowing as much as they could of it,' he said.

I asked, 'You mean the foreigners were filling their bags with art, filling their imaginations with cultural exotica, or ...?'

'Everything there was,' he said. 'The art question is a very difficult one to deal with. Too many people I knew took too many things out of here for the wrong reasons.'

I said, 'I'm interested in the fact that the people who first studied the material culture of Kathmandu are the same people who pinched it all.'

He laughed at that. 'The world's a very funny place,' he said. 'What you just said is true. They pinched it. They got it out of here in the diplomatic pouch, or in these cylinders that were provided by the US army. And imagine. It says "US Army" on the outside of these pieces of cardboard that the thankas are rolled up and stuck in. This isn't hearsay. I saw it.'

It wasn't only the Americans, either. A Polish diplomat was a notorious smuggler. Other people I spoke to, who were unwilling to go into details, mentioned other embassies. Nor was the diplomatic pouch the only way out. After they understood how much it was worth, Kathmandu's rulers cornered their end.[28] Rumours made Prince Gyanendra, the future king, into the big boss. He had been seen (some said it was his younger brother) in Bhaktapur's durbar square, with his men and a crane in broad daylight, trying to remove a famous statue from the top of a column.[29] A policeman who complained was imprisoned (some said killed). Certainly there were unsolved murders. Some said the police chief's mother-in-law was running the smuggling routes. The treasure was exported in marked baggage (people said), so the airport customs wouldn't touch it, carried by mules who ran stolen art and hashish to Hong Kong and Bangkok, and came back carrying gold and heroin.[30]

The Department of Archaeology certified that works were less than a hundred years old and fit for export. Old statues were coloured gold to make them look new, but even that might not be necessary. 'It's purely a matter of money. Fast money, that is the thing,' the old archaeology official told me. 'People with good access in the government, they are always behind the curtain. There won't be any proof. The telephone call comes to the Director General. Finished.'

Anyway, Kathmandu was engrossed in its bewildering social revolution. 'The level of my father's faith will always be greater than the level of my faith,' the old official said. 'My father will never sell the icon but I say, "oh, if I don't have money then I can sell it".'

The 'values crisis' gripped the city and the exodus of the manmade gods was just one consequence, not even one of the greatest. Reinforced concrete became cheaper than timber for building private houses, and the new technology obliterated a millennium of architectural continuity in a generation. At the same time people became less willing to live in joint families (of several brothers with their wives), leading to an upheaval in family life and the vertical division of family property. Houses were built on the old family plots in towering, narrow slices. Some people had jobs in the new offices. Some families were moving out of the old city centres into the new middle-class suburbs, and they had less time for the onerous religious obligations that once formed community life. Several other factors also combined to reinforce the change. In Buddhism, the foreign Theravada school became popular, and fewer people paid for the expensive tantric pujas of the gubhajus. The communal institutions known as guthis, which had maintained the temples and monasteries, and organized the festivals since Licchavi times, were weakened when King Mahendra nationalized their lands in 1964. Their resources

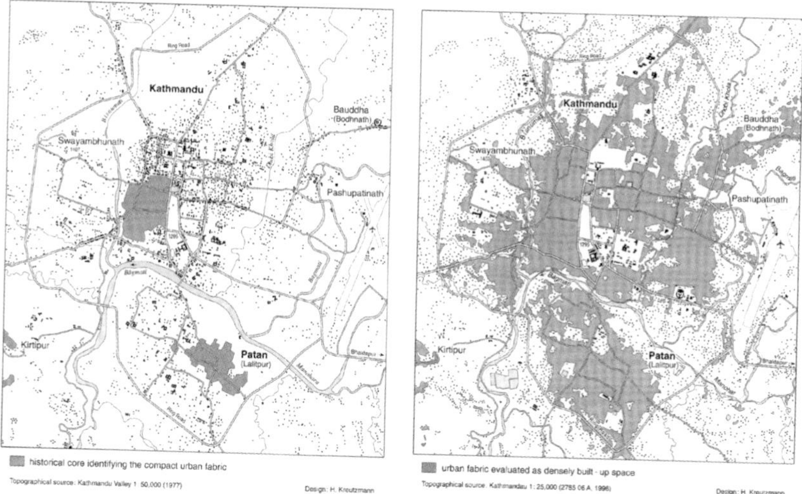

The spread of Kathmandu between 1977 (left) and 1996 (right).

passed to a corrupt and negligent bureaucracy. The lands were developed and encroached upon; the temples and festivals they maintained fell into dereliction and disuse.[31]

'It has become much easier to prove false things true …' an old man of the Valley, looking back on his lifetime, reflected in the early twenty-first century.[32] New economic forces brought more change in a few decades than the previous thousand years. No new civic values replaced the old ways. When the Ring Road was built with Chinese aid in 1973 it ran through fields. It looks like a country road in old photographs. By the late eighties, Kathmandu had one of the highest urban growth rates in the world, as the place filled with migrants from the rest of the country. It quickly became what it is today; a mixed-up small town, swallowed by a giant conurbation. It's an ancient city, in which most people were born in a village. 'Before, my parents would go out and they would meet people they knew everywhere they went,' a friend said. Her parents must still meet people they know wherever they go, but now they meet them while shuffling along pavements that are crowded with strangers.

Several people I spoke to described the eighties as 'a time of greed', although how you could call greed new in the city of the Ranas, or measure its increase, I wasn't sure. The political and social elite embraced Western pleasures and consumer ideals, I read, but not the ideals of democracy and human rights that might have grounded them.[33] Whereas the rulers had once endowed temples and upheld the caste system, now they merely paid lip service to Hindu values. The ideology of monarchist nationalism was just a cover story, to preserve a hierarchy that was only of power and money. Trash piled up in the temples and the gods took a plane to Bangkok in marked luggage. Everyone made a quick buck, I was told, as they sold anything, sold out whatever they claimed to stand for, hollowed out and stripped what was good, carved up or encroached on whatever they could, with a sacred thread across their chest and a bottle of whisky before them. Bhupi Sherchan wrote in his poem *This Is a land of Hearsay and Rumour* that Kathmandu was a bankrupted, philistine place,

Where deaf men wearing earphones
are judges in musical contests;
And people whose souls have turned into stones
are assessors of poetry;
Where wooden legs win races …
Where instead of our sacred rivers,
the Bagmati, the Bishnumati,
now beer and whisky flow.[34]

While the Department of Archaeology was supposed to identify antiques that shouldn't be exported, they were also sent modern objects made to look antique for the foreign market. Metal sculptures were dipped in urea to rust them, wooden ones in mild acid, and tika was daubed on to make it look as if they'd been worshipped. Most of these junk Buddhas were easily recognized and certified for export. A stone sculpture of exceptional quality, depicting scenes from the life of the Buddha, was submitted. It had an inscription in an extinct alphabet, identical to an inscription at an ancient, Ashokan site in India.[35] The exporter swore that it had just been made. The officials of the department formed a committee to discuss the case but he cursed them. '*Who are you to decide?*' He stormed off. He tried to take the sculpture through the airport without documents. It was confiscated and sent to the National Museum.

'Once confiscated it cannot be returned,' the retired official told me. There is no procedure for that. The decision was irrevocable. So it sits there still in the National Museum in poor bewildered Kathmandu, long after everyone concerned has recognized that it's a forgery, after all.[36] While the real stuff is in LA, Cleveland, Upstate New York ...

20

> Although revolutions often occurred, yet the country as a whole did not suffer more from such disturbances than England would from a change of Ministry; neither the army nor the peasantry taking any part in the disputes, and submitting without a murmur to the dictates of whichever party might emerge the victors.[1]

So the young Jang Bahadur Rana, fresh from the success of his own 'revolution', told an English companion during his visit to London in 1850. The revolutions he was talking about would be called *coups d'état* today: they were only violent intrigues among the rulers.

When the old woman Dhana Laksmi Shrestha heard the crowds in the streets shouting for 'democracy' it sounded to her like '*dom kwasi*', which means 'bull's balls' in Newari. Popular agitation had been practically unknown in Kathmandu during her young days, but as society developed that had to change. Different classes had different interests and the revolutions became more contentious, yet they still occurred roughly as often as when Jang Bahadur knew them. There were protests during the Panchayat years, but a major street movement first rocked the city in 1990.[2]

By the end of the eighties Kathmandu had a significant middle class. Wealthy people were no longer necessarily landowners or even merchants. They worked in the aid industry and bureaucracy, or were property speculators, hotel owners and tour operators. They had consumer ambitions, but if they were doing better than most they were still threatened by chronic high inflation. Graduate unemployment threatened their children's future.

The stagnant economy was controlled by royal cronies. A multi-party system offered more hope.

At the same time, more specific circumstances combined to enable a revolution. The regime was plagued by corruption scandals. A trade dispute with India escalated into a blockade on imports. The semi-underground opposition parties were weakened by internal feuds, as usual, but in the late eighties the Congress began to worry that the communists might be stronger than themselves. That argued for an alliance. Meanwhile, the largest section of communists saw the reforms in the Soviet Union and softened their stance towards bourgeois forces. Although some Maoist factions remained aloof, the way opened for a joint movement against the Panchayat. In particular, the overthrow of the Romanian dictator Nicolae Ceausescu in December 1989 had an inspirational effect in Kathmandu. Two years earlier he had visited the city as a guest of the king, and now his own people had toppled him. It became possible to imagine that the Nepali people could topple his host.

Protesters were killed in small numbers from the beginning. The police removed their bodies from the hospitals and took control of their funerals. Appalled by the injuries they were seeing, and by the high-handedness in the morgue, hospital doctors joined the movement. As weeks passed other groups also joined: lawyers, civil servants, bank workers, intellectuals and high school pupils, chanting for 'democracy' and 'human rights'. Eventually thousands of them were arrested. The repression seemed so out of character for the gentle, liberally inclined, Eton-, Harvard- and Tokyo-educated king. Perhaps he was deceived of the nature of his own regime by his scheming wife or wicked coterie of advisers? Or maybe that was just a rumour, put about to deflect criticism.

A day after the police opened fire near the durbar square, Patan was declared a 'liberated zone'. Trenches were dug and barricades erected at the vanished gates of the old city; young men and housewives patrolled the streets with farm tools and kitchen implements. Then, on 6 April, a huge crowd crossed the bridge, mingled with others in the centre of Kathmandu, and began to move towards Durbar Marg. As they surged within view of the palace the crowd attacked the statue of King Mahendra. Before they got much further the army opened fire.

The demand of the movement's leaders had been to lift the ban on their parties, not to abolish the monarchy or to make any other radical change. They had no social agenda, but the massacre on Durbar Marg inflamed the masses and threatened a more radical turn. Squeezed between the palace and the Maoist factions on the hard left, in a country full of desperately poor people, the party leaders preferred to do a deal with the king. And the king for his part may now have realized that he could not crush the movement without losing international support. Behind the scenes, the Indian and Western ambassadors were urging compromise, presumably fearing that if events slipped out of control the far left might come out on top.[3]

Two days after the massacre the party leaders presented themselves at the palace, where state TV showed them sitting before the king at his desk, accepting his offer. In due course a committee was formed to draft a new, multi-party constitution. The following year elections were held. The Nepali Congress, whose aged leaders had overthrown the Ranas, which had won the 1959 election but been toppled by the king eighteen months later, had risen again to lead the People's Movement, and was elected to rule as the party of democracy in Nepal.

Now there was the freedom to oppose the government, to call a strike and to block the road until your demands were met. People complained that democracy meant anyone could do whatever they wanted. But in people's minds, looking back, this democracy was a turning point in the character of the place not just politically. So a kid might see the roads, which had just been repaired, and think, 'so this is what change means'. Or, for example, global trade arrangements, which brought the garment industry to Nepal in the 1980s, also brought foreign fabrics. So a person who was growing up around that time might associate the changes of the period with people no longer wearing patched clothes, made of the coarse cotton from the Hetauda Cotton Mill. 'You don't hear mothers telling their children not to talk to this or that person because of their caste anymore,' I was told. 'People don't walk around sweepers in the street the way they used to.'

The rest of the country impinged ever more on the insular capital. In 1990 over 90 per cent of Nepalis lived in the countryside. In the hills, living standards had actually declined during the eighties. Around 40 per cent of people were unable to meet their daily food needs. Sixteen per cent of families owned 63 per cent of the land.[4] Men from the hills were involved in labour migration, often to work in India as security guards. Women and girls were trafficked to Indian brothels. Of 879 doctors in Nepal in 1990, 550 were in the Central Region, where Kathmandu is.[5]

The changing circumstances of the period quickened the tide of migrants to the city. They worked as domestic servants, factory and construction labourers, drivers, office peons, and street hawkers. They packed the sidewalks and cinema halls and lived in rented places, in new districts on the outskirts, several people, or a whole family, to a room. Sherpas and Manangis opened tourist businesses. Retired British Gurkhas established their own colonies in the suburbs. The land agents who bought and broke up the farmland came from different districts, and sold building plots to people who came from the same places, creating invisible patterns of settlement in the unplanned urban sprawl. Young, mostly Brahmin, men from the village elites came to Kathmandu to study. They lived as cheaply as they could, in rented rooms at first, because everything about Kathmandu was expensive. Later they became journalists, lawyers, government officials, and aid industry middle managers. They hitched their wagons to one or other of the two main parties and became the rising class of democratic Nepal.

I remember talking to a British research student who was attracted to revolution, anarchist theories and anti-globalization-ism. I'd probably been lamenting the destructiveness of the insurgency, or saying that the Maoists didn't understand economics. He thought I was deluded, duped by the dominant discourse of the corporate media. He was trying to persuade me of things I seemed unsympathetic to in a way I found annoying. 'According to Lenin,' he said, 'the first time history's tragedy, the second time it's farce.'

'I think that was Marx.'

'OK then. Marx.' If he was making a point I don't remember it. But Marx's cycle of tragedy and farce is a good enough description of the way events have crowded in on one another since 1951. Revolution has been followed by royal coup followed by revolution followed by royal coup followed by revolution.[6] The same errors are repeated. The vanquished are always allowed a comeback. Why should that be so? Everyone knows that someone else once said, 'Those who don't know their history are condemned to repeat it.' Nepali politicians are steeped in political history. Most of them are old enough to have repeated it at least once, personally. So why should they keep going round in farcical, tragic circles?

The new democratic rulers of the 1990s needed to transform their parties from semi-underground open secrets into national, mass-membership organizations.[7] They did it by distributing favours. In return for payment, or access to vote banks, they could arrange legal impunity, tax immunity, monopoly concessions and rigged tenders. Their services were in demand from provincial towns to the prime minister's office. Supporters of the old regime, including many of the landlords and petty rajas who still held sway in the countryside, rushed to join the Congress party. Pledges to protect the rights of the tiller and end bonded agricultural labour, which were first made in 1950, were dropped again after Congress entered government. A judicial report had been commissioned, to discover who was responsible for killing pro-democracy demonstrators during the People's

Movement, but to ease its accommodation with the old order the new government buried it.[8] Big wealth was accumulated by an expanded class of senior officials, party bosses, contractors and traders with political connections. More people than before had to be accommodated at every level of the system. The productive potential of the country was still sapped by rent-seeking, now on a larger scale.

Democratic Nepal remained dependent on foreign aid, as Panchayat Nepal had been. Writing in 1992, a development economist wondered aloud whether Western donors would continue to fund Nepal's enduring poverty.

> Would it yield sympathy to put all the blame on the *ancient regime* for the structural weaknesses, graft and corruption, and unaccountability in aid management? And will it be wise to do so given the fact that these very donors (save Sweden) were development partners of the past regime?[9]

He shouldn't have worried. The donors needed to keep giving whether the system worked or not, and aid held steady. NGOs mushroomed in Kathmandu to service the foreign agencies with feasibility studies, impact assessments, capacity building workshops, travel expenses, kickbacks and billing scams.[10] Parasitic Kathmandu, with its superior education and excellent networking skills, was adept at extracting resources and capturing aid. The city had few productive industries, but property values, private schools and private hospitals flourished while state services were dreadful and the economy flatlined. The countryside, where the actual development was supposed to be going on, remained one of the poorest places in the world.

Because distributing state resources was so important to politicians and their followers, but the resources were finite, patronage promoted factionalism, as it always had. While a party was in power more effort was spent on internal struggles than on policy or governance; and it was imperative for the opposition to bring the government down as soon as they could, by whatever means necessary, before its supporters benefited too much. The hung parliament elected in 1994 produced five different coalitions. The 1999 election delivered a Congress majority, and three successive prime ministers from the same party. On average, administrations survived for about one year.[11]

Party politics spilled onto the streets through proxies in the student unions. ('We need them to throw bricks,' a Congress politician told me.) The university, which was never great, was ruined. Public employees were divided along party lines. Every trades union, every organization, representing whatever group, appeared in duplicate; one to support, and receive the support of, each of the two main parties. If the parties split into further factions so did these organizations. Even the NGOs that received the donor funds sometimes split, along the factional lines of the mother party. The struggle for access to resources was repeated everywhere, to the exclusion of all else. In this way the system was able to produce a seeming contradiction: democratic government with no concern for the national interest, or even the public mood. The economy of political favours meant that the parties supported the most powerful petitioners on any given issue, whether awarding contracts or releasing gangsters from jail or writing legislation. 'We have a saying,' the old man from the Archaeology Department had told me. '*Thulolai chain. Sanolai ain*. For the powerful, ease. For the weak, the law.' (It is almost unknown in Nepali history to date for the claims of the weak to prevail over the interests of someone more powerful.)

Looked at one way, all that seemed to have happened was a renegotiation of the spoils, between a few courtier families (previously), to include newer and larger privileged networks associated with the political parties. These networks were dominated by members of the higher castes, reproducing established patterns of social inequality.[12] Many people (especially if these descriptions apply to them) would claim that this reading is offensively simplistic, but people did look at it that way. I met a New Road jeweller, drinking beer at the Police Club. In the old days, he said, many of his father's customers were from the old Chhetri families. 'They really knew about jewellery,' he declared, perhaps mindful that most of the group drinking there were from old Chhetri families. 'Now it's all *Kangressi* Brahmins,' he complained. 'They don't know anything. All they want is as much gold as possible.' The Chhetris murmured their approval.[13]

From the beginning the idea was put about by the radical Leftist factions (and by political scientists) that there hadn't been any revolution at all. The People's Movement wasn't as different from Jang Bahadur's type of revolution as it had seemed. There was no great restructuring of the social or economic order. High-caste domination of the bureaucracy actually increased after 1990.[14] There were even more high-caste people in the directly elected parliament than there had been in the more plainly fixed Panchayat assembly. In three elections during the nineties, only one Dalit was elected to parliament, once.[15]

A few years after democracy arrived, in the hills of Rukum and Rolpa, where the state was represented by the school teacher, the unmanned, unsupplied health post, and intermittent police brutality, an obscure Maoist party started sowing the seeds of a new revolution. 'A.) This plan of ours would be based on the lessons of Marxism-Leninism-Maoism regarding revolutionary violence …' the Central Committee of the Communist Party of Nepal (Maoist) declared in their 1995 *Plan for the Historic Initiation of the People's War.*

> … G.) The war will develop according to its own laws not in a straight line but in a complex zigzag path. It is necessary to acknowledge the importance of Lenin's saying that the revolution always creates in its course of development an unusual and complex situation. The people's war will triumph after going through cycles of victory and defeat and gain and loss. We shall be able to lead the people's war only by correctly grasping the law of contradiction, of transformation of wrong into right.[16]

The Maoists believed that Nepali history kept repeating itself because the country was caught in a long struggle between the forces of revolution (in the form of 'bourgeois democracy') and counterrevolution ('feudalism'). So far neither side had won, but the final victory of the people was guaranteed. When the Maoists issued their ultimatum threatening war at the beginning of 1996 (demanding an elected constituent assembly and 39 other things), it was largely ignored in Kathmandu. Insofar as they thought about the Maoists at all, each of the mainstream parties suspected that the rebellion was a conspiracy of their rivals to undermine them. The rebellion spread. The war escalated. In a random event that seemed to come out of nowhere, the crown prince mowed down most of the royal family, leaving King Gyanendra on the throne. A state of emergency was declared. Parliament was dissolved. The king took over again ... 'This royal *coup d'état*,' wrote the Maoist deputy leader and chief theorist, Baburam Bhattarai, after the king sacked the prime minister in 2002,

> has unmistakably validated the principled stand of the revolutionary left that the 1990 change had not consummated the bourgeois democratic revolution ... it is just confirmation of the law of materialist dialectics that the advancing revolution would give rise to the corresponding level of counter revolution until revolution finally triumphs.[17]

I flew to the mid-western district of Rukum in 2005, in a small plane that wormed and burrowed between the hills, the wind whistling in a gap in the door. The district headquarters was a tiny place called Musikot, on top of a hill, full of soldiers and surrounded by razor wire. The rest of the district was controlled by the Maoists. The rebels had driven members of Congress and the UML out of the villages, into Musikot. Since the king took over the army had painted out the slogans for multi-party democracy that the democrats had written on Musikot's walls.

In the tin shack on the roof of my hotel, which was the dining room, it was a nightly ritual to tune into the Maoist radio station, 99.9 FM. The signal was excellent. The bulletin had news of the democratic parties recognizing the error of their ways; and of an anti-king protest, by Nepalis living in Washington D.C. There were songs; a beautifully sung duet:

> 'The poor people are emerging like the light of the full moon.'
> 'Sleeping villages are rising for their rights.'

And there was a programme about the revolution's martyrs, featuring a crackly interview with a fighter's widow. 'Revolution is the demand of history,' the presenter declared.

I met the raja of Musikot, whose family had once ruled the area, at the government guest house. He was a big, affable man, sitting on the bed with one leg tucked under himself and the other leg pendant. He described his family history and marital alliances back to the eighteenth century. The raja had been a minister during the Panchayat. In 1990 he joined the Congress party and in the 1991 election he narrowly defeated (by fraud,

people said) a communist named Janardhan Sharma. The raja became minister of state for industry and Sharma became the Maoist military commander known as Prabhakar. Some of the raja's relatives came in, touching their foreheads deferentially, sat at his feet and presented him with a jar of pickles. Both of his children, he proudly told me, were accountants in Wembley.

There were also other rajas from other parts of the district. One was a general in the army, and a third was married to the king's sister (a village had been named after her as a wedding present). I left Musikot with my two companions, for another grim week among the rebels in the countryside.

In the royalist view, democracy was an un-Nepali, anti-national travesty that had brought the country to the brink of collapse. King Birendra's compromise with the political parties in 1990 had been a disaster. Unbounded corruption, the failure of discipline and authority, the Maoist war: everything bad flowed from it. Satchit Shamsher Rana was the army chief during the 1990 People's Movement. When I interviewed him in 2005 he was the chairman of the Privy Council. 'Birendra?' he said, 'What do you say? Some people say he was not fit to be king of Nepal – too democratic! You see he went to school in Darjeeling, Eton College, Harvard. His ideas were too advanced for the Nepalese set-up.'

The old general's mouth was twisted upwards at one corner, as if by a stroke. His sitting room was decorated with a stuffed peacock, perched on a branch screwed into the wall. There was a large portrait of the king and queen, hung above a decorative khukuri; and a glass case the size of a wardrobe, full of dolls wearing saris. He said, 'In the Panchayat time ministers, corrupt people, could take twenty to thirty lakh. Now they are taking billions. Politicization has destroyed the police, intelligence. One minister put three hundred party people into intelligence in one day. Imagine! To nurture one intelligence man takes years! If you understand what went wrong in the last fifteen years you will understand that the king is trying to defend Nepal's independence and sovereignty.'

'You stopped military aid,' another retired general told me, referring to Britain generally. 'You know a country cannot afford to let itself become a failed state because of democracy and human rights. A country is greater than democracy and human rights.

'It's not cricket, you know,' he added stupidly. 'It's not cricket.'

But it wasn't Western squeamishness about human rights and democracy that brought the king's regime down. The king had been calling the shots since 2002 and Western governments had backed him against the Maoists. They wanted a negotiated solution, in which the government set the terms. After the king took full control with his coup in 2005 governments such as Britain's and America's were caught between rhetorical support for democracy and human rights on one hand and their anti-terrorism and development agendas on the other. They could see that the king was failing, but they also saw him as on the better side of a struggle between terrorism and long-term stability. So they trimmed their support in an attempt to force him into compromise with the parliamentary parties; cutting military aid while offering a measure of diplomatic cover, continuing financial aid but making private and public statements of concern.

The reason for the king's downfall was that he broke the settlement of 1990 between the palace and the political parties. Offered a choice between the palace's story of 'terrorism versus democracy' or the 'democracy versus monarchy' dialectic of the Maoists, the parliamentary parties were obliged to accept the Maoists' version second time around. The Maoists had plenty of rhetoric to terrify Nepal's democrats, but their demand for an elected constituent assembly was democratic, and had been raised on and off for more than fifty years. The Maoist leaders had publicly theorized many times that true 'bourgeois democracy', without the feudal hangovers, was the next necessary stage of Nepal's historical development, and they said they wanted to live by it. It was a risk for the other parties to work with them, but the king left them no alternative. In November 2005, at a meeting in Delhi (brokered by India, and to the dismay of the United States), the Maoists and the other parties signed a 'Twelve Point Understanding' that would be the basis of a joint street movement against the monarchy.[18]

When I think about the second People's Movement of April 2006 I remember things like coming home covered with dust, shocked by the violence I'd seen. But when I went through my few photographs from those weeks, I found that most were taken in my girlfriend's garden, reading magazines and playing with her dog. I tend to remember the tension and the elation on the streets at the movement's climax, rather than the particular atmosphere of pressure I experienced staying in a hotel full of other journalists; the glass of whisky in a hot bath at midnight, before catching six hours' sleep and going out again.

The movement began with a four-day strike. The Maoists suspended military action inside the city so that the government had less justification to clamp down. Nevertheless the government

did clamp down, citing Maoist infiltration. And the sense at the beginning was that, although the king was doomed, the security response would work for now. Similar protests had failed three months earlier. Even the parties weren't confident that their strike would hold, and yet protesters appeared. They threw bricks, burnt tyres and shouted, 'Fuck the king!' They chanted, 'Gyanendra thief, leave the country!', 'Lock up your statues, Gyanendra is coming!' and 'Long live democracy!' On the third day of protests the government ordered a day-time curfew inside the Ring Road. Protesters would be shot on sight, so the Ring Road became the frontier. The protesters chopped down trees and arranged concrete blocks to stop police vans and armoured cars, but it wasn't only in response to the regime's tactics that the movement focused there. The newest migrants were concentrated on the city's outskirts, clamouring to be allowed inside. These were the neighbourhoods near the bus park and the roads leading into town from the countryside, neighbourhoods that had been fields a few years earlier. Now they were warrens of muddy lanes and high buildings, sleeping several people to a room; unfinished concrete frames of houses; heaps of bricks and sand and gravel.

The regime's claim that Maoists had infiltrated the movement infuriated people. The home minister said that 'new faces' on the streets proved the rebels were active, but it didn't seem to prove anything. Kathmandu had become full of new faces. A young man was arrested from a hotel and paraded on TV, but he turned out to be a member of the Congress party. Shots were fired at the home of a retired police superintendent, in a Ring Road suburb I'd never heard of called Gongabu. But after a search the protesters retorted that no such person lived there.

Because of the home minister's claims, Gongabu became the scene of the first big incident that the movement memorialized and fed upon. I arrived there at about three-thirty on the afternoon of the sixth day, parked my bike on the Ring Road, and bumped into my friend Sam, who was the correspondent of the French news agency AFP. There were gunshots coming from inside Gongabu. At the edge of the Ring Road, where unburied concrete pipes were lying beside unfinished earthworks, armed police had taken up firing positions. It was the latest wisdom among journalists that putting toothpaste under your eyes lessened the effects of tear gas and so, leaving our motorcycle helmets on, passing a tube between us, Sam and I walked into the lane where the shots were coming from. The shops were shuttered and the rooftops were lined with spectators looking down at us. I wrote in my notebook:

> Mob attacking home of DIG [Deputy Inspector General] of police and nearby shops owned by him. Throwing bricks. All glass broken. Lit fire in front of gates, posting burning bamboos over gate.
>
> Shots fired from inside into air.

We knocked on a neighbour's door and climbed the stairs to their roof. From there we could see uniformed cops inside the compound, and a man holding a rifle, who was talking to a squad of police who had crept up outside the back wall. On the street in front a line of riot police came up and then withdrew, to be replaced by a line of soldiers. I started writing down quotes from the family we'd imposed ourselves upon:

'We are much frightened,' said a 19-year-old daughter of the house.

'It's too scary. All the children are crying,' said her 20-year-old sister.

'A CID [plain clothes policeman] from next door came and he knocked on the gate but we didn't open it,' said the first girl.

The story began to emerge. A police spy had been discovered among the protesters, who had beaten him up. He fled into the DIG's house. A Nepali human rights activist and two French diplomats joined us on the roof. It was a hot day and we asked for some water to drink, which the family gave us.

'Today's incident proves that it was not terrorists – the terrorists were the police,' the activist declared. 'The home minister said it was the Maoists but it was plainclothes police!'

The crowd below was rampaging through a plant nursery at

the side of the building, pounding the DIG's house with potted marigolds. The men in the street could see us on the roof and were shouting to be let in too, the better to bombard the besieged police. The family asked us to leave, and were affronted when the French offered them a thousand rupees for their trouble.

In the street the police charged. They used a good deal of tear gas. There was a shower of bricks from the rooftops. Shots were fired. I saw people carried away, beaten unconscious. I was taken into an unfinished building, behind a steel roller-shutter, where the injured were being sheltered, slumped against the bare bricks and lying on the concrete floor. There were rubber bullet wounds. There was an unconscious young woman in the gloom. There was a child, under ten, with blood running from the corner of his mouth.

I went outside again. The police fired tear gas. The protesters picked up the hot canisters, fizzing white smoke, and threw them back. They threw bricks, which the police threw back. The missiles struck the overhead power lines and blue sparks cascaded into the street. Police chased people up the skeletons of unfinished buildings and threw them off the upper floors. I lost count of the stretcher cases. The battle lasted all afternoon. When I got back to my girlfriend's house, covered with dust and toothpaste, I started gabbling. Only after she stopped me did I start making sense.

Not every day was like that. There were lulls. And anyway, there isn't a newspaper in the world that will take news from Nepal every day. Some days there seemed no point in chancing the curfew. It only became apparent gradually that this really was the overthrow of the royal regime.

It was an irony that no one believed the home minister's stories, because the Maoists certainly had infiltrated the movement. Rebels mingled with the protesters and led the crowds in shouting republican slogans. They disguised themselves as members of other parties. They planned to attack royal statues, or snatch weapons from security forces, anything to provoke violence and exploit the ensuing chaos. It was almost certainly the Maoists who chopped down trees and dragged concrete obstacles onto the Ring Road. When it was over I interviewed their commanders. They described the number of mobile teams they had, and how they used emails and text messages and runners (because the phones were sometimes shut down) to direct their people to the flash points around the Ring Road, to fire up the crowds, lead the confrontations, and make them more intense.

The king, meanwhile, was out of town, because a partial eclipse had made it inauspicious to return to the capital. Like our counterparts during the first People's Movement, the foreign press delighted in the superstitious mysteries of the Shah dynasty. The government spokesman didn't deny that the king consulted an astrologer. 'I do too,' he said, reasonably enough. 'If you'd been in Nepal for a while, so would you.' The finance minister told thrilled foreign journalists that the king was a 'religious leader ... people have a religious respect for him.'

As the strike and the curfew wore on, fuel and food became scarce. Prices began to rise. Civil servants joined the protests. Staff at the national bank refused to cash the home minister's cheques, so he sent soldiers to open the vault and remove the funds he needed to pay his spies and thugs. Commercial banks went on strike in solidarity, so now there was a shortage of cash. I was with other journalists, on a rooftop again in Gongabu, doing radio interviews on the phone while we watched the fusillades of missiles and the beatings in the street. A white helicopter passed over. It inflamed the crowd, because they assumed that a member of the regime was on board, inspecting the battles around the Ring Road. The next place, flying anti-clockwise, was Kalanki. When the helicopter reached there the police went berserk. They opened fire and killed three people.

The next morning I went to Pashupathinath. On the south bank there was a small group of protesters waving opposition flags, chanting 'Long live democracy.' Near them was a group of journalists and TV crews, wearing fluorescent jackets. A helicopter flew overhead.

On the north bank three pyres had been made below the temple, but there was only one corpse. The police had seized it from the hospital mortuary. It was laid out on the steps beside the river, covered with a white sheet and the Congress party flag. Half a dozen cops were staring at its face with what seemed idle curiosity. The victim's wife had refused to come until his parents arrived from their village. An officer was remonstrating with her brother to let the funeral proceed. A pair of crematory workers were pressed forward, to light the pyre without ceremony, and as the white smoke rose the protesters chanted, 'End the murderous regime!'

When news of the travesty reached the crowds already forming at Kalanki they attacked a tax office and burned its contents in the street. Then they set off on a march around the Ring Road's 17-mile circumference, attracting more people until the crowd swelled to hundreds of thousands. A few hours later I was returning from a meeting at the American embassy. The crowd was an extraordinary sight as it came into view, between the high buildings at Tinkune and the cannabis forest on the airport perimeter. Self-appointed marshals were jogging at the front, trying to keep the mass united. Excited young men were rushing forward, waving party flags, branches of trees, shouting 'Down with Gyanendra!' whistling, waving and jumping around. Soldiers and police retreated before them. There was a billboard bearing the royal claim: '"Constitutional monarchy and multi-party democracy is the main belief and unchangeable commitment of all Nepalis." – His Majesty King Gyanendra'. They tore it down.

To judge a marching crowd you have to see the front, estimate the density, and see how long it takes until the last people pass. It was like waiting for a river to run dry. The marchers themselves appeared almost disbelieving at the scale of it. There were so many of them that it was obvious they had won. People came out of their homes with water for them and applauded. It was very moving, after everything that had happened in the last few years. It was the moment I realized that the king had lost, some kind of peace process would surely follow, and the war might end.

The American ambassador had called foreign reporters in an hour or two earlier, to warn that the Maoists could take over. He was a lean, gangly basketball-lover, strewn across a white armchair in his study. It was his last chance to jolt the king into reaching out, and drive a wedge in the Maoists' alliance with the democratic parties. (He'd been summoned to the foreign ministry once already that week, to explain his prediction that the king would be forced to flee, perhaps clinging to the wheels of a helicopter. The image seemed to imply which war the ambassador was fighting.) We sat, notebooks in hand, on the white sofa before him. 'The king will lose his kingdom if he doesn't move fast,' he repeated now. Nothing short of an unconditional, immediate return of power to the political parties would avert a 'very tricky endgame'. 'I think [the king] kinda likes power and he thought he'd be good at it. It hasn't worked,' he said, with the on-the-record candour that journalists find most endearing. 'Maybe I'll be called in by the foreign ministry again, if they're still doing business.'

That night there was a televised address from the palace, in which the king justified his actions and praised the security forces. He offered to make a member of the protesting parties prime minister, but only on the same terms as the three prime ministers whom he'd fired in the last four years. When the broadcast was over, the crowds chanting in the streets showed that the offer had been rejected. The people had warned the leaders for days that no compromise would be acceptable. Politicians told journalists that they'd be lynched if they made a deal with the palace this time. In the morning, the British ambassador led a delegation of European diplomats to meet the party leaders and urge them to accept the king's offer.[19]

☀

Now it did seem to be the messy endgame. Half the foreign press moved from its base in a hotel outside the curfew area to a hotel on Durbar Marg, in time to witness the massacre, or else the storming of the palace gates. Genuine black thunderclouds actually gathered above the city. The people on the Ring Road marched into the city from every side, to find the centre closed by razor wire and soldiers. The endless crowds flowed around the prohibited area, probing for a way in.

At Tripureswar I climbed up beside the statue of King Tribhuwan to watch them pass, and spoke to the soldier who was also standing there. 'I tell you one thing,' he said. 'If you look at these people, so many of them have been bought by money. Many of them have come from remote parts. There is infiltration of Maoist people.'

I could tell by his short-barrelled rifle that he was from an elite unit. We were about the same age, and he'd been to one of the best schools. It wasn't surprising that we had a few friends in common. We talked about them. He told me he was in the Special Forces, had been trained by the Americans. A man wearing civilian clothes but a military haircut drove up on a motorcycle, exchanged a few words, and was off again on his reconnaissance. I asked if the monarchy could survive.

'Yes, it will,' the soldier said. 'These people are going to get nothing, whoever comes. The problems we face in this country were brought by the political parties. Lots of people still respect the monarchy.' It began to rain heavily but we were dry under the marble canopy of the king's statue. 'I really feel pity for our country that it's going through a hard stage of life and things are like this,' said the soldier, who then tried to be upbeat. 'Let's see what happens.' He indicated some bedraggled labourers on a building site. 'These poor people. They are paid from day to day. How will they survive?' A tourist coach passed, a row of alarmed white faces pressed to the wet, steamy glass. 'These poor people,' he repeated, this time of the tourists.

There were streaks of lightning and the rain grew heavier. Protesters, police, and soldiers were pressed together, taking shelter beneath the same buildings. Within a few minutes there was an inch of water in the road. It was dark at three in the afternoon. 'Now the riots will be controlled,' the soldier said.

When the storm was over I drove around the Ring Road. Near Swayambhu women and girls were hacking firewood from the trees that had been felled across the road. Further on, a small group was demolishing a police post and making a roadblock from its razor wire. Still further, another smoking police post. People were dancing on the branches of felled trees, sometimes falling off. Black smoke rose from burning tyres. An effigy of the king swung from overhead cables. 'Nepal,' one of the protesters told me, and I wrote it down, 'it's a messed up country.'

I went to the City Police Office, to see who was around and what they were talking about. The men in the inspectors' bunk-room were people who knew me and they allowed me in. The place was strewn with tea glasses, laathis, bottles of aftershave, pieces of body armour. There was a tennis racket and a rudraksha rosary hanging on the same nail in the wall. These were the junior officers who led the riot squads and they were tired. An inspector was in bed with his boots on. No one wanted to stir in this lull, for who knew what would happen next?

'We are now the police of a democratic country so we don't have to worry,' an inspector said.

'Why are you saying that? You must be worried or you wouldn't be saying that,' said another.

Two inspectors who were attached to the palace as police aides de camp came in, out of uniform. They must have been sent out to test the mood. One of them was nearing the end of his posting, and the men began to talk about the kind of jobs that former aides de camp might receive. Commanding the police station at Boudha would be a good one, because some of the Tibetans who'd settled there had become rich in the carpet industry. 'You don't even have to be that corrupt. They just give you money.' And there was the casino at the Hyatt hotel nearby, which would make gifts to the station commander. What about the station on Durbar Marg? That had two five-star hotels with casinos on its patch. The conversation seemed a little forlorn to me, like they were kidding themselves to feel better. Things were about to change, I thought, but the way it turned out I'm sure those guys were well taken care of.

The protesters were exhausted too. The lull lasted another day and then the king's capitulation came. He appeared on television to read a statement written by his opponents, offering condolences to the families of those killed, reinstating parliament, and accepting that the parties would now pursue a peace process with the Maoists. I remember the crowds around the Ring Road, marking their victory by chanting that the parties should not let them down again. Parliament met a few days later, with protesters outside warning the politicians not to betray them this time.

The universal slogan was for a 'New Nepal'. The parties formed a unity government to negotiate with the Maoists. A special United Nations mission came to support the peace process. It took two years to settle a series of agreements and hold elections to a constituent assembly. The king sat it all out quietly, perhaps hoping that if he gave no more offence then some kind of accommodation might still be possible. But the People's Movement had forced every party to become republican. Even if some politicians might have preferred to save the king, the public gave them no opportunity. At its first sitting in 2008 the Constituent Assembly voted overwhelmingly to abolish the monarchy. Gyanendra gave a dignified statement at a press conference (his first-ever press conference), while journalists climbed over the palace furniture and heckled him. He said 'May the Lord Pashupati bless us all,' then he left to become a private citizen. 'Taxi for Mr Shah!' joked the guy on the *Telegraph* foreign desk that day, and time was up for the monarchy.

PART THREE

Without End

21

By the time the king gave his press conference and left the palace I'd left Nepal for Thailand, to be the *Telegraph*'s South-East Asia correspondent. On that day I filed my copy on the king from a small island in Indonesia, where I was chasing a story that never got published, about a scuba-diving accident.

In Bangkok I lived in a downtown apartment, near the sky-scrapers and the go-go bars and a sky-train station. I never really got a taste for it. My new beat was huge. I spent so much time in South-East Asian airports, I filled two large passports with visas in a bit over two years; they were probably the last years that a British newspaper would pay for something like that. I missed Kathmandu, and as I travelled I collected things for the house that my girlfriend was building there, which we would live in together. Glass lampshades from a junk shop in Jakarta; boxes of lacquer-ware from Rangoon; a print from Vientiane. I kept returning to Nepal as well, either to cover the news, or on the pretext of covering the news to visit her there.

She also came to Bangkok sometimes. I took her to a fashion-able restaurant on her birthday. The place had exposed concrete, lush vegetation and throbbing ceiling fans. I ordered martinis, with a slice of sashimi on the glass. I think there was squid in its own ink, or something like that, stuffed in ravioli. I ordered a bottle of Riesling. For the main course there was a heap of lamb chops (herb-crusted), and presumably a bottle of red. Subi had an upset stomach that weekend so I ate everything myself. I was well paid for the first time in my life and, since I was trying to give up cigarettes, I liked to smoke a cigar after dinner. Whatever party spirit I thought I'd conjured was ruined by a text message from Kathmandu. Two bombs had exploded, on a moving bus and at a bus stop, killing at least two people and injuring several others. Many of the victims were school children.

☀

The Comprehensive Peace Agreement, which was signed at the end of 2006 between the Maoists and the mainstream parties, was quite a vague document. It was premised on balancing concessions by the two sides: the Maoist army would be integrated into the national army, which would be reformed. Until then the former fighters would wait in camps monitored by the United Nations. The Maoists would return the land they had captured, mostly from absentee landlords, and there would be 'scientific land reform' in return. As the Maoists had demanded, there would be elections to a constituent assembly which would write a new constitution, to address historic iniquities and create a 'new Nepal'. In return the Maoists would abandon violence and accept the constraints of a multi-party system. Until the new constitution was complete politics would proceed on the basis of cross-party consensus.

I used to think that when the war ended Nepal would begin to address its problems. Politicians and commentators had declared this time, between the end of the war and whatever comes next, to be another transitional period, as if it were just a staging post the country would occupy for a few years before completing itself. In the first winter of the new transitional period the scheduled power cuts started and the reality became clearer. Shopping malls and multiplex cinemas began to open for the first time, like up-country versions of the glittering malls in Bangkok. The first luxury apartment blocks rose, transforming the skyline again. They promised an escape from the filthy air, the water and power shortages, and the hordes of unmanageable people in the rest of the city.

'Panipokhari Heights project,' says the website, 'is primarily designed for the upper middle class families for modern trendy living in the most sophisticated manner. Pure joys of living differently, higher up within the clean sunny atmosphere, in total

harmony with the unmatched ambience, elegantly eminent, exclusive architecture decorated classy housing units for an endless time.'[1] Likewise, Baluwatar Residency is quite centrally located, but it has 'an atmosphere so pristine and quiet, far from the chaotic traffic snarl-ups and insurmountable pollution coupled with the ubiquitous population of the city core.'[2]

The rage that the people's movement had exposed dissipated only slowly; or it never completely dissipated, and instead Kathmandu settled into a new, more uneven temper. The Maoists quickly began to build their organization in the city by recruiting the mostly migrant poor to their trades unions. The newly Maoist workers were impervious to any form of managerial logic or persuasion. If there were any cases in which members of that class weren't cheating them, they refused to recognize it. Sometimes they made the bosses wear garlands of shoes, or blackened their faces. To middle-class city people, the Maoist unions seemed to be going after anyone who had money, with furious militant self-righteousness. The former rebels turned their militia into an intimidating youth wing, called the Young Communist League. 'They want to take our property and send us back to the village,' a friend told me, who was a journalist from the generation of village elites that had come to the city around 1990. Individual middle-class insecurity became a kind of rage against the poor in return. The fact that this radical politics was now openly conducted inside the city, capturing the remaining space of the old parties, and seemingly able to overrun the system from within, made the Maoists far more intolerable than they'd been when they were fighting in the countryside.

Everyone was raising their voice, demanding one thing or another. It is a mark of how unruly the country was at the beginning of the peace process that picketing villagers around Kathmandu's landfill site could fill the city's streets with garbage a dozen times a year while they escalated their demands of the government. Squatters were said to be taking advantage of the weakness of the government as they built their wretched homes on the riverbank at Thapathali. Especially, many people demanded respect, and the courtesy of their traditional superiors. Taxi drivers (a category of people from the countryside whom the middle class resented almost as much as it resented the Maoists themselves) started to answer back. Nasty little arguments broke out. Rude passengers found themselves abruptly abandoned at the side of the road. The old woman, Dhana Laksmi, who'd been waiting for her turn to be served at a shop counter, asked, 'Why were you letting him touch everything?' The previous customer had been a Dalit. 'There's nothing you can do about it,' the shopkeeper told her. 'It's democracy now.'

I noticed for the first time that a few expensive, recently completed buildings had secured as tenants the honorary consulates of small, faraway countries. I supposed that they hoped, if the city lost control of itself again, they would be offered diplomatic security by the police. On the other hand, previously unknown armed groups emerged, such as the Nepal Defence Army, which seemed to be serving a far-right agenda to postpone change by simulating chaos and stalling the Constituent Assembly election. Probably, as people said, such groups could be traced back to some influential drawing room in one of the older suburbs of the city, and that would be why no one ever got to the bottom of the bombings.

☀

But by far the most important development of those years was the Madhes Movement, involving a large (and itself internally diverse) community known as Madhesis, who live in the southern plains. There had been 'identity politics' in Nepal since the 1950s (and before that), but the tendency was suppressed during the Panchayat in favour of a supposed social harmony which privileged some groups over others. The committee that drafted the 1990 constitution received more submissions on communal and religious issues than on anything else, but it dismissed them (and the dominance of the state by members of the hill upper castes had increased).[3] Madhesis, and many other communities, considered themselves the victims of discrimination and were, on average, poorer and less healthy than members of 'the dominant group'.[4] The issue wasn't anywhere on the mainstream agenda, but it was ripe enough that the Maoists had drawn support for their insurgency by promising autonomy to marginalized people. Even despite the Maoists, it remained the case that political issues were rarely presented in primarily communal terms.[5]

So in 2007, when Madhesis rose up demanding their share in the New Nepal, everyone, including the movement's own leaders, was surprised by their intensity. When I went to the plains (the ashes still warm in ruined buildings) I found that some of the angriest men had worked in Kathmandu for a while, and endured the complacent racism of the capital's housewives and policemen. They were furious with journalists, and with human rights activists, who treated their movement according to the prejudices of the hill high-castes to which they overwhelmingly belonged. And suddenly it was obvious that not only the government, but also civil society, the media, the international community and foreign development agencies had completely

overlooked the Madhesis. The hill-dominated state treated the aspirations of the plains as a law and order problem. The police shot dead over thirty.

It therefore happened that almost as soon as the Maoist insurgency was over, and before its issues were settled, class struggle was unexpectedly joined, and increasingly replaced, by caste and ethnicity as the salient category of political differences. As soon as the Shah monarchy was defeated the settlement that Prithvi Narayan Shah had imposed (of a unitary Hindu state controlled by and for a relatively few, mostly Brahmin and Chhetri families) was challenged and threatened to unravel. Much of what followed can be read as a struggle over Prithvi Narayan's legacy; renewing him on posters, placards, and social media as a conservative icon of immediate contemporary relevance.

After the Madhesis, other ethnic groups quickly imposed strikes and brought their own demands. The agenda for the 'liberation' of all the peoples of Nepal stepped from the countryside into the streets, then the seminar rooms, and in presentations and reports there was a new set of buzzwords referring to 'identity' and 'marginalization' and to 'included' and 'excluded groups'. The major political parties – all of which, including the Maoists, were led by hill-Brahmin men – were forced to concede, after much evasion and renewed protests, that there would be a proportional electoral system, that the new constitution would establish a federal structure, and guarantee the rights and representation of excluded groups, who between them constituted a majority of the population.[6] After two postponements the election was eventually held in 2008. The conventional wisdom in town was that the Maoists, who had done so much to inspire this chaos, would be punished. They took 40 per cent of the seats – twice as many as their nearest rival, the Congress, and it was now that the peace process ran into serious trouble.

After two years in Bangkok I moved back to Kathmandu and got married. We lived in the house my wife had built and we had two servants. One woman, Sabitrididi, who had worked for us before, was shuffling and tired in her late 30s. Now we hired a young neighbour to help her with the laundry, the maid's maid. This pretty, blushing woman, shyly turning her face away when I met her in the kitchen, happened to be the same girl who was terrified on page 120, by the shivering mask of the goddess

Kumari, who felt a shiver and a thrill every time she saw a mask dancing in the neighbourhood, or an animal being given to the god. I was shocked that she'd never tasted mutton. She spent her first wages from our house on the first mattress she'd ever slept on, ten years since she married.

I told Sabitrididi, 'We've got too much stuff in this house.'

'No you haven't,' Didi said, 'except you've got too many books.'

In her own tiny home Didi lived in ordinary discomfort, with her husband and his mother, their son and his wife, and her granddaughter. Didi admired luxury, but she couldn't understand anything that was written on paper. To her the piles of books I left in every room were futile. I sat around all day making disorganized jottings; sifting various scraps and notes into layers on the sitting-room floor; leaving notebooks and diaries open at certain pages; putting useful press-cuttings where I wouldn't lose them; hammering on my computer with two fingers at the kitchen table. Sabitrididi reshuffled the papers and put them in tidy piles on my desk. I was rereading histories of Kathmandu, and in something like their own selective approach I was constructing my own; a history in which I would try to simulate the jumbled, layered, endlessly interconnected and repetitive structure of the city. It would be a new history, but like the first ones in which the chronology of the composition was unavoidably complicated. It would be addressed, like all the others, to entirely contemporary concerns.

'When you have a daughter,' Sabitrididi said, 'I want to look after her.'

'And will *she* get pregnant when she's sixteen?' my wife asked. Didi thought it was genuinely funny.

Our son was born in a hospital by the Dhobi Khola, just upstream from the Licchavi centre at Hadigaon. Like the rest of the hospital, our deluxe private room was slightly scruffy, and smelled of something besides disinfectant, although it was more or less clean. The water in the taps of the en suite bathroom was clear but not colourless. From the deluxe private window I could see the layers of plastic bags exposed in the riverbank that previously recorded strata of Licchavi pottery shards. Cleaning staff wandered in and out with their mops and buckets, complaining that the air conditioner was on, and offering their views on the correct number of blankets with which to smother a newborn child at the height of summer.

Sabitrididi loved the baby. And she thought that our neighbours, seeing how beautiful he was, would give him the evil eye. It's normal to put a black spot on a child's forehead to protect against the eye, but she put it behind his ear, thinking that if I saw it I would wash it off. She didn't doubt that magic spells were bouncing around the chowk. When the baby lost his appetite she probably had a suspect. She threw milk three times on the terrace and spat on it.

The Maoists' surprising election victory was at first unpalatable, and then indigestible to their opponents. The Nepali Congress abandoned the principle of consensus on which the peace process was based, refused to leave office for months, then refused to join the new government led by the winners. India, which had helped to create the peace process, was aghast; especially when the new Maoist prime minister chose to make his first foreign visit not to Delhi but to Beijing.

Newspaper columnists shrieked that the Maoists were the new Khmers Rouges, but in office they only launched (to the dismay of would-be tax-payers) an effort to tighten revenue collection. The public rhetoric of the Maoist leaders was somewhat moderate, but the rhetoric they addressed to their party cadres was revolutionary, giving reason to doubt their commitment to pluralism. The former rebels' budget was welcomed by the World Bank and the IMF. Kathmandu's intelligentsia howled against their national literacy scheme, their self-employment scheme, and their farm-loan-waiver scheme, as populist stunts and conspiracies to 'capture the state'. The Maoists didn't commit any major ceasefire violation but their cadres were scary. They did beat people up sometimes, and occasionally murder someone, yet Maoists appear to have been killed more often in these years than the members of any other party.[7] Their attackers were from the muscular youth wings of the NC and the UML, or new armed groups that were given political protection by those 'democratic forces'; for the truth was not that different parties occupied different points on a spectrum between violent and open politics, but that each party adopted methods ranged across that spectrum.

It seemed to me then that whatever was violent or undemocratic about the Maoists wasn't unique, but they were the only major party advocating progressive social change. All the reform agendas of 'new Nepal' came from them. They had more supporters than anyone else. That's why Kathmandu's middle and upper classes hated them, wrapped themselves in the rhetoric of democracy and screamed against dictatorship. Whatever insincerity the Maoists showed towards 'democracy' was at least matched by their opponents' insincerity in denying that they were a legitimate force. They were denounced more passionately as irredeemably violent after they won the election than when they were waging their rebellion. And however commentators shrieked that the former rebels were a vicious anachronism, indistinguishable from the brainwashed ultras of the Cultural Revolution, they were no less anachronistic themselves; in wilfully repeating the error of the cold warriors, who had failed to recognize in national communist movements the authentic expression of local aspirations for justice. If Maoism was a weird throwback, it reflected the enduring conditions in the countryside, and the character of the ruling class.

Rage became the new spirit of Kathmandu; puffed up, blustering bourgeois outrage, and the repressed, sometimes volatile anger of the poor.

The Maoists made missteps and overreached; their complicated relationship with the Valley's traditions revealed some of the contradictions of the time. Through their ethnic front organizations, the party was more active than any other in cultivating Newar support, tapping into the communist sentiments of Jyapus in particular. To please them, the party proposed (with no expectation that it would ever happen) that the old Newar calendar would be restored as the national calendar; mid-2065 BS (Bikram Sambat) – which fell in late AD 2008 – would be the early months of 1129 NS (Nepal Sambat). As the fact that this could ever seem a populist policy shows, many Newars were culturally conservative, even as they were politically 'left'. The Maoists were partly sympathetic, or at least willing to exploit those feelings.[8]

On the other hand, at the beginning of the peace process Nepal had been declared a secular state, at the Maoists' demand. The Maoist finance minister therefore saw nothing wrong with cancelling the state subsidy for sacrificial animals at the annual Indra Jatra. 'The Maoist government is trying to stamp out cultural and religious festivals,' claimed Rajan Maharjan, who had a role in the celebrations. 'It's their first step towards a cultural revolution!'[9] There was rioting, stone throwing and teargas. The government was forced to back down, and pick up the protesters' medical bills (which showed how far they had to go in establishing a dictatorship).

Or, for almost three centuries, it had been the tradition that South Indian priests would minister at Pashupati. Many Nepalis wanted that to change, and there were complaints about the management of the temple's revenues. Notwithstanding the newly secular status of the government, the Maoists replaced the Indian chief priest with a Nepali. Early reports were muted, but a campaign geared up. The Supreme Court issued a stay order. Lawyers were wheeled out to declare, 'There is total constitutional breakdown in the country. Constitution, constitutional order and constitutional norms seem to have no place in the Maoist regime.'[10] There were respectable calls for the prime minister's ouster. Anonymous Indian diplomats briefed their national press that the sinister affair of the Pashupatinath priests was part of a Chinese design to spread Beijing's influence south of the Himalaya. The Indian priests were reinstated.

A coalition was being assembled to contain the Maoist threat, including the old parliamentary parties, much of the media, the army, judiciary and other sections of the many-headed Kathmandu establishment (monarchists, the conservative intelligentsia

...); powerfully backed by India, which once again perceived a security threat on its northern border. The crisis arrived in the summer of 2009 when the Maoist government tried to sack the army chief, citing insubordination.[11] Alarming newspaper articles foresaw a grab for absolute power. People were asked to believe, and apparently they could believe, that replacing the top general with the second man would throw open the last door to communist state-capture.[12] Only the intervention of the ceremonial president could save democracy; and he stepped forward, to countermand the general's sacking. The Maoists' coalition partners quit, the Maoist prime minister resigned. A government largely resting on the votes of the poor was hustled out of power by a coalition of elite interests in the name of democracy. A new government was put together by the Indian embassy (rather in the manner of Brian Hodgson operating from the same ground 170 years earlier), in which the prime minister, deputy prime minister, defence minister and peace minister had all lost their seats in the last election.

Kathmandu's craven and factionalized power structures offer excellent scope for manipulation. There were many stories in the newspapers of threats and interventions by 'the south', many more than usual. And while they denounced India in public, Nepal's rulers were forever whispering to the embassy, seeking aid against their rivals. They'd all taken favours and instructions from Delhi at one time. The Indian customs authorities held up newsprint imports to newspapers that harped on these kinds of things.[13]

In the spring of 2010 the Maoists announced a huge programme of protests in Kathmandu, demanding that the government step down, to be replaced by one led by the largest party. The government threatened to call out the army. At the beginning of May thousands, or maybe hundreds of thousands, of young men and women arrived from outside the city and imposed a bandh. They stood and sat around on the shuttered and traffic-free streets, some of them playing music, or dancing and singing, some of them carrying sticks. They were hungry and bored. The weather was alternately hot and unseasonably wet. At night they ate and slept in empty buildings, and were ravaged by mosquitoes and an epidemic of diarrhoea. For several days the young Maoists kept the city shut down; then, in a formidable demonstration of popular power, and organization, they lined both sides of the 17-mile Ring Road, literally surrounding Kathmandu, and cheered their leaders in light rain as they drove past waving.

The Maoists were taught the importance of the middle class to a successful street movement. Smart city people scorned them as imposters from the countryside (the fact that they were not from the city was constantly cited as a reason that their demands were illegitimate). The demand was raised for harsh measures against them. Champions of liberal democracy in the newspapers denounced the Maoists' politics of violence, and taunted them with 'the Sri-Lanka solution'. The business community organized a 'peace rally' in Kathmandu's durbar square, and packed the place in their uniform of white T-shirts. A popular actor addressed the gathering: 'I see big industrialists, doctors, engineers, teachers, intellectuals and journalists here. You are the respectable, intelligent and law-abiding section of this society. You shape the destinies of simple, ordinary folks. Aren't you the ones most entitled to have your say?'[14] Then they set off on a march, 'Nepali flag in one hand and iPods in the other', to reclaim the streets. It was a very large crowd. The younger, more spirited ones taunted the Maoists. And I noticed that not only were the city people paler, and of course better dressed than their fellow countrymen, they were taller as well. The peasants were defeated.

By keeping the largest party out of power, India and the domestic forces it backed proved, as they probably needed to prove, that the Maoists couldn't win against their strength combined. For the two years this demonstration lasted the peace process appeared at the edge of collapse. By the time the point had been well made, any lingering doubt that the Maoists could really 'capture the state' had been removed, and with it the anti-Maoists' own best argument.

22

Word went round that some excellent rice was on sale from the national godown at Thapathali. Everyone seemed to be talking about how good it was. The grains were fat and round and slightly sticky. We had a sack dropped off at the house. On it there was a sticker, displaying a red disc on a white rectangle, and the message, 'A gift from the people of Japan,' but this seriously good rice was much too nice to give to hungry people.

It is well recognized in Kathmandu that it is the agents of development, not the targets, who benefit. If you have the power and opportunity, the best thing is to get a job in a donor agency, or develop a good line in consultancies, or found an NGO, or work for one, and use donor funds to teach people how to improve their lives. Failing that your best chance would be to capture a position on a donor-ordained users' group, or some other kind of 'locally owned' committee, with access to resources. Anything's better than merely being an ordinary person, a poor member of the public. If you're receiving the development message, about washing your hands after you've had a shit, or the sustainable use of resources, or whatever, but you're not giving that message to someone else, then you're not taking any money home, and you know you're screwed.

The Nepali development laboratory was inaugurated by the Americans' 'community development' concept in 1951, which was implemented through their Village Development Projects. They regarded Nepal as a blank slate (the notion of awakening villagers to improve themselves apparently owed something to the self-help manuals of the time).[1] The first Five-Year Plan was launched in 1956, designed by a UN expert and three-quarters funded with American, Indian, Chinese, and Russian contributions.[2] Foreign money built the rapidly expanding bureaucracy.

Foreign aid's contribution as a percentage of GDP blossomed during the Panchayat years.[3] Multilateral donors and lenders such as the UN, World Bank and Asian Development Bank joined the scene; and new bilaterals, such as the Japanese, the Germans, and the British joined the Indians, Swiss and US. In the sixties capital investments would let Nepal 'take off'. 'Poverty reduction' was the mantra in the seventies, but less for any reason specific to Nepal than in consistency with global currents, such as renewed concern at the spread of communism in peasant societies. There would be 'growth with equity' and 'the basic needs approach', and Integrated Rural Development Projects not unlike the old Village Development Projects, except this time they were integrated. The projects had little benefit of course, for reasons including that powerful people ate the cash. By the eighties, new old ideas were going around again, like 'community empowerment' and 'participation'. Development workers were 'change agents', working with communities to form 'users' groups', or to teach villagers that they'd asked for the projects that were about to be given to them.

The eighties and early nineties also brought Structural Adjustment, which was being pushed everywhere by the World Bank and the IMF to create growth through privatization and liberalization. The benefits would trickle down. As it turned out the anticipated results didn't materialize, the benefits were captured by a few, and rural incomes went into absolute decline. The cold war ended and the 1990 People's Movement happened. The donors that had supported the monarchy supported democracy instead. A 1992 USAID publication, marking the anniversary of *Four Decades of Development* the previous year, reckoned that

> With the changed political circumstances of the past few years, and an increased understanding of the need to follow market principles and to rely more on the private sector to

> stimulate economic growth, we are hopeful that by the year 2001, the 50th anniversary of Nepal's entry into the modern era, we will see Nepal graduate from the ranks of the world's relatively least developed countries.[4]

By now there were 32 bilateral and multilateral donors, but the poor were still there, in increased numbers. GDP growth per capita hovered around 2 per cent and economic inequality was widening. Four years later a journalist wrote:

> The powerful aid-givers, all strong believers in the trickle-down theory, are of the belief that when the dust settles the public as a whole will benefit. More likely we will have a revolt on our hands, but by then of course the aid agencies will be on to the fad of the next half decade – which will in all probability be, and not at all incongruously, the rediscovery of the role of government in national development![5]

So it proved. Structural Adjustment didn't cause the Maoist insurgency, but as those words were written the first shots of the war were being fired in the mid-western hills. Rural poverty and discrimination, failed development and dysfunctional state institutions helped to incubate an uprising that would exceed all expectations. Between 1977 and 1996 the number of Nepali people in absolute poverty had nearly doubled.[6]

The next donor paradigm was Human Development, which was a worldwide move away from neo-liberal theories towards 'community self-reliance' and 'local management', rejoining the battle for 'poverty eradication'. Under foreign tutelage a Poverty Reduction Strategy Paper was produced, which was 'nationally owned' and 'country driven' and became the country's tenth Five-Year Plan. Projects addressed infrastructure and 'social sector development', 'social inclusion' and 'good governance'. Growth and poverty reduction targets were set and missed.

Throughout these years a parallel development had been taking place, and lending itself to whatever happened to be the donors' best practice at the time. Since the eighties NGOs had been established in growing numbers, which were private, supposedly non-profit agencies devoted to social work. The NGOs would help to build 'civil society' and make power answerable to the community, deepening the democratic culture.[7] As Kathmandu opened up in the nineties the NGO sector boomed. There were, and still are, thousands of them.[8] (It's been said, going by the number of signboards of development organizations in the city, that Kathmandu must be the most developed place on earth.) The NGOs produced studies and reports and mid-term evaluations, and ran training programmes and awareness raising workshops, and did human rights advocacy, and provided whatever other services were required, to and on behalf of the donors. Those NGO people who were successful in attracting funds could speak English, which allowed them access to the donors. They were adept at using the jargon of the moment ('code phrases'), which won the foreigners' trust and made their project proposals attractive. They also spoke Nepali, which meant they were operating in networks the foreigners couldn't understand.[9]

Many of the new NGO wallahs were associated with the moderate communists of the first people's movement, the Unified Marxist Leninist party. The NGO boom helped pave their way into the political mainstream, with gold, as it were.The common view was that many of them were 'farming dollars'.

In the late nineties the Millennium Development Goals were seized upon as the solution, committing the world to cut a swathe through the spreadsheet of grim poverty statistics by 2015. ('Of course the next problem will be the MDGs,' a lower-level European aid official told me in 2011. 'For years we've been showing progress towards ending X, Y, and Z. What's going to happen in 2015 when X, Y, and Z still exist?')

The al Qaeda attacks on America in September 2001 inaugurated the war on terror and made third world poverty a global security issue again. The US secretary of state came to Nepal, and the Nepali prime minister visited the White House. The American administration believed that 'Nepal could easily turn into a failed state, a potential haven for terrorists like that which we have transformed in Afghanistan.'[10] British development aid was bundled with military aid, to fight the insurgency. Thanks to the king's stupidity, and some clever Indian fixing (and despite American misgivings), the war ended in 2006. The Western spooks and military advisers left and the democracy experts and mediation gurus came, to teach the Nepalis about constitution writing and conflict resolution. The city swelled with peace-building advisers and post-conflict specialists, organizing conferences and junkets to study the peace processes in South Africa and Northern Ireland and Sri Lanka and Guatemala. In 2007–08 the donors (by now called 'development partners') numbered forty-five.

The experts talked about governance, and institutions, and 'building state capacity', or 'building a more inclusive state', as if they had no idea (in fact, they had no idea) that the state's institutions had been built, funded and twisted out of shape with the help of foreign aid for the last sixty years. They were understandably confused by Nepali politics and society, but they knew what they were doing. They punched 'root causes' and 'triggers' into their conflict analysis formulas like they were casting a horoscope. 'We just persuaded them to buy us a new sports centre,' a friend in the police said. 'They've got all this money to spend, they'll say yes to anything, as long as it's for peace building.'

There's no doubt that foreign aid has been instrumental in gaining many achievements since 1951, such as constructing the weak and limited infrastructure (from roads to telecoms and power generation).[11] Improvements in health and education, especially for women and children, have come about through donor aid, even if the country does remain near the bottom of many global rankings.[12] If the donors withdrew, some needy people who benefit from some projects would undoubtedly suffer. The discourse for human rights has been led by donor-funded NGOs. Activists draw valuable moral support and political protection from the international community, even if legal impunity is rife in every field, and no one has yet been prosecuted for wartime abuses. The UN did play an important part in the peace process. Even if it couldn't promote 'sustainability' or 'planning', donor aid helped finance the rapid urbanization of Kathmandu, and middle-class consumption, making political change possible. If the donors left, and took $1 billion a year with them, Kathmandu's economy would suffer (although the majority of rural Nepalis would surely be less affected). An unknown but presumably large share of aid is paid in foreigners' wages and never comes to Nepal anyway.

The charge against foreign aid in Nepal isn't that it's achieved nothing, but that it's achieved little at great cost, bearing little relation to the donors' claims. Six decades and billions of dollars, thousands of man-years of expert advice, have failed to build functional institutions or productive economic structures. They couldn't stop the spread of communism and may have facilitated it, since for the Maoists' 'revolution of rising expectations' to take root at least a little education was required.[13] Measured in per capita income, Nepal stands in 189th position in the global wealth tables, 24 places off the bottom, the poorest country in Asia except Afghanistan. People make on average $700 a year. Income inequality may be the most severe in all of Asia.[14] Nepal now hopes to graduate from the bottom class, of Least Developed Countries, by 2022.[15]

'There are *some* good projects, and many good people,' a thirty-year veteran of the scene reminded me. But the system makes most efforts worthless. 'The excuse Nepalis make is that this country is small, poor and landlocked. Thirty million people's not small. It's not poor. Have you seen the price of land in this town? And landlocked, so what? It's between India and China.

'You don't need donor funds to clean up the human shit outside your district hospital,' he said. 'You don't need donor funds to give people a place to wash their hands beside the toilet. Why can't the donors say, "We've had enough. You guys get your thing together and come to us when you're ready. Until then, we'll concentrate on stopping the spread of fascism in Greece"?'

It was a version of the same question everyone is asking. Then he described how an instance of massive (and hardly unsuspected) corruption had recently come to public light, in a sector funded by his organization, and it hadn't even been discussed in their internal meetings, which showed he could see where the answer lay.

> It may be that what is most important about a 'development' project is not so much what it fails to do but what it achieves through its 'side effects'. Rather than repeatedly asking the politically naïve question 'Can aid programmes ever be made really to help poor people?', perhaps we should investigate the more searching question, 'what do aid programmes do *besides* fail to help poor people?'[16]

The fact is that the international community and the Nepali state are bound together as tightly as two halves of the same walnut. The shell of a walnut admits no light, and its structure is resistant to external shocks. The fruit is stuck inside.

The starting point to think about Nepal's failed development is that the country's rulers have never been motivated by the national interest. The defining characteristic and raison d'être of the political economy are the practice of patronage for the purpose of resource extraction: through the sale of offices and political favours, bureaucratic graft, commissions on public contacts, lucrative but unproductive donor programmes, politically protected business cartels, or any other opportunity for rent seeking. Economically useful assets, like the national airline, or the electricity board, are hollowed out for the benefit of a few officials and their patrons, and left derelict at immeasurable cost to the nation. Political protection is accorded to orphanages that traffic children, and the licensing of sub-standard medical schools. The transport sector is controlled by transport syndicates, tripling the price of road haulage and killing bus passengers. The syndicates insist that their drivers are exempt from the traffic laws. (If the police keep issuing fines they'll block the road: the government backs down.) Food wholesale is controlled by fruit and vegetable cartels, driving down farmers' incomes and generating food-price inflation. Union bosses create a monopoly on factory workers, then use it to enrich themselves, crippling industry against the interests of workers. Fuel is distributed (and adulterated) by fuel cartels, which shut off supply when their interests are threatened; drinking water is supplied by drinking-water cartels because the water board is dysfunctional (they'll stop delivering water if the government tries to regulate them). Goldsmiths have a syndicate (they reject the testing of their scales). Taxi cartels defend the right to rig meters. Construction companies have contractors' cartels, which build the country's substandard infrastructure at inflated costs, from the development budget.

In short, the words 'development' and 'democracy' do not so much describe what's going on as conceal the system that exists.[17] There was a feeding frenzy in the early years of the 'transition', as the donors pumped money in in search of the peace dividend. Donor aid increased as a percentage of GDP.[18] Nepal plummeted down the international league tables for corruption. Members of political parties, which were at each other's throats in Kathmandu, sat together in each district to carve up the local development budget. Old buildings were repainted and passed off as new schools, or the new schools were paid for but never built. Schools that didn't exist received regular operating costs. Users' groups were stuffed with political proxies; politically protected criminals and party youth wings skirmished over contracts. In some parts of the country officials guessed that 80 per cent of the development budget was stolen.[19]

It was the same story in education. Some people said education was the most corrupt part of the government, which would be startling if it was even nearly true. In 2014, sixty years after the donors first got involved in education, fifteen years and hundreds of millions of dollars after the latest donors' group started making the sector their own, after the 'moderately satisfactory'[20] Education for All Programme, and past halfway through the vaunted School Sector Reform Programme, 28 per cent of government school candidates passed their School Leaving Certificate exams.[21] The rest ended ten years of schooling with no qualification. There is probably no greater indictment of international development in Nepal than the derelict state of public education.[22]

Everybody knew about all of this, but the donors worked hard not to fully acknowledge it, while insisting they had 'zero tolerance' for corruption. Why would they do that?

Foreign aid to Nepal is worth about $1 billion a year (exact figures aren't available) and provides a quarter of the government budget,[23] but remittances from migrant labourers are worth about $4.8 billion a year, or a quarter of the national economy. This contribution is rapidly increasing.

Circumstances in Nepal, the demand for labour in Gulf countries, and a change in the rules for issuing passports, combined to get the remittance boom started around 2000. By 2010 about 10 per cent of the population were working abroad, and 56 per cent of households received income from remittances.[24] These remittances are the main reason that the proportion of people living on less than $1.25 a day declined from 68 per cent in 1995, to 53 per cent in 2003, to 24 per cent in 2010.[25] Because these payments went mainly to poor households, income inequality began to fall for the first time. Remittances from migrant labourers have done more to reduce poverty in Nepal in a decade than foreign aid could in six, yet the donors are almost silent on the migrant labourers, even while they slyly claim credit for recent gains.[26]

The migrants have to work abroad because the dysfunctional politics and stagnant economy ensure that there are no jobs in Nepal. They take out high interest loans or mortgage their land to pay the middlemen, who fleece them, and the manpower agents, who sometimes send them abroad without proper documents.[27] The Labour Ministry is another of those often described as among the most corrupt parts of the government.[28] At each government office where they queue for paperwork the labourers are extorted and treated with contempt. Maybe two thousand of them leave every day.[29] No reliable total is available, but many hundreds die every year on their construction sites and in their workers' camps.[30]

Their contributions make cartels and dysfunctional, extractive politics sustainable. The more screwed up Nepal is the more remittances and the more foreign aid pour in. Domestic businessmen make their money in the middle, on arbitrage and scams. The 'growth sectors' of the economy, such as banking, finance, and upscale housing developments, are far removed from most people's lives. Hardly anything is invested in domestic production because of all the extortion, the power cuts, and the militant trades unions. Remittance money helps millions of people meet their daily needs, and it also helps to fund real estate bubbles, private schools, and private healthcare.[31] Sales taxes and import duties, paid for with remittances, form the government's tax base, which, combined with the contribution from foreign aid, removes financial pressure on the government to provide effective management, or implement policies to promote growth. Many of the young people who might be angry (and force change) are labouring outside the country to raise their families out of poverty, which helps to take the political pressure off.

The result is a 'rentier state', called a 'fragile', 'frail' or a 'failing state' to justify more aid, but which is actually stagnant and surprisingly stable. Development, peace, and conflict experts assume that the government is there to provide services, and must derive its legitimacy from that or collapse; but it's clearly not true. And what appears to be disarray is (for the most part) the functioning of a resilient system in which power and resources flow outside the structures that ostensibly regulate them; where informal networks are more powerful than public accountability; and where the incentives reward the destruction of value. The system has endured and deepened through periods of royal autocracy and multi-party rule, then through the

Maoist insurgency and the peace process. All of the parties are engaged in it – struggling to protect their share, or increase it at the expense of others – because this is a game in which the spoils to be divided don't grow. Bureaucratic incomes derive precisely from not reforming. Which politician truly wants to empower his vote bank, or empower the people his backers exploit? Nepal is 'dysfunctional by design'.[32]

Marx and Engels wrote, 'the executive of the modern State is but a committee for managing the common affairs of the whole bourgeoisie.'[33] In Kathmandu that means the traders and salaried office staff, the journalists and intellectuals, the homeowners, carteliers, monopolists, speculators, brokers, manpower agents, rent-seeking bureaucrats, and absentee landlords. Whatever it may fail to do, the state succeeds at protecting these people's core interests. If the country started to work by the system to which lip service is paid then all the kickbacks and commissions and monopoly profits, the permissive legal environment, the unwarranted privileges and the social iniquities that help sustain anyone who is doing well, would end; and people wouldn't need private schools or water deliveries or diesel generators or housing colonies or a development industry to employ the middle class and throw money at NGOs.

As society has changed, violence and disorder have increased. The system of power has changed more slowly. The vision of the ruling classes lags far behind people's expectations. The poor are blamed for their own backwardness and Kathmandu's middle class is caught between demanding that the country become more modern, and resisting demands for social change. Hardly any office worker denounces rural slavery, for example, or landlessness, as loudly as she denounces the annoying protests of its victims.[34] It's questionable how long this situation is tenable. Clearly the donors can't be blamed for all of this. But they do help to reproduce and entrench it, by funding the status quo for decades, with limited measurable achievements. And why would they do that?

☀

I used to think of the development experts as like blind people taking shots at billiards, with no idea what was happening on the table.

'It's wilful ignorance, more like,' said a friend who works in the business, because despite appearances the experts do partly understand what's going on.[35] For example, a Conflict Assessment Report sponsored by Britain's Department for International Development in 2000 found that foreign aid had 'sustained Kathmandu's elite patronage systems'.[36] Most research in the development sector is done on behalf of the donors, by consultants who understand that reaching unsupportive conclusions is professionally maladroit, but the war years may have been a time when a little more independence was called for. Other reports of the period made similar points.

> Society's caste employment and income inequalities are indeed strikingly reflected in many [development] agency structures ... in spite of the emphasis given to rural employment, the management of programmes is still overwhelmingly placed in the hands of a gatekeeper group.[37]

There are plenty of cocktail circuit millionaires who receive donor funding for some scheme or another.

Or, according to a European Union Conflict Assessment Mission,

> The problem of politicization, caste and ethnic inequality are the context of civil society activity. For donors, civil society is a very small group of English speaking elite operating in Kathmandu.[38]

And, as an official at an international agency told me in 2011, 'Corruption is a fundamental systemic issue ... In terms of the political economy we provide the fiscal space for them [corrupt officials and politicians] to do what they want to do. The donors don't want to speak openly because each one is into "let's give peace a chance". I'm quite sure they know what is happening but they are willing to turn away.'

How is it that this fiasco carries on, with so little accountability?[39]

☀

To understand the robust, walnut-like structure that binds the donors to Nepal in persistent, mutually reinforcing failure it's necessary to recognize the modular repetition. Over six decades the slogans and acronyms have changed regularly but the system and its basic premise (that the solution to Nepal's underdevelopment lies in foreign money and expertise) has not, although it remains unproven. The changing and recycled theories justify more aid to their constituency, which is the same development experts. The statistics, studies, and evaluations must be flawed (as practitioners privately admit), or they wouldn't give encouraging support to the latest concept, until it fails to work and it's time to quietly move on again.[40]

'Everywhere it's the same story,' according to an activist for women's economic empowerment, finally disgusted at the series of failed, purportedly successful projects she'd been roped into. '"*No tangible results*".'

Several things are constant. Since the beginning the industry has relied on short-term consultants, or staff who lead insular expatriate lives during their two- or three-year postings.[41] The events of five or six years ago are background details they're too busy to study, but their Nepali counterparts sat in similar meetings with their predecessors' predecessors.[42] The staffing rotation, and the fancies of passing agency chiefs and ambassadors, plays into the project cycle which, of all Nepal's cycles of repetition, is the tightest. The latest batch of foreign officials don't personally remember how their organization has tipped a couple of million a year into the same ruined institution, always claiming it is about to turn the corner. They have to believe the change is about to come, instead of asking, *if our money's not making this work, are we paying for it not to?*

Obfuscating jargon allows the donors to believe they're saying more than they are, while stopping other people from understanding. They fool themselves the better to fool others. According to a friend, 'the repetition of these phrases is exceptional, and no one seems to agree on what they actually mean. I read and re-read a sentence the other day,' he told me in an email, 'in which the author promised their organization would start "addressing the causes of conflict in a manner that is conflict sensitive." I have my own long list.'

I asked him to send it to me. He wrote:

> The current list Tom (all taken from recent meetings, some explanations/ actual meanings added in brackets).
> Are you free for lunch tomorrow?
> Ground-truthed
> Fiduciary risk (corruption)
> Managing expectations (no)
> Deliverables
> Upliftment
> Stakeholder
> Going forward
> Low-hanging fruit
> The parking lot (issues which we don't want to discuss now, we will put them aside in the parking lot)
> Supersizing budgets
> Game-changer
> Crossroads
> Cross-fertilization
> Real trade-offs (as opposed to fake ones) …

I wrote back:

> That's fantastic! What does ground-truthed mean? Measured against reality and given a pass? Love to have lunch…

My own favourite phrase is 'visiting the same place twice'. It means, 'showing long-term commitment to the facts on the ground'.

'This sounds very crude,' said a development worker, whom I took out for dinner, 'especially from someone working in the development sector. But the fact is that a lot of the people in these agencies are just doing things to save their asses. It has to do with their capacity for understanding. I don't think the quality of their work matches their pay cheque. That's why they're always reinventing the wheel.'

It's essential for the international bureaucrats to believe that expertise in governance, or microcredit, or conflict, or mediation or the 'rule of law', or whatever, is more important than expertise in Nepal, which few of them have. (Some of them are expert in nothing besides their own bureaucracy.) Foreigners are paid more than locals and hold all the senior jobs.[43] It is on these tenets that massive organizations are built, and which careerists must preserve. Staff live in lovely villas, with gardeners and maids. They pass weeks, possibly entire postings, scarcely meeting anyone who doesn't derive their income from development.[44] Many consultants are on $500 to $1,500 a day. (The office flies them over business class to give a power-point presentation.) If the consultant is doing an evaluation, she's hired by the people she evaluates. I'm not aware of any measures to address this staggering conflict of interest.

All the incentives sustain the money-go-round. Senior aid executives measure their success, and move on in their careers by their ability to increase and disburse their budgets. (They are dependent on their recipients.) If they ceased to fund projects because they were corrupt or failing, then their budgets would have to shrink. The recipients know this.[45] Britain, Nepal's biggest bilateral donor, nearly doubled its aid from £55.9 million in 2012/13 to £103.8 million in 2013/14. The budgets increase even though the government consistently fails to spend the aid it already receives: it is an astonishing fact that due to the government's weak capacity, actual expenditure is consistently a fraction of the development funds available. As the end of the year draws close there are frantic deliberations in the donor offices, as the development experts search for ways to spend the millions left over from unspent commitments to the government, before next year's (increased) budget arrives.

Genuine scrutiny is necessarily weak, notwithstanding the equally necessary rhetoric of 'transparency'. ('When the project goes tits-up we just blame the partner organization!' a friend explained.) The donors don't appear before the Public Accounts Committee or any other committee of the Nepali parliament. The National Planning Commission is supposed to represent the government to the donors and set national priorities, but it also receives donor funds. (The donors were even in the prime minister's office until recently.) The donors do have a set of basic operating guidelines (BOGs), committing themselves to uphold unspecified standards of political neutrality, transparency, and accountability, to help the poor, be egalitarian and so on, but as far as I can discover, in all their hundreds of projects and programmes they have never found any of their own activities not to be in compliance.[46]

Very little academic research is done in areas concerning the donors that isn't funded by them.[47] If findings are deemed controversial they're not published. A donor might commission a study of transport cartels, but not publish it, perhaps because, if all that's true, how is their hundred-odd million a year ever going to stimulate growth? An official estimated to me that over half of all donor-commissioned studies, costing tens of millions of dollars a year, go unpublished.

Please take the European education expert who complained to me, during the latest scandal in the education ministry, that a local journalist had telephoned her at home to enquire what was going on. Imagine it! She was outraged.

In fact the local media mostly leaves the donors alone, for several reasons. The financial structures, fusing a dozen or more foreign agencies with national ministries and a cascading structure of committees and users' groups, are so complicated that (even development workers admit) nobody really understands where the money's going. This means it's impossible to attribute responsibility for anything. There's also harassment. For example, when a young reporter described a newly formed NGO in the forestry sector, composed of ex-donor staff, getting a multi-million-dollar contract without fulfilling the criteria, the donors called her editor and alleged that she'd been bribed to smear them. (He stood by her, the NGO's contract was later cancelled.)

'Editors don't like to pick too many quarrels with power centres, and the donors are a power centre,' said another journalist, who'd had his own run-in. '"*Don't rock the boat.*"'

'That's a phrase I hear quite often in connection with the donors,' I said.

'I couldn't have written five articles like the one I wrote and stayed on at the paper,' he said. 'Or even two or three. More than most things I've written, people came to me and said they really appreciated that piece. And everyone was telling me, "Don't you want to work in Kathmandu any more?" Everyone sees the donor industry as the only way you can have a middle-class or upper-middle-class career in Kathmandu. There's nothing else.'

In Kathmandu alone the donors surely spend more on public relations than all but a few British news organizations spend covering the whole of Asia. ('Telling the story' of how their programme work is an increasingly important preoccupation, even in internal reporting.) Most British foreign editors now have never worked abroad, and they have a professional need for cliché, so they're glad to believe that Western money and advice is what poor people lack. When I did a story on how DFID, the British government's development agency, had spent thirty thousand pounds renovating a small palace for their country director to live in, I couldn't persuade the *Daily Telegraph* to print it, until I told them the *Daily Mail* were going to, which wasn't true.[48] The article got more attention than most things I've done. DFID was furious, and soon several people were passing me messages, each peddling tales of waste or failure, each in a different project.

The editor of a local paper told me he was going to rerun my *Telegraph* piece. He had it laid out on the page, until he got a call from management and pulled it. Apparently they were worried they might lose the large ads donors place every time they're hiring drivers.

*

It was Dashain, the great harvest-time festival of the victory of good over evil. The roads were empty. The newspapers said that 450,000 people had left the city to celebrate in their villages. In their place thousands of goats had entered, to be sacrificed by those who remained. I was at my in-laws' house and a friend, Ujjwal, came round to fly kites from the roof; it was a ritual that had somehow remained missing from my Nepali education.

The day was hot. Under a blue sky and high white clouds the suburban houses stood in gardens, with trees or clumps of bamboo between them. Before us was the massive, jungle-clad hill of Shivapuri. We dropped our pile of paper kites, opened bottles of beer, and tied the first one on, carefully using the string to measure the centre. Ujjwal got the kite up at the third attempt. 'Right,' he said, 'where are those guys?' and we looked around.

There was a black and red kite identical to ours, high in front of us. It clearly belonged to the group of teenagers a few roofs behind. Ujjwal moved, rattling and diving, in their kite's direction. 'It's best to strike from above', he said, 'that's what they say. I don't know why.'

Ujjwal is a development wallah. According to him, the current global paradigm says that donors have weakened governments in recipient countries by routing their funds through non-state channels. Now the Paris Declaration and the Accra Agenda for Action were going to make donors work through recipient governments, and be accountable to parliaments and people.[49] 'The Paris declaration is coming in but when you have a country like Nepal that's fucked up, working through the government means nothing gets done,' he said. 'The problem is there's this whole collusion and corruption in the procurement thing, it's all these contractors' cartels. Look at the roads they're building. They're obviously not up to the technical standards.'

'All these ministries were partly created by the donors anyway,' I said.

'Yup,' said Ujjwal.

The kites' strings crossed and they struggled, then moved apart again. The duel lasted a minute or so, to the noisy pleasure of the kids on the roof behind, until Ujjwal shouted '*chet!*' The other kite drifted slowly away. The boys turned quiet. We drank our beer. 'The main thing's the string then?' I said. 'Can't you get different ones?'

'Yeah, there are loads of different types,' said Ujjwal. 'We used to make it ourselves. You can make sharp ones or slippery ones. You know sabudana?'

'No.'

'It's a grain, a bit like rice. You boil it for hours then you just put it on the string, by letting it run through your fingers. People use aloe vera. The best is to grind fluorescent tubes into a very fine powder. We used to spend all day.'

There were some children on a roof a little further off. By their style of flying Ujjwal inferred that they were playing with all the string they had. He set off after them and cut their kite easily away. He called *chet!* again. The kids left.

'Money from remittances along with access provided by roads – that leads to improvements in maternal mortality,' he said. 'The living standards survey shows that something's going on. There have been dramatic improvements coming from remittances and urbanization.'

'But that's not coming from government development policy or from the donors,' I said.

'It's unintended. Maybe those jobs could have come here, but it didn't happen that way.'

We drank our beer. Our original victims' new kite had never really got started, and it was now becoming entangled and broken on the rebar of an unfinished house. The best target seemed to be at least 200 metres away, a tiny speck. We couldn't even make out the position of the people flying it.

'I don't think corruption is so detrimental to development,' Ujjwal said to my surprise. 'I think the problem's the inability to make decisions. If the work gets done the benefits are worth more than the ten or twenty per cent you have to pay in corruption. I mean, if you're paying eighty per cent then that's bad …

Of course, everyone says zero tolerance on corruption, but internally I've heard the bosses say that twenty per cent is acceptable. Why not just formalize it, make the commissions open? These guys are running away,' he muttered, but eventually he reached the distant kite. There was a struggle, then he said *chet* without enthusiasm, and we watched our own kite drift away. 'It's true, you see? He was on top.

'It's all the syndicates, man,' said Ujjwal. 'The transport costs in Nepal are some of the highest in the world. Thrice what they should be! You were the one that sent me that report, right?'

'I don't think it was ever published.'

'There was a lot of good information in that report,' said Ujjwal. 'Why can't we threaten the government?' he wondered. 'Why can't we say, "If you guys don't get your act together we're not going to give you any money"? That would make them change. I don't know why we can't do that.'

I repeated my point, that the bureaucracy wasn't some alien institution from the donors. It had been moulded by them through decades of joint programmes, 'capacity building', 'partnership', and 'SWAps'.[50]

'I can train you and you might be the best engineer,' said Ujjwal, 'but unless you have the contacts with the politicians you're not going to get promoted. It's all the fuck-ups and the arse-kissers that are going up. It's not that there aren't good people out there, but it doesn't matter how much capacity building we do, it's not going to have an impact until the whole system in the bureaucracy changes, and that's not going to happen unless we do something radical.' He meant, like turning off the cash spigot.

I said, 'The donors'll never do it. How can they? If they didn't give money they wouldn't be donors,' and I explained to him my walnut theory of how the foreign and domestic 'development partners' are bound together in mutually reinforcing failure.

Ujjwal grunted, and told me a story that a foreign consultant had told him, about how big organizations work. 'It's like a raft,' he said, 'floating down a rocky river, and all the bosses can see their pension on the other side of the finishing line and they don't want to rock the boat. South Asians are clever man. We keep giving them the money. They know the money's coming. They can keep doing whatever they want. Don't quote me on this man, because everybody knows that I'm your friend ...' and then he told me one of the secrets that everybody knows.

I crashed a couple of kites into trees and Ujjwal had another one up before the kids behind had got a good beginning. 'Shall I get them now?' he joked, but he let them get theirs soaring properly before he cut it loose.

There's some evidence, Ujjwal reminded me, that just giving money to the poor works better than elaborate programmes.[51] It seems they don't spend it on booze, as everyone assumed they would, but on whatever they most need. Administrative costs, salaries, intermediaries, and corruption would be reduced, and maybe fewer poor people would miss out if the schemes were simpler. 'What's the point of means-testing in these villages?' said Ujjwal. 'Everyone's poor there. Who cares if a couple of rich peasants get grants too?'

We'd put the kites down and we were sitting in the small shade of the low wall around the rooftop. I said, 'You know, it turns out that idea's not new.' I'd found something written twenty years ago: for forty-one years, the author had written in 1992, the development approach had been wasteful and ineffective, pursuing the creation of supply rather than demand.[52] Why not channel money for health and education directly to poor households, whose rights were currently assailed by the collusion of political and business interests? As far as I know, it wasn't tried.

'If you just give money to the poor you don't need all these consultants,' said Ujjwal. 'That's what Mike was working on. He lost his job. Think about it. Running around identifying poor households is going to cost more than the five hundred rupees a month we're giving them. But everyone is giving out "poverty cards". There are three agencies doing it at the same time! There's a term for that too. Empire building. A good bureaucrat has to build his empire. Go and talk to Jane,' he added gloomily. 'She's a fucking idiot.'

We talked a bit about Mike's case. I'd got the feeling he didn't exactly lose his job because he'd started pushing unpopular ideas, but rather he'd started criticizing policies and partner organizations, and become generally disaffected.

'Yeah. His boss was one of those don't-rock-the-boat types.'

'What are the foreigners like?' I asked. 'Is it a problem that they don't know about stuff?'

He screwed up his face and thought for a while. A couple of times I thought he was about to answer. 'It's a lot of words, a lot of paradigms, a lot of meetings,' he said.

'I mean, is it a problem that they don't understand?'

'It's a lot about personalities,' he said. 'I don't find, "I'm a fucking Westerner and I know better than you." I think that's a thing of the past. I don't think that's the problem, Tom. But the organizations don't change. It's not that the realization isn't there, but these organizations have not been able to change.'

Some small children were playing with a kite they'd found in the garden below, running up and down, pulling it behind them on its severed string. I asked about the attitude to internal criticism.

'You don't get reprimanded but they don't like it,' he said. 'They don't like it. There's a fine line. I think if you pinpoint people then it's not acceptable, but if you talk about the system, that seems to be ok. Nothing happens of course, but that's bureaucracies. The buzzword now,' he added, 'is climate resilient and gender friendly …'

'There's hundreds of millions,' I said, 'being pissed against the wall for climate resilience, right? Where's that money *gone*?'

'I know man. And that's money taken away from actual conservation like saving tigers. There's no money in that now. It's all climate resilience, whatever the fuck that means. Anyway,' he said, 'tens, hundreds of millions. In the end it's so small, it's not going to make any difference.' We got back to our feet and put up a final kite. For his last trick Ujjwal crossed the sky again and cut the one that had cut him earlier. As he worked the line he must have been brooding on development, or conservation. 'Have you been to China?' he said.

'A bit. Not much.'

'Shanghai must be amazing.'

'Yeah, it is,' I said. 'It's amazing.'

'But they're still eating fucking tiger penises man. To get a hard-on.'

☀

'The perception is that every project is partly corrupt,' said a senior official at the constitutionally ordained anti-corruption commission. (At the time, the commission had had no commissioners for several years.) 'There is a smell of corruption' in the donor sector, he said, but no specific studies. 'I think the donors are not so serious about corruption,' he added. 'They never bring pressure to immediately appoint the commissioners or chief commissioner of this department.'

'Mostly they just refuse to admit it,' said a commissioner of the National Planning Commission. There were 'whispers' about corruption inside international agencies, he said, but never any formal cases.

The whispers, if you care to listen, are quite loud. NGO people privately allege that kickbacks of up to 50 per cent are sometimes paid in exchange for grants. Local consultants and contractors say they have to pay bribes to the procurement and human resources guys. All you have to do is start asking questions to hear half a dozen lurid tales. '[X international office] is one of the most corrupt buildings in the country,' a respected local consultant told me. 'I can name the people taking kickbacks if you want, but of course there isn't any proof. And like anywhere else, when you want to get paid, you have to pay the accountant.'

It is partly questionable how far the foreign officials are aware of this kind of thing. It may be that when the rumours reach them they simply assume that Nepalis mistakenly see corruption everywhere, because that's how Nepalis think everything works. Some of them know better. I remember a diplomat remarking that his embassy fired a visa clerk for taking bribes about once a year, yet the donor agencies, with far more staff and huge budgets, fire nobody. They say they have zero tolerance, but since they don't have serious initiatives to identify and pursue cases they never find any. The donors can offer very few examples of when they've taken action in a specific case of corruption involving a member of staff or a partner agency, or halted payments over concerns; much less taken evidence to the police, although presumably that would promote their objective of 'strengthening the rule of law'. Everybody knows all of this. It promotes public cynicism.

To keep it all going you have to ignore things that might cause a problem. Bare-faced denial is the force that holds the two halves of the walnut together. All of the criticisms repeated here have been around for decades, and they still apply. Everybody knows what's going on but the well-meaning agencies stand by their claims, such as that local communities can hold the powerful and corrupt accountable. What choice do they have? If it wasn't true, how would their projects work? Apparently, during the First World War, the German Kaiser ruled out peace talks, because it would disrupt the railway timetables on which victory depended. Likewise, the donors demand to carry on, without interference or disruptive scrutiny, because the poor depend on them. Everybody knows that international development, like many of Nepal's failures, persists the way it is because some people depend on it. Obviously, that doesn't include the poor.

23

I had dinner with some friends, mostly foreigners, who had taken an intense and detailed interest in Nepali affairs for many years. They worked on politics and human rights for international organizations and NGOs. We were sitting around on the floor with glasses of wine and bowls of olives, and humus and pistachio nuts and sticks of cucumber. There was almost certainly some esoteric music playing, which would have passed me by. Someone mentioned a secret intelligence operation codenamed 'Mustang'. The others all had, but I'd never heard of it.

While I'd been away a detailed article appeared in a Nepali-language magazine called *Nepal*, which captured the attention of all the foreign missions.

Going to Mustang
Foreign friends have gotten lost in Mustang
There is a meeting in Mustang

the article began. 'Such conversations used to take place among the spies at the National Investigation Department (NID), the primary secret espionage department of the government of Nepal. But the word Mustang virtually hanging off their lips was not the name of the mountainous district in Nepal. It was in fact a covert operation which ran for more than four years before the peace agreement in 2006. Foreigners would come in vehicles with black windows to the supplies department and would meet secretly with the chief then leave', it quoted an NID officer as claiming. 'The construction of the new building inside the department and all other requirements of the operation were met by the British Government.'

The Maoists were the target. MI6 were said to have used three safe houses (the article gave their addresses). They supplied 35 motorcycles, 36 sets of night-vision binoculars, 35 desk-top computers, 35 stills cameras and 35 cassette players as well as a varying number of cars, television sets, video cameras, laptops, mobile phones, faxes, fridges, air conditioners and items of furniture. A radio mast was installed on top of Pulchowki hill, on the Valley rim, and another on top of a newly constructed building in the NID headquarters, creating a secure network for the 35 special radio sets. The article was less specific about the bugs and other listening equipment the British supplied. (Apparently they insisted that the Nepali government pay for the 35 pistols required from its own funds.) A handful of British civilian and military officers attached to the embassy, as well as a varying cast of visitors, trained the NID officers and ran the Kathmandu end of the operation.[1]

The fact that by 2004 the king was planning a *coup d'état* created a problem for Operation Mustang, because the British government would obviously have to condemn it. So an environmental NGO named, with a glimmer of public schoolboy wit, the High Altitude Research Centre (HARC) was established to provide extra cover. Every signature on HARC's registration document was provided by an NID officer.[2]

'There's a certain black comedy,' one of the guests at the dinner remarked, 'in the fact that the Brits got ripped off by a dodgy NGO.' Because the reason all of this is known is that someone, or some people within the NID leaked it all, claiming that the British equipment – the cars and motorcycles and the air-conditioning units – had been stolen and sold off by the spies they ran. The Indians apparently bought up the bugging and intercept gear. The disgruntled officers produced a 24-page document detailing these frauds, which they circulated to all the political parties, including the Maoists, to the parliamentary public accounts committee, to two tabloid weekly newspapers, and to *Nepal* magazine.[3]

When I heard these things described at that dinner party several thoughts ran through my mind in an almost instantaneous succession. I'd known the spies and military types at the British embassy during the war. I liked some of them. (One of them offered to recommend me for a career in his office.) We socialized, and talked about what we thought was going on in Nepal. But because I'd known what my friends were I took the things they told me seriously, but not always literally. I suspected they sometimes flattered me (a freelance journalist in his mid-twenties) with scraps of information that seemed exciting; so I received them with interest, but I didn't put them in the newspaper – except once. The day after the coup in 2005, I was told that British military aid to Nepal was being suspended. That information now appeared in a different light.

Another occasion came instantly to mind, an occasion to which I could hear the dinner party conversation now turning. In 2004 the Maoist Valley Commander, whose name was Sadhuram Devkota, whose *nom de guerre* was 'Prashant', died in custody at the Balaju barracks in Kathmandu. It had struck me at the time as odd that my British friend was so keen for me to believe him when he insisted, casually, that Prashant really had hanged himself. Apparently, he was suicidal because his comrades had betrayed him, and because his comrades had come to suspect him, although in fact he was loyal. Something like that. I hadn't been especially interested in the case. Everybody knew, they'd known for years, that the army tortured and killed prisoners all the time. And now my mind was reprising every conversation I'd ever had with certain people. Had I ever told them anything that now seemed so much more important?

I knew as soon as I heard of it that I would write about Operation Mustang. I'd forgotten many things that now took significance. It was only later that I rediscovered the observation, recorded in my diary after an embassy dinner in October 2002, which I quoted in chapter 5: 'It becomes clear that the military assistance that the minister did not want to be specific about is in setting up an intelligence capability.' I'd forgotten it completely.

I interviewed politicians and officials; Maoists who'd worked underground in Kathmandu; members of every security agency, retired and serving; Nepalis and foreigners. They included many of the men who'd led the war. Some of them would be good candidates for a war crimes trial. Most of them seemed to dislike one another, which they expressed by singling one another out to imply *So-and-so was the one who knew what was going on, He authorized it, His money's finished too! I wasn't so much involved.* They all had agendas. They all lied. But they all talked, and I was able to corroborate parts of it. I trawled through American diplomatic cables on Wikileaks and British policy statements in Hansard, to try to understand what the policymakers were doing, or what they thought they were doing. In what follows there are large gaps and some omissions, including the names of everyone involved, but it's an unusually detailed glimpse of a recent MI6 operation. The consistent testimony of senior figures speaking anonymously gives an impression of what went on. It's for the British government to explain what happened; and especially, what happened to the victims.

It's obvious that Kathmandu is a nest of spies. The South Koreans and the Japanese are there to watch the North Koreans, who use the same tradecraft everywhere. The North Korean embassy is so poor it has to run a restaurant (called Pyongyang) to finance itself. The NID trails Pyongyang's manager as he travels halfway across town, to save a few rupees on the price of melons and mangos in the bazaars south of New Road. The North Koreans also make money by selling Viagra, which they apparently produce themselves. According to Nepali assessments, it works. Nepali surveillance reports that the North Koreans are the only embassy that troubles to sell its empty beer bottles (always Carlsberg) to the man who comes around on a bicycle buying old newspapers and glass.

The Chinese are there to watch the Tibetan refugees. They are said to run extensive networks under the cover of volunteer teachers and language institutes, NGOs, restaurants, and small businesses; and they place agents among the refugees themselves before they escape across the mountains. A neighbourhood like Boudha, where the refugees gather, is jumping with informants and watchers.

The Indian intelligence agency RAW operates a station of scores of officers, because the Pakistani ISI uses Nepal to infiltrate counterfeit currency into India. Explosives have been found in Kathmandu in houses linked to Pakistani diplomats, and when an Indian Airlines flight from Kathmandu was hijacked in 1999 Pakistani diplomats were implicated. But mostly the RAW works on infiltrating and manipulating Nepali political parties, and many other institutions. 'RAW's not like a normal intelligence agency,' a Western intelligence officer said. 'It doesn't do intelligence, it does political interventions.'

Restaurants and coffee shops where diplomats do their business are kept under domestic surveillance, but this is mostly to see which Nepalis are talking to whom. Nepalis don't seem to spy on foreign governments very seriously, but they spy on each other with vigour. The buzz-cut young men who loiter near the homes of power players might be from the Directorate of Military Intelligence. They often wear a tika on their forehead, so the police say, thinking it makes them look more innocent. Those who mourn the final failure of the monarchy believe the palace had become an abyss of intrigue, in which everyone was serving a double or a triple agenda. In happier times, before a lack of belief turned it inside out, the palace used the NID to spy on its democratic opponents. (Some people claim that Operation Mustang did a bit of that as well.) 'Many party leaders worked for our department at one time,' an NID officer told me. 'We still have the reports they submitted. If our boss wants to blackmail them he still can. Cash was hard to come by in the Panchayat, and four thousand rupees was big money. A top-level Congress guy now used to draw an agent's salary of four thousand then.'

About half of the NID is apparently still dedicated to spying on the government of the day's political opponents, which must create a bewildering maze of personal calculation, because the organization is stuffed with political appointees, and the government changes so often.

I arranged to meet an NID man at an Italian restaurant in Thamel, the tourist district. 'We're friends,' he kept saying. 'I like you, Tom.' The streets at night were jammed with taxis and rickshaws and whistle-blowing cops, dreadlocked hippies, serious Dutch trekking groups and trashed kids selling hash. The Maoists made use of this area in the war, because no one pays attention to strangers. Upstairs in La Dolce Vita there weren't many customers; it was all checked tablecloths and pictures of Anita Ekberg.

The intelligence man was fat, with short bulging fingers bound in gold rings; the rings bulging with coloured stones. He'd brought an underling along. We ate nothing, but quickly went through several gins and tonic while the underling clutched a bottle of beer. When I made a joke, that the guys playing carom outside a certain politician's house were probably his colleagues, the NID man seemed to think I was being serious, and turned to his underling to ask if it was so. Then he offered me a story, about a man on surveillance duty who was getting his shoes cleaned while he loitered outside the Teaching Hospital. The target moved, and he had to take to his motorcycle with one shoe missing.

'The shoe-shine guy was probably a spy too,' I said.

'Yeah, a static post for the Indians! It's like that now, so many people watching the same target, and when he's gone to bed they're always the last ones around: our guy, the Nepal Police, the APF, the army, RAW … '

This new source of mine was among those trained by the British. 'Everyone has the same surveillance manual,' he said. 'The Chinese, the British, the Americans. There's nothing about that that's different.' The NID has been trained by them all. The Westerners were more intelligence minded, he said (instructors didn't like their trainees to greet them in the street), but in the end (and this was a point several people made) the Westerners were Western, whereas the Nepalis had to work in Nepal as they knew it to be, so they discarded part of their training at the conference room door.

I imagined the spies in an endless round of power-point briefings in five-star hotels. I asked him, 'How do you know if you're being followed?'

'If you are being followed?' he said, and looked at me closely.

'Yes, for example.'

'Whenever you go out of your house,' he said, 'assume you are being followed. But don't worry about ghosts.'

'What do you mean by ghosts? Something that's not there, or something …?'

'If you notice the same person, if something happens again at the same time of day, if you really have a hunch that you are being followed …' he gripped the front of his shirt, which was hanging open to show a gold chain, to demonstrate how a hunch feels, '… then you are,' he said. He continued less passionately. 'But they have to write a report. If you've got to exchange important information, like,' (he tried to excite me) 'if I'm going to exchange sensitive information with you, of course you don't compromise the source. You have to have a fallback. You go to visit your in-laws. After a week the guy writes his report. If you're not doing anything, they follow someone else.'

In exchange for this I told him a story about thinking I was being followed while I was reporting in Burma, stopping to look at a shop and switching back, glancing around indiscreetly all the while.

'The surveillance officer wants to feel in the dominant position. Don't do anything that might challenge that,' he said. 'He could become aggressive.' It seemed ridiculous to imagine the supposedly unseen watcher blowing up in your face because you'd noticed him. 'People do things like throw something away for them to pick up.' (He implied there was nothing clever about this trick.) 'You can ask him directions, then it will be you following him!'

I was wondering about his hearty protestations of friendship and why he'd agreed to meet me. We carried on talking this crap. After some time he said, 'There are new rules. No one's allowed to fuck around anymore. That's why I brought him along.' He gestured to the underling, who grinned at me, seemingly unable to understand more than the simplest English. 'He might be able to understand names like…' the fat man reeled off some of the people who'd been involved in Operation Mustang, 'but that's all.'

'I was wondering about that,' I said. I was still wondering.

He asked the underling to pass his bag and produced a file, containing a list which he passed to me. Amid three pages of names, about a dozen people had been highlighted with different coloured pens. In the dim yellow gloom of the pizzeria the faintly printed characters were difficult to resolve. The NID man asked me to help him learn what these Britishers were doing, because he didn't believe they should be on business visas. Maybe hash smugglers, maybe paedophiles. I politely declined.

'No-no-no, of course not. You're far too busy.'

'If you give me a British paedophile I'll fuck him up in the newspaper,' I offered, but I didn't really think that was his interest. Eventually we parted.

Later that evening he turned up alone in the place where I was sitting with friends. He also knew some people there, as he knew he would, although they didn't seem to like each other. He was drunk, slamming his radio on the bar, where they said he had unpaid bills, and he was shouting, 'What can you do to me?' He also said this, as I was later told. 'My boss said, "There's this kid who's very clever who's poking his nose around, but he never goes outside. The only time we found him was in New Road having an ice cream with his wife, or visiting his in-laws".' So I probably had been followed, although I didn't remember the ice cream. But I probably hadn't given much away about what I'd learnt so far, or who'd told me, because I still didn't have very much, and I was proceeding very slowly. I would have been busier then with something like the Mallas, or Brian Hodgson.

During the war, Kathmandu's characteristic modes of treachery naturally achieved full expression.

I interviewed a senior NID man in his house, amid all the paraphernalia of a senior public servant's visiting room: framed certificates, trophies, framed photographs of ceremonies, silver and gold models of Pashupati and Swayambhu in glass cases, drinking tea his wife had made, and he told me how the war got started from the bureaucratic point of view. 'Our political leaders, they have good sides, but they have bad sides much more. Their corruption, their power-hunger. So the Maoists used the Congress and the UML and the king at different times. When they attacked Congress party members in the districts the UML thought, "They are our brothers." After some time they started to attack the UML and the Congress thought, "It's OK, they are attacking the UML." Sometimes they didn't speak against the monarchy. Then the king thought, "They are attacking only Congress and the UML." Gradually they became successful.'

One could see Mao's tactical doctrine in this, or read it as an application of the age-worn formula for political mastery; *saam daam danda bhed*; conciliate, bribe, coerce, divide. When everyone is applying it to everyone else, *saam daam danda bhed* creates an opaque environment. There are retired army officers and home ministry officials who maintain that members of the royal family channelled funds to the Maoists in the early days, to undermine the democrats.

Shortly after the insurgency began the prime minister, who was an elderly veteran of the Congress party, told a meeting of security officials, 'It is difficult to revolt with catapults. The Congress had guns but we couldn't revolt. How can they revolt with catapults?' The NID was less sure, and produced a report showing how the rebellion could spread to ten districts. It called for the recruitment of security personnel from those districts, to improve the agencies' access to information. 'The home minister came with a list and told the Chief, "We have accepted your proposal. Here are the names, enrol them." So what happened, the minister recruited his own people. We needed people from Rukum, Rolpa, and Jajarkot, but we recruited only from Dang. I am telling you how the government failed,' he said. The price was 5 lakhs for an inspector's job and 3 lakhs for an Assistant Sub Inspector (the NID uses police ranks). By the turn of the millennium the Maoists in the Valley 'were more informed than us. They had deep penetration in our department also.'

Just after the war ended I'd interviewed the commander of the Maoists' Special Task Force, which operated covertly inside the

Valley. He was still semi-underground at the time, and we met in a room of one of the bleak hotels at Sundhara. His arrival was preceded by his Special Task Force bodyguard, the usual stocky tracksuited type. The commander was short and young and personable. He described something of his organization, and how it gave force to the crowds confronting the police around the ring road. I asked him if they'd had senior people in the royal government paying them off or giving them information. 'Generals, ex-generals, government secretaries, ex-secretaries, ministers, MPs, all pay the Party,' he said. 'A general informs us that another general has a lot of money. Even industrialists and ministers do that. We get secret information from generals, from the palace, from the prime minister's office and the cabinet. People are driven by personal selfishness and they inform us. How could we survive until now if we didn't get this kind of information?'

A few years later I paraphrased these remarks to the NID man in his sitting room.

'They were more informed than us,' he repeated, 'because actually our loyalty was not with the government. Our attitude was only for money money money money.'

'You cannot imagine who is involved with the Maoists,' another senior spy told me. 'They all want power and money only.'

'There's big money at stake in these rivalries,' a former royal adviser explained.

The Maoists, on the other hand, killed suspected informants, which made informants difficult to recruit, even if many of those the party killed were only the victims of personal vendettas. The war provided an opportunity for settling all sorts of antagonisms and, more than usual, people of every status and throughout the country had to live by their political skills.

British support to the Nepali security apparatus was already long-standing. The generation of men who led the NID during the war had received training from MI6, and the CIA, as new recruits during the Panchayat. Renewed British interest in bolstering the Nepali state against terrorism preceded 9/11 by a couple of years. The British supported the establishment of a National Security Council Secretariat, which was also a pet project of King Birendra in the last years of his life. It seems the army and the palace hoped the NSC would be a useful administrative smokescreen between the palace and the army. The British saw it as the equivalent of their Joint Intelligence Committee in Whitehall. It would be a clearing house for intelligence and the coordination of security agencies, nestled right beneath the cabinet. A procession of generals and senior spies was taken to London to see how the JIC works and to be shown around the MI6 headquarters. According to Nepali generals, MI6 paid for the NSC building, and the CIA was also involved in the project. Amid all of the British support to Nepal recorded in Hansard, establishing the NSC secretariat is not mentioned anywhere that I could find.

Around the same time, the British army was helping the Royal Nepal Army to establish the Military Intelligence Support Group (MISG). More people went to the UK for training and to be shown around MI6. In 2001, before the army entered the war, a British team came to Nepal to help set up the MISG within the Directorate of Military Intelligence. British officers instructed recruits at an intelligence training school near Bhaktapur. The MISG, with a unit in each regional division, was involved in surveillance operations, agent handling, handling defectors and operations to snatch or kill Maoist targets. Some of the British officers involved with the MISG were later involved in Operation Mustang. Important figures in the British embassy retained close links with the DMI throughout the conflict, and so did the CIA.

The British also suggested that the Royal Nepal Army produce a counter-insurgency 'bible', which they assisted in drafting, drawing on their experience in Northern Ireland and Malaya and recent covert operations in Sierra Leone. So, by the time the army entered the war at the end of 2001 British military and intelligence support was already being provided. Nevertheless,

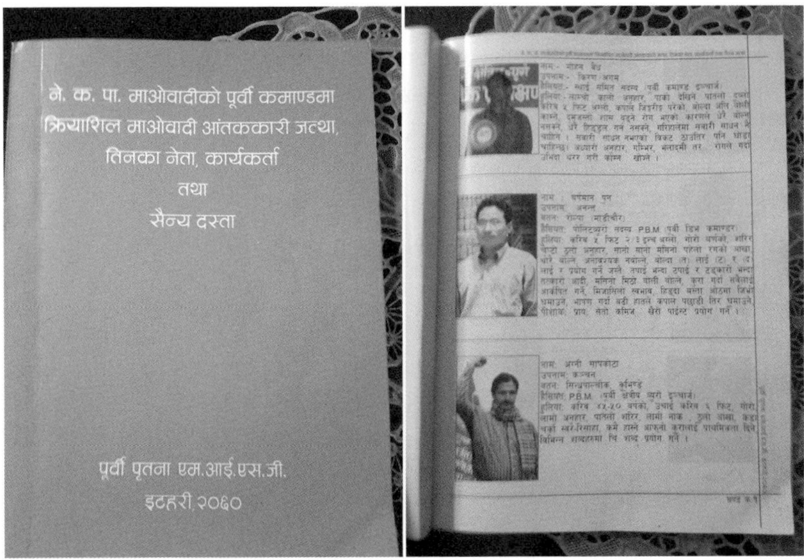

ने. क. पा. माओवादीको पूर्वी कमाण्डमा
क्रियाशिल माओवादी आंतककारी जत्था,
तिनका नेता, कार्यकर्ता
तथा
सैन्य दस्ता

पूर्वी पृतना एम.आई.एस.जी.
इटहरी,२०६०

the army was spectacularly unprepared. According to a general, there was not a roll of barbed wire in the stores.

It was a busy time for generals. 'There used to be the ICRC [International Committee of the Red Cross] raising hell, Amnesty International, all the embassy officers, and the merchants of death coming round.' This last was a half-jocular reference to the arms dealers who now descended on Kathmandu. There was a procurement spree. 'Every night there was some party I had to attend.' At these parties the defence attachés made their offers of military support.

Operation Mustang was being set up at the same time. The original initiative seems to have come in 2001, but it took time to prepare (the safe houses, the radio network, the new bug-proof building inside Singha Durbar for which, according to the disgruntled spies, those involved on the NID side managed to double the costs). This preparatory work was undertaken by a different man from the one who took charge of the Nepal end once it was ready to go. The training of the Nepali officers in such topics as the principles of counter-insurgency, surveillance, and agent handling took place at the Ambassador or the Yak and Yeti Hotel, and at the safe houses. When an instructor observed his students conferring in the car park after a session he realized they didn't understand English properly, so some were sent to the British Council for lessons. The specialists who planted the bugs needed special training. It's not clear exactly when Mustang became operational. Staff deployments indicate it may have been around late 2002 or early '03.[4] It was 'a big operation', 'all singing, all dancing', 'the full works', 'very expensive', and apparently 'signed off by the secretary of state', who was Jack Straw at the time.

The peace talks began at the beginning of 2003. According to a Western official, King Gyanendra was keen at first but then he cooled off and the talks stalled. By the summer the question was how to break the ceasefire while giving the Maoists the blame. 'There was a view, "we can beat these people",' a general confirmed. Gyanendra was lingering in London when the talks collapsed.[5] Then the army went to work without restraint. And it appears that counter-intelligence in Kathmandu turned the corner. There was a cluster of arrests as soon as the fighting resumed.

Early on I was keen to establish how intelligence was shared by the NID with the other security agencies, because I saw Mustang as an operation to arrest people, and I wanted to know what had happened to them. In principle NID reports were shared with several offices, the home minister's and the prime minister's among them. There were weekly, sometimes daily, meetings of the security chiefs (including the NID chief) at the palace, and the NSC secretariat provided a mechanism for intelligence sharing between all the agencies. British intelligence officers spent a fair amount of time at the NSC, it being a British initiative of sorts, but senior officials of the time say that most actionable intelligence was shared more informally, according to the principal people's relationships and political judgement. After the 'Unified Command' structure was introduced at the beginning of November 2003 the civilian security agencies came under the military in what a general described as 'a sort of semi-army rule'. Anyway, it appears that for the NID the most important relationships were with the palace and the army.

'At that time the army and the NID had a special pact,' according to a senior policeman, involved in counter-terrorism. The same thing was attested by many others. 'The British I think helped the NID a lot,' said a general. 'Whatever success or whatever you call it that we had, maybe it was down to that. Otherwise, it would have been worse.'

'The NID never acted, they just gave information,' said another general. According to him, the main conduit for NID intelligence was through the Palace Military Secretariat. 'The NID were involved in many incidents,' he said. When the information came to the army it would most likely be passed to the DMI or the elite 10 Brigade, headquartered at the Rana palace of Laksmi Niwas in Maharajganj. This is often referred to as the Bhairabnath Battalion: 'They used to snatch people and do all those things,' explained a general. Thanks to a UN report, Bhairabnath has become the most notorious interrogation centre, from which 49 people were probably extra-judicially executed in the space of three months alone at the end of 2003.

'How many people were arrested on NID intelligence?' I asked a senior NID man.

'So many,' he said. 'Actually, of the four security agencies, only we had deep penetration of the Maoists.'

There's no doubt that MI6's contribution was appreciated, and the British spies are still fondly thought of. 'They were trying to protect democracy against the Maoists,' another senior NID man said. 'These people must be punished, who exposed the operation and embarrassed the British government.'

'It was sincere help for the enhancement of the NID in regard to international terrorism,' said another.

A senior NID officer lamented that the army didn't always share material from interrogations with his department in return for its tip-offs. 'So many senior people were arrested on the basis of our information,' he said, 'but the army didn't share what they got from them. Time and again [the British officers] used to say to them, "You have to share that information, because the army can't do this job, but the NID can."'

A general remembered one of the British intelligence officers as 'a very fast chap … a very nice man, a very intelligent man. He knew whom to talk to'. And according to a close confidant of the king during the period, another British intelligence officer 'was a great friend of mine. He had a great sense of humour, and he was a great help. We were coordinating. It's just a pity that they left.' He searched his memory for another name but couldn't reach it. He picked up his phone, dialled, waited, and spoke in Nepali. 'Who was that person who used to email the weekly reports?' he said, 'Ah yes,' and repeated the name of another British spy. 'He was great,' he assured me, 'and he coordinated. He helped us organize our intelligence, and the kind of information that he made available worked wonders!'

'I thought the British were working very secretively through the NID,' I said.

'As far as this is concerned, these are not clear-cut sort of things,' replied the courtier. 'NID, NSC, the palace, they were all the same.'

On a chilly day at the end of winter I met a senior NID officer in a deserted hotel garden, on the deck chairs by the empty swimming pool. He'd had a central role in Operation Mustang. We were wrapped in our jackets. The waiter brought us tea and left. I asked him how many people were arrested on NID information in Kathmandu.

'Likely one hundred,' he said.

'About a hundred? More, or less?'

'In between,' he said.

'And who made these arrests?'

'The Unified Command.' The British were always 'very pleased' to hear of these successes and to see that their support was 'getting some result'. 'We never nabbed any people, we just gave the information. Sometimes the police quick response team did it ...'[6]

'And if the army?' I asked.

'If the army ordered them, "Send the prisoner in my barrack," the police used to send them. The army used to beat them. And if someone dies that's another thing. They used to send the dead body back to the police, then the headache will come to them.'

'How many people who were arrested on NID information were tortured or disappeared?' I asked.

'I don't know,' he said, 'because the army had camps in different places in the Valley. You know Maharajganj? Some forty-nine people in a common grave, in a single grave, in Shivapuri.'

'Did they include some of your targets?' I asked.

'I don't know,' he said. 'I don't know all the names. So many people were arrested on our information. The police arrested them. The army arrested them. Some were disappeared, some were, some were, you know, they were left.'

'Left? What? Freed?'

'They were freed.'

At a fast food restaurant I told a general, who'd been in the thick of it, 'The Brits must have been aware that the people who were arrested because of their operation ended up getting abused.'

'I'm sure they knew,' he said, 'They knew. Being British they must have thought about human rights also, but they knew exactly what was happening to them.'

After a while he said, 'The thing must have been approved at a high level.'

'It must have been,' I said. 'Maybe by the foreign secretary.'

'It must have cost a lot of money.'

'Yes, plenty of money.'

He said that the British had suffered frustrations, including over human rights. He questioned how well they understood the local context ('there may have been something lacking there'). He regretted that the whole thing had been exposed. 'They kept it secret for a long time,' he said. 'Even now not many people talk about it, and they talk only in vague terms. We just know there was this Mustang operation going on. Nobody asks, "Who were the victims?" It never came out.'

'Right,' I said. 'It's quite difficult to pin down. I suppose it's in the nature of these things.'

'Very difficult,' he agreed.

There is no question that the British knew how the army treated prisoners. The British ambassador protested strongly to the Chief of Army Staff around the beginning of 2002, after a man who was collecting his father's Gurkha welfare pension was arrested from a British Gurkha Welfare Centre, taken to an army camp, and summarily shot. The Doramba killings were raised at a meeting between the king and the British foreign secretary in London in August 2003. In December of that year, Amnesty International circulated a list to all the foreign embassies of nine people who had 'disappeared' in Kathmandu in the previous three months. A few days later the National Human Rights Commission published a list of hundreds of 'disappeared' people in the newspapers. In February 2004 Amnesty International declared that government forces 'seem to be pursuing a strategy of disappearance'.[7] The UN Special Rapporteur on Torture and the UN Working Group on Enforced Disappearances both reported on the abuses at the time. Nepal was said to have the highest rate of 'disappearance' in state custody in the world. The UN's report on torture and disappearance at the Bhairabnath Battalion in late 2003 came out in May 2006, five months before Operation Mustang was closed down.

British public statements, and private discussions with the Nepali authorities, repeatedly expressed concern, and emphasized the need to protect human rights. Funding was provided to human rights NGOs. 'At that time, every single person who was released from custody would claim that they had been severely tortured,' recalled a prominent human rights lawyer, who himself received British funding. 'Everyone knew there were hundreds of prisoners in army barracks.'[8] The Red Cross registered 1,122 detainees in the Kathmandu Valley between 2001 and 2006, but less than a third of their visits were to military establishments, to which they were rarely granted access. According to the Red Cross, 1,401 people were still missing from all parts of Nepal in 2012, six years after the war ended. There are eighty missing people in the Kathmandu Valley whose fate is unknown and a further seventeen for whom there is information that they are dead but whose remains have not been found.[9] If there are ever prosecutions or a truth commission examining what happened, the British will surely have a good deal of evidence to contribute.[10]

On 4 November 2004 the Maoists' Valley Commander Sadhuram Devkota, alias 'Prashant', was arrested by the army. Several NID and army officers confirmed that Operation Mustang was involved. According to a general, the NID had passed the information to the army through the Palace Military Secretariat, including photographs of the target and his address. The DMI then added their own surveillance before he was taken in. The prisoner was held at the Balaju Barracks in Kathmandu, near where he'd been living. Four days after the arrest the British junior foreign office minister (now shadow foreign secretary) Douglas Alexander visited Nepal. It seems likely that he was briefed on this success of British counter-terrorism.

On 19 December Prashant was dead. He'd apparently hanged himself from a low window in his cell. There was a panic. Someone tried to convince me that he really had committed suicide. I later confirmed with the autopsy doctors that it is possible for a man to hang himself from a point lower than his own height: it's called partial suspension. They said that two kilos of pressure on the jugular are enough to cause the loss of consciousness, and the constriction continues.

'I was surprised,' recalled a senior army man. 'They say he committed suicide with a bootlace from a low window, and they showed his almost naked body on TV. I still tell this story to others, whenever some junior people come to me to take advice. I say, "Don't hide, do as they have done to Prashant." If that body was not shown then people would have come against the army saying, "Where is that body? How did it happen?" All the human rights chaps would have come ... On TV there was a dead body, they started shouting for a day or two, and it was over.'

This turn of events, he believed, was simply good fortune, owing to the fact that the colonel in command at Balaju was 'particularly thick-headed'. 'When he showed that body on TV I said, "Look at that fool, what is he doing?"' Whether through luck or judgement, the row quickly faded.

A senior foreign official put it this way. 'Why did the army panic when Prashant died? They'd done this to hundreds and hundreds of guys. It's because he was one of the great successes of Operation Mustang.'

The British often referred to their experience in Northern Ireland to explain their expertise in counter-terrorism. I remember they said they feared that the Maoists' next step would be mass-casualty bombings, like the IRA's. In imagining how Mustang worked it helped me to read about counter-intelligence operations in Northern Ireland.

After identifying a Maoist operative the team would run background checks, watch his or her activities, study their routine in detail, identify their contacts, and try to assess their position and role in the organization. The first contact would be carefully planned. Did they attempt to bribe them, or did they simply say 'Come and work for us, or go and get tortured by 10 Brigade'?

Obviously the safe houses were for meeting the agents that Mustang turned. Developing and protecting these assets required an enormous amount of work. It was a twenty-four-hour operation. Sources told me that I should imagine the more junior British staff turning up for shifts in an operations centre that never slept, where the radio transmissions and the signals from the electronic equipment were received and the telephones were answered. There was a battery of equipment at a property near the Shangri La hotel, where generals were shown around and briefed. (This was the site operated under the cover of an environmental NGO, the High Altitude Research Centre, after the royal coup.) The computers used pirated software from New Road, because it's harder to trace.

'I don't think it's just about arrests, is it?' I said to one of the men who ran the operation. 'Once you've got a way into the organization then the real work starts, right? Then you can start deceiving them, finding out what they are going to do next, turning them against themselves in different ways.'

'An intelligence officer always wants to do their responsibility and duty at their best,' he said. 'It was a war, you know. Nothing is fair,' and we both laughed, he evasively and I, so I hoped, encouragingly.

I said, 'I gather in Northern Ireland, well, for example, sometimes you might have a choice. Do we use this information, or do we not want to reveal what we know? Maybe you can get your agent promoted within the organization. That was the kind of thing the British were into, I'm sure.'

'Sometimes,' he said very quietly. 'Actually, many Nepali people are forgetting all these parts, and the whole nation is committed to political reconciliation.'

'It's a very interesting career,' I told him, 'I should think it's one of the most interesting careers you can have.'

'Intelligence is not a charming job,' he said.

'No? What kind of job is it? How would you describe it?'

'In our society,' he repeated, 'intelligence is not a charming job.'

The NID headquarters is by the south gate of Singha Durbar, where most visitors enter. The spies have their own separate gate beside it. Their compound is fairly extensive. It is known as Baraph Bagh, the ice garden, because in the days of palaces the buildings there (which are still shaded by tall pine trees) were cool in the summer. A small temple can be seen above the high perimeter wall and, standing on a hillock among the pines, an old building where the Begum Hazrat Mahal of Lucknow is said to have lived in her exile. The present structure is plain and from the street it looks like it might not be old enough for the Begum herself to have known it, but it's fairly handsome and I can imagine how it appealed to the British. It was in a dilapidated state until MI6 paid for renovations. The main building today is a modern, squat white block. On a half-landing on the stairs a recent chief has installed two wall-sized mirrors facing each other, so that a person standing between them is surrounded by reflections.

'Is that some sort of joke?' I asked him.

'Does it look like a joke?' he said, but he seemed pleased with the idea.

'This glass is a glass,' a Maoist who worked underground in Kathmandu told me. 'If you start believing it might not be a glass then you're finished.'

We were in a restaurant drinking lemon-soda. Being a revolutionary in the white zone was a constant strain, he said. They knew they could be arrested and tortured or killed at any time.[11] They maintained contacts with members of the security forces. They warned them about times and places that would be dangerous, and apparently the police and the APF in particular were often willing to take the hint. In this way the antagonists were able to avoid one another when they wanted to. They knew that many in the army were anxious to avoid combat postings ('They told their relatives. Eventually the whispers would come to us.') They sent threats to army men who were known to kill civilians, and they attempted to prey upon the minds of Congress and UML people, by urging them that the time for monarchy was gone. And they collected money.

'We won because of the information they gave us,' he said.

All of the security agencies had their relationships with the Maoists, and protected their Maoists against the other agencies. Senior people sometimes had Maoists stay in their homes (the chiefs were all playing their own end). The NID field officers would be observed with the Maoists by the other agencies (sometimes they thought they were at risk from the army). It was very complicated.

One of the senior men in Operation Mustang told me a story about a prominent Maoist leader, who was staying at a businessman's house in Gongabu. The house and its owner had been under surveillance for a long time. 'And the army people used to go to that man's house and used to relax and entertain there. Drinks and dinner there, in Gongabu. Once they were caught by the army, our people who were on surveillance,' he said.

'On that day, [the Maoist leader] had come to take the money he used to keep there. Protection money. The police did the raid, but the army was there and the army saved him. The briefcase with the money, and also some plans, was thrown in the water tank under the house. We had that information at that time, but the army picked up my officer, and he was beaten badly. The army people were taking money from the Maoists.'

The Maoist who believed that a glass is a glass should have been more sceptical. He used to stay in army officers' houses sometimes, he said. He was arrested shortly after the ceasefire ended, taken to the Bhairabnath Battalion and severely tortured. A piece of luck saved him from a grave on Shivapuri.

It seems to have been a cleverly assembled illusion that trapped Prashant. I thought I'd been told that he was suicidal, because his comrades had betrayed him, and because his comrades had come to suspect him, although in fact he was loyal, or something like that. There probably was a core of truth in something like that, if some of his comrades were agents of Operation Mustang. After his death the Maoists' new Valley Commander issued a statement, thickening the plot by acknowledging that Prashant had surrendered, but disputing that he had killed himself. Whatever was going on, the Maoist organization in Kathmandu probably no longer understood what was happening to it, and whether he hanged himself or not it was this deception that killed Prashant.

By late 2004 it seemed that King Gyanendra was planning a coup to seize power outright. MI6 had strong indications of this from sources inside the palace and army, but one only had to read the newspapers to realize it was a distinct possibility. Through their senior contacts the British spies tried to pass their advice to the king, that a coup would be a bad move for the monarchy. An extra layer of cover was added to Operation Mustang when the High Altitude Research Centre was formally registered as an NGO on 11 November. Around December that year the British and American ambassadors both sought assurances – and received them from the king personally – that no coup would take place, and some people in the British embassy may have given too much credence to this. Certainly the final timing of the coup, on 1 February 2005, seems to have been a surprise to the British, otherwise MI6 would not have chartered a cargo plane to deliver a consignment of equipment the same week. (Despite frayed nerves, the delivery was made without attracting attention.)

In fact, the timing of the coup played havoc with all kinds of shipments. There were tons of military hardware waiting to be delivered, but the king forfeited it to the suspension of military supplies that Nepal's vexed allies now imposed.[12] Within months the army was running low on ammunition. 'If he'd waited a few weeks the trucks would have been in Nepal,' a general lamented. 'But it was an auspicious day, an auspicious time, given by the astrologers.'

The same general said, 'The king must be wise enough to understand. He must have a good ear for listening, but he lacked that. He had many advisers, but one has to understand also. He saw many things as, "Either you are with me, or you are not."'

On the whole, in their willingness to accommodate themselves with the new republic, members of the royal regime can't agree whom the king listened to. 'Unfortunately King Gyanendra couldn't manage the political strings,' said a top policeman. 'I must say that he was a failure to manage the political strings. I don't know how he was briefed by his advisers.' The king's ineptitude even made it difficult to turn Maoist agents, who couldn't believe they'd be joining the winning side. 'It's what we call counter-intelligence,' the cop explained, 'but that didn't work in the later phase, because the king's political string didn't work.'

Another general put it simply: 'The Maoists had a better agenda.'

The war was a political issue, and in the end India managed the political strings. A US embassy cable of 15 March 2006 has a visiting State Department official sitting with the Indian and British ambassadors at a lunch hosted by the American ambassador.[13] The British and Indian ambassadors were sanguine about the 12-point understanding recently reached in Delhi between the Maoists and the parliamentary parties, which the Americans still opposed.[14] All the ambassadors had long hoped that the king would 'reach out' to the mainstream parties, but grown pessimistic that he would ever do the clever thing.[15]

The American ambassador announced the disquieting news that the army's ammunition shortage had reached 'crisis point'. The British ambassador expressed concern, but the Indian demurred; they could still manage by moving their supplies around, he thought, and anyway the army's real problem was morale. One unit hadn't been paid for three months. Meanwhile, the senior officers were enriching themselves on a procurement spree. They'd recently asked China to add an extra 30 per cent to their invoices for small arms. (The reason the top brass hadn't seemed to care much when India, the US, and UK halted shipments after the coup was that they made no money from such government-to-government transfers, and preferred to operate on the grey market.) So poor was the army's training, leadership and morale, the Indian ambassador reckoned, that foreign governments could provide ten times what they previously had and they still couldn't defeat the insurgency.

The British ambassador disclosed a plan the EU was working on, to challenge both the king and the Maoists to accept democracy and a negotiated solution, in exchange for vast sums of donor aid. The Americans pointed out that it hadn't worked in Sri Lanka. But there seems to have been a general sense at the lunch that there might soon be some sort of peace process for the international community to pay for, because the ambassadors started chatting about international experience in arms monitoring and disarmament.

At the same time there was great complacency in the regime's high command. A top-level NID officer said that in the weeks before the People's Movement of April 2006 began his agency provided the palace with intelligence that the Maoists were moving large numbers of people into the city, but the generals around the king assured him, 'There is no such problem your majesty.' The final crisis could have been avoided, he insisted, if the government had announced a ceasefire, or called everyone for talks, but the king didn't see the need.

A few years after the outcome was settled, now that everyone realizes that they personally will be OK, it's more pleasant to reflect on these things. 'Foreign intelligence,' a general told me, 'one of the big questions they always used to ask was, whether the Maoists were linked to al Qaeda or not.'

'It seems a crazy question,' I said.

'Yup. Especially the Americans. This is how it used to work. The Americans always used to come to us thinking, "The Maoists are terrorists, we've got to fix them, what aid do you need?" The British used to come and say, "What is the problem?" and the Europeans used to come and say, "Well, they are also citizens of Nepal. They have a cause. Today's terrorist is tomorrow's, you know, patriotic leader."'

'It turns out to be true,' I said.

'Troo,' cooed the general. There was a Maoist prime minister at the time. 'So, these were the versions I used to get in different places.'

No doubt it all made sense to the British while they were doing it, as a judicious balancing of exigencies. But one of the reasons we know about the torture and disappearances MI6 seems to be implicated in is because of the human rights work that the British also supported. Possibly they would say that their military and intelligence support to the government helped bring the Maoists to the table and end the war; but then the terms of the peace in 2006 were essentially the same that the Maoists were offering in 2003, when Britain and others were strongly backing the king's government, which was in turn probably most responsible for the collapse of negotiations.[16] The British supported a negotiated solution, but right to the end they hoped the king and the parties would be on one side dictating terms to the weakened Maoists on the other.

So this kind of diplomatic influence upon the course of the war is as ambiguous as the impact of development aid, which calls for change while underwriting the status quo. In Nepal at least, and presumably in other countries, it's questionable whether governments such as Britain's are really able to promote the democratization, the respect for human rights, the sustainable development, or the peace and security that are the backbone of their foreign policy rhetoric. The misunderstandings, the unintended or unacknowledged consequences of their policies are more evident than the benefits. No doubt the rhetoric can be disingenuous, but I suspect this divergence is partly because clever modern Westerners are unable to escape from what they think must be, instead of understanding what is; or, in other words, they look upon a place like Nepal with assurance in the universal validity of their terms of analysis, and misread it to fit their categories. They have an unwarranted belief in the rightness of their line because they received a fine education in a country that works; and something must be done; and their feelings are validated by an elite employer, from which they derive personal prestige.

As a friend, who was himself British, put it, 'The Brits are the worst. They've got an answer to everything.'

To wade through parliamentary statements on Nepal in Hansard is to find that the British response to the war in Nepal was unwittingly ideological, or misled by partial sympathies, while its authors had no doubt that they upheld universal good sense, democracy and human rights. While I was researching this chapter I arranged to meet a British minister of the period, at the Costa Coffee in a suburban London shopping mall, because I wanted to understand at what level British policy was formed. I didn't ask him directly about Operation Mustang because I didn't think he'd tell me, and I didn't want to frighten him, and I wasn't sure that anyone in Britain knew I was looking into it yet. The minister's own concern about the situation in Nepal had derived largely from a favourite restaurateur, in a neighbouring constituency to his own, who'd informed him about the depredations of the Maoists. During his time in office, with the wars on in Iraq and Afghanistan, a junior minister had one and a half hours a week for Nepal policy. He recalled a cabinet-level meeting discussing the situation in Nepal once.

He described a visit to the UK Department for International Development's Kathmandu office, during a trip to Nepal, and in their conference room 'the biggest mahogany table I have ever seen in my life. The amount of money spent on frivolities,' he said, 'I was really very upset. What we had was a bunch of consultants who were useless and a bunch of people going around in white jeeps who were just not engaging with the local people.' He wrote a damning memo about it when he got back to London, but in those days DFID had recently been established as a separate ministry, and the secretary of state believed that if you want the best you have to pay for the best.

'Was it good to have ministers taking an interest in Nepal?' he asked. 'In the end I'm not sure it did a fat lot of good. In the end, I think what happened is what we were looking for. We had a clear foreign policy view about how the war should be ended but we were not able to deliver it.'

Operation Mustang continued until the Comprehensive Peace Agreement was signed in November 2006.[17] When it was closed down, and MI6 withdrew to Delhi, the palace, which by now was supposedly cut off from power, used whatever contacts it had in the British establishment to lobby for the spies to stay. MI6's apparent complicity in torture in Nepal had not been any of the things apologists talk about: 'a tough compromise' 'on the front line of the war on terror' 'with national security at stake'. It was an unnecessary operation in support of an unpleasant and misguided regime. The details were leaked, of course, because the faction in the NID of the outgoing chief had enjoyed all the spoils, as part of a conspiracy among the rivals to replace him.

24

A couple of years ago there was a whole month of bad luck. The chariot of the red god Bungadya was parked at the roadside until it could be pulled again. Newlyweds didn't sleep together. 'Every two years a month like this comes,' said Sabitrididi, our maid. 'I don't know why.'

I asked her, 'What does it mean?'

'This time it's about husbands and wives. They can't sleep together, they shouldn't even sit together. The next one is about mothers-in-law and daughters-in-law. They can't drink water from the same tap.' And while my wife was pregnant with our daughter there was a partial solar eclipse. 'Don't touch your stomach,' Didi said, 'because, wherever you touch, the baby will have marks. You're not supposed to eat today either.'

My wife said, 'Why not?'

'It's like eating something given to you by a cobbler.'

'But I've eaten plenty of things given to me by cobblers,' she claimed.

'You never listen to me.'

I overheard poor Sabitri talking to one of the neighbours, on her rooftop terrace, through our kitchen window. The neighbour wanted to borrow our pump, and therefore use our electricity, to pump water from the well in the small yard between our houses. 'We'll do it because of dharma,' Didi was telling her in her account of our godless household. 'It's the only type of dharma we do here, because it's the only type of dharma that counts.'

The neighbours bickered about who was pumping the most water, how they hung the laundry in the chowk, and how they stored the heaps of planks that moulded the poor concrete houses they built for a living. We had a dispute when a next-door shed was leased to a copper foundry and the house filled with metallic fumes. The neighbours brewed and distilled moonshine in their yards, and they had harrowing marital rows in the middle of the night. They lived packed into crumbling, derelict heirlooms, a brother and his wife in every room, or (where a homeowner had moved to the suburbs) the rooms were leased to families from outside. These tenants had no say in neighbourhood matters, such as, who may use the chowks, and how. The locals called them 'khey', which means a Nepali who is not a Newar in Newari.

I overheard a conversation in the chowk. 'You shouldn't call us khey,' a woman was saying, 'because even a tailor or a blacksmith, you would call them khey.' She meant, 'We are high-caste and you should recognize it.'

One of the generals had told me that during the war the army never knew what safe houses the Maoists had in the old parts of Patan. To that extent, two and a half centuries after its conquest, the old Newar city held out.

In his book *English Social History* the historian G.M. Trevelyan wrote, 'In everything the old overlaps the new – in religion, in thought, in family custom.'[1] Someone else put it differently: 'the tradition of all the dead generations weighs like a mountain on the minds of the living.'[2] The new circuitry is imposed on the old without disconnecting it, creating mazy new routes. All of Kathmandu's history, true and false, all the texts and gossip, are the city's modern fabric, like the timber and the concrete are, and it all lies in a mutable heap.

The city's social revolution, and the political demands of ethnic and caste groups which the Maoist war elevated, made people renew their relationship with their traditions and repoliticized the nation's history. This group-consciousness, which was also a sensitivity sometimes bordering on rage, occurred at just the moment when the old ways were being challenged and the culture seemed in danger of disappearing. In fact the very act of re-emphasizing traditions changed them, and reference to the past was made to justify modern political positions. The slender stone monolith, which had been the leprous farmer Lalit's bamboo staff, now attracted a crimson decoration and a painted sign proclaiming its identity.

Every ten years it was the turn of our neighbourhood to provide the drummers during the festival of Matya. The temple of Nasahdya for our neighbourhood was in our chowk, so the drummers must practise there. For a whole year running up to Matya they worshipped the god of loud music day and night. The young men fulfilled their duty to the culture and to the locality with a zeal that was special to their generation.

None of the drummers actually lived in the chowk itself, and their rehearsals placed a strain upon everybody who did. Normally mild husbands lashed out at their wives and mothers at their children, and it was easy to imagine how torture with loud sounds can disrupt a victim's reason. After several months, amid the heavy drinking that surrounds the festival of Bungadya, a family of our neighbours lost control. 'I can drum better than that – anyone can drum better than that!' one of the brothers raged. 'It would be possible to sleep if they had a rhythm!' Yet the brothers were unwilling to confront the drummers. Instead they threw bricks from their windows onto the tin roof of the shed where they practised. When the brothers were drunk they crashed into the shed, brandishing the planks from their building business, frightening the younger children who were learning the cymbals. Death threats were exchanged. The rest of the neighbourhood took the drummers' side, and the brothers didn't come out of their house for days.

When we tried to talk to the members of the older generation, who composed the Matya committee, which was responsible for the neighbourhood's preparations, they told us they understood our feelings completely. We suggested that they limit the hours of rehearsals to notified times, and stopped at a certain time in the evening, and told us in advance when the calendar indicated a midnight session. But the elders didn't know how to reason with the younger generation, who were not deferential,

but whom they needed for the maintenance of tradition. The young leaders said that if we had a problem we could move out. They refused to discuss anything in any language except Newari. They planned to start a second shift, to learn another piece of music. After my wife tried to talk to them we found the glass broken in our car. They said that as the festival (still four months off) approached their rehearsal hours would lengthen. As babies, our children learned to sleep through anything.

After ten months of practice – an old man flapping time – the kids weren't very good, but they were very proud. We all awaited Matya with sincere personal investment. As the festival neared the committee put bunting in the alleys. A letter came under the door, invoking Matya's history and requesting donations: '1,400 years ago …' it claimed. We were moved enough to contribute quite generously.

A few days before Matya, which occurs on the second day of the waning moon in around August or September, there was a feast for the whole neighbourhood, and we were warned that there would be music at two in the morning. When I woke to it I went to the window and saw the musicians standing in a circle,

illuminated by temporary floodlights, and I recognized several of our neighbours, hastening past. There were only a few hours in the middle of each night, and only five nights left for them to visit every nook of the city, and somehow open the way for the procession that would follow them. The musicians departed and another group, playing flutes, took their place, to be replaced by another. I went back to bed but several times I returned to the window to wonder at them, and their determined nocturnal energy, poured out once a decade on a few nights of the year.

The spirit of defensive/aggressive cultural pride that affected the drummers was part of a broader sentiment that came to prominence during the peace process, and was crystallized in the demand for 'identity-based federalism'. According to this view, which was proposed by the Maoist party, the unitary Nepali state and the caste hierarchy were inseparable. Bitter experience had shown that, whatever the verbal commitments of national leaders, the 'dominant group' would never relinquish its grip. The only way to gain recognition and dignity, as well as access to political power and economic resources, for traditionally 'excluded' groups was to create federal states named after those groups. In a country of great social complexity and diversity, where the different castes and ethnicities live among one another throughout, this demand came to be seen by some as almost a panacea, to remake the country in the image of all its people. It was framed in a discourse of half-formed concepts, and in particular there was an attempt to build identity-based federalism around an international instrument known as ILO 169, which was drafted with the Amazon rainforest in mind to provide 'indigenous people' with 'prior rights' to natural resources. Nepal became the only country in Asia to ratify ILO 169, as if asking whose ancestors migrated to a tract of land first, maybe a thousand years ago, was a meaningful way to address Nepal's modern inequality, and decide who should control the community forest.

This identity politics gave rise to an equivalent anxiety and rage on the part of many members of the 'dominant group'. Typically, people on this side of the argument denied that there was any such problem as caste or ethnic discrimination, pointing out that in the Far West many high-caste people are poor, and that there are a couple of Madhesis on the Supreme Court. Or, if there was a pattern in who held the spoils (as even some newspaper columnists were willing to argue), it was because high-caste people are more educable. Privileged people argued without irony that 'inclusion' would only mean creating a new 'creamy layer' within the 'excluded groups'. The whole inclusion agenda was condemned as 'racist' and 'communist' in Kathmandu, denounced as disturbing the nation's unity and social harmony, and ruled out for threatening ethnic conflict and the dissolution of the state. Whereas India had had Temple Entry Acts and so on for more than half a century, and identity politics for decades, whereas the Indian constitution reserves government jobs and places in education for disadvantaged castes, no such thing was necessary to address Nepal's enduring discrimination; so the bureaucracy, the courts and supposedly centrist political parties stoutly resisted laws that might mitigate these inequalities.[3] Identity politics challenged the ideological foundation of Nepal, and many high-caste people in particular sincerely felt that their culture, and their place, was in danger of being sacrificed to the demand for 'inclusion'.

In Kathmandu there was a concerted and largely successful campaign to deny the social causes of the insurgency; to evade peace-process commitments to land reform, 'democratization' of the army and 'progressive restructuring of the state'; to pretend that caste differences and even violence itself hadn't been an issue until the Maoists came along. In an inversion of the documented reality, it now became the rebels who had committed the worst abuses of the conflict, and 'human rights' was refashioned as a political weapon against them. All of this gave ironic confirmation to the old Soviet joke, that not only the future is unpredictable but the past as well. The proponents of identity politics or social change found their views confirmed, of the 'dominant group's' commitment to preserving inequality. There was mutual incomprehension, even as the two sides knew each other too well, and anger rose.

You could go mad over the politics, and several people did. Simply living in this place is depressing and infuriating by turns, to anybody who does it. Now I've got a car, as well as children. It's me sitting in a white jeep in the traffic, taking the kids to the pool; raging against everything that doesn't work, like a tourist who can't understand why foreigners don't behave the way he would. The banal questions never received an answer: why do drivers try to get two cars through a small space at the same time? Would it kill one of them to give way? What makes fruitful cooperation so hard? Everyone's furious and willing to believe the worst of everyone else.

I was under-slept, overworked, stuck in traffic with the window down, driving my child home from hospital. 'Eh, kuire,' a gormless-looking Madhesi taxi driver told me through the window before he moved away. 'Fuck off,' I said to his departing car. ('Kalé, muji,' I thought.) 'Why did you say fuck off?' said the 4-year-old. The traffic moved and we advanced a little.

In this atmosphere of suppressed aggression and mutual contempt I was riding with some policemen, in a civilian car on the Ring Road. At night, when dazzling oncoming lights alternate with deep darkness, flickering shadows in the bands of floating dust are the only warning you receive of a pedestrian. I don't think the driver had had any beer, but the rest of us had, and some barbecued meat, at a restaurant attached to a butcher's shop which I'd wanted to show them. From my position pressed against the back left window I could see that we were passing quite close to a motorcyclist, who was driving more slowly at the edge of the road. I might have said something, except that this relation lasted only a moment, and then the tip of his handlebar touched the side of our car. He wobbled and after we passed him the bike and rider tumbled, and crashed into the road. We all looked back, shocked. After a moment someone said, 'Did he fall?'

'Drive! Drive! That wasn't your fault.'

'The motherfucker was drunk.'

'The muji was talking on his phone.'

Someone's phone rang and he answered it. 'We just killed some motherfucker on the Ring Road,' he joked, his voice a bit too loud, and the words came into my head: *I can't run no more, with that lawless crowd...*

These small incidents, such as occurred while I was thinking about the nature of the place, which struck me as standing for it somehow, are indispensable. They are the part of the character that shows. Like when I was thinking about the unplanned development, the lack of street names and so on, and I overheard two professional men talking in a bar. 'What's my address?' one asked the other. 'I dunno,' said his friend. 'I don't even fucking know mine.'

Quite recently we had a dinner at our house. Suman the cop came and so did Ujjwal the development wallah. They came with their wives. At that time, when we'd recently got a new and better telephone line, we were receiving a lot of wrong numbers, from people who were trying to reach a government minister. When the phone rang I mentioned this, and one of the guests said he'd take it.

'Yes?' he said. 'No ... Ministerjee is sleeping. He enjoyed *too* much this afternoon! Playing cards and all that ... What? Aunty? No, aunty left two weeks ago. "Any more of these young girls in the house and I'm leaving" she said, and now she's gone ... That's fine ... Yes, yes ... Of course, don't mention it. Call in the morning. After nine. Bye.'

He replaced the receiver. We laughed, and drank and talked, about people we knew, and what we were doing. I tried to show them some passages of my manuscript. And we talked about booze and revelry, possibly trying to recapture the atmosphere of when we were slightly, but decisively younger, or promising that we would do all that stuff again soon. Suman said he'd been writing a song.

'What's it called?' asked Ujjwal. '"Wasted Life?" Mind you, in Kathmandu I suppose we all feel that way.'

'Everywhere,' I said. 'Everywhere people feel like that.'

It's not clear from the pieces I typed into my computer, and cut and pasted, whether it was on that evening or another that we listened to the chatter on the police radio. A microbus driver was running amok somewhere in the city. He'd gone through a police check without stopping. For a moment I wondered what on earth the police could do. The drama was over in two minutes, when the micro reached a traffic jam. My wife said, 'When you listen to this it sounds like the city's going crazy.'

Suman answered, 'It's the kids by the rivers that are the worst. So sad!' He was referring to the bodies of abandoned babies that the police find in increasing numbers on the banks.

I was driving my bike across the footbridge at Shankamul, towards the Mother temple of Chamundamai. The sediment and garbage the bridge had trapped formed a partial dam in the early spring, when the water was low, and the river passed beneath the bridge through a single channel, almost narrow enough for a man to jump across. In the pool up-stream shifting banks of trash had formed. The bridge was congested too, with motorcyclists and pedestrians craning to look down at the river. After I'd crossed it I parked my bike and stepped onto a low wall, where more people were watching.

'What happened?' I asked.

'A kid's fallen in.'

A group of people were standing by the channel beneath the bridge, probing the deep water with sticks they'd found. More people were running towards them, or searching for sticks. A policeman was taking his clothes off.

After another minute or more they found him, and although I couldn't see them bring him out I saw them carrying his limp body under its arms. His trousers had slipped down to show his small bum-crack. The policemen laid him on the dry garbage of the former riverbed and crowded round. I could see them pumping his chest. Then a policeman picked him up and came toward the crowd on the bank, moving quickly, trailing the others behind. He was holding the boy's feet in one hand and his wrists in the other, the body and the head hanging down. The boy had been wearing a faded T-shirt. He might have been four or five. There was yellow crap on the side of the face, which must have been picked up in the river.

Without waiting any longer I got back on my bike and drove up the hill into Patan. A short distance away everything was normal. People were walking around normally, holding their children's hands, unaware and possibly never to know the shattering disaster that had just occurred. It was sunny, the really pleasant warm weather of early spring.

Kathmandu is lovely in the spring. The flowering jacaranda trees really look lovely around Durbar Marg, Tri Chandra College and Tundikhel; and even on the Ring Road, where they haven't been cut down yet. The dry, warming air is thick with dust and exhaust fumes, and the river is beginning to build up its highest stink. I was surprised by the public response to the second Maoist government's road-widening scheme.

The government reminded the public that an item printed in the government *Gazette* in the 1970s had ruled that property owners must establish their boundary a certain distance from the centre of the road, according to the class of road it was. Nobody had complied. Now the government was going to tear down garden walls, or the first two metres of the building, or whatever, to establish the proper width of the carriageway. It might have been a minor premonition of what the next earthquake will look like; miles and miles of smashed concrete and twisted metal. Those who lost the front of their buildings simply stuck a new wall on what remained, and perhaps they inserted some new concrete columns and beams. New buildings were built inside the remains of buildings that were just a decade old.

There was some resistance to this, on the part of the owners of roadside shops and houses, who were due compensation only if their house had been built before the crucial item appeared in the *Gazette*. But most people applauded it. 'Wah!' they said. 'My cousin lost his garden wall! Serves the bastards right. They bribed the officials to encroach on the road – maybe they should ask for their money back? This is progress. Finally! A government that's got the balls to do something.' I thought, 'This is interesting.' And I also thought, 'While they're brutalizing the place, couldn't they replant some trees?' And I looked at the pavements that were being made, two feet wide and cluttered with electricity poles, with twenty yards of road between them, and I raged to myself, 'Nothing expresses the attitude of the rulers to the ruled better than that!'

'The intoxicating high that tall buildings and wide avenues give to the people who have only seen them in pictures is beyond description,' a newspaper columnist explained.[4] Blue mirror glass was the latest architectural fashion. The newspapers cheered the news that the city's first flyover was planned.

☀

After the second People's Movement a judicial report had been produced, describing who was responsible for the killing and suppression of protesters, but, like the first time round, the winning side buried it.[5] The parliamentary parties and the Maoists accommodated themselves again with the old elite. In fact, within a few years the Maoists began to resemble the parties they had fought to replace, especially in their financial corruption. The leaders took kickbacks, extracted rents and, in the most notorious and possibly the largest scam, stole what were supposed to be the wages of their former fighters, now languishing in UN-supervised cantonments. The Maoists, the Nepali Congress, and the army discovered a common interest in blocking war crimes investigations.

I went to dinner at a senior policeman's house, who was famous for his incorruptibility. He spoke from the experience of many UN peacekeeping tours. 'I've seen it everywhere,' he said, 'Timor-Leste, Sudan, Bosnia, Sierra Leone, Haiti, Kosovo. In all of these post-conflict countries, it's about money and power – nothing else. In Kosovo the different sides were into the flesh trade together,' he made the money sign with his fingers. 'They were into …' he took hold of his love handles and paused.

'The kidney business?'

'… organ trafficking together,' he said, 'and still they were fighting each other. It works the same here. I've seen it everywhere.'

He turned to me in particular. 'Do you find Kathmandu interesting?'

'Kathmandu has it all,' I said.

'Yes,' and he raised his voice exultantly over the noise of three couples having dinner, and their children running around, 'Kathmandu has everything! Everything is here!'

After every 'revolution' the ruling class had simply expanded as little as it could get away with. Something similar was happening again. The parties' economic policies were very much alike. They all said they supported enterprise, trade, and foreign investment. (The Maoists wanted to create Special Enterprise Zones, and new goods terminals along the borders.) They all endorsed multi-party democracy (which they attempted to practise in similar ways), and secularism, republicanism, and federalism. They all paid lip service to 'social inclusion'.

As the peace process had settled down into a bitter stand-off between the older parties and the Maoists, politics was presented as a titanic struggle between democracy and communism. It was never really convincing and became progressively less so. Many people identified themselves as communists or democrats, and those terms did signal genuine differences, including in the way people spoke, dressed, and decorated their homes or offices. But the truth was that few people truly fitted either description, and neither side cared to emphasize that both sides were similarly engaged in the same political economy of patronage and corruption.[6] As the latest transitional period became the new normal, the rival ideologies became a mere social romance, or deliberate mystification. People were angry and disillusioned because they weren't fooled, but they still talked about it all the time, because Kathmandu is obsessed with politics.

If the rival ideologies held any practical meaning it was mainly in that the Maoists claimed to represent constituencies that were still trying to gain access to power, whereas the older parties sought to protect the interests of constituencies that had already gained admission. And it was in this that the current changes were different from the non-revolutions of 1950 or 1990. During those upheavals enlarged sections of the national and provincial elites were admitted to the circle of power. This time quite different sorts of people were demanding entry. It wasn't the fake bogey of a communist dictatorship that was really upsetting conservative Kathmandu. (The Maoists had actually created greater pluralism in politics, making authoritarianism harder.) The spectre stalking the bourgeoisie was social inclusion, which was profoundly threatening. In addition to those who called themselves communists, other people who only supported progressive change were also labelled 'communists' and 'Maoists' by 'democrats'.

For the top leaders themselves, even the social inclusion agenda wasn't what it was really all about. What's more important than any other principle in Nepali high politics may simply be the number three: three Malla city states, three sides in the war, three major parties in the peace process, three major factions in each major party, two queens plus Bhimsen Thapa. Three allows you to switch sides and play two against one.

The constant small crises create an illusion of greater instability than actually exists.[7] There has been no political revolution, not since 1768. Nepal is not a failed state, as foreign analysts periodically warn.[8] It is, for now, in a sub-optimal equilibrium. So it was that when the Constituent Assembly expired without completing a new constitution it actually eased a situation that had begun to grow tense, over the chance that a last-minute decision would actually change something. And it was suggestive of the underlying stability of the system that (like in previous intervals when there'd been no effective government) having no effective constitution for a while made no obvious difference, besides that the nation's leaders had a new short-term crisis to engage them.[9]

The constitution couldn't be completed because of the demand for identity-based federalism. Calls for prior rights to natural resources for indigenous groups had been dropped (draft provisions said all citizens would have equal rights). The issue had come down to whether each state would be named after an ethnic group, and how many states there would be (the parties had each demanded various numbers, but never the same number at the same time). Proponents of identity-based federalism had a majority in the Assembly, but their moderated demands were still unacceptable to the old parties. Amid private deals between leaders, made and broken; press reporting, that the nation was about to endure the next Balkan/Rwandan-style genocide; and genuine tension between rival communities in some parts of the country (including Kathmandu), the Assembly's mandate expired.

The Western donors had been modestly backing some groups, and sponsoring some reports, which espoused ethnic and caste grievances, and which sliced inequality along those lines. They faced a powerful backlash. And now that they saw the trouble social inclusion could cause, the internationals put the issue down more quickly than they politely could, like they'd found a worm in the food they'd been given.[10]

When I lie in bed and look at the ceiling the stains in the concrete sometimes look like a camel, or a weasel, or a whale; they resemble the face of a bear, or of a man, or Jesus. The death of the first Constituent Assembly was like that. All the many people who were in the building as the time ran out have irreconcilable versions of who killed it: it was the immoderate demands of the identity-federalists (egged on by Christian evangelists!); it was the undemocratic intransigence of the status-quo-ists (the issues were never put to a vote); it was the speaker's fault; the prime minister wanted to avoid a confidence motion; he wanted to establish a dictatorship; it was a conspiracy of the Indian embassy – the Indians were to blame! The Assembly must have been killed ten times at once.[11]

In the monsoon, oblique evening light makes the brick walls glow a lovely colour below the gunmetal sky. A group of sparrows swarms from a bush to the top of a wall and back again. A crow wheels from one water tank to another, flying the black flag of himself. In the winter, when the power cuts last more than half the day, millions of people are sitting in the dark, without heating, without even television, in their drafty concrete boxes.

I went to see a friend at Pashupati, paving his mother's way to heaven during the thirteen days of mourning. In the ashram he sat isolated, at the far end of the concrete room his family had taken, where nobody would touch him. He had no water to drink, because some relatives had argued that bottled water wasn't pure, since people had touched the bottle. Flowing water must be pure, and they had a blue plastic jar with a tap at the bottom; but this made no sense according to the grieving son, since someone still had to touch the tap before he captured the water in his brass bowl. He sat thirstily while a suitable solution was sought. Furthermore, he hadn't eaten yet today because he was still waiting for the priest to arrive. His wife touched a piece of newspaper spread on the floor, which touched his bed, and he said gloomily, 'If anyone sees there'll be another big row, and we'll have to start again from yesterday.

'If it's like this now,' he said, 'after the Maoists, after the king is gone, after the secular state, after everything, imagine what it was like before, even ten years ago,' and I was struck that he associated those changes as feeding back into the performance of such private family business.

The division of undeveloped land into building plots for sale shows that the city will soon consume the fields that are left. The gap is widening between the tops of the new, tall buildings and the bottom of the new tube wells, which pump ever more water out of the deep lakebed aquifers. One day, experts say, the ground beneath the city will subside. The owner of the shed where the drummers practised pulled it down and built a five-storey house for his family, with enough room for one room on each floor. The view of the hills and of the roofscape is disappearing behind higher buildings.

Often, in fact obsessively, when I'm walking in a narrow gully I look up and wonder where I'll be when the earthquake comes and the walls open like curtains of bricks. I look at the people who are walking around me and I think, 'Which of us is going to make it?' In Haiti they could dump it in the sea, but where will they put the rubble in a valley like Kathmandu, connected to the outside by slender mountain roads? Will the camps where the relief agencies collect the starving survivors (amid the flawed disbursement of massive funds) become permanent settlements, the crowded slums of the next Kathmandu? What crowds of people will pick their way around the line of the Malla city wall at the Indra Jatra after that?

I asked Dhana Laksmi about the past and future of Kathmandu. Before, she said, you could buy four manas of daal for a rupee. A pathi (eight manas) of rice cost just fifty paisa (half a rupee). 'How expensive it is now! One tin of potatoes – you know a tin? – would be a rupee. Saag! For five paisa you got *this much*. Do you know what a paisa is?'

I did, but she asked her daughter to bring a cloth bag of coins and spread them on a sheet of newspaper. 'These have all been given to Laksmi,' she said, 'so you can't take any.'

The newest was minted after the republic, when the image of Mt Everest replaced the royal devices on all the money. There were also old silver fifty-paisa pieces; the tiny twelve-paisa piece, like a little finger nail; and the five-paisa piece that was bigger than any of them. There was a silver Indian rupee dated 1840, showing the young Victoria; and a copper coin of 1941, so worn that it was hard to decipher the emperor George VI. 'But when you look at the changes,' I tried to press her, 'has Kathmandu got better, or worse? How are people different?'

'There's no comparison,' she said. 'When we were young we weren't allowed to step outside without wearing a shawl. Now, even if you don't have boobs you wear a bra and show them off. I saw one of those bras once – full of sponge!'

'Is it good,' I asked, 'that people are free to enjoy their boobs?'

'I want to beat them up!' said Dhana Laksmi, and adopted the tone she would use while she did so. 'Everyone has it! Why are you flaunting it?'

'There must be some things that have got better,' I said.

'People know how to eat nowadays.'

'They didn't know how to eat before?' But she just said something about the price of eggs, and how embarrassed she felt by the trousers women wear, which show the shapes of their bottoms.

When she was young, some young men wore trousers that showed the position of their ... she indicated a penis with her thumb. The trousers were made in such a way that you could see the penis swing from side to side as they walked: 'Like this, like that, like this, like that,' with her thumb. 'You could see it, everyone could see it, and the young girls would giggle and say, "Look how good that looks."'

And did she regret that this custom had died out? Was it at least of some benefit?

'With men it's better they hide it,' she said, 'but now women have started showing their ass, and that I don't like at all.'

Now, the newspapers report, there are popular clinics in Kathmandu offering paternity tests. 'Did people have affairs before?' I asked.

'There'd be plenty of affairs,' she said, 'but there was no cover for the dick. Nowadays, you can put a lid on it.'

And what will Kathmandu be like in the future? At that she chuckled, then laughed. 'It's impossible to figure out,' she said, then referred again to the incredible change in the price of potatoes. 'Sometimes when I go to bed I think about it, and it's because there are so many people and no land. Now there are medicines that save people. Before there would be smallpox and a hundred died. People don't die any more.'

In the evening there was a festival outside, with flutes and drumming, and everyone wanted to see it except my son. So I put him to bed while Amita, the younger maid, took my daughter to the jatra. When they came back she tried to tell me what she'd seen, but she was too young to talk, so she stuck her tongue out, said 'Maaa, maaa', and made her other sounds. According to Amita they'd seen a goat be given to the god. 'She wasn't even scared,' Amita said in wonder, since all that stuff gives her the shivers. 'Maaa, maaa,' said Nani, and shook her head in furious delight.

Later, when I went out to the shop, I heard in the darkened gully the sound of 'John Wesley Harding' playing in an upstairs room.

Epilogue

A few minutes before midday on 25 April 2015, the Main Himalayan Thrust ruptured 15 kilometres beneath Gorkha district, about 80 kilometres north-west of Kathmandu.[1] This fault runs right across the hills of Nepal, where the northward-creeping Indian continental plate strains to slide at a shallow angle beneath the Eurasian continental plate, and is locked by friction. That Saturday, for the seventh time since the thirteenth century, the Indian plate in this section slipped, by between 4 and 6.5 metres and at speeds of up to a metre a second. It caused an earthquake with a magnitude of 7.8, the seismic waves propagating eastwards from the epicentre as the slip unzipped a section of the fault 120 kilometres long.

About twenty seconds after the rupture began, it flashed across the fault 10 kilometres north of Kathmandu. The Valley is a basin filled with five to six hundred metres of former lake bed sediments, in which the seismic pulse resonated to produce strong shaking, but with an usually low frequency of about five seconds. This may be because the Indian plate had slipped quite smoothly, and that seems to have saved the city. The land moved like a sea swell. In some places, such as Balaju and Gongabu, the vibrations rearranged the air, water and soil particles beneath the ground to cause 'liquefication', whereupon the ground really did become like a fluid, sand and water oozed from the surface, and some buildings tilted over or sank.

Within 65 seconds the main event was complete. During that period a section of the earth's crust 120 kilometres long and 60 wide, with Kathmandu standing on it, had risen by a metre and moved two metres south. Not only did it seem like being at sea, what we also felt was like being among the towering, rattling objects on a giant table that is picked up and put down in a different place. In the same moments the mountain range to the north sank lower. Over the next few weeks hundreds of aftershocks were set off across this region, as pieces of the crust found their new equilibrium, causing continuous alarm. Rumours spread that a new huge quake, of magnitude 8 or 9, would occur at certain times on particular days, and on at least one occasion two people were arrested for making such announcements with a loudspeaker from a taxi. A friend who camped out in Sindhupalchowk district at that time, more or less right over the rupture, said that all night she heard sounds from the earth, like big boulders being dropped off a cliff far away.

When the shaking started I climbed into the back of the parked car where I'd just strapped my children, and closed the door. The chowk quickly filled with horrified people, and I could see a tree thrashing like in a storm, but none of the houses came down, as I expected them to. Bouncing on the car's springs was like driving on a bad road. Other people mostly experienced it as a swaying motion upon which it was difficult to keep one's feet, like being on a boat, or, as one man who fled into his garden (to find the iron gates clashing like the Symplegades) described, it was like running across a series of conveyor belts which were driving in alternate directions.

That night I slept indoors. Since our house hadn't cracked yet I didn't think it was going to, and with a couple of pegs of whisky in me I turned over with a true sense of security when the room banged from side to side. We invited many neighbours to stay inside, but they didn't feel safe, and every time the tremors rose I heard the women in the chowk calling 'Haa! Haa!' I later learned that when they did this they pressed the paving with their thumbs to calm the shaking. I would like to know whether this relates to the belief, which I once read about, that earthquakes are caused by the weight of sin upon the world, but I haven't yet found anyone who knows. There was a large aftershock from the eastern end of the rupture on the second day,

when the ground swayed and I watched a hotel swimming pool wash from side to side before it began to spill.

My friend Ujjwal said that when he was finally able to stumble out of his house he didn't find himself, as he expected, standing still in the garden watching his house shake, because the garden was shaking just as much. He said, 'This is the strange thing, because you always think of the ground as firm.' It was only after the next day's aftershock that he grasped the strangeness of the whole world moving like a boat. 'It was the noise,' said another friend, Niranjan, who on that morning was in an upstairs room at an oral history workshop. 'Prawin got up and started waving his arms around, saying not to panic and to get under the tables' – which Niranjan had already done, while others crowded round the door. All he remembers after that was a Tk! Tk! Tk! Tk! sound like a train going fast over points.

This conversation took place more than one hundred days after the earthquake. Other people who were present said that an earthquake begins with a sound like an explosion, or a loud deep hum. That morning there had been a tremor, the first I'd noticed for several weeks. It was relatively weak but shallow, and had its epicentre right under the Valley, and I experienced it upstairs in my house as two firm jolts, that I somehow heard before I felt them, although there was no audible sound. It was agreed that that morning's event had a particularly sonic quality.

'Gongabu's seedy underbelly has been laid bare!' said a friend, whom I bumped into at a weekend brunch fund-raising auction for the victims in the countryside. I imagined the corpses of some secret Gongabu murder victims divulged upon the surface, but she was only talking about lovers 'going out with a bang'. 'Do you want to hear something heartbreaking?' she said, and told the story of a man whose wife had gone to the shop fifteen minutes before it happened, whose body was found naked with a different man in a Gongabu hotel. The husband refused to understand, and almost went mad. Out in the hills, where the same storyteller had a relative, it felt as if the mountain was jumping up and down, she said, and then it began hurling rocks from its summit onto the houses. From cracks in the earth green worms appeared, which ate all the maize and made people's skin itch. Apparently these worms were also reported in a newspaper. In this lady's own garden in Kathmandu they found enough frogs to fill twelve buckets, whereas usually they hardly have any, and 'since we couldn't kill them' they put them over the neighbour's wall.

The earthquake destroyed the sixteenth-century Charnarayan temple in Mangal Bazar, which was the oldest temple in the square, and the thirteenth-century Kasthamandap, at the junction of Kathmandu's trade routes, which was a symbol of the city. Large parts of the old Kathmandu palace, and several temples in the square before it, collapsed. Earthmovers with mechanical shovels were scraping the debris into heaps when I visited three days later. Several of the structures on the Swayambhu hill were broken. Bhimsen Thapa's tall white minaret collapsed again, killing perhaps 150 people, but a teenage couple who were on the viewing platform fell eight stories and survived, with quite minor injuries.

Several of the new, towering apartment blocks suffered severe cracks, and now stand deserted. They didn't meet the building

codes. Apparently the developers took insurance in order to get loans, but now they're looking for a payout from the government, and the money to be made on such a scam makes me think it might have a future.

Out of a population of perhaps three million, about 1,700 people in the Kathmandu Valley were killed by the earthquake. This is not enough for most residents to have been deeply personally affected by the disaster. Some of the victims were buried under the rubble of temples in the durbar squares. Scores were killed when churches collapsed, because Saturday is the Christian sabbath in Nepal. Brick houses with load-bearing walls were ruined in far greater proportion than the new ferroconcrete pillar-system structures, which had become more common in Kathmandu and Patan. The most concentrated damage in the Valley was therefore in Bhaktapur, and in smaller old towns outside the Ring Road, such as Harisddhi, Bungmati and Sankhu, which had largely preserved their old fabric. In Bungamati over seven hundred houses collapsed, yet only five people died; a miracle that local people attributed to the blessings of Bungadya, the famous rain god of the place, whose chariot had recently set off on the extended journey it makes once in a twelve-year cycle.

In fact the disaster was not in Kathmandu, where everyone expected it, but in the countryside, especially in districts directly above the rupture. Landslides were set off in many places. The village of Langtang, 60 kilometres north of Kathmandu, was obliterated by an avalanche that buried three-storey houses and killed each of the 300 people who were there at the time.[2] Most rural houses were of two or three storeys, built of stones bound together with mud, and in many villages most houses were destroyed.[3] It was very fortunate that at midday on a Saturday most people were outdoors. Altogether about 9,000 people were killed and over two million were made homeless, a few weeks before the monsoon.

In the weeks that followed many people from Kathmandu joined with others whom they knew to deliver whatever relief they could arrange to the stricken villages. On two separate days about a week after the earthquake I joined a group of friends who were delivering rice and other items to a village in Sindhupalchowk. This district, a couple of hours' drive north-east of the city, appeared to have been the worst affected, which ultimately proved to be so, although at that time the extent and distribution of the disaster was still a mystery. The three men whose trip I joined were all successful businessmen; my friend Samden, who is in tourism, his brother-in-law Mingma, whom I knew, and a third man called Kaji, who had apparently made three huge fortunes, and lost two, in real estate and the garment industry. He was often cited, I learned, by the grandparents of his community as an unrepeatable anomaly, and he looked like Chairman Mao – a fact, he admitted, his Chinese trading partners also remarked on.

Being currently at the high-point of his economic cycle, we rode in Kaji's luxury SUV, which he drove properly but in a way that was careless of its value, onto appalling tracks that, if they'd been even slightly worse, might have claimed his car for ever. Behind us followed one of his delivery vans, a more practical vehicle, loaded with almost a tonne of rice, and some blankets from his factory. This group had identified a village called Langarche, which they believed was as remote as any we could reach.

There were stories by this stage of crowds of desperate people trying to capture the few supplies that were passing on the roads. As far as we knew, the government had banned people from offering supplies and demanded that everything be turned over to them. The authorities were getting a bad name for intercepting aid, and so we developed lies that we would use in case the police interfered. Nothing like that happened. The way only deteriorated into a dreadful track for the last forty minutes or an hour, and before that, although the houses and settlements we passed were shockingly ruined, there was no difficulty. We saw no relief traffic except a few likeminded people doing the same thing.

All day there were helicopters overhead, but only small ones, unable to carry appreciable freight, so presumably they were rescuing injured people from the north of the district.

Shortly before we reached Langarche we passed a group of students hiking with backpacks, to whom we gave a swig of bottled water. They turned out to be associated with a party of motorcycle enthusiasts, who had reached Langarche slightly before us with a cargo of medical items. The place was wrecked. There was at least one family absorbed in grief, as well as a woman with a broken leg, who had been left behind by a helicopter two days ago – the crew had said they would return for her but hadn't. The people were mostly idle or waiting. They were shocked, no doubt. My private speculation, which may not have been very relevant, was whether they could summon themselves to harvest the ripe barley in their fields, or plant rice when it rained, and whether that was even possible to do without a house.

The government had dropped off a quantity of rice the previous day, roughly equivalent to what we had in our van, but since it wasn't enough for everyone, and no instructions had been given, it was lying under a tarpaulin by the ruin of the police post. The police, who had presumably lost their boots, or at any rate were wearing slippers, had also lost their home, yet they had spent the last several days tramping across their area assessing the damage. They helped us to make a list of the households there, which was compared to our quantity of rice, the households were divided into groups to equally share a number of sacks by a practical fraction, a line formed, names were read out, and whatever we had was equally distributed. Ninety families received nine and a half kilos each, which was enough for a couple of days. In fact, at that stage, although it already seemed important, a shortage of food wasn't their main problem.

There were members of two Dalit families present, with distressing stories, whom I took pity on, but because they had walked there from another place it was impossible to include them in the distribution without causing dissent. My companions helped me to give them some cash without attracting attention.

You could still buy things. We hadn't thought to bring anything with us to eat, so before we left we had some noodles from the woman brewing tea in the village. Nevertheless, we were quite uncomfortable by the time we stopped, late in the evening, at the roadside halfway home. The single room, which was open to the road on one side, was crowded with members of youth groups and social organizations from Kathmandu, who'd all been doing their part. We sat at a table outside, and kept ordering plates of fried chicken, and more beer than I ultimately wanted, and while we sat there in the dark the first significant relief convoy we'd seen went past.

A Nepali village – which is an administrative unit – is composed of several settlements spread over many kilometres. Two days later I returned to the same village with different members of the same group of friends. This time I was travelling in Siddharth's powerful Land Rover. Word had been spread across various networks in Kathmandu (classmates, relatives, Facebook friends) and we had collected over a tonne of rice, a couple of hundred kilos of daal and beans, and, most significantly, several dozen plastic tarpaulins, practically unobtainable in Kathmandu, which is what people actually needed, their houses having been destroyed. We intended to visit a different part of the same sprawling village, and we had the phone number of the head constable who had helped us before.

It was fortunate that we now had a more powerful car, because as the track went further, where it had only been cleared the previous day, it was extremely steep. We struggled to get through to the police on the phone. We understood that they were in a different part of the area. When we briefly spoke they particularly requested that we reserve for them one tarpaulin. We slogged up the hill, giving out stuff at each cluster of houses, and evening it up by giving out more on the way back down. We didn't forget the police, but one woman grabbed more than we wanted her to, and then we met an elderly couple we'd missed, whom we pitied, and we gave them two plastic sheets because they said they needed them both. At the bottom we met and greeted the policeman. He asked if we had a tarpaulin for him and I told him through the car window that we hadn't, and felt shame when he turned on his shoeless heel in unconcealed disgust.

The earthquake had been anticipated – preparing for it had become a touted sector of the development business – but the emergency response got off to a poor start. It had been so widely expected that the city would be flattened, that for a couple of days it was reported abroad that that is what had actually happened. The inaccessible countryside was devastated. Planning failed. Especially, there were severe bottlenecks at the airport, which was unable to cope with the number of aircraft and the volume of cargo, and where the government began laboriously taxing relief supplies.[4] If material could escape, there were not enough helicopters, trucks or drivers to distribute it. There were instantly allegations that members of the government, and local politicians, were stealing aid; and the government and international agencies began feuding over who should control the resources that the world was trying to send.[5] In the affected districts, officials began a vexatious process of identifying genuine victims, which had the effect of barring vulnerable people from access to relief.[6]

Two months after the earthquake, on the eve of an international donor conference, the government declared that the relief phase was over, and the reconstruction phase had begun.[7] Representatives of foreign governments and multilateral agencies came to Kathmandu and pledged over $4 billion for Nepal's reconstruction. Yet at the time of writing – now six months after the quake – the government authority that will spend this money has not yet been formed, and none of it has been spent.

In the wrecked villages, the relief operation, much of it carried out by international agencies, has distributed significant materials, but is still struggling to address the most elementary requirements of food and shelter; and the villagers, emerging miserably from the monsoon, are facing the imminent onset of winter. Most places have received something, and many people may have had their barest needs met, but some have still received almost nothing or nothing. It isn't a coincidence that many of those worst affected by the disaster, and worst served by the response, belong to groups of low social status, such as Tamangs.[8] Reaching these places is very difficult, because many walking trails have been destroyed. It is also clear that the data is flawed, both as respects people's needs and what has actually been distributed to specific places.[9]

By July the earthquake had largely disappeared from the Kathmandu newspapers. This was partly because, after the

first fit, the city reverted to not really caring about these people. (Some radically neglected settlements, a few dozen miles from the capital, have never produced a high school graduate.) But besides that, the three major parties chose this moment to rush out a new constitution, and the earthquake disappeared from the mind of almost everyone whose life hadn't been wrecked by it. There seems to be a gaping disjunction here, but the political crisis flowed directly from the natural disaster. The conservative establishment took the chance to capture the new constitution.

The first constituent assembly had a majority for parties, including the Maoists, which (in the current terms) favoured progressive political change and were sympathetic to identity politics. The establishment parties, the Congress and UML, won the second election in 2013. They interpreted this as a mandate to reverse the agenda for the 'inclusion' of marginalized groups that had become the central issue of the political transition. However, despite their large majority, the constitution-drafting process remained deadlocked, because it was appreciated that a constitution promulgated without the support of the Maoists could not successfully conclude the peace process. After the earthquake the Maoists changed sides, and backed the Congress and UML. Their motive was the subject of convoluted speculation, but all accounts agreed on their need to join the new coalition government that would be formed when the constitution was complete. (Three years out of power saps a party's finances, and its powers of patronage and political protection.) A 'fast track' process now began, which drafted and promulgated the new charter in a little over three months.[10]

The 2015 constitution established a republican, parliamentary democracy and seven federal states.[11] It was promulgated on 20 September, after being endorsed by an overwhelming majority of the assembly. It was therefore argued to be very democratic, and it included some progressive terms – such as being notably accommodative to transgender rights. However it deeply polarized the country, both because of some of its provisions, and the manner in which it was done. Important civil liberties, such as freedom of expression, are undermined by broadly drawn caveats. But most opposition has focused on a few particular issues.

The new constitution makes women unequal citizens, by denying them the right to pass full citizenship to their children, unless the father is a Nepali man. (When a foreign woman marries a Nepali man the case is different.) This also affects single mothers.[12] It is part of the charter's larger patriarchal and ethno-nationalist identification of citizenship with Nepali 'seed', particularly motivated by the prejudice and paranoia of some hill people towards the cross-border marriages that are common among Madhesis. The constitution also reduced the parliamentary representation of the plains, partly through the composition of the upper house, and partly by playing on the fact that although the plains are home to just over half the population they compose a much smaller proportion of the country's area. Constituencies in the lower house would now be drawn on the basis of 'geography' in addition to population. Further, the constitution diluted provisions for the 'proportional inclusion' of marginalized groups in public employment and official posts. In these respects it reversed progressive provisions in the 2007 interim constitution, and abrogated agreements previously made by the government with marginalized groups.[13]

The second assembly had earlier voted to carry over the large portions of the draft that had been agreed by the first. It also had a committee which negotiated compromises on some outstanding issues. In the event much of that was discarded, and the constitution was drafted in private by around half a dozen men – a few politicians and a couple of bureaucrats – of the same caste and political persuasion. There was a public consultation exercise, lasting a couple of days, the draft slightly adjusted, then it was endorsed in a whipped vote, in which members of the parties that backed it were not allowed to register amendments.

The issue that caused the greatest uproar reflected both the content and this dubious process, and was the delineation of federal states. The Congress and UML had long argued that states should not be drawn to reflect the demographic concentrations of the larger marginalized groups, which would undermine social harmony, but on the basis of 'mixed identities' and 'economic viability'. Yet they drew the boundaries in a manner that ensured a hill-caste demographic advantage in six out of seven states, and in particular bolstered the electoral constituencies of a few key leaders. (There is, of course, little evidence that 'economic viability' is almost any politician's real concern, except in protecting thievery, which is the basis of their political economy.) The result was protracted strikes and protests across the south during the final weeks of drafting; involving Tharus in the west, and Madhesis in the eastern plains. The leaders at the centre refused to pause the process to negotiate with the dissenting groups, but rather addressed insulting language to them, and deployed the security forces. Around 45 people, including ten policemen, were killed.[14] In Kathmandu there was an outburst of open racism towards Madhesis, on social media, in the newspapers, and on the tongues of politicians, which shocked me. It was in the midst of this crisis that the constitution was promulgated. The government decreed national celebrations that night, which were observed by some with lamps, but by others with a blackout.

It was dismaying, to me, to see the opportunity of the constitution squandered. It repeated the pattern in which previous periods of democratization had been partially reversed by a resurgent establishment, making the basis for future conflict. My sympathies lay with those whom I saw as seeking their rightful place in a more generous, forward-looking new Nepal. But there was a significant, and overwhelmingly influential, section that couldn't see it that way. Among them there was a genuine fearfulness that Indians – which is to say Madhesis – or that Christian missionaries, Europeans, or other castes, were out to take Nepal and Nepaliness away from them. The argument that is taking place is over provisions of the constitution that defend a vision crafted by King Mahendra during the Panchayat, of a Nepal which belongs especially to high-caste men from the hills.

Those who supported the new constitution in public debate were almost exclusively high-caste men. The writer Pranaya Rana described the attitude of some members of his own community. 'I am a Chhetri man, born and raised in Kathmandu. Today, the new constitution of the Federal Republic of Nepal will be officially promulgated and it is my constitution – it has been drafted by people who share my gender, my complexion, my language, my customs, my religion and my traditions. It is a document that preserves my standing in society. It takes pains to ensure that my kind, we Bahun-Chhetri men, will not lose much, if anything. And it sends a message to those pesky Madhesis, Tharus, Janajatis and women – all those who oppose this "historic" "epoch-making" document – that we will prevail, whether by ballot or by bullet ... We are the state and when it is opposed, so are we.'[15] This is a rather more convincing analysis than that of those who wrote that the dissenters were merely uneducated, or manipulated, and mistaken, and that the constitution was in fact a truly inclusive and democratic charter.

If the struggle over identity, and a high-caste vision of Nepali nationalism, was one of the big things that the past decade's politics were about, the other was the struggle for power-sharing and the control of resources, among a few top leaders and their followers. The rush to complete the constitution was also a rush to form a new power-sharing government, and not least to control the \$4 billion of earthquake relief. Who would be prime minister, who would get the presidency, and the speakership? What would the Maoists get out of it? Who would get the \$4 billion? This is what people also talked about, and this seems to be why establishing the earthquake-reconstruction authority has been made to wait until the new government is in place. This is the practical reason that the constitution-drafting process, finally ending like this, had earlier been so confounding and protracted. It is the reason that part of the country was encouraged to believe that others' gain would be their loss. When the top level of politics is an oligarchy extracting resources from the public, how can the bosses accept reform? Why would their followers want them to risk it? In so far as they are engaged in rent seeking and so on, others' gain *would be* their loss. So there is nothing in the constitution that could threaten the existing system, of extractive oligarchs. If anything, it seems to have weakened accountability. And the caste polarization foxed many high-caste people in Kathmandu, who might otherwise have wanted a better politics.

Before they'd gone through with it, while it was all still headed for disaster, a foreign scholar joked to me, bleakly, that the leaders hadn't failed to make an opportunity from the crisis of the earthquake.

They grabbed their victory when their inadequacy was most evident. But in the moment of their triumph, and for the first time in the latest drama, something that couldn't have been anticipated occurred. India, which had said the constitution should accommodate everyone, but had otherwise become unusually disengaged, responded furiously to the conflict that had been sown along its border. On the pretext of the Madhesi protests, it imposed an informal blockade. The squandered opportunity of the constitution became a full-blown crisis, within just a day of its promulgation, and now the atmosphere was really sour. Nationalist paranoia found full vindication. In the plains the police were on special duty, and in Kathmandu there was no traffic, but the roads were blocked by people queuing for fuel. Schools started closing, and hospitals running out of drugs. How would Kathmandu's generators run without Indian diesel? The reality that Delhi had miscalculated Kathmandu, and Kathmandu miscalculated Delhi, became in Kathmandu the false fact that India was responsible for the mess that Nepal had become.

Out in the hills there are three 'humanitarian hubs' from which supplies are being distributed to earthquake survivors. There are apparently between 65 to 80,000 households in need of aid, living above 2,500 metres in elevation, who must receive materials to help them endure the winter, which will begin to advance in a month or so. Each hub needs seven tankers of fuel for a month. But the government isn't giving them priority over the clamour for fuel in the city. As traffic returned to Kathmandu's streets it was evident that some officials and politicians were making a lot of money on the black market. For the second time in a decade, city folk were cooking on firewood.

I'm hearing about a new batch of foreign suits sitting in donor meetings, discounting realistic assessments of what's going on here, who are smugly convinced that their optimism is pragmatic.[16]

It is one of the most dismal times I've known. The same men who are in charge of the country now were in charge a quarter-century ago. Prejudice and the chance to steal money have led them to create a deep political crisis. It's not only me, I hear many people, of all sorts, dreading bleak scenarios. The best case is that things muddle on, but it's hard to escape the implications of this analysis: only if Nepal's problem was the marginalized demanding their place has the peace process succeeded by rejecting them. And those who believe that have won.

In the week before the constitution was promulgated I was travelling in the plains, collecting information on how people had been killed in the protests. I went to see a noted Madhesi intellectual, a moderate man, who, others say, has spent his career seeking the approval of patrons in Kathmandu. There's no doubt that he's a nationalist. On his desk was a Nepali flag, and on the wall of the book-cluttered, concrete cell of his study there were framed pictures of Nepali heroes, such as the poet Laxmi Prasad Devkota and the democrat B.P. Koirala. 'One question that Madhesis will ask for a very long time,' he said, 'is that when there was an earthquake in the hills they sent in a lot of food, a lot of medicine, a lot of supplies. They were grieving with the family. But when so many people in the Madhes are dying, why are the hills so silent? The future of this country is in the answer to this question.'

Kathmandu, 27 October 2015

Notes

Preface

1 Cited by Percival Landon, vol. 1, p.171.

2 Many non-Nepali accounts maintain that Sati's *yoni* fell to earth at the site of the Kamakhya temple in Assam.

3 Paraphrases K.P. Malla (1973), *The Intellectual in Nepalese Society:* 'They are also a displaced stratum of society, because by their training and education (as against their upbringing and origins) they have suddenly been compelled to live in the latter half of the twentieth century without due ceremony. They woke up one fine morning from the sleep of the Middle Ages and found themselves exposed to the neon lights of an electronic age.'

Chapter 1

1 Pablo Neruda, 'Poor Creatures'.

2 Dor Bahadur Bista, *People of Nepal,* p. 24.

3 John Locke in his study of the festival writes: 'Accidents resulting in the death of people crushed under the wheels of this *ratha* [chariot], as well as the ones in Kathmandu and Bhaktapur, are a frequent but little publicized fact.' *Karunamaya*, p. 270, n.35.

4 Locke, *Karunamaya*, p. 272, n.38. See also p. 276.

Chapter 2

1 Michael Hutt (ed.), *Himalayan 'People's War'*, p. 17.

2 'Plan for the Historic Initiation of the People's War' by the central committee of the Communist Party of Nepal

(Maoist), 1995. Cited Thapa, *A Kingdom Under Siege,* pp. 46–47.

3 See Sam Cowan, 'Inside the People's Liberation Army: A Military Perspective', *EBHR 37*, Autumn–Winter 2010.

4 Thapa, *Kingdom Under Siege*, p.72.

5 Hutt (ed.), *Himalayan 'People's War'*, p. 49.

6 Sara Shneiderman and Mark Turin in 'The Path to *Jan Sarkar* in Dolakha district: Towards an ethnography of the Maoist Movement', in Hutt (ed.), *Himalayan 'People's War'*, p. 89.

7 Prince Gyanendra's radio address, 3 June 2001, cited Isabel Hilton, 'Royal Blood', *The New Yorker,* 30 July, 2001, p.46.

8 See Baburam Bhattarai, 'The New Kot Massacre', *Kantipur*, 6 June 2001.

9 *Kathmandu Post,* 23 January 2002.

Chapter 3

1 Bendall, *A Journey of Literary and Archaeological Research*. p. 3.

2 *The Dictionary of National Biography* remarks on the gentleness of his nature.

3 The first man to do modern research on Kathmandu's ancient inscriptions had been Dr Bhagwanlal Indraji in 1880.

4 Bendall, p. 4.

5 Bendall, p. 14.

6 Bendal, p. 15.

7 Bendall, p. 5.

8 This inscription of King Amsurvarma is now dated by scholars to AD 610.

9 Bendall, pp. 80–81.

10 This theft (including beautiful photographs of the missing statue) is documented in Bangdel's *Stolen Images of Nepal,* pp. 61–64. Bangdel gives the date of the theft as 16 May 1985. When I noticed this discrepancy and went back to check, the bottom line of the inscription on the replacement

statue was illegible. Presumably we had misread the last digit of the date.

11 Bendall, p. 94.

12 Daniel Wright, *History of Nepal*, p. 97 n.1.

13 Wright, pp. 115–116.

14 References to Indian rulers imply that Mishra arrived sometime before 57 BC and Lhasa was not founded until the seventh century. In the Tibetan chronicles there is a record of a holy man, a 'Venerable Mishra', who arrived to teach Buddhism in Lhasa in 1210. See Todd Lewis, 'A Chronology of Newar-Tibetan relations in the Kathmandu Valley', in *Change and Continuity: studies in the Nepalese culture of the Kathmandu Valley,* edited by Siegfried Lienhard.

15 Wright, pp. 135–36.

16 Wright, p. 154.

17 Wright, p. 182.

18 Wright, p. 184 n.1.

19 Wright's chronicle lists 64 castes categorized by Jayastithi (pp. 185–86) but other chronicles state there were 36 categories (see Gellner and Quigley p. 8).

20 Wright, pp. 185–86.

21 Wright, preface. p. v.

22 Wright, pp. 203–05.

Chapter 4

1 Kaevrne, Pat (transl), 1979. 'The Visit of Prince Waldemar of Prussia to Nepal in February and March 1845', *Kailash* 7(1), p. 39.

2 Niels Gutschow, 'Urban Patterns in Patan', in *The Sulima Pagoda*, pp. 81–86.

3 'Prayers Read at the Consecration of a House', published in Slusser, *Nepal Mandala*, pp. 420–21.

4 Prayer for consecrating a house, reproduced in Slusser, *Nepal Mandala*, pp. 420–421.

5 'A mandala is an arrangement of deities conceived of in sets (of four, eight, sixty-four or more) laid out along the axes of

the cardinal points around a centre.' David Gellner, *Monk, Householder and Tantric Priest*. p. 190.

6 'A mandala is a circle, a mystic diagram of varied form, and in ancient Indian usage signified an administrative unit or country. From at least the sixth century AD., in conjunction with the word "Nepal" it signified to the Nepalese the Kathmandu Valley and surrounding territory.' Mary Shepherd Slusser, *Nepal Mandala*, p. vii.

7 Gellner, *Monk, Householder and Tantric Priest*, p. 48.

8 'Adya mahadana' ('And now the great gift') cited by David Gellner, *Monk, Householder and Tantric Priest*, p. 191.

9 This structure must have looked similar to the child's swing (*ping*) which is erected at Dasain.

Chapter 5

1 'Manparne euta sali, ali kali chha' by Rekha Shah and Nabin Dhungel.

2 Wright, p. 201.

3 For an example of typical attitudes at the time see Seira Tamang and Anonymous, 'Nepali View, Foreign View', *Nepali Times*, 11 October 2002.

4 Cited International Crisis Group, *Nepal Backgrounder: Ceasefire – Soft Landing or Strategic Pause?* 10 April 2003, p. 17.

5 Mike O'Brien, 'Terrorism can never be allowed to win', *Kathmandu Post*, 12 October 2002.

6 'Armed police chief shot dead', by Kiran Chapagain, *Kathmandu Post*, 27 January 2003.

7 When I reread these notes I realized the man belonged to the Tharu ethnic group, which was particularly severely exploited by landowners, and his description of feudalism may have been no exaggeration.

8 A Maoist position paper on the negotiations, published in April 2003, resembled their position during the previous brief ceasefire in 2001, which the Maoists had broken off. It included the demand for an elected constituent assembly, establishing Nepal as an officially secular country

and integrating their 'People's Liberation Army' into the national army. Reproduced in Deepak Thapa, *A Kingdom Under Siege*, pp. 219–27.

9 The army's strength rose from 50,000 when it entered the conflict at the end of 2001 to 70,000 less than two years later. During the 2003 ceasefire the Royal Nepal Army took delivery of two troop-carrying helicopters gifted by the British government and was receiving $17m in US military aid. It completed the commercial purchase of 5,000 M-16 rifles and 5,500 Belgian Minimi machine guns. The royal government concluded an anti-terrorism treaty with America and received public and private assurances from Britain of continued military support if the peace talks collapsed. The king's negotiating position, finally laid out in August 2003 (reproduced in Thapa, *A Kingdom Under Siege*, pp .228–39), was publicly endorsed by Western diplomats. See International Crisis Group reports, *Nepal Backgrounder: Ceasefire – Soft Landing or Strategic Pause*, 10 April 2003; *Nepal: Obstacles to Peace*, 17 June 2003; *Nepal: Back to the Gun*, 22 October 2003.

10 Many health posts were scarcely functioning before the insurgency began, after which many health workers fled the villages. Rural health services were further undermined by the army's tactic of blocking medical supplies to Maoist-affected areas, to prevent them from falling into the hands of the rebels.

Chapter 6

1 Sylvain Lévi, *History of Nepal*, part 1 (trans. Riccardi), *Kailash* 3(1), p. 35.

2 See András Höfer, 'On re-reading *Le Nepal:* what we social scientists owe Sylvain Lévi', *Kailash* 7(3&4), pp. 175–180.

3 Lévi, *A Notebook of Sojourn*, p. 28.

4 Lévi, *A Notebook of Sojourn*, p. 12.

5 Lévi, *A Notebook of Sojourn*, p. 35.

6 Lévi, *A Notebook of Sojourn*, p. 20.

7 'Shoes! Shoes!' *Sojourn*, p. 17.

8 *Sojourn*, p. 29.
9 All quotations as provided in Riccardi's translation, *Kailash* 3(1), pp. 39–40.
10 Cited Höfer, 'On re-reading *Le Nepal:* what we social scientists owe Sylvain Lévi', *Kailash* 7(3&4).
11 Weber, *The Religion of India*, p. 20. Weber presents an account of assimilation into Hinduism similar to Lévi's, although Lévi is not cited.
12 See for example Kamal P. Malla, 'Linguistic Archaeology of the Nepal Valley, Preliminary Report', *Kailash* vol. 8, No. 1 and 2, pp. 5–23, 1981.
13 See Locke, *Kurunamaya*, pp. 296–97.
14 Nepali historical traditions, still widely held, refer to the existence of pre-Licchavi dynasties such as the Gopalas and Kiratas, but there is no contemporary evidence for their existence and they are only known from vamshavalis composed a millennium or more after they were supposed to have existed.
15 The 171 cm tall statue of King Jayavarman, dated AD 185, was unearthed in 1992.
16 D.R. Regmi, *Inscriptions of Ancient Nepal*, p. 46.
17 Friedrich Engels, *The Origin of the Family, Private Property and the State* (1884, pp. 234–35 in the 1972 edition), cited K.P. Malla, 'Epigraphy and Society in Ancient Nepal: a critique of Regmi 1983', *Contributions to Nepalese Studies* 13(1), p. 82 (Dec 1985).
18 Wang Hsüan-t'sê, cited Slusser, *Nepal Mandala*, p. 5.
19 Buchanan, pp. 43–44. (This eyewitness account is not Buchanan's own, but was provided to him by his companion on the short-lived 1802 residency, Captain Crawford.)
20 For instance Guita, in the north-east of Patan. Yala, the name of Patan in the Newari language, was the name of a Licchavi village that stood near the cross-roads at Mangal Bazaar.

Chapter 7

1 When the bodies were found by investigators, strewn down a slope, their hands were still tied. *Kathmandu Post*, 'Army questions rebels' attack', 19 August 19 2003. See also the report of the National Human Rights Commission, and Advocacy Forum's account 'Doramba Incident'.

2 Colonel Basnet, who died, was associated with the Special Forces and was head of counter-terrorist interrogations. Colonel Chettri, who was paralysed from the waist, was blamed by the Maoists for killings in Gorkha District before being transferred to the east, where he was in command when the Doramba massacre occurred. Both were American trained. See wikileaks cable 03KATHMANDU1648, 28 August 2003. The minister was Devendra Raj Kandel, who had offered cash for dead Maoists' heads.

3 *Kathmandu Post*, 11 September 2003.

4 See for example Colonel Kaji Bahadur Khattri's press conference, widely reported in the Kathmandu press, 24 September 2003.

5 See, for example, wikileaks cable 03KATHMANDU1692, 2 September 2003, in which the British and American ambassadors exert pressure on the parliamentary parties not to protest against the palace.

6 He was a member of the UML student union.

7 In other words, give back the government or lose the palace.

Chapter 8

1 All quotations from Kesar Lal, *Legends of the Kathmandu Valley*, pp. 11–12.

2 K.P. Malla's phrase in his review of Petech's *Medieval Nepal.*

3 Anyway, according to Niels Gutschow, perhaps none of the Licchavi chaityas remains in its original location.

4 In *The Antiquity of Nepalese Wood Carving*, pp. 35–46, Slusser argues that this finding, by radiocarbon dating, shows that the monastery probably was founded in the reign of Shivadeva II (694–705), as tradition attests.

5 Slusser, *Nepal Mandala*, p.162.
6 For instance, an illustrated Pala Buddhist manuscript made in Bengal c.1150–1200, was annotated with the Nepali date in 1234, indicating that it was brought to the Nepal Valley and used there. Joseph Dyer, *The Arts of India, Virginia Museum of Fine Arts*, pp. 190–91.
7 *Gopalarajavamshavali* (trans. Vajracharya and Malla), p. 160.
8 The *Gopalarajavamshavali* had not entirely disappeared. For example, the now lost 'Kirkpatrick vamshavali', recorded by a British visitor in 1792, appears to have been related to the *Gopalarajavamshavali*. However, major events such as the raid on the Valley by the Bengali sultan Shamsuddin in 1349 had been lost from the historical record and are only known from the *Gopalarajavamshavali*. See K.P. Malla's introduction, pp. i–xxvi.

Chapter 9

1 Maya Laksmi Shrestha says that she is possessed by Kumari, of the Nava Durga of Bhaktapur. The number of women who are possessed in similar ways, and their popularity, has increased in recent decades. See Gellner, 'Priests, Healers, Mediums and Witches: the context of possession in the Kathmandu Valley', in *The Anthropology of Buddhism and Hinduism, Weberian themes*, pp. 197–221.
2 Tucci, *Rati-Lila*, p. 114, citing *Brhatsamhitã*, LXXIV, 20.
3 Locke, *Karunamaya*, p. 300.
4 K.P. Malla, 'The Earliest Document in Newari: the palm leaf from Ukubahah NS 235 / AD 1114', *Kailash* 16 (1&2), pp. 15–25.
5 There are 308 of these Newar monasteries in Kathmandu and Patan, many of which one wouldn't recognize as monasteries, except for the fact that the place name ends with *-baha* or *-bahal*. This does not include the scores of monasteries in the celibate Tibetan tradition that were mainly established on the outskirts of the city following the

exodus of refugees from Tibet after 1959 (although Tibetan Buddhism has been represented in the Valley for many centuries), nor the imported Theravada tradition whose presence in the Valley dates from the mid-twentieth century.

6 Tucci, *Rati Lila*, p. 43 and p. 62 without citing sources. An observation of Max Weber, made in a different context, is suggestive: 'This secrecy is not due solely to the monopolization of magical formulae, a practice originally characteristic of all priests ... One is tempted to think of the Occident. The New Testament contained passages of an ethical substance which first had to be explained away by priestly interpretation (and thus in part turned into their exact opposite) before they were suitable for the purposes of a mass church in general and a priestly organization in particular.' *Religion of India*, p. 26.

7 *Saktisangama Tantra* II, p. 57, cited Tucci, *Rati Lila*, p. 41.

8 *Prajnopayaviniscayasiddhi* III, pp. 6ff, cited Tucci, pp. 41–42.

9 Tucci, p. 42.

10 Tucci, p. 44.

11 Unnamed Tantra, cited Tucci, p. 49.

12 *Guhyasamãja*, pp. 128 ff, cited Tucci, p. 62.

13 Wendy Doniger's phrase, *The Hindus*, p. 428.

14 This ignorance may become more common in future, but in 2004 it struck a young reporter as exotic.

15 Yarsagumba is *Cordyceps sinensis*.

16 Wright, p. 209.

17 Gellner, *Monk, Householder and Tantric Priest*, p. 256.

18 Wright, p. 130, cited Slusser, p. 338.

19 See Michael Allen, *The Cult of Kumari*, p. 85.

20 A mixture of beaten rice and yoghurt.

Chapter 10

1 See Petech, *Medieval History of Nepal* (1984).

2 See for example 'Probe commission a pretext for government's weakness: Koirala', *Kathmandu Post*, 5

September 2004 and 'Govt infiltrated mobs: parties', *Kathmandu Post*, 6 September 2004.

3 A theatre state was claimed by Clifford Geertz to have existed in nineteenth-century Bali. Like Kathmandu, Bali is a fertile and densely populated area, bounded in Bali's case by mountains and the sea. According to Geertz the elaborate rituals of the theatre state were designed to dramatize the Balinese obsession with inequality and status pride, and to equate the hierarchy of the kingdom to the hierarchy of the Hindu universe. However, this was not done as a means to state power, but as the end of state power. 'The state cult was not a cult of the state. It was an argument, made over and over again in the insistent vocabulary of ritual, that worldly status has a cosmic base, that hierarchy is the governing principle of the universe, and that the arrangements of human life are but approximations, more close or less, to those of the divine.' (Geertz, *Negara*, p. 102.) A Balinese kingdom was a sacred space: all the people living in it and 'benefiting from its energies, were collectively responsible for meeting the ritual and moral obligations those energies entailed … [the nation was not a] social, political, or economic unit – but a religious one' (p. 129). The parallel between the Kathmandu Valley and Geertz's Bali is made by David Gellner, *Anthropology of Hinduism and Buddhism, Weberian Themes*, pp. 276–283.

4 The most important source of these stories, the *Swayambhupurana*, which describes the draining of the lake by Manjushree and associated events, cannot be traced further back than the 15th or 16th century (the oldest known copy is of 1558). Hindu equivalents such as the *Pasupatipurana* and *Nepalamahatmya* (1653), which associate the sites of Hindu shrines with miraculous events, belong to the sixteenth and seventeenth centuries.

5 See Locke, *Karunamaya*, pp. 300–309.

6 Stiller, *Prithwinarayan Shah in the Light of the Dibya Upadesh*, p. 39.

7 Stiller, *Dibya Upadesh*, p. 43.
8 Mao, *On Guerrila Warfare*, Chapter 7.
9 Mao, *Basic Tactics*.
10 Giuseppe, 'An Account of the Kingdom of Nepal', *Asiatick Researches* 2, London 1805, p. 317.
11 Giuseppe, p. 319.
12 Niels Gutschow points out that although the walls are often referred to, and the sites of gates can be identified, no archaeological trace of the walls themselves, of either Kathmandu or Patan, has been found. The walls may have consisted mainly of the backs of houses that faced inwards.

Chapter 11

1 In the early Shah years there were also some Gurungs and especially Magars in senior military positions.
2 Stiller, *Dibya Upadesh*, p. 44.
3 *The Nepalese Army: a force with history, ready for tomorrow*, Directorate of Public Relations 2008, p. 83.
4 According to Kiyoko Ogura's exhaustive account of the battle, both these bodies belonged to men who were returning home after working abroad. *EBHR* 27, p. 107.
5 See Sam Cowan, 'Inside the People's Liberation Army: A military perspective', *EBHR* 37.
6 Altogether 19 policemen, 14 soldiers, 19 civilians and probably around 80 Maoists were killed in the battle and immediate aftermath. The Maoists took around 39 prisoners who were later released to the International Committee of the Red Cross. Ogura, *EBHR* 27, pp 113–14.
7 British military aid was described as 'non-lethal' and provided under the Conflict Prevention Pool, a fund shared by the FCO, MoD and Department for International Development (DfID). The STOL Islander surveillance planes were used as spotters before the army dropped mortar bombs on suspected Maoist positions by helicopter. These raids, which often targeted villages and schools where the rebels were believed to be present, were among the military tactics most feared by Maoists and

civilians alike. The British helicopters were Mi-17 troop transporters, given at a time when the army had very limited capability to deploy soldiers by air, in exchange for assurances that they would not be used to bomb ground positions. American military aid included M-16 assault rifles.

8 See Yogesh Raj, 2012, *Expedition to Nepal Valley: the journal of Captain Kinloch August 26 – October 17, 1767*, Kathmandu, Jagadamba Prakashan. This recent publication overturns the long-held view that Kinloch was militarily defeated by the Gorkhalis at Sindhuli.

9 Kirkpatrick, p. v.

10 Kirkpatrick, p. 53.

11 Kirkpatrick, p. 57.

12 Kirkpatrick, pp. 63–64.

13 The shortest route from Kathmandu to the plains was finally blacktopped in 2012.

14 The identity of the mountain Kirkpatrick called Jibjibia is not known (see Harka Gurung, 'Nepaul to Nepal: Place names in two early accounts', *CNAS*, vol. 23, no. 1, Jan 1996, pp. 47–64), but the word is written on several drawings by Henry Oldfield in the collection of the Royal Geographical Society in London, apparently referring to the Gosainkund ridge, but perhaps implying that there was some confusion over the distinction between Gosainkund Lekh and Langtang Lirung, which stands immediately behind Goasinkund when viewed from the south. (Drawing numbers X410/022715, X410/022719, the superb panoramic drawing of the Valley X410/02790, and X410/022702, which is annotated 'Highest point of the Gosainkund mtn, seen over the summit of mount Jibjibia …' It appears that here Langtang is referred to as 'Gosainkund' and Gosainkund is referred to as 'Jibjibia'.)

15 Kirkpatrick, p. 69.

16 Kirkpatrick, pp. 163–164.

17 Kirkpatrick, p. 150. Niels Gutschow in *Architecture of the Newars*, p. 119, calculates that there are over 1,000

'meaningful' holy sites in Patan (and presumably a comparable number in Kathmandu) including all classes of temples and shrines.

18 Kirkpatrick, p. 210.

19 Kirkpatrick, p. 152.

Chapter 12

1 Buchanan, cited *Historical Records of the Survey of India, Vol II, 18001815*, p. 70.

2 Buchanan, pp. 22–23.

3 Buchanan, pp. 234–36.

4 Buchanan became increasingly solitary and disillusioned in later life, his scientific discoveries overlooked or unappreciated, and passed over until the very end of his career for the position he coveted, of Superintendent of the Botanic Garden in Calcutta. He finally returned to Scotland, changed his name to Hamilton and inherited a clan chieftaincy from his mother's family. He died a Scottish laird, mostly unrecognized for his contributions to Asian history.

5 Perceval Landon's observation, vol. 1, p. 86.

6 *Papers Regarding the Administration of the Marquis of Hastings in India*, vol. 1. Enclosures attached to the 'secret letter' of December 1814.

7 *Papers Regarding the Administration of the Marquis of Hastings in India*, vol 1. Letter to Charles Crawford, July 1814.

8 Called Kalunga or Kalanga in the British records.

9 Quotations from documents collected by Cox in the Hastings papers (1825). Prinsep's relatively brief contemporary British account of the war, excerpted from the first volume of Hastings's papers, has been republished as *The Gurkha War: the Anglo-Nepalese Conflict in North East India 1814–16* by Leonaur.

10 See Pratyoush Onta, 'Ambivalence Denied: the making of rastriya itihas in Panchayat era textbooks', CNAS 23(1), pp. 213–254.

11 For example, the Sugauli treaty imposed a British resident at Kathmandu and curtailed Nepal's right to conduct independent foreign relations. During the mid-nineteenth century, Britain mostly treated Nepal as an independent state but also sometimes exercised influence in domestic politics. Towards the end of the century British officials began to formally question Nepal's sovereignty. In 1905 the British Viceroy described Nepal's status: 'Nepal is definitely not an independent state. The degree of its incorporation in the Indian Empire and subordination to the British crown is somewhat indeterminate...' (cited Tamang 2013, p. 271). In 1923 Britain rewarded Nepal for the contribution of Gurkhas in the First World War with a treaty recognizing its independence (although still placing restrictions on its relations with neighbouring states such as Sikkim). Independent India inherited Britain's role. For example, Jawaharlal Nehru stated in 1950, 'Frankly we do not like and shall not brook any foreign interference in Nepal … No other country can have as immediate a relationship with Nepal …' (cited Tamang 2012, p. 272). In 1951 Nehru told the Indian parliament, 'where India's security is concerned, we consider the Himalayan mountains our border' (cited Mihaly, p. 52).

12 It has been said that in the nineteenth century the Anglo-Nepal war was the Indian campaign the British most wanted to forget, but now it's the only one they want to remember.

13 In a curiously ill-informed public diplomacy initiative, the British embassy in Kathmandu chose 2014–16 to celebrate the bicentenary of Nepali-British bilateral relations. Kinloch's invasion of 1767 (at the invitation of the Kathmandu raja), the commercial treaties of 1792 or 1801, Kinloch's embassy of 1793 or Knox's stint as resident in 1802 might have provided better alternatives, except of course that they had already passed. The impression was of a rather vague imperial nostalgia. A conversation with a diplomat suggested that the details of the history of

Britain's relations with the country, including the enduring unpopularity of the Sugauli treaty, were not a subject the embassy was particularly aware of.

Chapter 13

1 It was a peculiar coup in that the king overthrew a government he had himself appointed, over which he exercised large influence. It was in fact the culmination of a takeover that had been in progress since he first sacked Sher Bahadur Deuba as prime minister three years earlier, on 4 October 2002.

2 Thomas Bell, 'Britain halts training for Nepal's army as king seizes power from politicians', *The Daily Telegraph,* 3 February 2005. The British Foreign Secretary, Jack Straw, issued a statement on 22 February announcing the suspension of military aid.

3 Thomas Bell, 'Nepal's king threatens to seize assets of political rivals', *The Daily Telegraph,* 6 February 2005.

4 According to Hodgson's friend and biographer William Hunter (1896), p. 23.

5 See Theodore Riccardi, 'The imaginary orient of Richard Wagner', *Himal Southasian*, March 2006.

6 The Wright chronicle is in fact the best known among a group of vamshavalis composed in the early nineteenth century. Some of its information clearly derives from accurate earlier material of various sorts, and medieval mythological texts such as the *Swayambhupurana.* Even Wright seems to have dimly perceived its anachronistic quality, noting of one episode, 'This proceeding is exactly what would take place under similar circumstances at the present day'. Furthermore, the translation Wright published was very inaccurate. Only now is a second, authoritative, translation under preparation. Parts of the historiography of the past century (such as the incident of the priest in the jackal mask, cited as evidence of human sacrifice by Slusser, and on p. 118 of this book) are therefore based on a mistranslation. See the article by the translators of

the forthcoming new edition, Bajracharya and Michaels, 'On the Historiography of Nepal: the "Wright" chronicle reconsidered', *EBHR* 40 (2012), pp. 83–98.

7 Bhimsen Thapa moved to his more famous later residence, Bagh Durbar, after it was built c.1810.

8 In fact the building had long been used to store antique weapons, some apparently dating from Bhimsen's time. These were sold, in an allegedly corrupt deal, to an American antique dealer in 2000. See 'Lost history: Gehendra-made guns sold off to US company', *The Kathmandu Post*, 25 August 2011.

9 Whelpton, *A History of Nepal*, p. 43.

10 Letter of 24 June 1937 to J.R. Colvin, Secretary to the Governor General, cited Hunter, p. 153.

11 Hodgson, *Miscellaneous Essays*, pp. 211–223.

12 Landon, vol. 1, p. 99.

13 Leonard Adam, 1950, 'Criminal Law and Procedure in Nepal a Century Ago: Notes Left by Brian H Hodgson', *Far East Asian Quarterly* 9, pp. 146–168.

14 Cited Hunter, p. 140.

15 Hodgson to the Political Secretary in Calcutta, 18 February 1833. Cited Hunter, pp. 132–36.

16 Thomas Smith, *The Nepal Years*, vol. 1, p. 167.

17 Henry Oldfield, who was in Kathmandu in the 1850s, offers a pro-Bhimsen account. *Sketches of Nipal*, vol. 1 p. 316.

18 Letter to government of 30 May 1839, cited by Whelpton, *Kings Soldiers and Priests*, p. 71.

19 Letter to government of 30 July 1839, cited by Hunter, p. 176.

20 Letter to government, 14 April 1839, cited Hunter, pp. 171–173.

21 Hunter, pp. 185–187.

22 Whelpton, *Kings, Soldiers and Priests*, pp. 77–84.

23 These letters were first published by Oldfield, vol. 1, pp. 318–319. Also Hunter, pp. 187–89, Whelpton, p. 82.

24 Hodgson's letter to Government of 3 July 1840 is reproduced in full in Stiller, *The Kot Massacre*, pp. 14–23.

25 Hodgson's letter of 3 July.
26 Hodgson to Government, 10 October 1841, published by Stiller, *The Kot Massacre*, pp. 116–117.
27 Landon, vol. 1, p. 101.

Chapter 14

1 Of the flurry of prime ministers in these years, one, Ranajang Pande, escaped execution in 1843 because he was already dying when the rest of his family were sentenced to death.
2 Ottley's letters (along with much other residency correspondence of the period 1840–47) are published by Ludwig Stiller, *Letters from Kathmandu: the Kot massacre*, pp. 295–302.
3 Laurence Oliphant, *A Journey to Kathmandu*, p. 7. '... which pithy sentences he used to rattle out with great volubility, fortunately not making an indiscriminate use of them.'
4 Robin Cook was condemned in the Tory press for this assault on tradition. E.g. Charles Moore, *The Spectator*, 4 June 2008.
5 Oldfield, vol. 1, p. 399.
6 Personal letter by Dalhousie, May 1852. Cited Whelpton, *Kings, Soldiers and Priests*, p. 206.
7 This area, known as the Naya-Muluk (new country) consists of Banke, Bardia, Kailali and Kanchanpur districts. The indigenous Tharu people of the area suffered some of the worst abuses of Nepali feudalism. Some joined the Maoists, and the Tharu community consequently suffered some of the worst army atrocities of the conflict. (See report of UN OHCHR, *Conflict-Related Disappearances in Bardiya District*, December 2008.)
8 Other refugees, such as the family of the rebel leader Nana Saheb, also settled in Kathmandu. See Upadhyaya, *Indians in Nepal during the 1857 War*. It appears that Nana Saheb himself may have died in the jungles of southern Nepal shortly after the defeat of the rebellion, although the British

were not able to confirm this and suspected that reports of his death might be fabricated.

9 Lévi, *Notebook of Sojourn*, pp. 14–15.

10 A high gateway of the Thapathali palace spanned the road beside the Ram temple until it was deemed unsafe and demolished c. 2008.

11 Cited by Prayag Raj Sharma in his introduction to András Höfer, *The Caste Hierarchy and the State of Nepal* (second edition, 2004), p. xvi.

12 The Jaganath temple, 1782, and Laksmisvara, 1813. See Gutschow, *Architecture of the Newars*, p. 126; and Amatya, *The Bagmati: a monument guide.*

13 Oldfield, *Sketches from Nipal*, vol. 1, pp. 238–45.

14 Oldfield, vol. 2, p. 5.

15 Oldfield vol. 1, p. 252.

16 Oldfield, vol. 1, pp. 249–50.

17 Oldfield, vol. 1, p. 247.

18 Oldfield, vol. 1, pp. 248–49.

19 Oldfield vol. 1, p. 98.

20 Oldfield vol. 1, p. 100.

21 Oldfield vol. 1, pp. 115–16.

22 Wright, p. 2.

23 Wright, p.11, n. 1.

Chapter 15

1 The early history of photography in Kathmandu involves many others besides the well known Chitrakar family of Bhimsenthan. The first Nepali photographer may have been Dambar Shamsher Rana (1858–1922). See Pratyoush, Onta, 'Photographic Consumption in Kathmandu c.1863–1960', *EBHR* 15–16 (1998–99), pp. 59–68. The first person to photograph Kathmandu was Clarence Comyn Taylor in 1863–4. See J.P. Losty, 1992, 'Clarence Comyn Taylor (1830–79): the first photographer in Udaipur and Nepal', *History of Photography* 16(4), pp. 318–335.

2 Between 1880 and 1951 over forty palaces were built adjoining Kathmandu and Patan.

3 In 1856–7, while Jang Bahadur was abroad, two of his brothers deputized for him as prime minister for a few months each. Jang resumed the office on his return. For the sake of simplicity these are omitted from this count.

4 The present-day Gurkha recruitment reflects historical perceptions of which ethnic groups are 'martial' (or suitable for soldiering) and which are not. British officers openly spoke in such terms at least until the first decade of the twenty-first century. The groups principally recruited are not Gorkhalis in the sense that the national elite were Gorkhali (i.e. members of the Chhetri caste whose families were associated with Prithvi Narayan Shah's conquests), but rather members of hill ethnic groups legally defined as being of middle status, who filled the lower ranks of the army, especially Gurungs, Magars, Limbus and Rais. Other groups were previously prohibited from joining and are still rarely recruited today. Much of the rhetoric about the supposedly intrinsic character of these 'Gurkhas' (simplicity, bravery, 'fierce loyalty', etc.), such as can be read today even in liberal British newspapers, and which is espoused by the British champions of Gurkha rights, is remarkably little changed from colonialist writings of the nineteenth century.

5 Cited Puroshottam Banskota, *The Gurkha Connection*, pp. 101–2.

6 Cited Puroshottam Banskota, *The Gurkha Connection*, p. 89.

7 Interview, Bhaikaji Ghimire, 1 November 2005.

8 *Report of investigation into arbitrary detention, torture and disappearances at Maharajgunj RNA barracks, Kathmandu, in 2003–2004*, United Nations Office of the High Commissioner for Human Rights, May 2006, p. 50.

Chapter 16

1 See Mahesh Chandra Regmi, *Thatched Huts and Stucco Palaces*.

2 Kesar Shamsher Rana's Garden of Dreams, now a tourist attraction on the edge of Thamel, is said to have been built from the proceeds of a successful night's gambling.
3 Maharaja Chandra Shum Shere Jung Bahadur Rana, *Appeal to the People of Nepal for the Emancipation of Slaves and Abolition of Slavery in the Country*, Kathmandu, 1925.
4 M.C. Regmi, *Historical Miscellany*, pp. 131–159.
5 For example, in 2000 the government 'freed' the Kamaiyas – a type of bonded agricultural labourer of the Tharu community. A government survey found 101,500 Kamaiyas from 18,400 households. (Many of these families entered slavery in the 1950s and later, after high-caste migrants to Dang district appropriated the Tharu's land, with the blessing of the government, and lent them money they couldn't afford to repay. The land had become newly habitable to hill people following an American malaria eradication project.) Since 2000, after they were 'freed', some Kamaiyas received small amounts of land from the government (reportedly enough for 1–2 months' subsistence per year), but most did not receive even that. The Kamaiyas soon returned to their former 'owners' for survival. In July 2006 the Kamaiyas held protests in Kathmandu, demanding that the government provide land and other assistance – the government asked them to wait, formed a committee, and delivered nothing. See Adhikari (2008), pp. 51–52. In June 2013 there were protests in Kathmandu at the treatment of Kamlaris – young women and girls of indebted Tharu families who are traded by land owners, effectively as slave girls. The police had failed to investigate several cases of Kamlaris who had become pregnant, been abused, disappeared or died in suspicious circumstances while working as maids in middle- and upper-class Kathmandu homes. After police failed to violently suppress the Kamlaris' protests the government signed an agreement promising to address their demands. Kamlari activists alleged that many (unnamed) senior officials, politicians

and judges kept Kamlaris in their homes, and complained that the government did not deliver its promise to address Kamlari demands.

6 The first public screening of a film in Kathmandu is said to have been *Ram's Wedding* in 1949 – the audience threw petals at the screen.

7 This life is described by Krishna Bhakta Caguthi, a Newar peasant from the Bhaktapur area cultivating the land of high-caste Newar landlords, in Yogesh Raj's *History as Mindscapes*.

8 See Yogesh Raj, *History as Mindscapes*.

9 In 1918 Chandra Shamsher opened the first college in Kathmandu, Tri-Chanda College, to educate the sons of Nepal's leading families. Apparently his concern was that they not be exposed to progressive political ideas at Indian colleges. However, Tri-Chanda graduates did play a part in the coming political changes in Nepal.

10 Reprinted in Prem R. Uprety, *Political Awakening in Nepal*, pp. 186–91.

11 Krishna Bhakta Caguthi in Yogesh Raj, *History as Mindscapes*.

12 Ram Chandra Pokhrel, 'Leaflets from Heaven', *The Kathmandu Post*, 3 November 2011.

13 Tribhuwan's speech of 18 February 1951, cited Malagodi, *Constitutional Developments in a Himalayan Kingdom: The Experience of Nepal*, p. 5.

Chapter 17

1 The Rana *Muluki Ain*, giving legal force to the caste system, was formally replaced in 1963 but had fallen into disuse after 1951.

2 This promise was made by King Tribhuwan at the first meeting of the joint Rana/Nepali Congress cabinet, 18 February 1951.

3 All quotations from the translation by Larry Hartsell (1998).

4 In 1951 the national literacy rate was said to be around 2 per cent and there were around 300 college graduates in the country, many of them educated in India.

5 The politics of what was sometimes called the 'transitional period' of the 1950s is so reminiscent of the politics of the current 'transitional period' that it is worth quoting a description at length (from L.S. Baral, *Autocratic Monarchy, Politics in Panchayat Nepal*, Ch. 2, 'Nepal's Apprenticeship in Democracy 1951–1960', [originally published in *India Quarterly*, 27(3) 185–202, 1971], pp. 92–93). The interim period, ostensibly meant to prepare the ground for introduction of liberal democracy, dragged on bringing with it the stresses and strains which the Nepali people, impatient for their betterment, found so perplexing ... The policies of the interim governments were sometimes very progressive, but no tangible results could be achieved when opposition became intense ... [the leaders] compensated their lack of political base by their skill in operating cliques and conspiracies of one sort and another. Each of them claimed for his party, or even for the splinter group, national status deserving representation in the ministry, if not the chance to run the government ... (p. 94) Mutual rivalries and jealousies, prejudices and passions, and finally personality clashes...' were more important than ideological differences (there was broad consensus on constitutional monarchy and parliamentary democracy, reform of the birta system, a free press, human rights, etc.) 'Nevertheless, political actors were hardly ever prone to compromise. They failed to realize freedom of expression and accommodation to diversity of opinion were not merely an intellectual demand but a political necessity as well ... Understandably anxious that Nepal should remain within its sphere of influence, the government of India may have been more concerned with individual rather than institutional interests ensuring pro-India elements at the helm of the administration in Nepal rather than real development of the prerequisites of democratization.

(p. 101) Indeed, the problem for Nepal was finding ways and means for bringing about radical social and economic reform that would open the society to political reform. Without such change political participation of the people could not be effective. (p. 102) … in a situation where old values had not in the least been effaced, there were forces that were determined to whittle down radicalism of political leaders.'

6 Cited Louise Brown, *The Challenge to Democracy in Nepal*, p. 29.

7 *The Rising Nepal*, 18 March 1970.

8 Billboard on New Road, c. 2005.

9 There were some attempts to introduce socially progressive legislation, such as the Land Reform Act of 1964, based on the toppled Congress government's draft legislation. However, this was seen as largely cosmetic, being watered down so as not to disrupt the social structure of the countryside. The land ceiling was set so high, and implemented so slowly (allowing affected landlords to conceal their holdings), that only 1.5 per cent of all land was redistributed. Rent was set at a maximum of 50 per cent of the harvest. A compulsory farmers saving scheme was set up to provide agricultural loans but it collapsed in 1969, reportedly because senior government figures had stolen the money. 50,000 farmers had their debts cancelled (Adhikari, *Land Reform in Nepal*, pp. 61–64). No major land reform has been implemented since.

10 Niels Gutschow, *Architecture of the Newars*, p. 963.

11 What is now known as USAID was called USOM until 1961. USOM first acquired the ornate Phora Durbar (on Kantipath, later demolished by the Americans and replaced with an expat sports facility) in 1951 and moved to Himalaya Shah's Hari Bhawan in 1953. Hari Bhawan was sold and demolished by developers in 2012.

12 In the 1980s the suburb of Sanepa, on the Patan side of the river, had a similar evolution. The United Nations' office, UN House, was built there in an area that belonged to

Juddha Shamsher's family. The Ranas built houses and rented them to the development experts and international bureaucrats. Today it is a wealthy suburb of detached villas with gardens; bars, restaurants and European bakeries; kindergartens, mothers' groups and international schools, for the international experts and the Nepali elite who live there.

13 See Skerry et al., pp. 20–23.

14 Hugh Wood's 1987 memoir, cited Skerry, p. 22.

15 Anirudha Gupta, *Nepalese Interviews*, p. 119. Mahendra's coup was in December that year. The same author was astonished, and perhaps a little excited, at the sight of grand Nepali ladies smoking at parties. Today, sexual relationships between foreign development workers and Nepalis are, perhaps surprisingly, rare; 'international' and 'national staff ' mix little in their free time.

16 American support to education began in 1953. 'For well over a decade USOM/USAID financial assistance accounted for approximately 70 percent of all funds allocated for education development in Nepal. The U.S. remained the most influential donor in the education sector until 1972, leaving an indelible imprint on the education system.' (Skerry et al., p. 57.)

17 See Pratyoush Onta, 'Ambivalence Denied: the making of *rastriya itihas* in Panchayat era textbooks', *Contributions to Nepalese Studies*, vol. 23, no. 1 (January 1996).

18 Malagodi, 'Constitution Drafting as Cold War *Realpolitik*: Sir Ivor Jennings and Nepal's 1959 constitution'.

19 Cited Malagodi, 'Constitution Drafting as Cold War *Realpolitik*: Sir Ivor Jennings and Nepal's 1959 constitution'.

20 The agreement signed with Nepal on 23 January 1951 (weeks before the Rana regime was toppled) was known as the Point IV Agreement for Technical Cooperation after the fourth point of President Truman's inaugural address in which he outlined his response to the communist threat, including combating third-world poverty.

21 See Andrew Nickson, *Foreign Aid and Foreign Policy: The Case of British Aid to Nepal*, in which he argues that Britain strongly backed the Panchayat regime in order to safeguard Gurkha recruitment, and Seira Tamang, 'Historicizing state fragility in Nepal', *SINHAS*, v. 17, n. 2, p. 279.
22 *Chiso Aishtre*, trans. Michael Hutt, *Himalayan Voices,* p. 131.
23 *Mero Chowk*, trans. Michael Hutt, *The Life of Bhupi Sherchan*, pp. 99–100.
24 This description is partly derived from K.P. Malla's *Kathmandu, Your Kathmandu*, 1967.
25 *Yo Hallai Hallako Desh Ho,* transl. Michael Hutt, *The Life of Bhupi Sherchan,* pp. 115–117.
26 Pizza Hut and Kentucky Fried Chicken opened outlets in Kathmandu in 2009. Before that it had been one of a dwindling number of capital cities without major global fast-food franchises.
27 Yogesh Raj, *History as Mindscapes*, p. 51.
28 Government employees increased from 7,000 in 1951 to 90,000 in 1990. World Bank study, cited Brown, *The Challenge to Democracy in Nepal*, p. 66.
29 See Prayag Raj Sharma, *The State and Society in Nepal*, chapter 17.

Chapter 18

1 The information in this paragraph and in some passages below is derived from two lectures given by Mark Liechty, at the Social Science Baha, 9 January 2013, and Martin Chautari 13 June 2013, and his article 'The 'Age of Hippies': Nepalis make sense of Budget Tourists in the 1960s and 1970s', *SINHAS*, vol. 17, no. 2, Dec 2012.
2 All quotes are from Hollingshead's autobiography, *The Man who Turned on the World*, chapter 10, 'The capital of kingdom come', www.psychedelic-library.org/ho1110.htm; a relatively rare published text of hippie Kathmandu. Other recent visitors to Nepal, especially mountaineers but

also other tourists, have created a far larger literature. Even the early high-end tourist scene has its classic text, *Tiger for Breakfast* by Michel Peissel (1966). There is now an online crop of reminiscences by recently retired ex-hippies creating websites.

3 *Sanjhko Naya Sadak: Jindagiko Jatra*, transl. Michael Hutt, *The Life of Bhupi Sherchan*, pp. 118–19.

4 K.P. Malla, 'Kathmandu, Your Kathmandu'. Serialized in *The Rising Nepal* 28–29, November 1967.

5 Hippies of all ages still visit Kathmandu, now less visible among the much larger number of other tourists. As a respondent reportedly told Mark Liechty during his research – what do you mean they've gone? They're still here!

6 The first Nepali rockers may have been Newars from the areas where the hippies mostly stayed; Jhochhen (Freak Street) and Swayambhu (which the hippies renamed the Monkey Temple). Other early members of the scene included Nepalis moving to Kathmandu from Darjeeling at around the same time. Younger generations were exposed to rock music and influenced by these pioneers; but also had other influences, including increasingly widely available recorded music, radio, and studying abroad.

Chapter 19

1 *Development Plan*, p. 22.

2 *Development Plan*, p. 23 'In its present form, with very few exceptions, the Physical Development Plan is unable to specify in detail the natures of the programmes and projects which comprise it ... This situation is the unavoidable result of a total lack of information regarding many spheres of socio-economic activity in the Valley ... Unless the people and agencies responsible for development research and implementation adopt a more contribution-orientated attitude, coordinated planning and execution of effective development programmes will be severely inhibited.'

3 *Development Plan*.

4 Kanak Mani Dixit, 'Foreign Aid in Nepal: No Bang for the Buck', *SINHAS*, vol. 2, no. 1, 1997, pp. 173–87. Kathmandu development plans to that date included the Kathmandu Valley Physical Development Plan (1963), Physical Development Plan for the Kathmandu Valley (1969), Kathmandu Valley Town Development Plan (1976), Nepal Urban Development Assessment (aka the 'Padco Report', 1984) and the Kathmandu Valley Urban Development Plans & Programmes Study (1991).

5 The 'Padco Report' estimated that the price of land in the Valley increased by 633 per cent between 1964 and 1978. To a significant extent this must be due to foreign aid, aid being a major source of income in a city where productive growth in manufacturing or the service sector remained very slow.

6 *Inventory*, vol. 1, p. 9.

7 *Inventory*, vol. 1 p. 15.

8 This prescription refers to Daksinvarahi, near Thimi, vol. 1, p. 166.

9 Among the critiques of development aid in Nepal see the works of Mary Des Chene, Kanak Dixit, Tatsuro Fujikura, Eugene Mihaly, Chaitanya Mishra, Andrew Nickson, Devendra Raj Pandey and Seira Tamang cited in the bibliography.

10 'Low Road through the Himalaya', www.economist.com, 31 May 2011.

11 According to L.S. Baral, the Yogi Naraharinath was involved in royalist conspiracies preceding Mahendra's 1960 coup. Baral suggests that the coup happened when it did partly for fear that details would come out in court, at the yogi's trial for fomenting disturbances. See *Autocratic Monarchy*, pp. 128–9. Perhaps similarly, in the period between the people's movement of 2006 and the declaration of the republic in 2008, there were press reports of a royalist conspiracy to foment disturbances using Indian yogis attending the Shivaratri festival at Pashupati. When I mentioned this to a well connected royalist friend he

said, 'How do you know about it?' Clearly he hadn't been reading the newspapers.

12 Prayag Raj Sharma recalled the Yogi Naraharinath as follows in an interview in January 2012: 'He was an unparalleled explorer and the amount he turned out from his trips to all parts of Nepal was beyond anyone's imagination. He didn't publish everything. I am dismayed by what must have happened to the rest of the documents which he collected, [I don't know] whether they are still preserved by someone, because what he published was just a small amount of what he collected. Because he was a yogi and a true ascetic people believed him and they were willing to give their material to him ... He also had a taste for politics. He had an ideology. He was for monarchy, he was for a Hindu state, a very strong, unpolluted, unmixed Hindu state ...'

13 The Ancient Monument Preservation Act 2013 BS (1956 AD).

14 Mary Shepherd Slusser, 2003, 'Conservation Notes on some Nepalese Paintings', http://asianart.com/articles/paubhas/index.html, accessed 9 April 2014.

15 Dr Slusser has written fascinatingly about this painting in 'On a sixteenth century pictorial pilgrim's guide from Nepal', *Archives of the Asian Art Society*, vol. 38, pp. 6–36. Reprinted in Slusser, *Art and Culture of Nepal: Selected Papers*.

16 Pratapaditya Pal, *Art of Nepal*, p. 92. The accompanying text reads in part, 'In Nepal such reliefs are worshipped in a little shrine. The effaced condition of this relief may have been caused as much by the elements as by the constant application of ritual unguents.'

17 Pratapaditya Pal, *Art of Nepal*, pp. 106–07. 'Such crowns are worn by Buddhist priests (vajracharyas) during the performance of religious rituals.'

18 Pratapaditya Pal, *Art of Nepal*, p. 129. 'The central figure dancing on a bull is Siva, and it can therefore be surmised that the tympanum once adorned a Saiva temple.'

19 Sotheby's sale catalogue, *Indian and Southeast Asian Art, New York, Thursday September 19, 1996*. The piece (13th/14th Century, estimate $8,000–12,000) was identified by conservationists in Kathmandu as belonging to a known monument but Sotheby's reportedly did not cooperate with a request to identify the buyer.

20 Pratapaditya Pal, *Art of Nepal,* pp. 98–99; and Cleveland Museum of Art online catalogue, 'Goddess Uma' accession number 1982.49.

21 Dates (often very early) are confidently ascribed to pieces. However, as K.P. Malla observes in a review of Slusser's *Art and Culture of Nepal: Selected Papers* (CNAS January 2009), 'On pp. 192–193, she has published a revealing table of the total corpus of 13 dated stone and 17 metal sculptures from Nepal belonging to the long span of seven centuries between A.D. 467–1167. Even when a work is dated and inscribed, the numerals or texts and readings are fiercely contested.'

22 Pratapaditya Pal, *Himalayas: An Aesthetic Adventure*, Art Institute of Chicago, pp. 84–85.

23 Pratapaditya Pal, *Art of the Himalayas: Treasures from Nepal and Tibet,* p. 8.

24 Pal, *Art of the Himalayas*, p. 7.

25 Pal, *Art of the Himalayas,* pp. 9–10. Works from the Zimmerman Family Collection were auctioned by Christies in New York in 2008, many pieces going for several hundreds of thousands of dollars.

26 Guild, J. (pseudonym), 'The God Market', *Mother Jones*, Oct 1988.

27 When the Nepali art historian Lain Singh Bangdel visited American museums and told curators that the objects they held could only have been stolen from his country the answer he reportedly received from some was, 'Prove it'. Because the looting began before Kathmandu's art could be studied or documented *in situ* there is no record of where most of the pieces in foreign collections came from. That kind of photographic documentation was

only systematically undertaken in the 1980s by Lain Singh Bangdel and Jürgen Schick. The former received death threats and the latter had his visa revoked. Their efforts probably helped to bring an end to the destruction, although it had to decline anyway for lack of targets, and there are still occasionally art thefts today. In 1999 stolen art was voluntarily returned to Nepal for the first time, after Pratapaditya Pal recognized four sculptures from Bangdel's book *Stolen Images of Nepal* in a private collection. Since then there have been a few cases of stolen art being returned, and also of collectors refusing to return works despite evidence of where they were stolen from. Hundreds of works that were documented *in situ* remain missing. Under international conventions the responsibility lies with the Nepali government to reclaim stolen art from abroad, but it has made very little attempt to do so. Returned pieces are stored out of public view, in a locked shed at the National Museum in Chauni.

28 Presumably this is what Dr Pal was referring to when he told *Mother Jones*, 'I would prefer that things stay in their countries of origin. I would expect, however, that the governments of these countries would have a sensible policy for protecting the work. But if the heads of the governments themselves are not interested in it, then fine, let it go! What are you going to do?'

29 This famous rumour is discussed in Burghart, *The Conditions of Listening*, p. 315.

30 These stories are still popular in Kathmandu. For some impression see J. Guild (pseudonym), 'The God Market', *Mother Jones*, Oct 1988, and Isabel Hilton, 'Royal Blood', *New Yorker*, 30 July 2001.

31 See 'Kathmandu City and the Guthi System Today', in M.C. Regmi, *Nepal: An Historical Miscellany*, pp. 291–295.

32 Yogesh Raj, *History as Mindscapes*, p. 85.

33 See Prayag Raj Sharma, 'Values in the doldrums: Does the West meet the East in Nepal?', in *State and Society in Nepal*, pp. 297–317.
34 'Yo Hallai Halako Desh Ho', transl. Michael Hutt, *The Life of Bhupi Sherchan*.
35 The Nepali archaeology officials suspected that it might have been plundered from the Buddha's birthplace, Lumbini in southern Nepal, by the German rogue archaeologist Anton Führer at the end of the nineteenth century.
36 His talent recognized, the modern sculptor has since been employed in restoration projects.

Chapter 20

1 Ofeur Cavanagh, *Reminiscences of an Indian Official*, p. 132. Cited Whelpton 'Political Violence in Nepal', in *Revolution in Nepal*, edited by Marie Lecomte-Tilouine, p. 27. The choice of the word 'revolutions' was Cavanagh's – he spoke with Jang Bahadur in Hindustani.
2 The important student protests of 1979, which forced the government to hold a referendum on the Panchayat system in 1980, may be seen as a forerunner of the more decisive movement a decade later.
3 Western governments were somewhat ambivalent towards the 1990 people's movement. The US issued statements criticizing the excessive use of force against protestors, but also stating that 'Nepal has its own system of democracy'. See Tamang, 'Historicising State Fragility in Nepal', *SINHAS*, 17(2), pp. 280–81. According to Andrew Nickson, the British issued no statement during the people's movement (which began in February) until 9 April, when an FCO statement avoided mentioning 'democracy' and wrongly implied that the king had brokered a compromise between rival factions, rather than being forced to concede power to parliament. Citing interviews with diplomats, Nickson writes that Britain only endorsed the emerging multi-party democracy after receiving assurances that

Gurkha recruitment would not be affected. See 'Foreign Aid and Foreign Policy: the case of British aid to Nepal', p. 34.

4 Louise Brown, p. 60, citing 1988 World Bank report.

5 Louise Brown, p. 60, citing 1991 World Bank report.

6 The 1951 democracy movement, followed by the 1960 royal coup, followed by the 1990 people's movement, followed by the 2002–05 royal coup, followed by the 2006 people's movement clearly shows the dialectical struggle between 'progressive' and 'regressive' forces, which has directed the course of recent Nepali history.

7 This process is described in detail by Krishna Hachhethu in *Party Building in Nepal*.

8 This enquiry was known as the Malik Commission. No action was taken against those implicated, many of whom soon returned to public life.

9 Madhukar Rana, 'Open Letter to the Finance Minister', *Himal*, vol. 5, no. 2, Mar/April 1992.

10 This list derives from Mark Liechty, *Suitably Modern*, p. 49.

11 Indeed, this has been the case throughout the period since 1951, although during the Panchayat the ultimate power in the palace remained stable even as the king constantly changed his prime minister.

12 Several of the leading personalities of multi-party politics, even from bitterly opposed parties, are distantly related by blood or marriage. Meanwhile many other families of the same castes have little access to power – high-caste status is important but not sufficient in gaining access to power.

13 Hill Brahmins (comprising around 13 per cent of the population) comprised 12.5 per cent of the National Assembly in 1981, compared to 37.4 per cent of the lower house of parliament in 1991. Chhetris (approximately 16 per cent of the population) comprised 36.6 per cent of the National Assembly in 1981, declining to 17.7 per cent of the 1991 parliament (Gellner 2008, p. 177).

14 The proportion of new bureaucrats drawn from the Brahmin and Chhetri castes combined increased from

69.3 per cent in 1983 to 96.9 per cent in 2000. Kanak Mani Dixit, 'Bahuns and the Nepali State', *Nepali Times*, no. 65, 19 October 2001.

15 The situation was comparable to the democratic politics of 1959 as described by Eugene Mihaly: 'The parties were not rooted in different social or economic groups. The fact was that the membership of all of them was drawn almost entirely from the same group – the educated members of the landholding elements of Nepalese society... That few politicians set any store by attempts to implement such policies [as land reform] was a reflection of the realities of a political structure wherein all were vying for the support of the very group which stood to lose most by profound reform. Even the Communist Party was drawn from the middle class and considered this class's needs first.'

16 'Plan for the Historic initiation of the People's War' by the central committee of the Communist Party of Nepal (Maoist), 1995. Cited Thapa, *A Kingdom Under Siege*, pp. 46–47.

17 Baburam Bhattarai, *Monarchy vs Democracy*, p. 76.

18 Especially following his coup in 2005, India had come to distrust Gyanendra; seeing him as 'playing the China card' to balance Indian influence (another attempt to emulate his father), and being unable to provide security on India's border. The United States opposed the 12-Point Understanding and worked to undermine it. Britain was initially opposed but soon became more open to the development. See for example Wikileaks cables 05KATHMANDU1192 of 3 June 2005, 05KATHMANDU2548 of 22 November 2005 and 06KATHMANDU465 of 16 February 2006.

19 '... and here, Watson, is illustrated one of those general truths concerning our relations with foreign nations that often go unnoticed: that what is common knowledge in the bazaar rarely reaches through the isolated confines of our diplomatic enclaves.' Ted Riccardi, *The Oriental Casebook of Sherlock Holmes*, pp. 64–65. See also International

Crisis Group report, *Nepal: From People Power to Peace?*, pp. 11–13 www. crisisgroup.org

Chapter 21

1 www.panipokhariheights.com.np Accessed August 2013. The first housing colonies appeared after a change in the law in 1998 and by 2004 there were over 20 (see Nelson 2010). According to my memory, the first luxury apartment blocks began to go up in around 2007, prompted by the real estate bubble of that time, and there were almost instantly a score of such projects. By 2014 there were probably over 100 housing colonies and luxury high-rises either complete or under construction (Nelson estimates over 70 by 2009).

2 www.cerealestate.com.np Accessed August 2013.

3 For example Radio Nepal started broadcasting news in Sanskrit. For statistics on the growing high-caste domination of the bureaucracy after 1990 see for example Kanak Mani Dixit, 'Bahuns and the Nepali State', *Nepali Times*, 25 October 2001. On the 1990 constitution drafting process see Michael Hutt, 'Drafting the 1990 Constitution', in Hutt (ed.), *Nepal in the Nineties* and Mara Malgodi, *Constitutional Nationalism and Legal Exclusion*.

4 Data expressing inequality in relation to caste and ethnic identity can be controversial, especially among members of higher-status communities. See Himal Books, *Gender and Social Exclusion in Nepal*.

5 Later, attempts were made to deny that identity issues have any place in politics, but this issue was of course always in people's minds. See for example the wikileaks cable 05KATHMANDU2657 of 30 November 2005, in which a former prime minister explains to a US diplomat that 'suppressed' ethnic groups are about to create anarchy by toppling the state, abetted by sympathizers in the lower ranks of the army.

6 At least 47 separate agreements were signed between the mainstream parties, Maoists, and various agitating groups between November 2005 and September 2010, as recorded

in *From Conflict to Peace in Nepal: Peace Agreements 2005–10*, Asian Study Centre for Peace and Conflict Transformation.

7 Twenty-seven Maoist cadres were killed in 'the Gaur incident' on 21 March 2007 and around a dozen more in 'targeted assassinations' in the Madhes during early 2007 (see ICG report 136, 'Nepal's troubled Tarai region'). At least eight Maoists were killed during the 2008 election campaign, during which the party probably engaged in more successful (but less lethal) intimidation tactics than its rivals. (The majority of cases of lethal violence in the 2008 election campaign were associated with the Congress or the UML.) As of September 2010, 79 Maoist party workers had been killed since the peace process began in 2006, second only to unaffiliated members of the public among over 1,800 victims of lethal violence (figures from INSEC, cited ICG report 194, 'Nepal's Political Rites of Passage', p. 2, n. 5).

8 The Maoist chairman, Pushpa Kamal Dahal 'Prachanda', who was a Brahmin, also made a show of embracing more contemporary Hindu practice by consulting celebrity god-men.

9 http://www.telegraph.co.uk/news/worldnews/asia/nepal/3049047/ Nepal-Riots-as-Maoist-governments-cut-sacrifice-subsidy.html 22/9/08.

10 Yubaraj Ghimire, 'Nepal Govt defies court order, Maoists assault Pashupatinath priests', *The Indian Express*, 5 January 2009.

11 General Rookmangud Katawal had been raised as a child in the palace. He was accused by the Maoist government, in justifying his attempted sacking as army chief, of refusing orders to halt a recruitment campaign (which was in breach of the CPA), instructing eight brigadier-generals to continue work despite the government's refusal to extend their service beyond their mandatory retirement, and withdrawing the army from the National Games because a Maoist team was participating. It was, besides, widely believed that he'd falsified his age to postpone retirement.

12 The deputy was no one's idea of a leftist, but it was briefly pretended that he was.
13 See for example ICG reports numbers 173 and 194; and Prashant Jha, *Battles of the New Republic*, pp. 124–153.
14 For a scathing account of the elite response to the Maoists' May 2010 protest see Shradha Ghale, 'All too predictable', *The Kathmandu Post*, 10 May 2010.

Chapter 22

1 Tatsuro Fujikura, 'Discourses of Awareness, Notes for a Criticism of Development in Nepal', *SINHAS*, vol. 6, no. 2, p. 303, December 2001.
2 Adopting the voice of the Nepali government, the plan declared: 'It is expected that during the first years of development efforts we shall, due to our limited resources, rely heavily upon foreign aid. But it is most important that we do not become over dependent on such assistance. Aid should never be regarded as a substitute for our own efforts… upon which our reliance must be based.' Mihaly, p. 76, citing *Draft Five Year Plan: a Synopsis* (1956), p. 1.
3 Foreign aid was 2.33 per cent of GDP in 1974–75, 5.74 per cent in 1979–80, and 6.48 per cent in 1983/84. It was above 6 per cent in five years of the 1980s, the only period it had exceeded that figure.
4 Preface to *Four Decades of Development*, USAID, 1992, p. ii.
5 Kanak Mani Dixit, commissioned and written in 1996 but turned down for publication by the German aid agency GTZ (now GIZ). Published as 'Foreign Aid in Nepal: No bang for the buck', *SINHAS*. vol. 2, no. 1, June 1997, p. 183.
6 Chaitanya Mishra, 'Locating the "causes" of the Maoist struggle', (first published *SINHAS*, vol. 9, no. 1, 2004), reprinted in *Essays on the Sociology of Nepal*, p. 103. In terms of inequality: the top 10 per cent of the population owned 52 per cent of national income and the bottom 40 per cent owned 11 per cent (p. 105). Partly due to the urban bias of development spending, the wealth gap between

Kathmandu and the countryside was widening. The top 6 per cent of households owned 33 per cent of agricultural land while the bottom 40 per cent owned 9 per cent (p. 106).

7 Donor money may have undermined volunteerism. Despite NGO rhetoric of representing 'the grass roots', NGOs' reliance on foreign funds increased from 42.2 per cent in 1977–8 to 86.9 per cent in 1990–91. Dinesh Prasain, '"In the Name of the People": Writing Bikas in Post-1990 Nepal', *SINHAS*, vol. 3, no. 2, December 1998, pp. 368–69. Government rules constraining NGOs' financial activity also have the effect of preventing them from being self-reliant and increasing their dependence on donors.

8 In 2013 there were 37, 972 NGOs in Nepal, including 175 (international) INGOs. This figure includes all manner of non-government organizations, such as football clubs and libraries, and many NGOs that are defunct.

9 Although thousands of NGOs were established in the hope of gaining access to these resources, an Action Aid report in 1997 estimated that 80 per cent of money went to only 100 NGOs which had good access to the donors. See Seira Tamang, 'Civilizing Civil Society: Donors and Democratic Space', *SINHAS*, vol. 7, no. 2, December 2002.

10 Remarks by Deputy Assistant Secretary of State Donald Camp at the Heritage Foundation, Washington, D.C., March 2003. Cited Tamang, 'Historicizing state "fragility" in Nepal', *SINHAS*, vol. 17, no. 2, Dec 2012, p. 267.

11 In the decade before scheduled electricity load-shedding began in the winter of 2006–07, electricity generation received more foreign aid than any other sector. This failure does not appear to be acknowledged in the latest donor pledges to aid the sector. It has been estimated that today the country has the lowest per capita electricity consumption in Asia.

12 In his contribution to *Nepal in Transition* (ed. von Einsiedel et al.) the former finance secretary and finance minister Dr Devendra Raj Pandey points out that the vaunted improvements in literacy and life expectancy (from a very

low base in 1950) mask wide disparities, especially because anyone who can afford to seeks health and education services in the private sector (donor-backed), state services being so poor.

13 A 'revolution of rising expectations' was what the first American experts mistakenly believed existed in Nepali villages in the early 1950s, leading them to assume that villagers would be more receptive to technical advice than proved to be the case. These expectations (leading to the communist insurgency that the Americans had originally feared) finally materialized in the 1990s. See Mihaly, chapters IV and XIII.

14 See Asian Development Bank, 2007, *Inequality in Asia: key indicators.*

15 In 2012 Nepal stood at 157 out of 186 countries ranked for their Human Development Index, aggregating data on health, education, income, etc.

16 James Ferguson with Larry Lohmann, 'The Anti-Politics Machine. "Development" and Bureaucratic Power in Lesotho', *The Ecologist*, vol. 24, No. 5, Sept/Oct 1994, p. 180.

17 An excellent short analysis of these dynamics is provided in Adhikari et al., 2014, *Impunity and Political Accountability in Nepal*, The Asia Foundation, Kathmandu.

18 Since the beginning of the decade foreign aid had contributed around 3.5 per cent of GDP. In 2007–08 it was 3.59 per cent, but rose to 4.17 per cent in 2009–10 and 4.24 per cent in 2010–11.

19 See 'Low road through the Himalaya', economist.com, 31/5/11. An analysis of these issues around donor misunderstanding of local political realities is given by James Sharrock, 'Stability in Transition: Development perspectives and local politics in Nepal', *EBHR* 42, Spring-Summer 2013, pp. 9–39.

20 In the assessment of the World Bank.

21 The overall pass rate, including private schools, was 43.9 per cent. The target for 2014, set by the School Sector Reform

Plan (2009–15), was 71 per cent. Given the drop-out rate, only 13 per cent of children who began government school 10 years earlier completed their SLC.

22 The education budget more than doubled between 2007–8 and 2011–12, with foreign aid worth about quarter of the total. See for example Binod Ghimire, 'Where does all the money go?', *The Kathmandu Post*, 6 November 2011.

23 In 2013, 67 per cent of foreign aid was estimated to be routed though the government's budgetary system.

24 This figure, from the 2011 living standards survey, includes households receiving both foreign and domestic remittances.

25 (Values at 2005 purchasing power parity.) See Chandan Sapkota, 'Remittances in Nepal: Boon or Bane?', *The Journal of Development Studies*, 2013, p. 7.

26 For example, the 2012 Nepal Portfolio Performance Review (the most important joint government and donor document surveying the entire development sector) mentions 'poverty' on 43 out of 219 pages (claiming achievements in poverty reduction for various projects), but does not contain the word 'remittance'. There are just three uses of the word 'migrant', two of them in the context of HIV. There are some NGOs, and there may presumably be a few small donor-funded projects, catering to migrant labourers, although they're not well known. As far as I could discover there is no major donor effort to protect the migrants' rights, or increase their earning potential.

27 Suitable financial services for would-be migrants and regulation of 'manpower' agents would do much to reduce this exploitation. Besides, one may wonder, since there is demand for their labour and they provide the backbone of the economy, why migrant labourers have to pay to get jobs at all.

28 The government's Foreign Employment Promotion Board and Department of Foreign Employment apparently occupy buildings that are rented from manpower agents. Devendra Bhattarai 'What the Guardian did not understand' first

published in Nepali in *Kantipur,* 2 October 2013, later translated online.

29 This figure does not include the even larger number of people who cross the border to India seeking work.

30 According to the *Guardian*, for example, at least 185 Nepali labourers died in Qatar in 2013, many of them working on infrastructure for the 2022 football world cup. 'Qatar World Cup: 185 Nepalese died in 2013 – official records', 24 January 2014.

31 See Chandan Sapkota, 'Remittances in Nepal: Boon or Bane?', *The Journal of Development Studies,* 2013.

32 This theory was famously propounded by ICG report no. 194, *Nepal's Political Rites of Passage* (Sept 2010). Extraordinarily, in evidence to the House of Commons International Development Committee, Professor Mick Moore, a development expert and DfID consultant, opined: 'I have rarely seen as corrupt a country as Nepal, in the broad sense of the term. That is partly just people stealing money but I also mean, when I say that, the extent to which it is a very exclusionary political system and there are small numbers of people who steal money, and they are setting the system up so they can stay in power to carry on stealing money. So it is awful at the local level. I think my pragmatic attitude to this – I think it is pragmatic – will be to say that, frankly, there is very little we can do... My own view is that given the size of the security and order problems, generally speaking, to really try to tackle corruption, at this stage, would be a waste of effort. I think there is very little we can do about it. What we need is a little more order and, hopefully, with a little more order if the Indian economy carries on growing the general economic environment will get better and I think it will be much easier to tackle that somewhere down the road, but not at present as a major concern. That would be my view.' He added, 'I think a very good short-term target would be that more of the corrupt money actually goes into the central coffers of political parties rather than into the pockets of individual politicians,

because the more parties we have with a decent amount of resourcing, who can actually employ staff and campaign, the better politics will be.' See the committee's report, *DfID's Programme in Nepal, Sixth Report of Session 2009–10*, vol. II, pp. 29–30.

33 *The Communist Manifesto* (Wordsworth Classics of World Literature), p. 5.

34 An example of metropolitan indifference or even hostility towards protests against traditional forms of exploitation was provided by the movement against the practice of keeping kamlaris (indentured domestic servants who are children or adolescent girls of the Tharu community) in 2013, which failed to attract any prominent support in Kathmandu. It was claimed by activists that 500 kamlaris were captive in the homes of prominent Kathmandu politicians, policemen, senior officials, and even aid agency employees.

35 According to the American writer Upton Sinclair, "it is difficult to get a man to understand something when his salary depends on his not understanding it."

36 Goodhand, 2000, pp. 32–33. Cited Seira Tamang, 2002, p. 323.

37 Emery Brusset and Raghav Raj Regmi, *Conflict and Development in Nepal*, 2002, p. 15 (sponsored by DfID). Cited Seira Tamang, 2012, p. 282.

38 Jan Hollants Van Loocke and Liz Philipson, 'Report of the EC conflict prevention assessment mission', January 2002. Cited Seira Tamang, 2012, p. 282.

39 It is a core donor strategy to acknowledge political economy problems only to the extent that they justify more aid, without placing the usefulness of aid in doubt. When they're applying for project approvals from head office, agencies do include 'political economy briefs' and 'risk assessments', but according to donor staff they are almost always over-optimistic. If they gave a more realistic assessment of the political economy, according to an insider, 'the board would question the return on investment or its impact, resulting

in the cancellation of projects, which could ultimately hit country performance and may endanger jobs and funding for future projects.'

40 For example, in the introduction to the second edition of their book *The Use and Misuse of Social Science Research in Nepal* (which had first described massive discrepancies in survey data in its first edition thirty-two years earlier) the authors (J. Gabriel Campbell, Ramesh Shrestha and Linda Stone) describe how their work had received international academic recognition, but 'our recommendations ... were not widely followed in Nepal's development-orientated research. Our message unheeded, we came to feel somewhat like atmospheric scientists trying to warn politicians about global warming.' p. xxii.

41 This need not necessarily be so: many people, from academics to business people to missionaries to the colonial administrators of the past, develop (or developed) a much deeper knowledge of and a longer-term engagement with the countries where they work.

42 In 2014 a blogger described 'some of the usual attitudes of internationals in Nepal: Nepali history only began with the Comprehensive Peace Agreement in 2006, they need us more than we need them, the state is chaotic and fragile, and so on...' http://www.lalitmag.com/2014/03/observing-the-observers/

43 Decades of 'capacity building' in the state sector have not been successful, but in international organizations there are now a large number of Nepalis with degrees from foreign universities, with more, and more relevant, experience and expertise than their foreign bosses. However, 'national staff' and 'national consultants' usually only qualify for more junior positions with much lower pay.

44 Three- or four-day field visits also typically bring foreign staff into contact with people who either perceive their own interest in, or are deliberately organized by project staff with the intention of, telling the foreigners what they want to hear.

45 Indeed, some Western governments, such as Britain's, pledged to progressively increase their overall development spending to reach a target of 0.7 per cent of GDP, which Britain met in 2013.

46 Of course the real intention of the BOGs is to define what the donors expect of others. In effect: 'We won't accept interference in our projects.'

47 In areas not concerning the donors, almost no research is done except through a few programmes involving foreign universities, the main university in Nepal being dysfunctional. Independent research organizations such as Martin Chautari struggle for funding.

48 'International Development department spent £32,000 renovating Nepal palace', *The Daily Telegraph*, 7 September 2011. The story didn't have space to mention that this was the third rented property expensively renovated for DFID country directors in Kathmandu in a decade, because a previous director renovated two.

49 Rather than being new, this resembles a return to the practices of the 1950s as described by Eugene Mihaly in *Foreign Aid and Politics in Nepal*. From the point of view of where the money ends up, the difference between routing it through NGOs or the government may not be as great as it seems, since both tend to be controlled by a similar class of people.

50 SWAp stands for 'sector wide approach', in which a consortium of donors place money directly into a government departmental budget in exchange for structuring the department and its policies according to the recommendation of outside consultants.

51 For example this approach is being followed on an experimental basis in Africa by the NGO GiveDirectly (see 'Is it Nuts to Give to the Poor Without Strings Attached', by Jacob Goldstein, *New York Times Magazine*, 13 August 2013). A similar approach is advocated by the book *Just Give Money to the Poor* by Joseph Hanlon, Armando Barrientos and David Hulme (2010). Presumably the

impact of these cash payments, possibly similar to welfare payments in the West, would be in some ways like that of remittances.

52 Madhukar Rana, Open Letter to the Finance Minister. 'Because of the extravagance and wastefulness of current foreign aid delivery, the other challenge is: how to curtail the cost of projects? Donors repeatedly call for the empowerment of the poor and enhanced accountability to the poor. In the interest of these aims and also in the interest of project cost-effectiveness, why not transfer aid directly to the households to enable them, with money on hand, to demand the designated goods and services?' *Himal*, vol. 5, No. 2, Mar/April 1992, p. 7.

Chapter 23

1 The operation was also supported by a team in London.

2 According to a letter entitled 'cleaning the operation' and dated 30 December 2004 (two months before the coup), purportedly from the NID chief to the officer in charge of Mustang on the Nepali side: 'Considering the changing times and the UK's financial, physical and human support, this operation shall now be conducted within HARC and therefore HARC has been registered at the district administration office on 11/11/04. A safe house has been established in Kathmandu Municipality ward 3 for HARC.'

3 All of the above information appeared in *Nepal* magazine, Bhadau 9 2064 [26 August 2007] 'Operation Mustang: Belaayat sarkaarko sahayogma sanchaalit jaasusi kaarbaahima karodau rupiyako ghotaala' (Operation Mustang: a scam of millions of rupees in an intelligence operation which was run with the assistance of the British government). A series of articles in the weekly tabloids *Jana Aastha* and *Sanghu* published around the same time contained similar information. Several well-placed interviewees, speaking anonymously, asserted that this information is accurate.

4 In that case Mustang would have been running before the notorious and well documented tortures and disappearances at the Bhairabnath Battalion in late 2003. It is important for the British government to explain whether any of Mustang's targets were among those victims, although the practice of torture and disappearance in state custody was by no means restricted to the events described in the OHCHR's Bhairabnath report.
5 The army killing of 17 Maoist and 2 civilian prisoners at Doramba, which took place as the last round of talks began in August 2003, was raised in a meeting between the king and the British foreign secretary at the end of August. The British warned that if proved true such allegations could endanger British military aid. See wikileaks cable 03KATHMANDU1723 of 5 September 2003.
6 The police anti-terrorism unit was supported by the American government.
7 Press release, 4 February 2004.
8 In wikileaks cable 03KATHMANDU2496 of 19 December 2003, describing a meeting between the American Assistant Secretary of State for South Asia and the Nepali army chief, the army chief describes intelligence gained by army interrogations of Maoists and explains that he would like to hold prisoners without notifying the civilian authorities. The cable states that 'Under the Terrorist and Destructive Activities Act, the RNA already has authority to hold prisoners incommunicado for 3 months as long as they inform the relevant Chief District Officer.'
9 ICRC, *Missing Persons in Nepal, updated list 2012*. It was symptomatic of the impunity with which the army operated that when the Supreme Court ordered army prisoners released they were frequently rearrested by soldiers from the court steps.
10 Other Western countries, most notably the US, also gave assistance to covert, 'anti-terrorist' units of the army, police and APF, and must also have information on the conduct of the war which is not in the public domain but would

be of interest, for example, to a Truth and Reconciliation Commission.

11 According to a human rights lawyer who has worked with many victims of army torture in Nepal, mentally prepared and ideologically motivated Maoists have been able to recover much more successfully from torture than innocent victims, who did not have those psychological resources.

12 The purpose of the halt to arms shipments (at least for the American government) was to put pressure on the king to reach out to the parties, without pushing him to the wall militarily. The US therefore hoped that others such as Israel would continue to supply ammunition. See Wikileaks cable 05KATHMANDU2572 of 25 November 2005. Western governments also faced political and legal difficulties in supplying arms to what was, after 1 February 2005, a nakedly authoritarian regime with a very poor human rights record.

13 Wikileaks cable 06KATHMANDU689.

14 According to wikileaks cables, although the British had been against such a pact in the summer of 2005, by the time the 12-point understanding was signed they were cautiously supportive (see cable 05KATHMANDU2548 dated 22 November 2005). Their preferred solution in early 2006 seems to have been three-way negotiations between the parties, the Maoists and the king (see cable 06KATHMANDU465). As the wikileaks cables show, MI6 maintained their own contacts with the Maoists throughout the period of Operation Mustang, sometimes passing messages on behalf of the Americans, who refused to have contacts, even at the level of intelligence agencies, with a terrorist organization.

15 The somewhat belated American realization that the king was 'more interested in power than democracy' is expressed for example in Wikileaks cable 05KATHMANDU2565 of 25 November 2005, citing events of that July.

16 The final peace agreement, involving elections to a constituent assembly, the integration of Maoist fighters

into the national army and the Maoists' entry into multi-party politics, essentially resembles the Maoist position in 2003. See Thapa, *A Kingdom Under Siege*, pp. 217–227. For evidence of British backing of the royal government at the time of the 2003 peace talks, especially the promise of military support in the event the talks failed, see wikileaks cable 03KATHMANDU552 of 27 March 2003, 'While the UK fully believes in the importance of pursuing a peaceful resolution, should negotiation efforts prove unsuccessful, [UK Defense Secretary] Hoon pledged full support for development and military assistance.' Clearly the party to the conflict which was arguably most responsible for the breakdown of negotiations in 2003 was not under strong British pressure to reach a negotiated settlement. Ironically, had such an agreement been reached in 2003, it is likely that the monarchy would have survived.

17 By chance November 2006 was also the month that MI6 issued its clearest internal advice to date on Britain's legal obligations on complicity in torture. See Gibson Inquiry report ('The Report of the Detainee Inquiry'), December 2013, p. 66. For earlier iterations of MI6's internal legal advice on torture (based on the same legal obligations) see pp. 60–61, 57 and 49.

Chapter 24

1 G.M. Trevelyan, *English Social History*, p. 13.

2 Marx, *Eighteenth Brumaire*, p.1.

3 Indeed India also has identity-based federal states. Perhaps Nepal ('India in the making' as Sylvain Lévi saw it) will follow India's example in these respects, after the customary (shrinking) time lag. An example of official resistance to acknowledging the role of caste in forming contemporary inequalities was provided by the negotiations in 2012 between the government and the UN over a UN development-planning document known as the UNDAF. The original text read: 'In Nepal the most fundamental socio-cultural root cause of vulnerability is the structural

discrimination emanating from socio-cultural traditions, norms and practices developed over centuries. Dominant religious and cultural practices including patriarchy, the Hindu caste system and its institutionalisation over time as well as the economic and political domination of certain ethnic groups over others have, to a great extent, determined the position of different groups in Nepal's socio-cultural and socio-economic hierarchy.' After revisions requested by the government's National Planning Commission the same passage read: 'Dominant cultural practices including patriarchy, and its institutionalisation over time, have, to a great extent, determined the position of different groups in Nepal's socio-cultural and socio-economic hierarchy.' See Prashant Jha, 'Walking the Talk', *The Kathmandu Post*, 22 August 2012, and; Seira Tamang, 'Sanitised Patriarchy', *The Kathmandu Post*, 7 January 2013.

4 C.K. Lal, 'The demolition man', *Republica*, 1 October 2012.

5 The investigation into abuses against the 2006 movement was known as the Rayamajhi Commission. The equivalent in 1990 was the Malik Commission. In both cases no action was taken and those indicted shortly returned to public life.

6 The current conflict between the political parties in Nepal may be described as the parties competing (quite bitterly) to exploit the resources of the state, even as they collude with their rivals to maintain the state in its current condition. At least by circa 2012 most of the parties, including the Congress, UML and Maoists, did not appear very different in ideology when judged by their actions. The Hindu/Monarchist right and the Maoist faction led by Mohan Baidya were more genuinely ideological, but had relatively few followers.

7 Many descriptions of 1950s politics, published in the 'fifties and 'sixties, contain passages that strike the modern reader as applying today, showing that there has been a high degree of continuity in the way the system

works. For example in *Foreign Aid and Politics in Nepal* (published 1965) Eugene Mihaly wrote (p. 207): 'After the 1950 revolution, far greater demands were made on the administration, but political turmoil and utilisation of the civil service as a source of patronage ensured that the service would not attain the stability and security needed to meet these demands.' This seeming instability has endured for sixty years.

8 For example 'Nepal, on the Brink of Collapse', *The New York Times*, 5 June 2012 by Seyom Brown and Vanda Felbab-Brown.

9 One imagines that if, say, America found itself without a constitution there would be instant mayhem. Nepal has had six constitutions since 1949 and on average a different prime minister about once every eighteen months throughout the same period. Yet the country's ruling class shows great continuity, including at the level of its individual members who often carry on for decades. The performance, interests, prejudices and culture of institutions also seem fairly stable.

10 See for example 'Duncan stands behind aid for ethnic groups', *Kathmandu Post,* 28 June 2012. Nevertheless, agencies including DFID were widely seen to be backing away from this agenda. See for example 'Pressure from hill elites halts DFID exclusion report' by Kosmos Bishwokarma, *Republica,* 20 August 2012. The development community should be prepared to face a similar backlash again if they offer appreciable support to marginalized groups in the future. On the other hand, those who object that development aid disproportionately benefits privileged groups might note the agencies' sensitivity to well orchestrated public criticism.

11 A second constituent assembly was elected 18months later, in November 2013. At the time of writing it is not clear what the outcome will be.

Epilogue

1 This description of the earthquake is based on Jean-Philippe Avouac et al., 'Lower edge of locked Himalayan Thrust Fault unzipped by 2015 Gorkha earthquake', letters, *Nature Geoscience,* 6 August 2015; J. Galetzka et al., 'Slip pulse resonance of Kathmandu basin during the 2015 Mw7.8 Gorkha earthquake, Nepal imaged with geodesy', in *Sciencexpress*, 6 August 2015; and 'Liquefication in Kathmandu Earthquake 2015' on Nepaliengineer.com.

2 See Anna Callaghan and Rabi Thapa, 'An Oral History of Langtang, the Valley Destroyed by the Nepal Earthquake', *Outside Online*, 28 September 2015.

3 According to the government's Post Disaster Needs Assessment, altogether 609,938 houses needed to be rebuilt. Such figures were informed guesswork.

4 For a summary of relief efforts in the first month see Thomas Bell, 'The Nationals and the Internationals', *Himalmag.com*, 19 August 2015.

5 "More ministers, officials under PAC scanner", *The Kathmandu Post*, 22 June 2015. See also 'Billions of rufees embezzled in post-quake relief drive, concludes CIAA', *Himalayan Times*, 29 November 2015.

6 See Yogesh Raj, 'Remembering to Forget', *The Kathmandu Post,* 9 June 2015; and 'Made to Jump Through Hoops', Editorial in *The Nepali Times,* 24–30 July 2015.

7 According to the UN, 2.8m people were still needing urgent humanitarian assistance. 'Nepal still needs vital humanitarian assistance: UN', *The Kathmandu Post*, 25 June 2015.

8 See Shradha Ghale, 'The Heart of the Matter', three part series on RecordNepal.com, September/ October 2015; Deepak Thapa, 'The Country is Yours', *The Kathmandu Post*, 2 July 2015.

9 Interviews with aid workers, August-September 2015.

10 For a summary of the end of the constitution-drafting process, and a preliminary assessment of the new constitution's provisions, see S.D. Muni, 'Nepal's New

Constitution, towards progress of chaos?', *Economic and Political Weekly*, 3 October 2015, pp.15–19.

11 The constitution also declared the country secular (article 4), but ambiguously so, defining secularism as the protection of traditional religion. Making the cow the national animal had the effect of banning cow slaughter.

12 Due to similar provisions in the past, a study by the legal NGO Forum for Women, Law and Development has found that 4 million Nepalis (approximately 13 per cent of the population) are currently without citizenship. See *Acquisition of Citizenship Certificate in Nepal: Estimating Prevalence*, *FWLD*, April 2013.

13 See especially the 8- and 22-point agreements with agitating Madhesi groups in *From Conflict to Peace on Nepal: peace agreements 2005–10* (Kathmandu, Asian Study Centre for Peace & Conflict Transformation, 2011). On the evolution of these issues in the interim constitution and during the first constituent assembly, see Mara Malagodi, 'Constitutional Change and the Quest for Legal Inclusion in Nepal', in *Divided Societies*, Colin Harvey and Alexander Schwartz (eds.), pp. 169–195. On objections raised by Madhesi activists to provisions in the 2015 constitution see Dipendra Jha, 'Talk to the Tarai', *The Kathmandu Post*, 20 September 2015.

14 'Like we are not Nepali', Human Rights Watch report, October 2015.

15 Pranaya SJB Rana, "Don't Talk, Just Listen", *The Kathmandu Post*, 20 September 2015.

16 The EU, for example, has $350m to dispose of each year for the next three years.

Bibliography

Acharya, Baburam. 2013. *The Blood Stained Throne: struggles for power in Nepal (1775–1914)*. New Delhi, Penguin (transl. Madhav Acharya).

Adam, Leonard. 1950. 'Criminal Law and procedure in Nepal a Century Ago: Notes Left by Brian H Hodgson'. *Far East Asian Quarterly* 9: 146–168.

Adhikari, Aditya. 2013. 'Nepal: the discontents after the revolution'. *Economic and Political Weekly* XLVIII(7).

Adhikari, Aditya and Bhaskar Gautam et al., 2014. *Impunity and Political Accountability in Nepal*. The Asia Foundation. Kathmandu.

Adhikari, Aditya. 2014. *The Bullet and the Ballot Box: the story of Nepal's Maoist revolution*. London. Verso.

Adhikari, Ambika. 1995. 'Environmental Problems in the Kathmandu Valley: some issues in planning and management'. *Centre for Nepal and Asian Studies* 22(1). 1–19.

Adhikari, Jagannath, 2008. *Land Reform in Nepal: problems and prospects*, Nepal Institute of Development Studies.

Adhikari, Saroj Raj. 2007. 'Operation Mustang: Belaayat sarkaarko sahayogma sanchaalit jaasusi kaarbaahima karodau rupiyako ghotaala' (Operation Mustang: a scam of millions of rupees in an intelligence operation which was run with the assistance of the British government). *Nepal* (Bhadau 9 2064). 26 August.

Advocacy Forum. 2003. *Doramba Incident*. http://www. advocacyforum. org/downloads/pdf/doramba-incident.pdf

Allen, Charles. 2002. *The Buddha and the Sahibs*. London, John Murray.

Allen, Michael. 1975. *The Cult of Kumari*. Kathmandu, Mandala Book Point (1996 edition).

Allen, Michael. 1996. 'Procession and Pilgrimage in Newar Religion'. In *Change and continuity: studies in the Nepalese culture of the Kathmandu Valley*, edited by Siegfried Lienhard. Turin, Edizioni dell'Orso.

Alsop, Ian and Jill Charlton. 1973. 'Image casting in Oku Bahal'. *CNAS* 1(1). pp. 22–57.

Alsop, Ian. 1996. 'Christians at the Malla Court: The Capuchin "Piccolo Libro"'. In *Change and continuity: studies in the Nepalese culture of the Kathmandu Valley* edited by Siegfried Lienhard. Turin, Edizioni dell'Orso.

Alsop, Ian. 1997. 'The Alsdorf Collection: highlights from the Himalaya'. *Orientations* 28(7). p. 51.

Amatya, Shaphalya. 1984. 'A Brief Note on Strategy of His Majesty's Government on Heritage Conservation'. *Ancient Nepal* 79. pp. 33–36.

Amatya, Shaphalya. 1994. *The Bagmati: a monument guide*. Kathmandu, Ratna Pustak Bhandar.

Amatya, Shaphalya. 2004. *Rana Rule in Nepal*. New Delhi. Nirala Publications.

Amnesty International. 2005. 'Military Assistance Contributing to Grave Human Rights Violantions'. http://www.amnesty.org/en/library/asset/ ASA31/047/2005/en/a866bcb9-d4e4–11dd-8a23-d58a49c0d652/ asa310472005en.html

Antonini, Chiara Silvi and Giovani Veradi. 1985. 'Excavation in the Kathmandu Valley'. *Ancient Nepal* 89. pp. 17–36.

Art Institute of Chicago. Online Catalogue. http://www.artic.edu/aic/ collections/

Aryal, Manisha. 1992. 'Women in Development. What's in it for me?' *Himal* 5(2). pp. 24–25.

Asian Study Centre for Peace and Conflict Transformation. 2011. *From Conflict to Peace in Nepal: peace agreements 2005–10*. Kathmandu.

Aung San Suu Kyi. 1985. *Let's Visit Nepal*. London, Burke Publishing Co.

Bajracharya, Manik and Axel Michaels. 2012. 'On the Historiography of Nepal: the "Wright" chronicle reconsidered'. *European Bulletin for Himalayan Research* 40. pp. 83–98.

Avouac, Jean-Philippe et al., 2015. 'Lower edge of locked Himalayan Thrust Fault unzipped by 2015 Gorkha earthquake', *Nature Geoscience*, letters, 6 August 2015.

Bajracharya, Ranjana. 1995. 'The development of Vihara Culture in Nepal'. *CNAS* 22(2). pp. 141–151.

Bangdel, Lain S. 1989. *Stolen Images of Nepal*. Kathmandu. Royal Nepal Academy.

Bangdel, Lain S. 1995. *Inventory of Stone Sculptures of the Kathmandu Valley*. Kathmandu. Royal Nepal Academy.

Banskota, Purushottam. 1994. *The Gurkha Connection*. New Delhi. Nirula.

Baral, Lok Raj. 1975. 'The Press in Nepal (1951–1974)'. *CNAS* 2(1). pp. 169–186.

Baral, L.S. (ed. Pratyoush Onta and Lokranjan Parajuli). 2012. *Autocratic Monarchy; politics in Panchayat Nepal*. Kathmandu. Martin Chautari.

Becker-Ritterspach, Raimund. 1996. 'Dhunge-Dharas in the Kathmandu Valley: continuity and development of architectural design.' In *Change and continuity: studies in the Nepalese culture of the Kathmandu Valley*, edited by Siegfried Lienhard. Turin, Edizioni dell'Orso.

Bell, Thomas. 2005. 'Britain halts training for Nepal's army as king seizes power from politicians'. *The Daily Telegraph*, 3 Feb.

Bell, Thomas. 2011. 'Aid and corruption in Nepal: low road through the Himalayas'. *www.economist.com* 31 May.

Bell, Thomas. 2011. 'International Development department spent £32,000 renovating Nepal palace'. *The Daily Telegraph*, 6 Sept.

Bell, Thomas. 2012. 'Diary of a disastrous campaign', *Himal*, 21 Dec.

Bendall, Cecil. 1886. *A Journey of Literary and Archaeological Research in Nepal and Northern India during the winter of 1884–5*. Cambridge.

Bernstein, Jeremy. 1970. *The Wildest Dreams of Kew: a profile of Nepal*. New York, Simon and Schuster.

Bhattarai, Baburam. 2005. *Monarchy vs. Democracy*. New Delhi. Samkaleem Teesari Duniya.

Bhattarai, Binod. 1992. 'A Bank Asian in Name Only?' *Himal* 5(2). pp. 19–20.

Bista, Dor Bahadur. 1967. *People of Nepal*. Kathmandu, Ratna Pustak Bhandar.

Boulnois, L. 1989. 'Chinese Maps and Prints on the Tibet-Gorkha War of 1788–92'. *Kailash* 15(1&2). pp. 85–112.

Brown, Louise T. 1996. *The Challenge to Democracy in Nepal*. Oxford. Routledge.

Burghart, Richard. 1996. *The Conditions of Listening, essays on religion, history and politics in South Asia*. New Delhi. OUP.

Burleigh, Peter. 1971. 'A Plea for Talapatras'. *The Rising* Nepal, 20 March.

Callaghan, Anna and Rabi Thapa. 2015. 'An Oral History of Langtang, the Valley destroyed by the Nepal Earthquake'. *Outside Outline*, 28 September.

Campbell, Gabriel, Ramesh Shrestha and Linda Stone. 1979. *The Use and Misuse of Social Science Research in Nepal*. Kathmandu. Mandal Book Point, edition 2011.

Cavenagh, Orfeur. 1884. *Reminiscences of an Indian Official*. London. W.H. Allen.

Colaabavala, F.D. 1974. *Hippie Dharma*. New Delhi. Hind Pocket Books.

The Comprehensive Peace Agreement, 2006.

Cowan, Sam. 2010. 'Inside the People's Liberation Army: A military perspective'. *EBHR* 37.

Darnal, Prakash. 2002. 'Archaeological Activities in Nepal since 1893 AD to 2002 AD'. *Ancient Nepal* 150. pp. 39–48.

Des Chene, Mary. 1996. 'In the name of *Bikas*'. *Studies In Nepali History And Society* 1(2). pp. 259–270.

Directorate of Public Relations. 2008. *The Nepalese Army: a force with a history, ready for tomorrow*. Kathmandu.

Dixit, Ajaya. 1992. 'Little Water, Dirty Water' and 'Melamchi Boondoggle'. *Himal* 5(1). pp. 8–11.

Dixit, Kanak Mani. 1997. 'Foreign Aid in Nepal: no bang for the buck'. *SINHAS* 2(1). pp. 173–186.

Dixit, Kanak Mani. 1999. 'Gods in Exile'. *Himal South Asia* 12(10). pp. 8–15.

Dixit, Kanak Mani. 2001. 'Bahuns and the Nepali State'. *Nepali Times* 65 (19 October).

Doniger, Wendy. 2010. *The Hindus: an alternative history*. Oxford, OUP.

Draper, John. 1986. 'Nagas'. *CNAS* 13(2). pp. 139–166.

Dye, Joseph M. 2001. *The Arts of India, Virginia Museum of Fine Arts*. Virginia. Museum of Fine Arts.

Engels, Friedrich. 1884. *The Origin of the Family, Private Property and the State*. New York. 1942.

Ferguson, James and Larry Lohmann. 1994. 'The Anti-Politics Machine: "development" and bureaucratic power in Lesotho'. *The Ecologist* 24(3). pp. 176–181.

Forbes, William P. 2000. *The Glory of Nepal: a mythological guidebook to Kathmandu Valley*. Kathmandu. Pilgrims.

Fujikura, Tatsuro. 1996. 'Technologies of Improvement, Locations of Culture: American discourses of democracy and "Community Development" in Nepal'. *SINHAS* 1(2). pp. 271–311.

Fujikura, Tatsuro. 2001. 'Discourses of Awareness: notes for a criticism of development in Nepal'. *SINHAS* 6(2). pp. 271–313.

Galetzka, J. et al., 2015. 'Slip pulse resonance of Kathmandu basin during the 2015 MW7.8 Gorkha earthquake, Nepal imagined with geodesy' in *Sciencexpress.org*, 6 August.

Gallagher, Kathleen. 1992. 'Squatting in the Kathmandu Valley: a historical perspective.' *CNAS* 19(2). pp. 249–259.

Geertz, Clifford. 1980. *Negara, the Theatre State in Nineteenth Century Bali*. Princeton.

Geertz, Clifford. 1973. *The Interpretation of Cultures*. New York. Basic Books.

Gellner, David N. 1992. *Monk, Householder and Tantric Priest: Newar Buddhism and its hierarchy of ritual*. Cambridge.

Gellner, David N. 1994. 'Introduction'. In *Contested Hierarchies. A collaborative ethnography of caste among the Newars of the Kathmandu Valley,* edited by David Gellner and Declan Quigley. Oxford. Clarendon.

Gellner, David and Rajendra Pradhan. 1994. 'Urban Peasants: the Maharjans (Jyapu) of Kathmandu and Lalitpur'. In *Contested Hierarchies. A collaborative ethnography of caste among the Newars of the Kathmandu Valley,* edited by David Gellner and Declan Quigley. Oxford, Clarendon.

Gellner, David N. 1994. 'Low castes in Lalitpur'. In *Contested Hierarchies. A collaborative ethnography of caste among the Newars of the Kathmandu Valley,* edited by David Gellner and Declan Quigley. Oxford. Clarendon.

Gellner, David N. 1996. 'A Sketch of the History of Lalitpur (Patan) with Special Reference to Buddhism'. *CNAS* 23(1). pp. 125–157.

Gellner, David N. 2001. *The Anthropology of Hinduism and Buddhism: Weberian themes*. Oxford. Clarendon.

Gellner, David N. 2008. 'Introduction: transformation of the Nepalese state'. In *Resistance and the State: Nepalese experiences*. Edited by David Gellner. New Delhi. Social Science Press.

Gellner, David N. 2007. 'Caste, Communalism, and Communism; Newars and the Nepalese state'. In *Nationalism and Ethnicity in Nepal*. Edited by David Gellner, Joanna Pfaff Czarnecka and John Whelpton. Amsterdam. Harwood Academic Publishers.

Ghale, Shradha. 2010. 'All too predictable'. *The Kathmandu Post,* 10 May.

Ghale, Shradha. 2015. 'The Heart of the Matter', three-part series on RecordNepal.com, September-October.

Gibson, Sir Peter. 2013. *Report of the Detainee Inquiry*. London. HM Stationery Office.

Fr Giuseppe. 'An Account of the Kingdom of Nepal'. *Asiatick Researches* 2. London 1805. pp. 307–322.

Government of Nepal Ministry of Finance. 2013. *Nepal Portfolio Performance Review 2012*. Kathmandu.

Government of Nepal Ministry of Finance. 2015. *Nepal Earthquake 2015, Post Disaster Needs Assessment*.

Graafen, Rainer and Christian Seeber. 1993. 'Important Trade Routes in Nepal and their Importance to the Settlement Process'. *Ancient Nepal* pp. 130–133. pp. 34–48.

GTZ. 1995. *Images of a Century: The Changing Townscapes of the Kathmandu Valley*. Kathmandu.

Guild, J (pseudonym). 1988. 'The God Market'. *Mother Jones* 13(7).

Gupta, Anirudha. 1997. *Nepalese Interviews*. New Delhi. Kalinga Publications.

Gurung, Harka. 1983. *Maps of Nepal: inventory and evaluation*. Bangkok. White Orchid Press.

Gurung, Harka. 1996. 'Nepaul to Nepal: place names in two early accounts'. *CNAS* 23(1). pp. 47–64.

Guta, Thomas. 1997. 'Arniko: image weaver'. *CNAS* 24(1). pp. 71–78.

Gutschow, Niels. 1979. 'Ritual Chariots of Nepal'. *Art and Archaeology Research Papers* 16. pp. 32–38.

Gutschow, Niels. 1990. 'Pucalijatra in Patan: the experience of an urban ritual in Nepal' (MS on KVPT file).

Gutschow, Niels. 2011. *Architecture of the Newars. A history of building typologies and details in Nepal*. Chicago. Serindia Publications. 3 vols.

Gutschow, Niels. 2012. *The Kathmandu Valley: new buildings, sites under construction and demolition 1990–2011*. Kathmandu. Himal Books.

Hachhethu, Krishna. 1990. 'Mass Movement 1990'. *CNAS* 17(2). pp. 177–201.

Hachhethu, Krishna. 1994. 'Transition to Democracy in Nepal: negotiations behind constitution making, 1990'. *CNAS* 21(1). pp. 91–126.

Hachhethu, Krishna. 2002. *Party Building in Nepal, organisation leadership and people*. Kathmandu. Mandala Book Point.

Hachhethu, Krishna. 2004. 'The Nepali State and the Maoist Insurgency, 1996–2001'. In *Himalayan 'people's war'*, edited by Michael Hutt. New Delhi. Hurst & Co.

Hachhethu, Krishna. 2008. 'Nepali politics: people-parties interface'. In *Resistance and the State: Nepalese experiences*, edited by David Gellner. New Delhi. Social Science Press.

Hamilton, Francis (Buchanan). 1819. *An Account of the Kingdom of Nepal, and the territories annexed to this dominion by the House of Gorkha*. London.

Hastings, Marquis of. 1824. *Papers regarding the administration of the Marquis of Hastings in India*, vol. 1. London. J.L. Cox.

Hilton, Isabel. 2001. 'Royal Blood'. *The New Yorker*. 30 July. pp. 42–57.

Hindman, Heather. 2002. 'The everyday life of American Development in Nepal'. *SINHAS* 7(1). pp. 99–136.

HMG Department of Housing and Physical Planning. 1969. *The Physical Development Plan for the Kathmandu Valley*. Kathmandu.

Hodgson, Brian Houghton. 1880. *Miscellaneous Essays Relating to Indian Subjects*. London. Trübner & Co. 2 vols.

Höfer, András. 1979. *The Caste Hierarchy and the State in Nepal: a study of the Muluki Ain of 1854*. Innsbruk (second edition, Kathmandu, Himal books 2004).

Höfer, András. 1979. 'On re-reading *Le Nepal:* what we social scientists owe Sylvain Lévi'. *Kailash* 7. pp. 175–180.

Hoftun, Martin, William Reaper and John Whelpton. 1999. *People, Politics and Ideology: democracy and social change in Nepal*. Kathmandu. Mandala Book Point.

Hollingshead, Michael. 1973. *The Man Who Turned on the World*. New York.

Human Rights Watch. 2015. *Like we are not Nepali, protest and police crackdown in the Tarai region of Nepal*. New York.

Hunter, William Wilson. 1896. *Life of Brian Houghton Hodgson*. London.

Hutt, Michael. 2010. *The Life of Bhupi Sherchan, poetry and politics in post-Rana Nepal*. New Delhi. OUP.

Hutt, Michael et al. 1994. *Nepal: a guide to the art and architecture of the Kathmandu Valley*. Stirling, Kiscadale.

Hutt, Michael (ed). 1993. *Nepal in the Nineties*. New Delhi. OUP.

Hutt, Michael. 1989. 'Reflections of political change in modern Nepali literature'. *Kailash* 15(3&4). pp. 135–156.

Hutt, Michael. 1991. *Himalayan Voices: an introduction to modern Nepali literature*. University of California Press.

Ingram, Martin and Greg Harkin. 2004. *Stakeknife: Britain's secret agents in Ireland*. Dublin. O'Brien Press.

INSEC. 2006. *Jana Andolan II: a witness account*. Kathmandu.

International Committee of the Red Cross. *Missing Persons in Nepal, updated list 2012*.

International Crisis Group reports, including: no. 50 (2003), no. 94 (2005), no. 126 (Dec 2006), no. 128 (Feb 2007), no. 136 (July 2007), no. 149 (April 2008), no. 156 (July 2008), no. 163 (Feb 2009), no. 173 (Aug 2009), no. 194 (Sept 2010), no. 199 (Jan 2011).

Jha, Dipendra. 2015. 'Talk to the Tarai', *The Kathmandu Post*, 20 September.

Jha, Prashant. 2014. *Battles of the New Republic: a contemporary history of Nepal*. New Delhi. Aleph.

Jordan, R.R. 2010. *From Missionaries to Mountaineers: early encounters with Nepal*. Kathmandu. Giri Lal Manandhar.

Joshi, Bhuwan Lal and Leo E Rose. 1966. *Democratic Innovations in Nepal: a case study of political acculturation*. University of California Press (2002 Mandala Book Point edition).

Joshi, Bikas. 1997. 'Foreign Aid in Nepal: What do the data show?' *Himal South Asia* 10(2). pp. 70–72.

Kaevrne, Pat (transl). 1979. 'The Visit of Prince Waldemar of Prussia to Nepal in February and March 1845'. *Kailash* 7(1). pp. 35–50.

Kircher, Athanasius. 1677. *China Illustrata* (transl. Charles D. Van Tuyl).

Kirkpatrick, William. 1811 *Account of the Kingdom of Nepaul: a mission to that country in 1793*. London. William Miller.

Kölver, Bernhard. 1993. 'Two notes on Malla Currencies'. *CNAS* 20(1). pp. 53–59.

Korn, Wolfgang. 1976. *Traditional Architecture of the Kathmandu Valley*. Kathmandu. Ratna Pustak Bhandar.

Kreijger, Hugo. 1999. *Kathmandu Valley Painting: the Jucker collection*. Boston. Shambhala.

Kshetri, Dil Bahadur. 1998. *Documents on Nepal: a collection of diplomatic correspondences with British-India, sanads and lalmohars*. Pokhara.

Lall, Kesar. 2007. *Legends of the Kathmandu Valley*. Kathmandu. Nepal Bhasha Academy.

Landon, Perceval. 1928. *Nepal*. London. 2 vols.

Le Bon, Gustav. 1883–6. *Voyage to Nepal*. Bangkok. White Orchid Press. (transl. Niloufar Maoven and Cecilia Leslie.)

Lévi, Sylvain. 1905–8. *Le Nepal*. (transl. in *Kailash* 3(1), various volumes of *Ancient Nepal*, and as *Notebook of Sojourn* by Harihar Raj Joshi, Kathmandu. 2006).

Lewis, Todd. 1986. 'The Anthropology of Development in Nepal: a review article on foreign aid projects in the Kathmandu Valley'. *CNAS* 13(2). pp. 167–180.

Lewis, Todd. 1996. 'A Chronology of Newar-Tibetan relations in the Kathmandu Valley'. In *Change and continuity: studies in the Nepalese culture of the Kathmandu Valley*. Edited by Siegfried Lienhard. Turin. Edizioni dell'Orso.

Liechty, Mark. 2003. *Suitably Modern: making middle class culture in Kathmandu*. Princeton (2008 Martin Chautari edition).

Liechty, Mark. 2012. 'The Age of Hippies'. *SINHAS* 17(2). pp. 211–262.

Locke, John K. 1980. *Karunamaya: the cult of Avalokitesvara-Matsyendranath in the Valley of Nepal*. Kathmandu. Sahayogi Prakashan.

Locke, John K. 1985. *Buddhist Monastaries of Nepal: a survey of the bahas and bahis of the Kathmandu Valley*. Kathmandu. Sahayogi Prakashan.

Losty, J.P. 1992. 'Clarence Comyn Taylor (1830–79): the first photographer in Udaipur and Nepal'. *History of Photography* 16(4). pp. 318–335.

Malagodi, Mara. 2010. *Constitutional Developments in a Himalayan Kingdom: the experience of Nepal*. SOAS School of Law Legal Studies Research Paper Series 9.

Malagodi, Mara (unpublished paper). 'Constitution Drafting as Cold War Realpolitik: Sir Ivor Jennings and Nepal's 1959 constitution'.

Malagodia, Mara. 2012. 'Constitutional Change and the Quest for Legal Inclusion in Nepal', in *Divided Society*, Colin Harvey and Alexander Schwartz (eds.). Oxford: Hart Publishing, pp. 169–195.

Malagodi, Mara. 2013. *Constitutional Nationalism and Legal Exclusion: equality, identity politics, and democracy in Nepal*. New Delhi. OUP.

Malla, Govinda Bahadur 'Gothale'. 1959. *The Window of the House Opposite*. New Delhi. Book Faith India (1998 trans. by Larry Hartsell).

Malla, Kamal P. 1967. 'Kathmandu, Your Kathmandu'. *The Rising Nepal*. 28–29 November.

Malla, Kamal P. 1979. *The Road to Nowhere: a selection of writings 1966–1977*. Kathmandu. Sajha Publications.

Malla, Kamal P. 1981. 'Linguistic archaeology of the Nepal valley, A preliminary report'. *Kailash* 8(1&2). pp. 5–23.

Malla, Kamal P. 1982. 'River-Names of the Nepal Valley: a study in cultural annexation'. *CNAS* 10(1&2). pp. 57–68.

Malla, Kamal P. 1983. 'Review article. The limits of surface archaeology: Nepal Mandala, Mary Shepherd Slusser'. *CNAS* 11(1). pp. 125–133.

Malla, Kamal P. 1984. *Impeccable Historiography in Nepal: a rebuttal*. Kathmandu. Nepal Study Centre.

Malla, Kamal P. 1985. 'Nepalavamshavali: a complete version of the Kaisher Vamshavali'. *CNAS* 12(2). pp. 75–101.

Malla, Kamal P. 1985. 'Review article. Medieval History of Nepal, Luciano Petech'. *CNAS* 12(2). pp. 121–135.

Malla, Kamal P. 1985. 'Epigraphy and Society in Ancient Nepal: a critique of Regmi'. *CNAS* 13(1). pp. 57–94.

Malla, Kamal P. 1996. 'Vestiges of Totemism in Newar Society'. In *Change and Continuity : studies in the Nepalese culture of the Kathmandu Valley*. Edited by Siegfried Lienhard. Turin, Edizioni dell'Orso.

Malla, Kamal P. 1990. 'The Earliest Document in Newari: the palm leaf from Ukubahah NS 235 / AD 1114'. *Kailash* 16(1&2). pp. 15–25.

Malla, Kamal P. 1992. 'The Nepala-Mahatmya: a IX-century text or a pious fraud?' *CNAS* 19(1). pp. 145–158.

Malla, Kamal P. 1996. 'The Profane Names of Sacred Hillocks.' *CNAS* 23(1). pp. 1–9.

Malla, Kamal P. 2005. 'Manadeva Samvat: an investigation into an historical fraud'. *CNAS* 32(1). pp. 1–49.

Manadhar, Thakurlal. 1974. 'A leaf from the Bendall "Vamshavali"'. *CNAS* 1(2). pp. 99–102.

Manandhar, Vijay Kumar. 2000. 'The Nepalese Quinquennial Missions of 1792 and 1795 to China'. *Ancient Nepal* 145. pp. 7–18.

Mao Tse-tung. 1937. *Basic Tactics. http://www.marxists.org/reference/archive/mao/selected-works/volume-6/mswv6_28.htm*

Mao Tse-tung. 1937. *On Guerrilla Warfare*. http://www.marxists.org/ reference/archive/mao/works/1937/guerrilla-warfare/

Marx, Karl. 1852. *The 18th Brumaire of Louis Bonaparte*. New York. International Publishers.

Marx, Karl and Friedrich Engels. 1848. *The Communist Manifesto*. Ware. Wordsworth Classics of World Literature.

Michaels, Axel. 1993. 'Siva under refuse: the hidden Mahadeva (Lukumahadyah) and protective stones in Nepal'. In *Flags of Fame: studies in South Asian folk culture*. Edited by H. Brückner, L. Lutze and A. Malik. New Delhi. Manohar Publications.

Michaels, Axel. 1998. *Hinduism Past and Present*. Princeton (trans. Barbara Harshav).

Michaels, Axel (ed). 1995. *A Rama Temple in 19th-Century Nepal: the Ramacandra Temple in Battisputali, Kathmandu*. Stuttgart. Franz Steiner Verlag (Publications of the Nepal Research Centre).

Mihaly, Eugene. 1965. *Foreign Aid and Politics in Nepal: a case study*. Oxford. OUP. (Kathmandu, Himal books edition 2003).

Mishra, Chaitanya. 2007. *Essays on the Sociology of Nepal*. Kathmandu. FinePrint Books.

Mishra, Tara Nanda. 2000. 'Dated Figure of King Jayavarma, the tradition of figure making and the historical importance of this discovery'. *Ancient Nepal* 146. pp. 1–23.

Muni, S.D., 2015. 'Nepals New Constitution, towards progress of chaos?' Economic and Politically Weekly, vol. L no. 40, 3 October, pp. 15–19.

Muller-Booker, Ulrike. 1996. 'Traditional Technology in the Kathmandu Valley: The utilization of soils and sediments'. In *Change and continuity: studies in the Nepalese culture of the Kathmandu Valley*. Edited by Siegfried Lienhard. Turin, Edizioni dell'Orso.

Murphy, Dervla. 1967. *The Waiting Land: a spell in Nepal*. London. John Murray.

Nelson, Andrew. 2010. '"No Horn Please": self-governance and sociality in a Kathmandu housing colony'. In *Urban Navigations: politics, space, and the city in South Asia*. Edited by J.S. Anjaria and C. McFarlane. Oxford. Routledge.

Neville, Richard and Julie Clarke. 1979. *The Life and Crimes of Charles Sobhraj*. London, Jonathan Cape.

Nickson, Andrew. 1992. 'Foreign Aid and Foreign Policy: the case of British aid to Nepal'. University of Birmingham Development Administration Group. Papers in the Administration of Development No. 48.

Ogura, Kiyoko. 2001. *Kathmandu Spring: the people's movement of 1990*. Kathmandu. Himal Books.

Ogura, Kiyoko. 2004. 'Realities and Images of Nepal's Maoists after the Attack on Beni'. *EBHR* 27. pp. 67–125.

OHCHR. 2006. *Report of investigations into arbitrary detention, torture and disappearance at Maharajgang RNA barracks, Kathmandu, in 2003–2004.*

OHCHR. 2008. *Conflict Related Disappearances in Bardiya District.*

OHCHR. 2012. *Nepal Conflict Report.*

Oldfield, Henry Ambrose. 1880. *Sketches from Nipal*. London. W.H. Allen. 2 vols.

Oliphant, Laurence. 1852. *A Journey to Kathmandu (an unforgettable experience with Jang Bahadur)*. London. John Murray.

Onta, Pratyoush. 1994. 'Rich Possibilities: notes on social history in Nepal'. *CNAS* 21(1). pp. 1–43.

Onta, Pratyoush. 1996. 'Ambivalence Denied: the making of rastriya itihas in Panchayat era textbooks'. *CNAS* 23(1). pp. 213–254.

Onta, Pratyoush. 1999. 'Photographic Consumption in Kathmandu c.18631960'. *EBHR* 15–16. pp. 59–68.

Onta, Pratyoush. 2004. 'Democracy and Duplicity: the Maoists and their interlocutors in Nepal'. In *Himalayan 'people's war.'* Edited by Michael Hutt. New Delhi. Hurst & Co.

Pahari, Anup. 1992. 'Villagers of the Valley'. *Himal* 5(1). pp. 13–16.

Pal, Pratapaditya. 1975. *Nepal: where the gods are young*. New York. Asia House Gallery.

Pal, Pratapaditya. 1985. *Art of Nepal*. Los Angeles County Museum of Art.

Pal, Pratapaditya. 1991. *Art of the Himalayas: Treasures from Nepal and Tibet*. New York. Hudson Hills Press.

Pal, Pratapaditya et al. 2003. *Himalayas: An aesthetic adventure*. Art Institute of Chicago.

Pal, Pratapaditya (ed). 2004. *Nepal: old images, new insights*. Mumbai. Marg Publications.

Pandey, Devendra Raj. 1992. 'The Enigma of Aid'. *Himal* 5(2). pp. 14–15.

Pandey, Devendra Raj. 1999. *Nepal's Failed Development: reflections on the mission and the maladies*. Kathmandu, Nepal South Asia Centre.

Pandey, Devendra Raj. 2011. *Looking at Development and Donors*. Kathmandu. Martin Chautari (edited by Seira Tamang).

'Pasang' [Nanda Kishore Pun]. 2008. *Red Strides of the History: significant military raids of the people's war*. Kathmandu. Agnipariksha Janaprakashan Griha.

Petech, Luciano. 1984. *Medieval History of Nepal (c.750–1482)*. Rome.

Petech, Luciano. 1996. 'Chinese and Tibetan Materials on the Nepalese Quinquennial missions'. In *Change and continuity: studies in the Nepalese culture of the Kathmandu Valley*. Edited by Siegfried Lienhard. Turin, Edizioni dell'Orso.

Pettigrew, Judith. 2004. 'Living between the Maoists and the Army in Rural Nepal'. In *Himalayan 'people's war'*. Edited by Michael Hutt. New Delhi, Hurst & Co.

Pradhan, Riddhi. 1990. 'Dhunge Dhara: a case study of the three cities of the Kathmandu Valley'. *Ancient Nepal* 116–118. pp. 10–16.

Prasain, Dinesh. 'In the Name of the People: writing bikas in post-1990 Nepal'. *SINHAS* 3(2). pp. 341–394.

Prinsep, H.T. 1825. *The Gurkha War: the Anglo-Nepalese conflict in north east India 1814–16*. Leonaur 2007 edition.

Prior, Katherine. 2004. 'Hamilton [formerly Buchanan], Francis'. *Dictionary of National Biography*. Oxford. OUP.

Pruscha, Carl. 1975. *Kathmandu Valley: the preservation of physical environment and cultural heritage Protective Inventory*. Vienna. Anton Schroll & Co. 2 vols.

Quigley, Declan. 1994. 'Sresthas: Heterogeneity among Hindu Patron Lineages'. In *Contested Hierarchies. A collaborative ethnography of caste among the Newars of the Kathmandu Valley*. Edited by David Gellner and Declan Quigley. Oxford. Clarendon.

Quigley, Declan. 1994. 'Conclusion: caste organisation and the ancient city'. In *Contested Hierarchies*.

Raj, Yogesh. 2010. *History as Mindscapes: a memory of the peasants' movement of Nepal*. Kathmandu. Martin Chautari.

Raj, Yogesh. 2012. *Expedition to Nepal Valley: the journal of Captain Kinloch August 26 – October 17, 1767*. Kathmandu. Jagadamba Prakashan.

Raj, Yogesh. 2015. 'Remembering to Forget'. *The Kathmandu Post*, 9 June.

Rana, Brahma SJB. 1934. *The Great Earthquake in Nepal* (trans. Kesar Lall 2013). Kathmandu. Ratna Pustak Bhandar.

Rana, Chandra SJB. 1925. *Appeal to the people of Nepal for the Emancipation of Slaves and Abolition of Slavery in the country*. Kathmandu.

Rana, Madhukar SJB. 1992. 'An open letter to the minister'. *Himal* 5(2). pp. 5–7.

Rana, Pashupati SJB and Kamal P. Malla (eds). 1973. *Nepal in Perspective*. Kathmandu. Tribhuvan University.

Rana, Prabakhar SJB, Pashupati SJB Rana and Gautam SJB Rana. 2002. *The Ranas of Nepal*. Geneva.

Rana, Pranaya SJB. 2015. 'Don't Talk, Just Listen'. *The Kathmandu Post*, 20 September.

Ranjit, Sushmita. 2009. 'A Thought over Narayanhiti Palace'. *Spaces Magazine* 6(1).

Ranjitkar, Siddhi B. 1998. 'Rath Jatra of Rato Machchhendranath'. *Ancient Nepal* 141(2). pp. 25–29.

Regmi, D.R. 1983. *Inscriptions of Ancient Nepal*. New Delhi. Abhinav Publications. 3 vols.

Regmi, Jagadish Chandra. 1981. 'The Cult of Bhimasena'. *Ancient Nepal* pp. 61–64.

Regmi, Mahesh Chandra. 1978. *Thatched Huts and Stucco Palaces: peasants and landlords in nineteenth century Nepal*. Delhi. Adroit Publishers.

Regmi, Mahesh Chandra. 2002. *Nepal: an historical miscellany*. Delhi. Adroit Publishers.

Rhodes, N.G. 1989. 'The Monetisation of Nepal in the Seventeenth Century'. *Kailash* 15(1&2). pp. 113–117.

Riccardi, Theodore. 1973. 'Some preliminary remarks on a Newari painting of Swayambhunath'. *Journal of the American Oriental Society* 93(3). pp. 335–340.

Riccardi, Theodore (transl). 1975. 'Sylvain Lévi: The History of Nepal: Part 1'. *Kailash* 3(1). pp. 5–60.

Riccardi, Theodore. 1996. 'The Archaeological Perspective.' In *Change and Continuity: studies in the Nepalese culture of the Kathmandu Valley*. Edited by Siegfried Lienhard. Turin, Edizioni dell'Orso.

Riccardi, Theodore. 2003. *The Oriental Casebook of Sherlock Holmes*. New York. Random House (2010 Himal Books edition).

Riccardi, Theodore. 2006. 'The imaginary orient of Richard Wagner'. *Himal Southasian* (March).

Riccardi, Theodore. 2006. 'Of scholarship and politics: the relentless pursuit'. *Himal Southasian* (July).

Riccardi, Theodore. 2007. 'Studies in the psychopathy of culture'. *Himal Southasian* 20(3). pp. 45–48.

Riley-Smith, Tristram. 1982. 'Buddhist God-Makers in the Kathmandu Valley'. Ph.D thesis, Cambridge University.

Roka, Hari. 2004. 'The Emergency and Nepal's Political Future'. In *Himalayan 'people's war'*. Edited by Michael Hutt. New Delhi. Hurst & Co.

Rose, Leo E. Nepal. 1971. *Strategy for Survival*. Berkeley. University of California Press (2010 Mandala Book Point edition).

Sapkota, Chandan. 2013. 'Remittances in Nepal: boon or bane?' *The Journal for Development Studies*.

Schick, Jurgen. 1989 (first English edition 1997). *The Gods are Leaving the Country: art theft from Nepal*. Bangkok. Orchid Press.

Sen, Jehar. 1973. 'Slave Trade on the Indo-Nepal Border in the Nineteenth Century'. *Kailash* 1(2). pp. 159–166.

Sharma, Bharat. 1992. 'Selling Dreams. Project appraisal: the Kathmandu Valley Urban Development Plans and Programmes Study'. *Himal* 5(1). pp. 34–36.

Sharma, Nutandhar. 1999. "The Legends of 'Gayabhajya' of Patan in the Kathmandu Valley." *CNAS* 26(2). pp. 239–256.

Sharma, Prayag Raj. 1973. 'Kirkpatrick's An Account of the Kingdom of Nepal'. *CNAS* 1(1). pp. 96–105.

Sharma, Prayag Raj. 1999. 'A Fresh Look at the Origin and Forms of Early Temples in the Kathmandu Valley.' *CNAS* 26(1). pp. 1–25.

Sharma, Prayag Raj. 2004. *The State and Society in Nepal: historical foundations and contemporary trends*. Kathmandu. Himal Books.

Sharma, Sudheer. 2004. 'The Maoist Movement: an evolutionary perspective'. In *Himalayan 'people's war'*. Edited by Michael Hutt. New Delhi, Hurst & Co.

Sharrock, James. 2013. 'Stability in Transition: development perspectives and local politics in Nepal'. *EBHR* 42. pp. 9–38.

Shneiderman, Sara and Mark Turin. 2004. 'The Path to Jan Sarkar in Dolakha District: Towards an Ethnography of the Maoist Movement'. In *Himalayan 'people's war'*. Edited by Michael Hutt. New Delhi. Hurst & Co.

Shrestha, Bijaya Lal. 1991. 'Patan: a city no more shining'. *Himal* 4(2). pp. 24–28.

Shrestha, Padma Prakash (ed.). *Nepal Rediscovered: The Rana Court 1846–1951: Photographs from the Archives of the Nepal Kingdom Foundation*. Chicago, Serindia.

Shresthacharya, Ishwaranand. 1977. 'Newar Kinship Terms in the light of Kinship Typology'. *CNAS* 4(2). pp. 111–128.

Skerry, Christa et al. 1991. *Four Decades of Development: the history of U.S. assistance to Nepal 1951–1991*. Kathmandu. USAID.

Slusser, Mary Shepherd. 1982. *Nepal Mandala: a cultural study of the Kathmandu Valley*. Princeton (1998 Mandala Book Point edition). 2 vols.

Slusser, Mary Shepherd. 1987. 'The cultural aspects of Newar Painting'. In *Heritage of the Kathmandu Valley: proceedings of an international conference in Lübeck*. Edited by Niels Gutschow and Axel Michaels. VGH Wissenschaftsverlag.

Slusser, Mary Sherherd. 2003. 'Conservation Notes on some Nepalese Paintings'. Asianart.com http://asianart.com/articles/paubhas/index. html

Slusser, Mary Shepherd et al. 2005. *Art and Culture of Nepal: selected papers*. Kathmandu. Mandala.

Slusser, Mary Shepherd. 2010. *The Antiquity of Nepalese Wood Carving: a reassessment*. Washington. University of Washington Press.

Smith, Thomas. 1852. *The Nepal Years: narrative of five years residence at Nepal*. New Delhi.Cosmo Publications edition 1994. 2 vols.

Sotheby's sale catalogue. *Indian and Southeast Asian Art. New York. Thursday September 19, 1996.*

Stiller, Ludwig. 1980. *Letters from Kathmandu: the Kot massacre*. Kathmandu. Tribhuvan University.

Stiller, Ludwig. 1989. *Prithvi Narayan Shah in the Light of the Dibya Upadesh*. Kathmandu. Himalayan Book Centre.

Stiller, Ludwig. 1993. *Nepal: growth of a nation*. Kathmandu. HRD Research Centre.

Stiller, Ludwig. 1995. *The Rise of the House of Gorkha*. Kathmandu. HRD Research Centre.

Stoddard, Robert. 1980. 'Perceptions about the Geography of Religious Sites in the Kathmandu Valley'. *CNAS* 7(1&2). pp. 97–118.

Survey of India. 1945. *Historical Records of the Survey of India, Vol II, 1800–1815*. Dehra Dun.

Tamang, Seira and Anonymous. 2002. 'Nepali view, foreign view'. *Nepali Times* 115 (11–17 October).

Tamang, Seira. 2002. 'Civilizing Civil Society: Donors and Democratic Space'. *SINHAS* 7(2). pp. 309–353.

Tamang, Seira. 2013. 'Historicizing state "fragility" in Nepal'. *SINHAS* 17(2). pp. 263–295.

Thapa, Deepak with Bandita Sijapati. 2004. *A Kingdom Under Siege: Nepal's Maoist insurgency 1996–2004*. Kathmandu. The printhouse.

Thapa, Deepak (ed.). 2003. *Understanding the Maoist Movement of Nepal*. Kathmandu. Martin Chautari.

Thapa, Deepak. 2015. 'The Country is Yours', *The Kathmandu Post*, 2 July 2015.

Thapa, Manjushree. 2005. *Forget Kathmandu: an elegy for democracy*. New Delhi. Penguin India.

Thapa, Manjushree. 2011. *The Lives We Have Lost: essays and opinions on Nepal*. New Delhi. Penguin India.

Thapa, Ramesh Jung. 1968. 'Kashtamandapa'. *Ancient Nepal* 3. pp. 41–44.

Theophile, Erich and Gutschow, Niels (eds). 2003. *The Sulima Pagoda. East Meets West in the Restoration of a Nepalese Temple*. Connecticut. Weatherhill.

Tiwari, Ashutosh. 1992. 'Planning: never without aid'. *Himal* 5(2). pp. 8–9. pp. 11–13.

Tiwari, Sudarshan Raj. 1992. 'No Future for the Urban Past'. *Himal* 5(1). pp. 5–8.

Tiwari, Sudarshan Raj. 1996. 'Ancient Towns of Kathmandu Valley: a survey of legends, chronicles and inscriptions'. *Ancient Nepal* 139. pp. 25–40.

Toffin, Gérard. 1981. 'Urban Space and Religion: Observations on Newar Urbanism'. In Toffin (ed.). *Man and His House in the Himalayas. Ecology of Nepal*. Paris (English edition, Delhi 1991).

Toffin, Gérard et al. 1981. 'The Pode House: a caste of Newar fishermen'. In *Man and His House*...

Toffin, Gérard. 1992. 'The Indra Jatra of Kathmandu as a Royal Festival: past and present'. *CNAS* 19(1). pp. 73–92.

Toffin, Gérard. 1996. 'The Moiety System of the Newars'. *CNAS* 23(1). pp. 65–88.

Toffin, Gérard. 2007. *Newar Society: city, village, periphery*. Kathmandu. Himal Books.

Toffin, Gérard. 2013. *From Monarchy to Republic*. Kathmandu. Vajra Books.

Tucci, Giuseppe. 1969. *Rati-Lila: an interpretation of the Tantric imagery of the temples of Nepal*. Geneva. Nagal (transl. James Hogarth).

Tucci, Giuseppe. 1960. *Nepal: the discovery of the Malla*. First English edition (trans. Lovett Edwards). London. George Allen & Unwin Ltd.

UNESCO. 1997. *Changing Faces of Nepal: photos taken by the Chitrakars of Bhimsensthan*. Kathmandu. Ratna Pustak Bhandar.

UNESCO. 2003. *Traditional Materials and Construction Technologies used in the Kathmandu Valley*. Paris.

UNESCO. 2007. *Heritage Homeowner's Preservation Manual*. Kathmandu.

Upadhyaya, Devendra Raj. 1992. 'Bad Advice from World Bank'. *Himal* 5(2). pp. 17–18.

Upadhyaya, R.D. 2013. *Indians in Nepal during the 1857 War*. New Delhi. Kaveri Books.

Uprety, Prem R. 1992. *Political Awakening in Nepal: the search for a new identity*. New Delhi. Commonwealth Publishers.

Vajracarya, Dhanavajra and Kamal P Malla. 1985. *The Gopalarajavamshavali*. Kathmandu. Nepal Research Centre.

Vajracarya, Dhanavajra. 1987. 'The development of early and medieval settlements in the Kathmandu Valley – a review of the inscriptional evidence'. In *Heritage of the Kathmandu Valley: proceedings of an international conference in Lübeck*. Edited by Niels Gutschow and Axel Michaels. VGH Wissenschaftsverlag.

Vajracarya, Gautamavajra. 1973. 'Recently discovered inscriptions of Licchavi Nepal'. *Kailash* 1(2). pp. 112–134.

Vajracharya, Chakramehr. 1977. 'The Medieval Settlements'. *Ancient Nepal. pp.* 30–39.

van den Hoek, Bert. 1990. 'Does Divinity Protect the King? Ritual and politics in Nepal'. *CNAS* 17(2). pp. 147–155.

Vansittart, Eden. 1906. *Gurkhas (handbooks for the Indian army series)*. Calcutta. Government Printing.

von Einsiedel, Sebastian, David Malone and Suman Pradhan (eds). 2012. *Nepal in Transition: from people's war to fragile peace*. Cambridge.

Weber, Max. 1916. *The Religion of India: the sociology of Hinduism and Buddhism*. New York. Free Press. 1958 English edition.

Whelpton, John. 1983. *Jang Bahadur in Europe*. Kathmandu. Sahayogi Press.

Whelpton. John. 1991. *Kings, Soldiers and Priests: Nepalese politics and the rise of Jung Bahadur Rana 1830–1857*. New Delhi. Manohar.

Whelpton, John. 2004. 'Hodgson, Brian Houghton'. *Dictionary of National Biography*. Oxford. Clarendon.

Whelpton, John. 2005. *A History of Nepal*. Cambridge. Cambridge University Press.

Whelpton, John. 2013. "Political Violence in Nepal from Unification to Janadolan I: the background to 'people's war"'. In *Revolution in Nepal: an anthropological and historical approach to the people's war*, edited by Marie Lecomte-Tilouine. New Delhi. OUP.

Wildavsky, Aaron. 1972. 'Why planning fails in Nepal'. *Administrative Science Quarterly* 17(4). pp. 508–528.

Witzel, Michael. 1987. 'The Coronation Rituals of Nepal: with special reference to the coronation of King Birendra (1975)'. In *Heritage of the Kathmandu Valley: proceedings of an international conference in Lübeck*. Edited by Niels Gutschow and Axel Michaels. VGH Wissenschaftsverlag.

Wright, Daniel. 1877. *History of Nepal* (translated from the Parbatiya by Munshi Shew Shunker Singh and Pandit Shri Gunanand). Cambridge.

Acknowledgements

Many people have helped me in writing this book, and during my years in Nepal which are partly described here. Only a few of them are mentioned in the text, some with their identities concealed. Some might not be grateful to be thanked by name. I am very grateful to them all, and I hope I have treated everyone fairly. Among those I would especially like to thank, for various reasons, are: Dhana Laksmi Shrestha, Gopal Man Shrestha, Sundar Man Shrestha, Shyam Badan Shrestha, Neelesh Man Shrestha, Deepika Shrestha, Maya Rai, Hirakaji, Sunil and the Shakya family, Sharon Gould, Jamie Cross, Dinita Chapagain, Surya Bahadur Mahat, Binod Aryal, Maarten Post, Sita Pariyar, Sam Taylor, Brian Sokol, Daulat Jha, Sid Gurung, Mamta Khatri, R.B. Khatri, Anand Gurung, Ratna Raj Bajracharya, Kiran Pun, Himalaya Shamsher Rana, Baikuntha Shamsher Rana, Sangeeta Thapa, Manushi Bhattarai, Ramyata Limbu, Durga Thapa, Siddha Raj Paneru, Dhruba Simkhada, Laksmi Prasad Kisi, Anagha Neelakanthan, Rhoddy Chalmers, Gunaraj Luitel, Rohit Ranjitkar, Bandhu Thapa, Era Shrestha, Chandan Sapkota, Ramesh Dhungel, Prashant Jha, Kiran Chapagain, Catherine Bell, Eleanor Bell, Kunda Dixit, Rabi Thapa, Kiran Chitrakar, K.P. Malla, Prawin Adhikari, Suvani Singh, Shradha Ghale, Bishnu 'Kalpit' Ghimire, Patrick French, Nikita Tripathi, Kiran Khadgi, Sabitri Khadka, Amita Maharjan, Durga Byanjankar, Prayag Raj Sharma, David Gellner, Soham Dhakal, Mara Malagodi, John Bevan, Fred Rawski, Duane Clifford-Jones, John Tyynela, Samden Sherpa, Niranjan Kunwar and Mike Searle. I'm indebted to editors and colleagues on several newspapers including Alan Philps, Francis Harris and Joe Jenkins at the *Telegraph* and Simon Long and Dominic Ziegler at the *Economist*. Thanks to Francis Elliott for introducing me to my agency, HHB, and to Elly James and Celia Hayley at HHB for their advice and encouragement. Several people read different sections of the manuscript, at various stages, sometimes more than once, and gave very helpful suggestions, including Manjushree Thapa, Ted Riccardi, John Whelpton, Devendra Raj Pandey, Aditya Adhikari and Deepak Thapa. I've tried, and they helped me, to avoid mistakes; but ranging over such material I'm afraid that some must still have occurred. Only I'm responsible for remaining vulgarities, errors and undue simplifications. Niels Gutschow, Rohit Ranjitkar and Wolfgang Korn kindly supplied several of the maps and diagrams, as indicated in the list of illustrations. Rajesh K.C. kindly supplied one of his cartoons. USAID gave permission to use the photograph of D.R. Regmi signing the teacher-training agreement. I'm very grateful for Michael Hutt's translations of Bhupi Sherchan's poems which are reproduced with permission of Oxford University Press India © Oxford University Press, and to the Royal Geographical Society for permission to use the drawing by Henry Oldfield, showing the Valley as seen from Swayambhu in around the 1850s, which appears on the end papers. Many thanks to my editors, Meru Gokhale and Archana Shankar at Random House India, for the great deal of work they did. I'm deeply grateful to my parents, Martin and Veronica Bell, for their love, for the opportunities I've had, and for their acceptance of my decision to live on the other side of the world. This book is dedicated to my wife, Subina, whose home town this is, who gave me great love and all manner of help, and put a roof over my head while I wrote it. And to my children.

Index